Meditations
on FAVORITE SCRIPTURES
DEVOTIONS FOR A YEAR

Curtis A. Jahn
Compiling Editor

Northwestern Publishing House
Milwaukee, Wisconsin

Second printing, 2009

Cover photos: ShutterStock and DesignPics
Art Director: Karen Knutson
Cover Design: Carianne Ciriacks

Library of Congress Control Number 2005933230
Northwestern Publishing House
1250 N. 113th St., Milwaukee, WI 53226-3284
©2007 by Northwestern Publishing House
www.nph.net
Published 2007
Printed in the United States of America
ISBN: 978-0-8100-1941-6

Preface

Christian people have always recognized the value of spending some devotional time with the Lord every day in prayer and with his Word. For fifty years the popular devotional magazine *Meditations* has brought daily devotions to its readers. Through the Scripture verses, devotional thoughts, and prayers of *Meditations,* God's people have been spiritually nourished in their Christian faith.

This commemorative volume brings together 366 devotions, one for each day of the year, from the half-century of *Meditations.* Each devotion offers the comfort and guidance of God's Holy Word, centering in the gospel promises of Jesus Christ.

The title of this book, *Meditations on Favorite Scriptures,* reflects the primary way the devotions were selected. Christian readers will recognize many of their favorite Bible verses at the beginning of the devotions. Scripture passages that were originally in the King James Version have been put into the New International Version. The language of the prayers has been updated into contemporary English, and hymn verses have been quoted as they appear in *Christian Worship: A Lutheran Hymnal,* wherever possible.

May God bless you, the reader of this book, as he has blessed so many readers of *Meditations* for fifty years!

"God so loved the world that he gave his one and only Son, that whoever believes in him shall not perish but have eternal life." (John 3:16)

God's love—reflected in his gift

Birthdays, Christmas, and anniversaries are just some of the special occasions when gifts are given by relatives and friends. Gifts are often signs of love. Gifts may come in many different shapes and sizes. Some may be of great value while others may have cost the giver very little. Or the giver may have made gifts by hand at a great expense of time and effort.

God gave us the greatest gift of all, the gift of his own dear Son. He did it to fulfill the greatest need we have as human beings, the need for a Savior from sin. This gift was given to us by our heavenly Father to fulfill a promise he had made to our first parents, Adam and Eve, in the Garden of Eden. At that time he had told Satan, "I will put enmity between you and the woman, and between your offspring and hers; he will crush your head, and you will strike his heel" (Genesis 3:15).

This gift was the result of God's love for sinful humanity. No one, from Adam and Eve to this present day, deserves such a gift. Yet God in his love knew that this was the only way to save a sinful and lost world. This gift was one of a kind, never to be repeated and impossible to duplicate.

No gift is more personal than the gift of God's Son. He fits the needs of everyone—babies, young children, teenagers, adults, and senior citizens. All of us have broken God's law in our own evil ways. Yet "the blood of Jesus, his Son, purifies us from all sin" (1 John 1:7).

The gifts we as humans give soon break, wear out, get used up, or are discarded in favor of other things. Yet God's gift to us is ageless, endless, and always useful. Only God in his love could—and did—supply us with all that we need to be saved from sin and hell.

As a result of God's gift of his Son, we ponder more deeply and appreciate more fully God's love. In giving us this gift, he has shown us what love is all about.

God loved the world so that he gave
His only Son the lost to save
That all who would in him believe
Should everlasting life receive. (CW 391:1)

≈

Dear Father, thank you for the perfect gift of your dear Son. May his sacrifice continue to be the center of my faith and my hope and my joy. Amen.

"God did not send his Son into the world to condemn the world, but to save the world through him." (John 3:17)

God's love—reflected in salvation

Have you ever been lost? It can be a terrifying experience. Ask any crying child lost in a shopping mall. Ask a confused hunter who has lost his sense of direction in a roadless forest. Ask the motorist who can't figure out where he is or which street or highway to take to get to his destination.

When God looked at this world, he saw a world lost in sin. God saw that every person on this earth had violated his law, which declared, "Be holy because I, the LORD your God, am holy" (Leviticus 19:2). God saw that everyone had gone his or her own way and had strayed from the path of perfect righteousness.

God could have ordered the whole world to appear in court before his Son and could have had the Son declare the world condemned to eternal punishment in hell. But God's love intervened and sought salvation rather than judgment. Our loving God accomplished this salvation by sending his Son into this world, not as its judge but as its Savior.

This act of rescuing the world from sin was not easy. It required God's Son to live a perfect life in our place. It required that God place the sins of the whole world on his Son and punish him for "the iniquity of us all" (Isaiah 53:6). It required that the innocent Lamb of God be nailed to a cross, where he would endure all the pain and suffering that God had reserved for sinful humanity.

Jesus' suffering and death rescued every man, woman, and child from the eternal fires of hell. The life of the Son of Man offered on Calvary's cross accomplished a rescue like no other in the history of the world. Many day-to-day rescues save the lives of the lost, the trapped, and the injured. But only the rescue mission of the Son of God saved souls lost in sin and destined for eternal death in hell.

God's mission was a mission of love. It was planned in love by our Father, who saw a world lost in sin. It was carried out in love by Christ, who gave his life for us.

Once you were lost in sin. But Jesus died for you. How does it feel to be rescued? How does it feel to be loved by God? Many are still lost in sin and unbelief. Go and share with them the joy of that salvation found in Jesus Christ.

Dear Jesus, thank you for rescuing me from sin and hell through your death on the cross. Amen.

"Whoever believes in him is not condemned, but whoever does not believe stands condemned already because he has not believed in the name of God's one and only Son." (John 3:18)

God's love—accepted in faith

Suppose you need to get to the roof of your house or apartment building. You stretch a ladder from the ground to the roof. The roof is now accessible, assuming, of course, you trust that each rung on the ladder will hold your weight. If you do, you confidently climb the ladder one rung at a time until you reach the roof.

What was necessary? You had to believe in the ladder. This is similar to what Jesus told Nicodemus. Jesus explained that he had come to redeem man from sin by giving his life on the cross. It was vital that Nicodemus believe what Jesus said in order for him to be saved from sin and inherit eternal life.

The same is true for you and everyone else. The only way to escape God's condemnation of sin is to believe that Jesus is your Savior. This you do—by the power of the Holy Spirit. God inspired the apostle Paul to write, "It is by grace you have been saved, through faith—and this not from yourselves, it is the gift of God—not by works, so that no one can boast" (Ephesians 2:8,9). Your faith is a gift from your loving God, who wants you to be saved. He gives you the confidence to accept what Jesus told Nicodemus—that whoever believes in Jesus is not condemned.

Many in this world choose to remain unbelievers. They fail to put their trust and confidence in Jesus and his atoning work. They foolishly choose to trust in their own works or merits to save them from God's condemnation. How sad this is. They stand condemned to hell with no possibility of ever inheriting eternal life.

John the Baptist told his hearers, "Whoever believes in the Son has eternal life" (John 3:36). Paul and Silas informed the jailer at Philippi, "Believe in the Lord Jesus, and you will be saved" (Acts 16:31). Paul wrote to his fellow believers at Rome, "We maintain that a man is justified by faith apart from observing the law" (Romans 3:28).

The Bible is clear. Whoever believes in Jesus is free from the condemnation of sin. Whoever does not believe remains condemned to eternal punishment in hell. Since forgiveness and faith are gifts from our loving God, we owe him no less than our eternal praise and thanks.

৩৩৩৩

Dear God, thank you for your gift of faith by which I am able to receive the results of your Son's redeeming work. Amen.

"Whoever lives by the truth comes into the light, so that it may be seen plainly that what he has done has been done through God." (John 3:21)

God's love—reflected in Christian living

We receive much help from people during our lifetimes. Someone helps us with a flat tire. A neighbor cuts our grass while we are on vacation. A friend nearby helps us shovel out after the worst snowstorm of the winter. We are thankful for what these people do for us.

Sometimes we find ways other than with words to express our gratitude. We might return the favor without being asked. We might purchase a small gift to show our appreciation.

But what do we do in response to God's gracious and loving activity of saving us from sin and hell? Surely we give thanks to God for his unending love in Christ. We may also want to repay him for making us his own through faith in Christ Jesus. But let's face it. We could never repay our God for all that his love caused him to do for us.

But there is something we can do. We can offer our lives to him. That is what Jesus was saying to Nicodemus in the Scripture passage for today. He was telling Nicodemus and encouraging us to let our lights shine in the world around us.

God made us his own. And he gives us the strength and ability to live as his dear children. Therefore, as a redeemed child of God, you will desire to "let your light shine before men, that they may see your good deeds and praise your Father in heaven" (Matthew 5:16). Children enjoy pleasing their parents. As a child of your heavenly Father, you also want to lead a life that is pleasing to him and that brings him honor and glory. You seek no praise or glory for yourself. You want it all to go to him who did so much for you. We follow the encouragement Peter offered in his first epistle: "Declare the praises of him who called you out of darkness into his wonderful light" (2:9).

As a Christian, continue to search for ways to reflect the love God has shown you in Christ. Read and study his Word. Listen to the instructions and encouragements the sacred writers give. Especially listen to how they encourage us to serve the Lord because of all he has done for us. Because no Christian lives a perfect life, there is always room for improvement in what you think, say, and do. By the grace of God, you have a lot of victorious living to do!

❧◌◌❧

Dear God, shine on me with your love in Christ. Help me reflect the light of your love, especially on those who still live in the shadow of death. Amen.

My times are in your hands. (Psalm 31:15)

5 January

God's hands determine my days

We are living in a society that no longer considers people taking life into their own hands as wrong. The cultists of death are all around us: abortionists, right-to-die advocates, gangs who murder in the streets. This is one result of the lie of evolution that tells us that man is god. If evolution is true, there is no higher author of life, no higher authority when it comes to life and death. The days of our lives and the times of our deaths become ours to control.

David knew better. He knew that life and death are not ours to control. They are in God's hands. God determines whether each of us recovers from an illness or remains sick a while longer. While he is not the author of sin, he determines how it touches our lives. His will determines if a car comes across a median and takes the life of a loved one or whether it falls harmlessly into a ditch. Because our times are in God's hands, even the sinful actions of others serve God's purposes for our eternal salvation.

All of our times are in God's hands—the good times, the bad times, the easy times, the hard times. God delivers us from our enemies each and every day according to his good purpose.

The way God deals with us is not unlike how a coach deals with his players. He determines the plays and who will run them. The coach's hands point to where the player is to go and push him or her in that direction. God's control, however, goes far beyond that of a coach. From 12:00 A.M. until 11:59:59 P.M., the second before midnight, our times are in God's hands.

What is more, the God who determines our days is a gracious God. This means that everything that happens to us works out for our eternal good. During each and every minute of our lives, God is serving us. He controls our lives so that we are moved to search his Word, pray for help, grow in a knowledge of his love, and develop Christian concern for the lives and souls of others.

Since God determines our days, we can be sure he and he alone has determined when we will die. When his work for us is completed, he will take us home. What a different view of life and death this is than that proposed by modern ministers of death!

With this in mind, we eagerly await that moment when we depart this life for the endless day of heaven, where we can spend every ounce of energy worshiping and praising God.

෴

O Lord, thank you for using the days of our lives to bless us. Amen.

Now there was a man in Jerusalem called Simeon, who was righteous and devout. He was waiting for the consolation of Israel, and the Holy Spirit was upon him. (Luke 2:25)

Praise God for the consolation of Israel

Today Christians celebrate the festival of Epiphany. *Epiphany* means, literally, "to shine forth." This is what God did when he let the glory of Jesus as the Son of God and Savior of the world shine forth among his people.

To help us celebrate Christ's epiphany, we turn to the "Song of Simeon" in the gospel of Luke.

It was "consolation" for which Simeon, a man of the city of Jerusalem, was waiting. With a believing heart, he knew that consolation would come through the Messiah. In the Messiah would come the comfort to fill Simeon's and all mankind's greatest need: a Savior from sin and all its horrible consequences.

Simeon is described as a righteous and devout man. This does not mean that he was any less a sinner than any other person. He was justified by faith, as are we and all who believe in Jesus Christ as their Savior from sin. Simeon's faith is evidenced in his "waiting."

It was the Holy Spirit who had brought him to faith in the Savior by the same means the Holy Spirit still uses today—the Word of God. How his heart must have been thrilled at the words of the prophet Isaiah (51:3): "The LORD will surely comfort Zion and will look with compassion on all her ruins." By faith Simeon knew that God was also speaking to him through these words of the prophet: "Comfort, comfort my people, says your God. Speak tenderly to Jerusalem, and proclaim to her that her hard service has been completed, that her sin has been paid for, that she has received from the LORD's hand double for all her sins" (Isaiah 40:1,2).

The one who brought such consolation to Simeon and his fellow believers of old is the same Jesus Christ who comforts us through Word and sacrament. The Spirit is given to us also so that we too may have consolation in Christ's blood-bought forgiveness and the oil of gladness to soothe us in our troubles and afflictions. With the Holy Spirit upon us, let us bring our daily sacrifice of thanksgiving and praise to God for the consolation of Israel.

❦

In you alone, Dear Lord, we own
Sweet hope and consolation,
Our shield from foes, Our balm for woes,
Our great and sure salvation. Amen. (CW 447:1)

It had been revealed to him by the Holy Spirit that he would not die before he had seen the Lord's Christ. (Luke 2:26)

Praise God for the Spirit's revelation

When people reach a ripe old age, many of them express a deep desire to see someone or something before they die. This was demonstrated recently in a conversation between several elderly people in a retirement home. The question was asked of all present, "What would you like to see before you die?" One lady replied, "I would like to see my grandchildren, but they live so far from here and I am too weak to travel." Another said, "I would like to see my son come back to church."

Both of these desires seem unlikely to be fulfilled; yet both, by God's grace, are possible.

Simeon, the man from Jerusalem, also had a desire to see something special before he died. It was really a desire that was common to all devout Jews. He looked for the consolation of Israel—the Savior—to come into the world. What was uncommon in Simeon's case was that God had specifically revealed to him that he would see the Messiah before he died. Exactly how the Holy Spirit revealed this to Simeon we are not told. But we are content to read that God had given him this promise.

Simeon was endowed with the Spirit and well versed in Holy Scripture. By it he had come to faith. In faith he looked forward to the Messiah's coming. The general time and place of Christ's birth had been foretold by the prophets. However, it would not have mattered one iota for his salvation's sake if Simeon had died in his faith without actually seeing the Christ Child with his own eyes. But our good and gracious God granted him this revelation so that we too might marvel at the wisdom, power, and goodness of God. Simeon was no great man in the eyes of the world—no candidate for Who's Who in Israel—yet God the Holy Spirit selected him for this honor.

To see the Lord's Christ with bodily eyes was indeed a great blessing. But even that was not as great as to see him with the eyes of faith. Later, many in Israel saw Jesus with their natural eyes and heard him speak the words of life with their own ears, yet it did them no good because they did not believe in him. To see the child Jesus as the Lord's Christ through the eyes of faith is still the greatest blessing of all. And the Holy Spirit continues to bestow this great blessing wherever God's Word is preached and read.

୶୦୭ଚ୬

Dearest Lord Jesus, by your Word and the Spirit you have revealed yourself to be the Christ; grant us the gift of faith to believe it and the courage to proclaim it. Amen.

Moved by the Spirit, he went into the temple courts. When the parents brought in the child Jesus to do for him what the custom of the Law required, Simeon took him in his arms and praised God. (Luke 2:27,28)

Praise God for bringing Jesus to his temple

Oh, what joy must have come to Simeon as he held the Christ Child in his arms! It is a wonder that he did not die of a heart attack in that most thrilling moment of his life.

What happened that day is also ours to share. We join Simeon in praising God for bringing Jesus to the temple. Jesus' entry into the temple is of considerable significance. The temple was the symbol of God's presence with his people.

Guided by the Holy Spirit, Simeon was led into the temple at the exact time that Mary and Joseph brought the child Jesus in to fulfill the requirements of the Old Testament law. God always has a way of bringing things together for the good of his people and to accomplish his purpose. So it was here.

Forty days after the birth of Jesus, Mary was required to present her offering of purification in the temple. It was also part of the law that every male firstborn be dedicated to the service of the Lord.

Historically, all the firstborn males were to be dedicated to serve the Lord as priests. With the giving of the law on Mount Sinai, however, the Lord set aside the children of Levi as substitutes for the rest of the firstborn in Israel. As a token of redemption, the non-Levite parents would buy back their firstborn sons for the price of 5 shekels.

The law of purification, however, really concerned only the usual course of nature where there is a human father. That which is born of flesh is flesh, and that which is born of the Spirit is spirit. Jesus was born of the Spirit. He was born the sinless, holy Son of God.

He who is the living Word, the giver of the law, here placed himself under the law in our stead. Therefore, Paul writes of him, "When the time had fully come, God sent his Son, born of a woman, born under law, to redeem those under law, that we might receive the full rights of sons" (Galatians 4:4,5). So that we might be adopted into God's family—for by nature we are the children of wrath—Jesus took upon himself the whole law in perfect obedience.

As we here view Jesus in the temple, let us also review his purpose in coming to the temple for *us*.

⌒⊙⌒

Praise be to you, Lord Jesus, for redeeming us from the curse of the law and making us children of God through faith in you. Amen.

"Sovereign Lord, as you have promised, you now dismiss your servant in peace." (Luke 2:29)

Praise God for his promises

The opening words of Simeon's hymn of praise to God at first seem to be coming from the lips and heart of a believing child of God who is ready to die. Simeon certainly was ready to depart this life in peace. This can also be said of everyone who believes that Jesus is the Lord's Christ—namely, everyone who sees in Jesus the promises of God fulfilled.

Simeon was not only aware of the promise God had made to him—that he would not die before he had seen the Lord's Christ—but was also aware of the consolation God had promised Israel. Simeon remembered the promises God had made to the fathers: Abraham, Isaac, and Jacob. He also thought about the promises spoken by the prophet Isaiah, such as, "For to us a child is born, to us a son is given, and the government will be on his shoulders. And he will be called Wonderful Counselor, Mighty God, Everlasting Father, Prince of Peace" (Isaiah 9:6).

The natural eyes of Simeon saw the parents, Joseph and Mary, who looked like any other parents in the temple that day. The child, Jesus, looked like any other child. But God had made great and wonderful promises concerning this child and his coming. These were being fulfilled. As far as Simeon's faith was concerned, they were all as good as accomplished.

It is the nature of our Christian faith to believe all that the prophets have written. We believe that the Bible is the Word of God, and faith accepts and embraces every word to be God's Word without error. Faith finds its greatest joy and delight in the promises of the Bible. God's promises kindle and inflame hope in us during our stay on earth. They prepare us for our future sinless life in the kingdom of glory. God's promises uphold and strengthen us in every kind of affliction, disappointment, and frustration. They give us courage and boldness to testify about Jesus Christ as the Lord and Savior of all people.

God's promise to Simeon also made reference to Simeon's death. But when that would come was of no great concern to Simeon. This much is true of every child of God, because the promises of God are true. And his mercy endures to every generation.

⁂

O Lord God, great and precious are your promises of forgiveness, life, and salvation in Christ. Uphold my faith in him by your Word, and let me live and die in your peace. Amen.

"My eyes have seen your salvation, which you have prepared in the sight of all people." (Luke 2:30,31)

Praise God for his salvation

"I praise you because I am fearfully and wonderfully made," says the psalmist (139:14). These words include everything that Luther placed in his explanation of the First Article of the Apostles' Creed: "I believe that God created me and all that exists, and that he gave me my body and soul, eyes, ears, and all my members, my mind and all my abilities."

The gifts of the body are precious indeed. Who can place a monetary value on the gift of eyes that see? Praise be to God for eyes that see!

It was with his own two eyes that Simeon observed the features of the Christ Child. But with the eyes of faith, he saw "salvation" in that Christ Child. He saw a salvation completely prepared for all people and openly revealed for all the world to see and to share. He saw a Savior dying for the sins of all people, without exception. He saw God justifying every sinner for Jesus' sake. He saw that salvation offered to all people through the gospel, which is able to kindle faith in human hearts. Those who believe in Christ and his salvation have and possess Christ and his salvation. Those who do not believe forfeit that great blessing which God secured for them in Christ. By their unbelief they make themselves guilty of rejecting God and his salvation.

It is heartrending to see with our own eyes the many who cast aside the gospel of God's salvation. And yet, let us not be discouraged in our work of bringing the good news of salvation to others. It is the will of the Father that no one should perish but that all should come to repentance and faith in Christ.

And as we share the good news of salvation with others, may we remain sincerely grateful for the eyes of faith that God has given us. Gratefulness for this free and glorious gift of salvation can best be expressed by using our opportunities to tell our friends, relatives, and neighbors, near and far, about it—beginning with the members of our own family. Let us help support, with our prayers and our money, the pastors and missionaries who take the Lord's salvation into other parts of the world. Other eyes are waiting to see the Lord's salvation, and other ears are waiting to hear it.

❧☙

O blessed Holy Trinity, open the eyes of faith among all people so that they may see your salvation, which stands prepared for all. Amen.

*"A light for revelation to the Gentiles and for glory to your
people Israel." (Luke 2:32)*

Praise God for light and glory

The salvation that Simeon saw in Jesus, the Christ Child, is the "light" of the Gentiles. Here we are reminded that all the nations of the earth would be blessed through the promise given to Abraham. The Gentiles were, as Paul says, "excluded from citizenship in Israel and foreigners to the covenants of the promise" (Ephesians 2:12). They walked this earth in the darkness of sin and unbelief, as many still do. But with a prophetic eye, Simeon saw that Gentiles too would see the light of the world. The light of the gospel would shine into their hearts, and many would come to faith in their Savior and find his salvation.

These words of Simeon have been fulfilled a million times over by all those who have heard the gospel and have been brought to faith in Christ. By the light of the gospel, they no longer walk in the darkness of sin. They have tasted God's gracious pardon and have the light of his Word to guide them in their daily service to the Lord. To them the Word of God is what the psalmist says it is: "a lamp to my feet and a light for my path" (Psalm 119:105). It is the beacon that guides us to our heavenly home.

The salvation prepared by Christ for all people is also a glory to God's true Israel. Jesus spoke of it as such to the woman at Jacob's well when he said, "Salvation is from the Jews" (John 4:22). Yes, by and through no other people or nation was this salvation planned and procured by God. God had chosen this people, the Israelites, to be the bearer of the Savior of the world. The very fact that this same nation, as a whole, rejected him does not change this fact. Actually, it makes even more startling the accuracy of Simeon's prophecy that Christ would be the light of the Gentiles.

The honor of bearing the Savior still belongs to Israel, even though all in Israel did not accept it or appreciate it. But on those who truly waited in faith—like Simeon, like the fathers and prophets of the Old Testament, and like Mary and Joseph, Zechariah and Elizabeth, and many other Jews of the New Testament era—the glory of Israel still shines.

Jesus, "the sun of righteousness" (Malachi 4:2) and the light of the world, still causes the light of his gospel to shine into every corner of the earth, bringing pardon and peace, hope and joy to all who believe, be they Jew or Gentile. These are now made one by faith in Christ.

❧⊙❧

O Christ, our true and only light, enlighten those who sit in night; let those afar now hear your voice and in your fold with us rejoice. Amen. (CW 569:1)

*"Sovereign Lord, as you have promised, you now dismiss
your servant in peace. For my eyes have seen your
salvation, which you have prepared in the sight of all
people, a light for revelation to the Gentiles and for glory
to your people Israel." (Luke 2:29-32)*

Praise God for the "Nunc Dimittis"

The "Nunc Dimittis" is the song in the liturgy that we often sing
toward the end of our Common Service with Communion. It is one of
the oldest hymns in our liturgies and is a fitting response of God's
people after they have communed with their Lord at his Holy Supper.

The "Nunc Dimittis" is actually the prophetic hymn of praise and
thanksgiving that Simeon spoke in the temple as he held the Christ
Child. In the same way he expressed his faith and gave testimony of
Christ and his salvation, God's people still do to this day.

The message of the "Nunc Dimittis" is, first and foremost, the
inspired Word of God. It is a proclamation of man's sin and God's saving
grace in Christ Jesus. It is not only a hymn of praise, glory, and thanks
to God for all the blessings of salvation but one of the most powerful ser-
mons ever to be preached by Simeon or any of God's people throughout
the days of the New Testament. It is a hymn of comfort and peace to all
God's people who worship him in spirit and in truth. They come to the
church service, bringing with them their many sins, and find in these
words the absolution for their sins. They may come burdened with
every kind of misery, frustration, and temptation and find in the "Nunc
Dimittis" a rich supply of soothing balm and strength. As God's worshiping people hear and sing the "Nunc Dimittis," they remind themselves and others of what a blessing it is to be servants of the Lord and
remind themselves of the work that they must do. They see in the
"Nunc Dimittis" what Simeon saw, the Lord's Christ.

As God's people today herald the thoughts of the "Nunc Dimittis,"
they reflect the light of God's love. They are stirred, with the help of the
Holy Spirit, to carry the good news of salvation into their daily thoughts
and words and actions.

A doxology like the "Nunc Dimittis" belongs among the hymns in
our worship lives and church services. Praise and thank God for the
"Nunc Dimittis"!

*Lord Jesus, may the salvation that you purchased with your own
blood for me and all people enable me daily to sing your praises
with joyful lips and a believing heart. Amen.*

*The next day John saw Jesus coming toward him and said,
"Look, the Lamb of God, who takes away the sin of the
world!" (John 1:29)*

The saving Lamb

"Don't point!" How many times have we heard a father or a mother say this to a child? "Don't point. They may see you pointing and think that you are talking about them." It is considered bad manners to point.

But such was not the case with John the Baptist. He was forever pointing, but only at one certain individual—the Lord Jesus Christ. This was John's calling as forerunner of the Lord. His God-appointed task was to prepare the hearts of the people for the coming Christ. John had plowed the deep furrows by his sharp preaching of repentance. Now he was standing and pointing the people to Jesus and talking about him. What John said about Jesus was good news: "Look, the Lamb of God, who takes away the sin of the world!"

John could not find a more meaningful name for Jesus than "Lamb of God." It speaks of our salvation. John used it to focus the attention of his hearers on the true purpose of Christ's coming. He was that innocent, unblemished, unspotted, meek, and patient Lamb. He was even prophesied in this way by the prophet Isaiah: "He was led like a lamb to the slaughter, and as a sheep before her shearers is silent, so he did not open his mouth" (Isaiah 53:7). All the sacrificial lambs that were offered before this were pointing to Jesus. He came to offer the perfect sacrifice. He became the saving Lamb. John states that in these words: "who takes away the sin of the world."

Our loving God still invites everyone to look upon the Lamb of God with the eyes of faith. No greater invitation can be extended because he is the Lamb who removes sin.

We need this saving Lamb in our lives. Our hopeless, sinful lives must be pointed toward him in order to be numbered among the saved. We need to look upon him with the eyes of faith, not only in the time of depression, trouble, hardship, and danger but also for our eternal salvation. We need to begin and end each day with our hearts pointed toward him, knowing that one day we will be with our saving Lamb in heaven. Yes, "Look, the Lamb of God!" Don't ever be ashamed of pointing to him as your Savior.

$$\infty\mathcal{G}\infty$$

*Just as I am and waiting not
To rid my soul of one dark blot,
To thee, whose blood can cleanse each spot,
O Lamb of God, I come, I come. Amen. (CW 397:2)*

14

*Praise the LORD, O my soul; all my inmost being, praise his
holy name. Praise the LORD, O my soul, and forget not all
his benefits. (Psalm 103:1,2)*

Forget not all his benefits

Forgetting can be a sin. No, we're not talking about forgetting to get
a loaf of bread on the way home from work but the kind of forgetting
that David speaks about in this psalm—the way all of us can so easily
forget about God and all that he has done for us.

David speaks to his own soul and encourages himself to remember.
Apparently he recognized the same forgetful tendency in himself that
we often notice in our own spiritual lives.

How is it that we so easily forget all that the Lord has done and is
able to do for us? When the family budget doesn't balance, we immediately begin to worry. We forget that we have a loving and all-powerful
provider who has promised to take care of us. When all seems to be
going well, we remember that "in all things God works for the good of
those who love him" (Romans 8:28), but when something goes wrong,
we forget.

This is the forgetfulness of which David speaks when he says, "Forget not all his benefits." He recognizes this as a sinful kind of forgetting,
and he encourages himself to remember. We join him in confessing our
forgetfulness, and we say with him, "O my soul, don't forget, but remember all that God has done for you. Remember that he sent his Son into
the world to pay for your sins with his own precious blood."

When we do remember, we can't help praising him. When we
remember, our prayers are no longer self-centered. When we remember,
we approach God's throne of grace with praise and thanksgiving and
expressions of concern for others—not just with recitations of our personal problems and needs.

When we remember all that God has done for us, our lives, our
speech, and our thoughts will all blend together in a 24-hour-a-day
hymn of praise.

All good things are gifts of God's grace given purely because he is a
merciful Father in heaven and not because we have earned or deserved
them. "Praise the LORD, O my soul, and forget not all his benefits"!

*Good and merciful Father in heaven, forgive our forgetfulness.
Make us see and remember all that you have done for us in
Christ. We praise you for being our loving Father in heaven and
for all your blessings and benefits. Amen.*

He forgives and heals

How often don't we hear people talking about doctors, special diets, exercise programs, and new miracle drugs? People are generally happy to speak highly of a person or product that has helped them overcome a special problem or disease.

In the psalm verse before us, David reminds himself of how the Lord had forgiven and healed him. What could doctors, health food diets, and miracle drugs accomplish if it were not for God's guiding and creative hand? The Lord heals us both spiritually and physically. No spiritual or physical ailment is beyond his ability to cure.

"[He] forgives all [my] sins," says David. He could remember the sins of his past and was perfectly aware of his daily transgressions of God's law, but he expresses his confidence that the Lord had forgiven them all. The Lord does not make distinctions between sins, forgiving some but not others. He forgives them all, even those of which we are not aware. Our Savior bore all our sin on the cross. The only sin left for which there is no payment is the sin of impenitence, that is, unbelief.

He also heals all our diseases. Can we recall any earthly doctor who has had the power to cure leprosy or to raise people from the dead? Was there ever another physician like Jesus? By speaking a word, he could heal the paralytics, the lepers, the demon possessed, and raise the dead. Is there anyone around today who can cure the common cold, much less prevent the death of every human being? The answer is the same in our day as it was in David's. It is the Lord who heals all our diseases.

Physicians, dentists, dieticians, and the like are gifts of God to society. They provide valuable services to people. God uses them as his instruments in healing, much as he uses pastors and other faithful Christians to bring forgiveness to the repentant sinner. This psalm verse reminds us that the real source of forgiveness and healing is the Lord. He is the one who deserves the praise. He is the one to whom the credit belongs.

So next time we hear ourselves praising a new diet or medicine or the accomplishments of a skilled physician, we should remember who is behind it all and praise the Lord, who forgives all our sins and heals all our diseases.

❦

Heavenly Father, we thank and praise you for our health and life, but especially for the forgiveness of sins and the hope of eternal life in your Son, Jesus Christ. Amen.

16

[He] redeems your life from the pit and crowns you with love and compassion. (Psalm 103:4)

He redeems and crowns our life

David, the psalmist, praised the Lord for the very fact that he was alive. During David's youth, God had saved him from a lion and a bear and had protected him in his battle against Goliath. The Lord had protected him when King Saul and the king's army were trying to kill him. He had fought many wars against Israel's enemies and had lived through them all.

Unlike other ancient kings, David does not brag about his skills as a warrior or his cleverness as a fugitive. He gives all the credit to the Lord: "[He] redeems [my] life from the pit." It is the Lord who keeps us out of the grave, even when death seems almost certain.

Psalm 103 teaches us that our life is not to be despised but treasured as a gift from God. In some psalms we find prayers that the Lord would preserve our life and not let us go down into the pit, that is, the grave. This life, of course, is not all there is, but the time that the Lord gives us on this side of the grave is to be received with praise and thanksgiving. In another psalm the author asks, "Who praises you from the grave?" (6:5).

The Lord gives us our time of life on earth so that we can praise and thank him. Let us use this time of grace not to gratify ourselves as though there were nothing beyond the grave but to praise our loving Savior while we have the use of our lips.

Perhaps we might think that David had more to live for than we do—after all, he was a king. But when we look at David's words, we see that, for him, the real joy of living was not the crown that made him king but the opportunity it gave him to show love and compassion to his fellow human beings.

As God's people, we are children of the King of heaven and earth. He guides our lives with love and compassion. No matter where we go or what our occupation, the Lord's love and mercy are always present. This knowledge fills us with joy and confidence and a sense of purpose. The Lord has made us kings and priests. That makes life worth living—down to the very last days and minutes that the Lord gives us. While we still have life and breath, we praise him because he redeems our life from the grave and crowns us with love and compassion.

❧

Dear Lord, thank you for preserving me from all harm and danger and preserving my life. Teach me how to use my time to praise and glorify you. Amen.

[He] satisfies your desires with good things so that your youth is renewed like the eagle's. (Psalm 103:5)

He satisfies our desires and renews us

King Solomon said, "All things are wearisome, more than one can say. The eye never has enough of seeing, nor the ear its fill of hearing" (Ecclesiastes 1:8). He recognized that the things of this world always leave us looking for more. Televisions get bigger; stereo speakers are made to be more powerful; and recipe books offer more variety.

David here tells us that the Lord satisfies our desires. The Lord knows what we really need and what we really want and takes care of it in a way that fully satisfies. What God does and gives never leaves us with that empty feeling that asks, "Is that all there is?"

Jesus says it in a slightly different way. He calls himself the Bread of Life that completely satisfies human hunger. He calls his Word the Water of Life and promises that those who drink it will never thirst. He fills the spiritual void. He gives inner peace, joy, and security—things the world cannot offer. He satisfies us with good things—with eternal blessings that do not rust or fade. He gives us things that do not lose their value and guides us on the pathway to eternal life.

His complete satisfaction of our needs and desires causes us to soar with the eagles. Our youth is renewed because our hearts are full of hope and anticipation of perfection in heaven.

People are always willing to share their new and exciting things with their friends. Invitations to come over and see the new big screen television, to hear the new stereo, or to take a drive in the new car are common. As people whose needs have been fully satisfied, we can extend similar invitations, praising our Lord who has renewed and satisfied us. We can speak often and openly about our Savior who never leaves us disappointed or looking for more.

Our satisfaction, however, is not based on what we touch and see in this world but on the unseen promises of God in Christ. Our peace is not of the world's variety, but it is the peace that exists between God and humans. That peace is found in Jesus' death and resurrection. It is the peace of God's forgiveness and promise of eternal life.

❧ ❀ ❧

Dear Lord, with you as our Good Shepherd, we lack nothing but are completely taken care of and satisfied. Open our lips, and our mouths will sing your praise. Amen.

18

Praise him for his righteousness and justice

God is holy. This is part of the definition of God. If God were not holy, he would cease to be God. People, on the other hand, are unholy—and inconsistent. While they readily admit that God is holy, they also become critical of him for his way of doing things. They blame him for everything that they see wrong in the world and accuse him of being unfair in his treatment of mankind, especially when something happens to go wrong in their own lives.

Today the psalmist encourages us to praise God because he is holy and "works righteousness and justice for all the oppressed." God is holy and just, but do we also believe that he works righteousness and justice for all the oppressed? That's what this psalm teaches us.

When we read the rest of the Bible, we see that God not only promises to work righteousness and justice but that he already has done so. Through his Son, Jesus, he has achieved holiness for all of mankind. Jesus atoned for the sins of the world. He obeyed the law perfectly and died to pay for all the world's wrongs and injustices. All people have been declared righteous and just by the divine judge. And this righteousness belongs to us by faith.

People who don't recognize this fact continue to criticize God for being unfair in his dealings with us. They feel that they deserve better treatment than they are getting. But in reality, if God were to give us what we deserve, none of us would be alive. We would be in hell. God would be perfectly fair and just to condemn us all to eternal suffering for our sins. But he does not.

Of all the good things, of all the benefits that we should not forget, the greatest and most meaningful is this: God loved the world so much that he gave his only begotten Son as the payment for our sins. The Lord Jesus took away our death and gave us his righteousness and eternal life.

❧❦❧

Jesus, your blood and righteousness
My beauty are, my glorious dress;
Mid flaming worlds, in these arrayed,
With joy shall I lift up my head.

Jesus, be worshiped endlessly!
Your boundless mercy has for me,
For me and all your hands have made,
An everlasting ransom paid. Amen. (CW 376:1,6)

He made known his ways to Moses, his deeds to the people of Israel. (Psalm 103:7)

He reveals his ways and deeds to men

People sometimes excuse themselves by pleading ignorance. They say, "How was I supposed to know?" In some cases it might be a legitimate excuse, but in other cases, just a lame excuse.

Today's psalm verse tells us that, with regard to God's blessings, we have no excuse to plead ignorance. God has revealed all his blessings and all that he has done for us. He has made known his ways and deeds.

The psalm reminds us of how God revealed himself to Moses and to the people of Israel. He called to Moses from the burning bush. He drowned Pharaoh's army in the Red Sea. He let the Israelites cross without getting their feet wet. He fed them every day with manna and provided water from rocks in the desert. With his own finger, God wrote down his commandments. He inspired Moses to write the books of Genesis, Exodus, Leviticus, Numbers, and Deuteronomy. He gave the Israelites their tabernacle and all the furnishings and ceremonies that pointed ahead to Christ's incarnation and suffering and death on the cross for the sins of the world.

After all this, the Israelites had no excuse to say, "We didn't know." God had done everything to make sure they knew that he was their God and that they were his people.

God has also made known his ways and his deeds to us. He has taken many steps to make sure that we know who he is, what he has done for us, and how we might benefit from it. God revealed himself to us in Christ. Jesus was born in Bethlehem and lived among us. John calls Jesus "the *Word*" (John 1:1) who was made flesh and lived among us to reveal God's grace, his saving love for sinners. We have the 5 books of Moses and 61 other inspired books in the Bible that all serve this same purpose. God still makes known his ways and deeds through the prophets, the apostles, and his Son.

Why does God do all this? John tells us in the conclusion of his gospel that this record was kept "that you may believe that Jesus is the Christ, the Son of God, and that by believing you may have life in his name" (20:31). Praise the Lord for revealing his ways and deeds so that we too may know and believe and have life in his name!

⁓⊙⊙⁓

Heavenly Father, we thank and praise you for all that you have made known to us about your love and our salvation in Jesus. Amen.

20

The LORD is compassionate and gracious, slow to anger, abounding in love. (Psalm 103:8)

Praise him for his love and compassion

Verses 1-7 of this psalm speak of the Lord's gifts and actions on our behalf. Today, in verse 8, we are encouraged to praise him for who he is and for the way he deals with us.

The Lord's compassion, mercy, patience, and love are all rolled together in John's beautiful saying "God is love" (1 John 4:16). God's forgiving *love* goes far beyond our normal concept of that word. The psalmist says that God is "abounding in love."

We are all familiar with the kind of love that human beings are capable of showing. People do favors for friends. Parents make sacrifices for their children. And some people will even stop to give a stranger a helping hand. These are all ways of expressing love, but God has taken love to a level that has no parallel in this world.

Paul put it this way: "Very rarely will anyone die for a righteous man, though for a good man someone might possibly dare to die. But God demonstrates his own love for us in this: While we were still sinners, Christ died for us" (Romans 5:7,8). This is more than love between friends or family. God sent and sacrificed his only Son for the ungodly, for those who did not deserve it or want it. In fact, all of us by nature still don't want it, even though it already has been accomplished. Our acceptance of God's love in Christ is the result of the Holy Spirit's work in our hearts. This too is the work of God's love.

Now we should also consider this: If God loved us enough to die for us when we were his enemies, how do you expect that he will treat us now that we have been forgiven and have been brought into his family?

Luther said in the Third Article of the Apostles' Creed, "[God] daily and fully forgives all sins to me and all believers." This is of great comfort to us in our weakness. God's love is patient and keeps us from day to day. He is compassionate, slow to anger, and abounding in love. Therefore, we have the confidence to return to him daily to receive his forgiveness and to say with David, "Praise the LORD, O my soul; all my inmost being, praise his holy name. Praise the LORD, O my soul, and forget not all his benefits" (Psalm 103:1,2).

❧◉◉❧

I will praise Thy great compassion,
Faithful Father, God of grace,
That with all our fallen race
And in our deep degradation
Thou wast merciful that we
Might bring endless praise to Thee. Amen. (TLH 384:5)

The LORD came and stood there, calling as at the other times, "Samuel! Samuel!" Then Samuel said, "Speak, for your servant is listening." (1 Samuel 3:10)

A faithful servant listens

Listening is a learned skill. We can be so concerned about getting our own ideas across and concentrating on what we're going to say next that we miss the point the other persons are trying to make. Friendships and marriages fail because the two people involved are more interested in talking than they are in listening. Listening shows love and respect for the persons to whom we're talking.

Young Samuel knew that listening was important—especially listening to God. Eli the priest taught him that skill. Three times Samuel heard the voice of the Lord calling him by name, but Samuel didn't recognize it as the voice of the Lord. The older, wiser Eli taught Samuel what to say when he heard the voice again: "Speak, for your servant is listening."

Samuel learned his lesson well. Imagine—the Lord calling Samuel by name! When it happened again, Samuel replied, "Speak, for your servant is listening." It is vital for one who will speak for God to first learn to listen to God. And it is a lesson best learned at a young age. A faithful servant listens to God as he or she speaks heart-to-heart with God's people.

God still speaks. He says to you as he did to his ancient people, "Fear not, for I have redeemed you; I have summoned you by name; you are mine" (Isaiah 43:1). We hear his voice in the Bible. There we hear words of forgiveness and life. Forgiveness and life that we have through the crucifixion, death, and resurrection of the Savior, whom Samuel knew by prophecy.

But doesn't it seem harder to listen today? There are conflicting voices screaming more loudly than ever before for our attention. These voices beckon to other philosophies, beliefs, and morals, and they speak a language foreign to God's. Yet it remains true that faithful servants listen to God. Jesus himself said, "My sheep listen to my voice; I know them, and they follow me" (John 10:27). They listen with humble hearts ready to mute all the other voices, even their own, in order to hear God's all-important message of sins forgiven—even the sin of having closed ears.

God is speaking to you today. Say, "Speak, for your servant is listening."

⌘

Lord, give me the ears and the heart of Samuel, who was eager to listen to you. Speak to me through your Word, because I need to hear what you have to say. Amen.

22

"Blessed are the poor in spirit, for theirs is the kingdom of heaven." (Matthew 5:3)

A mark of discipleship—poor in spirit

Jesus was fond of teaching by paradox. A paradox is a statement that, on the surface, seems to contradict itself. It is this very contrast that Jesus deliberately employed which makes so many of his teachings stick in our minds. They shock us; they bother us until we look beyond or beneath the surface of the statements in order to understand the points that Jesus is attempting to drive home.

If we judge his statements as the world might, or even as our own experiences might tempt us to do, the statements would have to be labeled contradictory. However, when we get beneath the surface meaning of life and apply the Lord's words to life's deepest and most crucial experiences, then the truth emerges very clearly.

Yes, what a truth Jesus places before us in these magnificent words from the Sermon on the Mount. Obviously he judges differently from the world. The world says, "Blessed and happy are they who have no worries and are carefree, confident, and secure in this life."

But Jesus pronounces his blessing on people who are poor in spirit. "Blessed are the poor in spirit" doesn't sound like a very flattering description until we see that Jesus didn't stop after the word *poor.* He added the phrase *in spirit.* That phrase takes us out of the economic world into the spiritual. There is a difference between being poor and being poor in spirit. There is no virtue in being either poor or rich in the material sense. It depends on how one uses what he or she has. Neither poverty nor riches makes a person ready for the kingdom of God.

Rich and poor alike can be "poor in spirit." The poor in spirit are simply those who know how "poor" they are in God's eyes—whose entire spirit is one of contrition, who know their frailties and recognize their sinfulness, who realize there is no help for them in the things or ways of the world, and who put their whole trust in God. The poor in spirit are those who realize they need God's help and who trust in his forgiveness and salvation, who know that without God they will fail the temptations that confront them, who know that without God they cannot accomplish the tasks they are called upon to do. In short, they are those who admit that they need Jesus as their Savior and that they need his help even to live life well.

୧ଡ଼ଡ଼ତ

Lord, may our lives mirror our need for your help in every aspect of our lives. Amen.

The disciple—truly sorry for his sins

We usually associate the word *mourning* with the grieving that people do at the death of a loved one. Is that what Jesus has in mind here? Yes and no. Jesus is obviously not talking merely about grieving, lamenting, and feeling sad—experiences on which people spend an unbelievably large portion of their lives. However, he is not encouraging any and every kind of heaviness of heart when he calls the mourners "blessed."

On the other hand, Jesus is using the picture of mourning in the spiritual sense. We as Christ's disciples are to be plunged into deep mourning as for the dead. This mourning comes at the recognition of our own sinfulness and unworthiness before God. The mourners Jesus describes are those who recognize and grieve over their sins and the havoc it has wreaked in their lives, the effect their sins have left upon other people, and even more significantly, what their sins have done to their relationship to God.

There are people who have sinned and are sorry or are filled with regret because they have been found out. Or they are sorry that they have had to face the consequences of their actions. But many of them would do the same thing again if they thought that the next time they would get away with it. Indeed, what an ocean of tears sin has produced. It promises pleasure but rewards those who give into its temptations with nothing but shame and guilt, fears and tears.

The tears of which the Savior speaks are those that flow from a humble and contrite spirit, not merely from shame and guilt at being caught. We have to be honestly and sincerely sorry for all the sins we have done.

Blessed are those who mourn for their sins. While others may regard sin as a trivial affair and are content to live the unexamined life, the mourners see that they have grieved God. Their consciences rise up and accuse them. They pray in heartfelt simplicity: "God be merciful to me, a sinner." They mourn for their neighbor's sins as well. They are grieved over crime in the streets and among the young, over the shady practices of the business world, and over the attitudes of some who profess to be their fellow Christians. And they go to God in prayer, not only on their own behalf but for others as well.

Such godly mourners will find comfort in the knowledge that Christ atoned for the sins of the world—their own included.

⌘

Gracious God, help us recognize our sins, confess them, and find that comfort we so desperately need in forgiveness through your Son. Amen.

24

"Blessed are the meek, for they will inherit the earth."
(Matthew 5:5)

The triumph of the meek in Christ

Meekness must not be confused with weakness. It is unfortunate that the English word *meek* has acquired a milk-and-mush connotation, suggesting a weak and cowardly person or a person who is afraid to fight for what he believes in. In our day, to be labeled as "a meek little person" is a title that no one covets.

But true *meekness,* in the scriptural sense of the term, is not weakness. Rather, in Scripture there are times when God calls us to speak out sharply, to defend the rights of others, to come to the defense of God's kingdom when it is under scurrilous attack—yes, even to be angry for a justifiable cause. Certainly the word *meek* would hardly be an appropriate title for John the Baptist, for the Savior when he denounced the religious leaders of his people for leading his people astray, or for the apostle Paul, whose fiery darts were thrown with pinpoint precision at those who attacked the teachings of his Lord.

Rather, the meek are those who realize how small they are in comparison with the almighty God, those who commit their way to the Lord and trust in him, those who suffer personal wrongs patiently, confident that he will vindicate them. The meek are those who follow the example of the Lord himself—the example of kindness and long-suffering.

We, as his disciples, are called upon to be like him. The Lord is well aware of how this world thinks and operates, and so he seeks to instill his spirit of true meekness and gentleness in us. It is his will that, prompted by the Holy Spirit, we might put aside those normal desires to push aside and crowd out others, climbing over them and forcing them to yield to our advantage.

Our human nature insists that if we don't fight back, using fire to fight fire or employing every dirty trick that has been used against us, we will be trampled in the dust by all the heavy heels around us. But the Lord says that not the hard-hearted or the heavy handed but the meek will inherit the earth. In spite of popular opinion, it is not force that determines who receives the benefits of God's creation. Quite the contrary! It is the meek who will possess this remarkable inheritance: the whole world.

⌘

Heavenly Father, cleanse me from all jealousy, ill will, and bitterness. Teach me to be patient, gentle, and kind to all. Ever hold before me the perfect example of your Son, and make me strong to commit all my cares into your gracious hands. Amen.

"Blessed are those who hunger and thirst for righteousness, for they will be filled." (Matthew 5:6)

Hunger and thirst for righteousness— a matter of survival

Most of us have never known what it is like to be even on the edge of starvation. Food may be high priced, but relatively few people are lacking the essentials. And not many of us have ever been on the verge of dying of thirst.

But the people to whom Jesus originally addressed these words did know about starvation. Food was hard to produce; water was scarce. A family was fortunate to have meat once a week. If a man was unemployed for more than two or three days at a time, he and his family would quite literally be starving. Or, with the hot winds and sandstorms peculiar to that region, if a person was caught in a wilderness area without an adequate supply of water, death was almost always certain.

The point of comparison Jesus draws is a straight line from the physical to the spiritual. As the body needs and desires food and drink, so the disciple of Christ recognizes his plight and feels keenly the need for God's righteousness, for God's verdict of acquittal, for God's declaring him righteous—in short, for God's forgiveness. And those who hunger and thirst for righteousness will be filled. Through repentance and faith, God grants the righteousness earned by Christ, the righteousness that continues to cover the daily sins of his believers.

Yet looked at from another angle, the disciple continues to hunger and thirst for righteousness. The disciple should never be satisfied with his present state. He should always be hungering and thus trying to live more like what God intends him to be: "growing in the knowledge" (Colossians 1:10) of his Lord and Savior Jesus Christ.

The first four beatitudes have a lot in common. Poverty of spirit, mourning, meekness, and hungering and thirsting after righteousness are all qualities or marks of discipleship. They describe those who have listened to the call of repentance and have believed the promise of the kingdom. And the same key thought runs throughout the promises made to the Lord's disciples. To those who have nothing and have need of everything, the Lord promises all that will meet their needs. The comfort and peace they need, the righteousness for which they hunger and thirst that only he can provide, and the inheritance of the kingdom that people can receive only through him—these things he promises for their eternal survival.

❧

Lord, may your righteousness be mine, now in time and forever in heaven. Amen.

26

"Blessed are the merciful, for they will be shown mercy."
(Matthew 5:7)

Mercy is Christian love in action

There is such a thing as two-sided mercy: You be kind to me, and I'll be kind to you. But that is not genuine mercy; it is more or less a simple business proposition. By contrast, the kind of mercy Jesus is instilling in his disciples is a one-sided mercy: a reflection of the mercies that the believer has received from the hands of God and that the disciple now is to extend to others without charge, without even the hope that sometime in the future that same mercy he has shown others will be returned. The disciple is not to show mercy to others with the idea that God must then show mercy to him. That too would be simply a business transaction.

What then is Christian mercy? In Jesus' time it was used to describe a person who could put himself in the place of others—to become completely identified with the others, to see life as those others saw it, to think as those others thought, to experience the others' feelings, and to know what they were going through.

To show mercy in those ways is not easy. And that is possibly the reason many people do not even try to do those things. They are selfishly concerned about their own feelings. True, they may be sorry about misfortunes that have happened to others, yet much of their sorrow is superficial. They are always looking at the other person from the outside. They do not attempt to get inside the other person's skin and see things from the other's perspective. But a Christian, desirous of showing mercy, must be as much concerned with other people's feelings and problems as with his own. What a great difference it would make in our homes, our schools, our churches, and yes, even our society if this mark of discipleship were widely prevalent.

To repeat: To be merciful makes great demands upon us. It is not the natural way for people to be or to act. Christian mercy is one-sided. That is, it helps, gives, and grants forgiveness without a thought of return. And it does this without respect of persons—whether the person to whom mercy is shown is a relative or a friend, a stranger or a foe. To be merciful, obviously, is an impossible task without the help of God. It is planted and nurtured in the soil of God's mercy already extended to us. And our Lord himself furnishes the light and heat and warmth for our mercifulness to continue to thrive, to grow, and to produce its fruits of joy and peace. Mercy is God's love in action through us.

⟡

Lord, cast out all unkindness, bitterness, and jealousy from my heart and warm it with your love and mercy. Amen.

"Blessed are the pure in heart, for they will see God."
(Matthew 5:8)

A disciple's motives are pure—doing what he does for the right reasons

It is the heart—the inner self—that is the seat of our emotions and the source of all our actions. If the heart is defiled, the poison spreads throughout the whole person. But if a person's heart is pure, his life will be likewise.

In describing the citizens of his kingdom, Jesus, therefore, marks purity of heart as one of the marks of discipleship. By using that phrase, Jesus is not describing his followers as morally pure, as though they never sin, though they may strive for such purity. Any Christian knows and is ashamed that much, much too often he has been insincere and dishonest both toward God and people. Yet the Christian also knows that he has been cleansed with the blood of Christ. And by the aid of the Holy Spirit, he will show his guileless and well-meaning intentions for all to see.

Disciples, then, are people who are open, upright, honest, and sincere in their attitudes both toward God and others. As God is pure, so they attempt to walk in his footsteps. God has no double purpose when he deals with people. He has the single aim of bringing them the gift of forgiveness and blessedness for time and eternity. The pure in heart show the singleness of heart that a man like Abraham did, leaving his country for the unknown and not staggering at the command to sacrifice Isaac or the incredible promise that Sarah would have a son. Or they show the singleness of heart of Noah, building the ark with only the bare promise of God to rely on; of the widow who gave her all to God; of men like Peter, John, and Paul, who were undaunted by threats, torture, imprisonment, or death as they preached to abusive and violent people the only truth that could save them.

To examine one's own motives is a trying experience. There are relatively few things even the "best" disciples do with completely unmixed emotions. In fact, we succeed not only in lying to God and to others but occasionally succeed in lying to ourselves. We daily need to pray to God for the cleansing of our hearts so that we might be "pure in heart." But notice the promise: Those who are pure in heart shall see God, shall see him in the world about them even when others are blind to his presence. In the end of days, they will not only hear God's Word but will see God face-to-face.

☙❧

Holy Spirit, cleanse our hearts so that we are always guided by singleness and sincerity of purpose. Amen.

28

In that day you will say: "I will praise you, O Lord."
(Isaiah 12:1)

Praise him today

The prophet Isaiah stands about midway in time between Moses and Jesus, at about the year 730 B.C. He was the great evangelist of the Old Testament. He spoke to the spiritual needs of the Israelites in his own time. He also preached the good news of what the Lord would do in the future to rescue his people from captivity. We are especially interested in his message because he prophesied about the virgin's Son, the Prince of peace, the Suffering Servant, our Savior. With Moses, the Prophets, and the Psalms, he proclaimed that "the Christ will suffer and rise from the dead on the third day, and repentance and forgiveness of sins will be preached in his name to all nations, beginning at Jerusalem" (Luke 24:46,47).

Isaiah spoke of "that day." That is the day when "the Root of Jesse will stand as a banner for the peoples; the nations will rally to him, and his place of rest will be glorious" (Isaiah 11:10). Jesus is the Root of Jesse, the banner who attracts people from all nations. He has won eternal rest for us. We live in "that day."

No matter how honest we may be or how good our intentions are, we simply have not kept all our promises. But God has done that in Jesus. No matter how hard we try to be kind and generous and forgiving, we are always poor imitators of our gracious God. No matter how sincerely we try or what personal sacrifices we make, there is no way to save ourselves or our children from the wrath of God, which we have brought on ourselves by our sins. God has won salvation for all people.

For this and for all the blessings he has added, we have reason to say, "I will praise you, O Lord." He does not need our praise, but it is good for us to praise him. He does not need our praise, but he is willing to accept it and use it in order to get the attention of those who do not know his name. He is willing to bless it in order to open the ears of those who have not heard of his salvation. He uses it to teach others to trust his mercy and praise his grace.

"That day" of God's grace and power in Christ Jesus has come, but it has not gone. We still live in the day of God's salvation. It is still the day of his favor. His first coming has passed, but it is not too late to praise him. His second coming is in the future, but it is not too soon to praise him. So let today and every day be days for praising him.

❧

"O Lord, open my lips, and my mouth will declare your praise"
(Psalm 51:15). Amen.

I will praise you, O LORD. Although you were angry with me, your anger has turned away and you have comforted me. (Isaiah 12:1)

God's anger turned away

God's anger is real, not a fiction or a figure of speech. That does not mean he loses his temper. It does not mean he sulks or pouts. It does mean that he punishes sin. When people reject him and rebel against his will, they must expect to suffer the consequences. The just and holy God does not wink at unbelief or disobedience.

God's Old Testament people had to learn this again and again. From the time the Lord led them out of Egypt to the days of Isaiah and beyond, they were "a stubborn and rebellious generation, whose hearts were not loyal to God, whose spirits were not faithful to him" (Psalm 78:8). They complained; they worshiped idols; they ground the faces of the poor.

Again and again the Lord chastised his people and punished the unbelievers among them. His anger was real, and his punishments were deserved.

But Isaiah promised a day when they would have reason to praise the Lord: "Although you were angry with me, your anger has turned away and you have comforted me." No matter what disaster came on the people of Israel, the believers among them were comforted by the knowledge that God would rescue them at last. Down to the days of Zechariah and Elizabeth, Joseph and Mary, Anna and Simeon, God always had his own who believed this. They were people who knew that he had reason to be angry with them. They were comforted by the knowledge that he would redeem them at last from every evil of body and soul.

Comfort for anger is a marvelous exchange. It is possible because of an even more marvelous exchange. God did not change his mind about his anger. He did not wink at sin. He did not stop being a holy God, justly angry at sin and sinners. No, he turned his anger from us to Christ. "God made him who had no sin to be sin for us, so that in him we might become the righteousness of God" (2 Corinthians 5:21). God does not count our sins against us. He punished them in the Righteous One, and he credits his Son's righteousness to us. Marvelous exchange!

God's anger is real. It is not a figure of speech. God has turned his anger away. That is real. He comforts us by telling us that this is so. We praise him for this comfort.

༄ఄఀ༄

Lord, if we become comfortable in our sins, remind us of your just anger and then comfort us with your gospel in order to remove our fears. Teach us to glorify you in time and for eternity. Amen.

30

Surely God is my salvation; I will trust and not be afraid. The LORD, the LORD, is my strength and my song; he has become my salvation. (Isaiah 12:2)

My salvation, my strength, my song

The song is my song. But I am not the subject of the song. The Lord is the subject of the song. He is the living God of our salvation. He is gracious and faithful, utterly dependable.

His name is repeated, "the LORD, the LORD," so that we do not forget it or forget what it means. It reminds us that we can trust him because he is trustworthy. It reminds us that we can rely on him because he does not change.

"I will trust and not be afraid." God has made me his child, but Satan points to my sins and says, "You can't be!" Jesus has won eternal life for me, but my sinful nature is still afraid of the darkness of the grave. Jesus is always with me, but I still feel lonely at times. He holds the future in his capable hands, but my old Adam still loves to worry.

Doubt and fear and worry will control our lives and ruin our relationship with God unless we remember what Isaiah is teaching us here: "Surely God is my salvation. . . . The LORD . . . is my strength." No one would think of saying, "Alcohol is my salvation." How foolish to turn to it in times of stress. It would be folly to say, "Illegal drugs are my strength," but even greater folly to turn to them to overcome weakness. They only further weaken those who do so.

More subtle and more damaging is the folly of turning to one's own resources, positive outlook, or sharp intellect in time of doubt or fear or temptation. "I will be strong; I will be brave; I will be wise." This misdirected confidence is really idolatry, trusting the sinful creature instead of the almighty God of our salvation.

Through Isaiah the Holy Spirit teaches us where to turn: "The LORD . . . has become my salvation." He became our salvation by coming to be our Savior. He overcame the temptation to doubt his Father's Word and overcame every other temptation of Satan. With our sins on his shoulders, he died, trusting and unafraid. And God raised him from the dead. He lives. Now what is there left to be afraid of?

⁓⊙⊙⊙⊱

Almighty and everlasting God, mercifully look upon our infirmities, and in all our dangers and necessities, stretch forth the right hand of your majesty to help and defend us through Jesus Christ, our Lord. Amen.

Wells of salvation

In Jesus' time these words of Isaiah were spoken on the seventh day of the Feast of Tabernacles. That was the festival that commemorated the Israelites' wilderness wanderings, when they lived in temporary huts or tents that they could move from place to place. On the seventh day of the feast, a priest drew water from the Pool of Siloam with a golden cup. Then he went up to the temple and another priest took the cup and poured the water on the altar. The priest spoke these words from Isaiah, and the people remembered how the Lord had provided water for his wandering, thirsting tribes at Meribah.

Now it is obvious that Isaiah was using the words *water* and *well* as figures of speech for the abundant blessings of God's salvation. More than once our Lord Jesus also used the picture of water to speak of spiritual blessings.

In fact, he once did so on the seventh day of the Feast of Tabernacles. "Jesus stood and said in a loud voice, 'If anyone is thirsty, let him come to me and drink. Whoever believes in me, as the Scripture has said, streams of living water will flow from within him'" (John 7:37,38). John goes on to tell us that Jesus was referring to the Spirit. Just as people need water to stay alive physically, they need the Spirit to be alive spiritually. Those who believe in Jesus have the Spirit.

Water is needed for life. In the wilderness of this sinful world, the Spirit gives spiritual life. Isaiah's words promise God's people of all time that they will have the Spirit in abundance. "Wells," he said, so the supply is not limited.

The Jews had a saying: "He who has not seen the rejoicing at the drawing of water at the Feast of Tabernacles does not know what rejoicing is." At the drawing of water they remembered how their ancestors, wandering in the desert, found springs bubbling up in the desert and rejoiced. How much greater is our joy that God has provided abundant salvation for us in his Son.

Let us not try to draw spiritual blessings from the world's philosophies and religions; they are "broken cisterns that cannot hold water" (Jeremiah 2:13). Let us draw on the Word that the Spirit has inspired, the Word through which he keeps us alive in Christ.

ᏽᎧᏽᏽ

Lord, refresh us daily from the well of salvation, the Word of your Holy Spirit. Amen.

In that day you will say: "Give thanks to the LORD, call on his name; make known among the nations what he has done, and proclaim that his name is exalted." (Isaiah 12:4)

Make known what God has done

These words are for us today; we live in "that day" to which Isaiah is referring. "That day" of God's grace and power in Christ Jesus has come, but it has not gone. Today is still the day of God's salvation, still the time of grace.

Therefore, these words are meant for us who are believers today. These words say that we are to encourage one another in worshiping the God of our salvation. More than that, they say that we are to encourage one another to witness to what he has done, to confess him before the world.

Giving thanks to the Lord and calling on his name are things we do in private, but not only in private. When we do this with our fellow believers, it becomes public and God's name receives publicity. Then others also hear that he is holy and just, forgiving and merciful.

The church's worship and confession of the Lord's name declare what he has done. These things encourage and strengthen believers, but they are not for them alone. The good news of what God has done is not something for Christians to keep to themselves. "Make [it] known among the nations," says Isaiah.

"Proclaim that his name is exalted." His name was profaned when the Israelites abused God's grace by ignoring his law. His name was despised by the heathen when the Israelites were conquered and led captive because of their unfaithfulness. His name was debased when his Messiah was rejected by his own people and put to death. But his name was exalted when he raised Jesus from the dead. His name is exalted, held high, when his people make this known among the nations.

Witnessing to neighbors, evangelizing unbelievers, missionizing the heathen make known what God has done. Make known the truth that he gave his only Son to live and die for all. Make known that Christ paid for all the sins of all people of all time. Make known that God raised Jesus from the dead and that this means he has declared all sinners righteous in his sight.

What is the best way for us to give thanks to the Lord for what he has done? Make it known among the nations!

⋐⊙⊙⊙⊙⋑

Lord, make us faithful and willing witnesses to what you have done to save us sinners from eternal death for eternal life. Amen.

Sing to the LORD, for he has done glorious things; let this be known to all the world. (Isaiah 12:5)

ℒet this be known to all the world

With these words the Lord's redeemed people were encouraging one another to praise the God of our salvation. He had done glorious things when he led them out of Egypt. He rescued them from slavery, carried out his judgment on their oppressors, and preserved them in the wilderness. He brought them across the Jordan and gave them the Promised Land as their possession.

He would do glorious things for them again when he brought Judah back from captivity in Babylon. Jerusalem would be rebuilt, the temple would be restored, and they would possess the land once again.

The things that God did to redeem his Old Testament people were only steps along the way to his most glorious act. The day was coming—the day did come—for God's rescue of the whole race. In Jesus Christ, God came to deliver every human being from the great tyrant Satan. By his perfect life and sinless death, our Savior redeemed every human being from the slavery of sin. He rescued us all from the torment of hell. He has given us an eternal inheritance in the promised land, in heaven.

When God did glorious things for Israel, he always had the salvation of all people in view. That is why his inspired prophet says here that God's people should encourage one another to "let this be known to all the world." These are missionary words. The mission concern was already there in the Old Testament, and this chapter 12 of Isaiah is only one example of that.

Even before Jesus gave his church its Great Commission at the end of his earthly ministry, he had made it clear that what he was doing for his own people was done for all people and should be shared with all people. A centurion, who was not a Jew but an officer in the Roman army, said to the Lord, "Just say the word, and my servant will be healed" (Matthew 8:8). Jesus commended his faith and said to those who were following him, "I say to you that many will come from the east and the west, and will take their places at the feast with Abraham, Isaac and Jacob in the kingdom of heaven" (verse 11).

How can that happen? It does only when the message of what God has done for all people is shared with all people, east and west. "Let this be known to all the world."

❧⊙⊙☙

Lord, increase our zeal to help the heathen by letting them know what you have done for the salvation of all. Amen.

*Shout aloud and sing for joy, people of Zion, for great is the
Holy One of Israel among you. (Isaiah 12:6)*

God lives among his people

These words complete the "Immanuel," or "God with us," section of
Isaiah's prophecy. We know that God fulfilled that prophecy most completely in the birth of his Son. We know that in the birth of Christ, God
came to be with us as one of us. We know that as one of us, he won out
against all temptation, fulfilled all righteousness, and suffered the punishment that we had earned by our sins and rebellion. We know that
God raised Christ from the dead as the proof that his life and death were
acceptable in God's sight—our sins are forgiven.

The risen Christ has promised to be with us till the end of time. He
has promised that we will be with him forever. Meanwhile, when we
gather around his Word, meet at his table, or bring our children to Holy
Baptism, the Holy One of Israel is among us. Where his gospel is, there
he is. Where he is, there is life and salvation.

There can be no greater cause for joy. Even in hard times, times of
illness, times of bereavement, he is among us to help, to heal, and to
comfort. No matter how the devil shakes you or how his followers
plague you, "the one who is in you is greater than the one who is in the
world" (1 John 4:4).

There is a time to reflect quietly on these truths and draw strength
from them. There is also a time to "shout aloud and sing for joy." When
the people of Zion, those who believe in Jesus, gather in God's house,
then it is time to sing for joy. When the people of Zion, those whose bodies are the temple of the Holy Spirit, gather for family devotions, then it
is time to sing for joy. Anytime a redeemed child of God realizes what
great things the Holy One of Israel has done for him or her, it is a time
to sing for joy.

This Sunday is the Lord's day. The people of Zion will gather in
the Lord's house. The Holy One of Israel will be among them. They
will remember and heed these words of Isaiah and those of the apostle Paul: "Speak to one another with psalms, hymns and spiritual
songs. Sing and make music in your heart to the Lord, always giving
thanks to God the Father for everything, in the name of our Lord Jesus
Christ" (Ephesians 5:19,20).

Let us be there and sing with them. If we cannot join them, then let
us still give thanks in our hearts to the God who lives in us.

*Holy Lord, continue to be with us, fill our hearts with the joy of
your salvation, and open our mouths to sing your praise. Amen.*

"I am the living bread that came down from heaven. If anyone eats of this bread, he will live forever. This bread is my flesh, which I will give for the life of the world."
(John 6:51)

A life-giving bread

When Jesus was talking with a Samaritan woman at Jacob's well, he said to her, "If you knew the gift of God and who it is that asks you for a drink, you would have asked him and he would have given you living water. Whoever drinks the water I give him will never thirst. Indeed, the water I give him will become in him a spring of water welling up to eternal life" (John 4:10,14). The water in Jacob's well was regular water. Using that as a picture, Jesus pointed to himself as a special water, a living water, a water that had life in itself, a water that was the source of life—life eternal.

Jesus did the same thing with the picture of living bread. There is much bread that is regular bread. But Jesus is a special bread, a living bread, a bread that has life in itself, a bread that is the source of life.

How can this be? Jesus explains by saying, "This bread is my flesh, which I will give for the life of the world." That is why Jesus had come to this earth. He had come to give his life as ransom. It is through his innocent and perfect life in our place and his fully atoning death in our place that God reconciled the world to himself. He did that by not counting people's sins against them. Instead, in his grace and his love, he made his Son who had no sin to be sin for us. In him the wages of our sins were paid. And now the gift of God is eternal life in Christ Jesus our Lord. He is indeed the living bread—God's life-giving bread for a world of starved-to-death sinners.

That is the gospel, the good news of God. Of that the apostle Paul in Romans 1:16 says, "I am not ashamed of the gospel, because it is the power of God for the salvation of everyone who believes." Yes, in the gospel of Christ there is a power. He is not just a regular bread but a special bread, a living bread, a bread that has life in itself, a bread that is the source of life.

Thank God that through this bread we have been given life, that the message of life in Jesus was used by the Holy Spirit to work faith in our hearts, because "faith comes from hearing the message, and the message is heard through the word of Christ" (Romans 10:17).

❧⦿⦿❧

Thank you, Holy Spirit, that we have been given life through the living and enduring Word of God, the Bread of Life. Amen.

Create in me a pure heart, O God, and renew a steadfast spirit within me. (Psalm 51:10)

A pure heart

The apostle Paul complained about his sinful nature. He said that it was "waging war" against his new nature and making him a "prisoner of the law of sin" (Romans 7:23). Even in a Christian, the human heart is a war zone. The sinful nature, an ally of the enemy, gives rise to sinful thoughts and plans.

King David knew this as well as anyone. When he spoke the words of our reading, he had come through a period of sin and unrepentance that had reinforced for him the truth that he was a sinner from birth. He had committed adultery with the wife of one of his soldiers. He had killed her husband after learning she was pregnant. He had shut up this sin in his heart for nine long months. But by God's grace he was called back to faith. Now, with the filth of his heart clearly fixed in his mind, he asked God for a pure heart. And the Lord cleansed his heart of its guilt.

Who of us does not yearn for a pure heart? We too have sinned. At one time we thought sin wouldn't harm us. We believed it was a good idea. We secretly hoped that all would be forgotten. But God pointed out the horror of our sin and called us to repentance.

When you repent of your sin, you sincerely want to change your heart. After all, *repentance* means "a change of heart." Your attitude toward sin is reversed. You regret what you did. You know it was foolish and hurtful. You know it was an offense against God. You don't want to repeat it. But knowing your sinful heart, how can you hope to change?

Your hope for a pure heart starts with God's forgiveness of sin. God's love and forgiveness create a new nature in us that is pure and clean. Does God forgive you merely so that you can start another round of sinning? No! Repentant David wanted nothing more than for God to give his new man one victory after another. He wanted a spirit that would not waver back to a flippant attitude toward sin, a steadfast spirit that would desire nothing other than to please his Lord.

~~~

Lord, I admit that I am weak and sinful. Since I will have my sinful nature as long as I live, encourage me not to surrender to sin and Satan, for I am easily discouraged. My heart has never been pure, and sometimes I have not even tried to overcome sin. Forgive me, Father, and purify my heart. Give me power to resist temptation and faith to look to you in my weakness. Grant your Holy Spirit to guide and sustain me though life. Amen.

Renew a steadfast spirit within me. (Psalm 51:10)

A steadfast heart

Monday blahs. Sometimes we feel them when we go back to work or school. What a contrast from how we felt after leaving church on Sunday. Why is it that we rarely feel spiritually recharged on Monday morning, only 24 hours after we were in God's house?

Sunday's message fades too quickly from our minds. I have a friend who says, "I have a good memory, but it's short." Monday blahs is a symptom that shows short memories are common among Christians. Our songs of praise to God, the words of absolution, the Scripture readings, and the sermon all have a way of falling into the backs of our minds.

So we pray along with King David: "Renew a steadfast spirit within me." We want to turn Sunday's gospel into Monday's confident joy. We want the sins we have renounced in the church service to remain repulsive to us until the following Sunday morning.

God doesn't have this problem. "I the LORD do not change. So you . . . are not destroyed" (Malachi 3:6). The Lord is steadfast. His grace never fades, never fails, never changes. There is one constant in our world: the Lord's forgiving love. The cross of Christ towers over every trial and temptation and assures us that the Lord will remain steadfast at our sides.

Our faithful God transforms our fickle hearts through the gospel. "It is good for our hearts to be strengthened by grace" (Hebrews 13:9). As we recall what God has done to save us, we find the strength and courage we need to remain faithful to him. It is not an accident that the great resurrection chapter of the Bible exhorts us to stand firm. After Paul praises God for victory over death, Paul uses this victory as the reason for us to remain steadfast: "Therefore, my dear brothers, stand firm. Let nothing move you. Always give yourselves fully to the work of the Lord, because you know that your labor in the Lord is not in vain" (1 Corinthians 15:58).

Remember the truths you learn in church each Sunday, and remember God's love and faithfulness. In him you will find the power that renews your spirit and makes it steadfast. In him you will find the strength to serve him throughout the week at home, at work, or in school—service that will yield eternal benefits.

Heavenly Father, in a changing world, what a comfort it is to know your changeless love! Renew a steadfast spirit within me. Keep me from shifting my allegiance to the things of this world. Give me the strength this week to remain faithful to you in all I do. Amen.

*You do not delight in sacrifice, or I would bring it; you do
not take pleasure in burnt offerings. The sacrifices of God
are a broken spirit; a broken and contrite heart, O God, you
will not despise. (Psalm 51:16,17)*

A broken heart

A broken heart is a changed heart. The thief on the cross who said,
"Jesus, remember me when you come into your kingdom" (Luke 23:42)
had a broken heart. He was neither smug nor sarcastic. He knew he
needed Jesus.

The world considers anything broken or crushed to be of no value. In
God's eyes, however, broken and crushed hearts are more valuable than
anything else we might give him. In fact, such a heart must be there if the
other things we give him are to have any value at all. For the Old Testament Israelites, this meant that before they brought their burnt offerings
and sacrifices to God, they first had to bring him their broken hearts.

What are hearts like before they are broken? They feel confident
and strong. They feel bold about sin and rebellion against God. But it is
a false confidence, a sham strength, a foolish boldness, and a foolhardy
rebellion. A heart that has not been broken seems strong—until something stronger comes along.

Sinners with the taste of failure in their mouths do not have the luxury of false confidence. Sinners who feel the strength of the almighty God
who is holy and just taste the foolishness of their rebellion. When the full
weight of sin slams down on a sinner, when the spotlight of God's law
reveals the true nature of his sin, he can no longer deceive himself and
suddenly realizes this: I have ruined it all; who will rescue me?

A broken heart is a blessed thing, because it is in position to understand the real nature of God when it hears the gospel of God's forgiveness. Once when Luther's heart was crushed by the knowledge of his
sins, his mentor, Dr. John Staupitz, told him this was exactly why God
had sent his Son: "You will have to get used to the belief that Christ is a
real Savior and you a real sinner."

When your broken heart reminds you that you are a real sinner, let
the gospel remind you that you have a real Savior. He does not despise
broken hearts; he forgives and heals them.

❦

*Lord, I have sinned against you. Forgive me, Lord, for the sake
of your Son. Wash away my sins, and heal my broken heart.
Show your love to me, because I yearn for your salvation. Help
me and comfort me when my heart is crushed. Lift me up with
the message of your grace. Amen.*

Restore to me the joy of your salvation. (Psalm 51:12)

8 February

A joyful heart

The rush of adrenaline, the roar of the crowd, the thrill of victory—those are the things that draw people to competitive sports. Of course, to experience the joy of victory, athletes must go through rigorous training and sometimes play even though they are injured. It's not all joy.

Christians experience the joy of salvation when they come to faith in their Savior. It's as simple as that. But for Christians on this side of heaven, it's not all joy. Sin can spoil our joy.

Picture the pure joy of the shepherd David standing triumphant over Goliath. Imagine King David dancing with joy when the ark of the covenant was brought into Jerusalem. Now see him weep with shame at his adultery. Those tears produced our reading for today: "Restore to me the joy of your salvation."

The Lord answered David's prayer. The joy David had experienced before he had sinned returned. God restored David's joy by forgiving his sins and reminding him of that forgiveness during the aftermath of doubt that followed his sin and unrepentance.

Joy comes from salvation. You may have experienced that joy in a special way, as David did, when you were forgiven a great sin that distressed your conscience. But the joy of salvation is the saved sinner's ongoing experience.

You have reason to be full of joy in every situation. The Bible says, "Even though you do not see him now, you believe in him and are filled with an inexpressible and glorious joy, for you are receiving the goal of your faith, the salvation of your souls" (1 Peter 1:8,9).

We know God has forgiven us, but sometimes the shame of what we have done remains. When that happens, remember that God is glad to answer this prayer: "Restore to me the joy of your salvation."

The victors' joy at a sporting event can't beat the joy we have as Christians. This year's World Series champs and Super Bowl champs have joy, but it will not last. We, on the other hand, are "more than conquerors" (Romans 8:37) through him who loves us. The joy of our Lord's salvation is ours forever.

⎯⎯∞⎯⎯

Lord, what a joy it is to be your child! Your mercies are new every morning. My greatest joy is that I will spend eternity with you. Although I know these truths, sin sometimes robs me of the joy of your salvation. When that happens, lift up my eyes to my source of joy and restore to me the joy of your salvation. Amen.

Grant me a willing spirit, to sustain me. (Psalm 51:12)

A willing heart

Sabrina wept when her parents caught her smoking. She was ashamed for disobeying and disappointing them. That was last week. Today her friend is pressuring her in front of other girls to "take a few puffs." Sabrina knows her parents won't find out this time. Last week's tears, however, reflect a change of heart about disobeying her parents. Sabrina hesitates for a moment because she's afraid of what the girls will say if she doesn't go along. But then she turns the offer down.

There comes a time after we repent when we have the opportunity to repeat that sin. David knew that there would be more battles between his sinful nature and his new self. King David knew he hadn't experienced his final temptation. What would he do the next time he had a similar opportunity? His fall into sin had been painful. He didn't want to repeat the sin. So he prayed for a willing spirit, a heart that was willing to follow the Lord, a heart that would sustain him the next time he was tempted.

Now, it is a good thing to ask God for the strength to endure temptation and to ask him to steer us away from temptation. After all, Jesus taught us to pray, "Lead us not into temptation." But in such a prayer, we sometimes focus more on the nature of the temptation than what God really wants us to focus on—the nature of his help. Concentrating on temptation may help us analyze when and where it might occur, but turning our thoughts to God and his help increases our faith and our ability to withstand temptation.

In a variety of ways, God can increase our ability to withstand temptation. The believer looks to the Lord and says, "I will run the course of Your commandments, For You shall enlarge my heart" (Psalm 119:32, NKJV). The Lord strengthens the believer's gratitude for his or her forgiveness. He helps believers see that Satan lies when promising that this or that sin has worthwhile benefits. He enlarges hearts by filling them full of the breadth and depth of his love. Such hearts have no room for sin. Such hearts are willing to resist temptation.

⁂

Heavenly Father, I am yours. You gave your Son that I might serve you and not my sinful desires. As I consider my life, I realize that you have been my rock when I have trembled in the face of temptation. You have been my shelter during the storms of Satan's lies. Enlarge my heart, and keep me from stumbling into sin. Amen.

The excellence of Christian love

In the care and concern of a mother for her child, there is love. In the tear of a sorrowing husband at the open grave of his wife, there is love. In the helping hand that reaches out to one who is in need, there is love. Love is the universal language of hearts drawn to one another.

But sin has a habit of tarnishing the luster of love. In fact, sin has cheapened the meaning of the word *love* to the extent that it often cannot be recognized as love at all. That is why the apostle Paul felt compelled to include the Christian love chapter in his first epistle to the Corinthians. This chapter renews and refreshens our understanding of the excellence of this Christian virtue.

Christian love is much more than physical attraction. It is more than an empty emotion, even more than avid affection. True love exists and grows in a heart where Christ dwells by faith. "God is love" (1 John 4:8). And the fullness of the Father's love is seen in the giving of his Son. "God so loved the world that he gave his one and only Son" (John 3:16). His supreme act of love took place on Calvary. The cross is the symbol of wretched death; Christ's death made it a symbol of love. By that love, Christ made us God's own. Now his love assures us: "Fear not, for I have redeemed you; I have summoned you by name; you are mine" (Isaiah 43:1). This love of Christ draws us to follow his path of suffering and to stand beneath his cross during the approaching Lenten season.

We who are God's children, who know his love in Christ Jesus, cannot but return love for love. "We love because he first loved us" (1 John 4:19). His love moves us to be loving toward others. "If we love one another, God lives in us and his love is made complete in us" (1 John 4:12). His love is the sun that shines through the dark clouds of life; his love directs our lives.

That love—as it is reflected in the life of a Christian—is fully described in the series of devotions for the next several days. We shall see what it is and what it is not, what it does and what it does not do. Christian love is the supreme virtue and the source of every other virtue, because it is rooted in the original love of Christ.

෴

Abide, O faithful Savior,
Among us with your love;
Grant steadfastness and help us
To reach our home above. Amen. (CW 333:6)

If I speak in the tongues of men and of angels, but have not love, I am only a resounding gong or a clanging cymbal. If I have the gift of prophecy and can fathom all mysteries and all knowledge, and if I have a faith that can move mountains, but have not love, I am nothing. If I give all I possess to the poor and surrender my body to the flames, but have not love, I gain nothing. (1 Corinthians 13:1-3)

Without love—nothing

Looks may be deceiving. A used car may look great, with no rust spots or dents and with a clean interior and good tires, but if the motor has a cracked block, the car may be a very bad buy.

Looks may be deceiving also in people's lives. The greatest gifts and the grandest deeds of humans are nothing in God's estimation if they are done without love.

Sounds too may be deceiving. One may say things in the nicest way—even as the angels would say them—but if there is not love in what is said, the words are nothing but a hollow noise. Without love they are nothing—just clanging cymbals.

If the gifts of unfolding and explaining truth, of understanding and comprehending it, of learning and knowing it are not used out of love to the glory of God, then all these gifts are not what they appear to be. Without love, they are nothing.

Even the faith that seemingly accomplishes great things, like moving mountains or casting out devils or healing, is nothing unless it is faith born of the love of Christ—faith that reflects his love.

Perhaps the strongest indicators, or earmarks, of true love are the desire to share and the willingness to sacrifice. Generosity may bring millions to the poor; self-surrender may lead to the supreme sacrifice of life itself. But, again, unless these great deeds are motivated by love, they are nothing.

All of this is not said to discourage us from using the special abilities with which God blesses us; we would not want to belittle or despise great deeds. To the contrary! Special gifts and abilities bring the added responsibility of using them to God's glory. Great blessings bring additional opportunities for sharing them with others. Unselfishness and self-surrender are virtues encouraged by the Scriptures. But in the eyes of God, without real love they are nothing. Oh that our hearts may be filled to overflowing with true Christian love—a love that flows naturally out of that wellspring of love that God has shown to us in Christ!

c*✿*Ꙃ

Lord, fill our hearts with the gift of Christian love. Amen.

Love is patient, love is kind. (1 Corinthians 13:4)

ℒℴℴℯ is:

Love is the mother of Christian virtues. In our Bible verse, Paul tells us that love is patient and kind. We see examples of these excellent fruits of love most clearly in our Lord Jesus himself.

Jesus was patient both with his friends and with his enemies. When his disciples were slow to understand the uniqueness of his person and his mission, Jesus showed patience and understanding. When his enemies were quick to condemn him, Jesus suffered long and was patient.

Especially during the season of Lent, we reflect on his patient love. In the courts of the religious before Caiaphas and Annas, Jesus was falsely accused and shamefully mistreated. In the courts of the state before Pilate and Herod, Jesus was scourged, crowned with thorns, and condemned to death. Jesus also suffered the agony of Peter's denial and of desertion by the other disciples. He followed the pathway of sorrow to Calvary, where his love and patience moved him to pray for his enemies, to stay on the cross, and to pay the penalty for our sins and the sins of all.

We also find examples of love showing itself in the form of patience in many of the Old Testament heroes of faith. In Egypt, Joseph passed up his opportunity to take revenge on his brothers, whose envy had led them to deport him as a slave. Joseph was moved instead to forgive them. Moses had every reason to become impatient with God's people, and at times he was. Yet Moses' love and long-suffering moved him again and again to plead for them and to pray that God would forgive them.

Sometimes we may suffer at the hands of ignorant or mean individuals. And there is a great temptation to be resentful, to become angry, to speak bitter words, to seek revenge. Because our sinful flesh is constantly inclined to be unkind and impatient, we need to learn patience from the great heroes of faith. We need to follow the example of Christ's long-suffering, patient love.

The second characteristic of love that Christ teaches us is kindness. His kindness in word and deed was evident in the way he treated both his friends and his enemies. And who can measure the patience and kindness he has shown to us in forgiving our many sins and in keeping the divine promise he made through the prophet Isaiah (54:10): "My unfailing love for you will not be shaken"?

May his abiding love move us always to be patient and kind to one another!

⌒⊙⊙⌒

Lord Jesus, increase in us your attitude of love. Amen.

Love is patient, love is kind. It does not envy, it does not boast, it is not proud. It is not rude, it is not self-seeking, it is not easily angered, it keeps no record of wrongs. Love does not delight in evil but rejoices with the truth. (1 Corinthians 13:4-6)

Love is not:

Christian love is like a glittering diamond. If you view it from a different angle, it takes on a new beauty. The words above give us different views of the same Christian love. By explaining what love is not, the apostle Paul actually unfolds new patterns of love before our eyes.

Love is not envious. Christian love does not covet or look with jealousy at what others possess. Others may enjoy more earthly success, more honor, more blessings than we do. But what reason have we to be jealous of them? God's love provides us with all that we need now and for eternity. We ought to be content with what he is pleased to give us.

Love is not proud. "It does not envy, it does not boast." Love has no room for boasting or bragging. After all, what does anyone have that he did not receive? Paul, the greatest apostle, called himself the "least of the apostles" and confessed, "By the grace of God I am what I am" (1 Corinthians 15:9,10). Christian love reflects the humility of that confession.

Love is not rude. A Christian is not to be thoughtless, tactless, or rude, forgetting about the feelings of others. Rather, Christian love is thoughtful and considerate.

Love is not selfish, self-seeking, or self-loving. Selfishness lies at the root of so many of this world's problems—problems between rich and poor, between capital and labor, between nation and nation, between a man and his neighbor, between husband and wife, between brother and sister. Unselfish Christian love moves us to look beyond ourselves and to seek the welfare of others.

Love is not easily provoked or angered. Instead, Christian love tells us, "Bless those who persecute you; bless and do not curse" (Romans 12:14).

Love does not keep a record of wrongs. It bears no grudge and takes no revenge, but it follows the example of God himself, who covers every sin with the righteousness of Christ. Finally, love does not delight in evil but rejoices with the truth; it takes pleasure in whatever pleases God.

❦

O Father, God of love, now hear my supplication;
O Savior, Son of God, accept my adoration;
O Holy Spirit, be my ever faithful guide
That I may serve you here and there with you abide. Amen.
(CW 460:5)

[Love] always protects, always trusts, always hopes, always perseveres. (1 Corinthians 13:7)

Love's golden chain

These four characteristics of Christian love—protecting, trusting, hoping, and persevering in all things—form a golden chain linked together by the love of Christ Jesus. This chain of gold is made to fit every child of God; these characteristics of love ought to adorn every Christian life.

Unbelievers are all too eager to ridicule the Christian way of life. And Christians may be tempted to complain that we are made to suffer too much. Whenever we are so tempted, we ought to look to the cross, where Christ suffered quietly and without complaint. "He was oppressed and afflicted, yet he did not open his mouth" (Isaiah 53:7). Remembering how the Lord suffered silently for us, we are moved to add the first link of "always protects" to the golden chain of love that decorates our lives in him.

The second link in love's golden chain reminds us always to trust, that is, to trust one another and to put the best construction on everything. Sometimes our ears itch to hear the latest gossip, and our sinful hearts yearn to be suspicious and doubtful of others. But that is not the course of love. Love seeks to excuse its enemies and to speak well of them.

The third link in this chain gives us the boldness always to hope. Is there a problem in our homes because of alcohol or other drugs? Is there a problem in our marriages because of inconsiderate spouses? Is there a problem disturbing the relationship between parents and children? Is there any problem at all in our lives? As Christians, our hope rests in the confidence that God's power can conquer every situation and that his grace will have its way.

The fourth link in this chain of love is the bold patience that "always perseveres." "We must go through many hardships to enter the kingdom of God" (Acts 14:22). Under heavy trials it is easy to lose courage. But our ability to endure comes with the certainty that "all things God works for the good of those who love him," those who are God's children by faith in Christ (Romans 8:28). The patient and forgiving love of Christ is the foundation for our endurance.

This golden chain, with these four links of love, is made to order for every Christian. May God enable us to wear it well!

༺☙ᏏᏏᎧ❧༻

**And let my love the answer be
To grace Thy love has brought. Amen. (TLH 170:7)**

Love never fails. But where there are prophecies, they will cease; where there are tongues, they will be stilled; where there is knowledge, it will pass away. For we know in part and we prophesy in part, but when perfection comes, the imperfect disappears. When I was a child, I talked like a child, I thought like a child, I reasoned like a child. When I became a man, I put childish ways behind me. Now we see but a poor reflection as in a mirror; then we shall see face to face. Now I know in part; then I shall know fully, even as I am fully known. (1 Corinthians 13:8-12)

Love never changes

Mere human love is often fickle—sometimes hot and sometimes cold. But Christian love does not change; it never ceases. "Love never fails," Paul writes.

While Christian love is permanent, all else will pass away. The time will come when all that prophecy reveals will be fulfilled. The time will come when "tongues" that proclaim him shall lapse into silence, because their witness will no longer be necessary. The time will come when the gift of "knowledge," of formulating and setting forth truth in a way so that people may understand it and by the power of the Spirit believe it, will disappear. That time will arrive when Christ appears in glory. Then we shall know and understand the mysteries of our salvation in a heavenly manner. But the gift of love will remain unchanged: "Love never fails."

Just as a child grows to adulthood and leaves childish things behind, so the Christian grows and reaches full maturity in heaven, leaving the things of earth behind—except for love.

As long as we are here on earth, we need to keep on growing in that love. For that continued growth, we need the spiritual nourishment of the Word, and we will need it until that great and final day. Then all the glories of heaven, which we can only glance at now in the mirror of his Word, will suddenly burst into full view. In heaven we shall see God face-to-face. This will be the height of joy—to be with our Lord and Savior forever and to see him as he is.

There our love, which here is strengthened by his Word, will reach its fullness. Our love of God and of the fellow saints will never be blemished, never grow cold, never be lost. Christian love lasts forever. That is its excellence and its beauty.

❧◉☙

O God, pour the gift of love into our hearts so that we may love you and one another more fervently each day until that great day dawns. Amen.

Now these three remain: faith, hope and love. But the greatest of these is love. (1 Corinthians 13:13)

Love is the greatest

God's grace provides so many gifts that we are inclined to take most of them for granted—legs that can walk, minds that can remember, eyes that can see, hands that can help. He cares for us daily by providing parents who love us, homes that shelter us, foods that nourish us, and protection from the danger that surrounds us. Even greater than all these blessings are the spiritual gifts of faith, hope, and love.

Faith is the hand that lays hold on Christ Jesus as the Son of God and embraces him as the Savior from sin. Faith is a most precious gift of the Spirit. "It is by grace you have been saved, through faith—and this not from yourselves, it is the gift of God" (Ephesians 2:8). Faith is the foundation for our hopes and the evidence of what we are not yet able to see in person, as we read in Hebrews chapter 11.

Hope is the second in this list of three very special gifts. Hope is the expectation of eternal salvation through Christ. Our hopes are built "on nothing less than Jesus' blood and righteousness" (CW 382:1). Paul wrote to the Thessalonians, saying, "May our Lord Jesus Christ himself and God our Father, who loved us and by his grace gave us eternal encouragement and good hope, encourage your hearts and strengthen you in every good deed and word" (2 Thessalonians 2:16,17).

"And now these three remain: faith, hope and love." Love completes this triangle of God's grace. In the devotions these last several days, we have been shown what a precious gift we possess in the love God has shown us in Christ. It is love that we have in no way deserved, love beyond our understanding, that led to his atoning sacrificial death. That love made us God's own. And that love reaches its fullness in heaven; it is a love that lasts forever.

"But the greatest of these is love," Paul concludes. Love is indeed the highest pinnacle in this triangle of grace. Here in time all three—faith, hope, and love—abide with us. They all have to do with the priceless salvation of our souls. But love outranks all the others; love is the greatest. Why? On the day of God's judgment, faith and hope will no longer be necessary. We will see God with our own eyes. But love will continue, as strong as ever. The love of God in Christ, which brought us into union with God, will preserve that union forever.

"And now these three remain: faith, hope and love. But the greatest of these is love."

❧◎❧

O Lord, may your love my hope renew, in Jesus' name. Amen.

17

A new song for a new message

There are times when you just can't help singing. The man you love finally asks you to be his wife. Or the woman you love says yes to your proposal. Your broker calls and tells you that the investment you thought was a lemon is suddenly paying off in a big way. Your favorite team wins a championship after spending a long time in the cellar. Or a very sick child passes a crisis and is on the way to recovery.

You just can't help singing at times like those. You've just gotten some really great news. It's the kind of news that fills your heart with glee, that makes your face glow, and that makes your mouth whistle, hum, and sing. This is especially true if you were expecting bad news to begin with.

Isaiah the prophet told his people to sing a new song to the Lord. He could tell them to do that because he had good news for them, the best news of all. This good news was a new message about new things that God would do for his people. The new message that Isaiah gave the people was a startling turnaround from what they had every reason to expect.

The people had every reason to expect that God would come to them with anger and punishment. Isaiah had accused the people of rebelling against God, of doing the very opposite of what he wanted. The people even bowed down to what their hands made rather than to the God who made them. They didn't turn to God for the help they needed; they turned to helpless idols that they had to prop up to keep from falling.

The people had every reason to expect that God would break them to pieces and choke the life right out of them. They had every reason to expect that God would lock them in a dark prison and throw away the key. But God did just the opposite. He promised to send his Servant, who would not break those who are bruised but would heal them. The Servant would not yell at sinners or threaten them with what they deserve; he would speak soothing words of love and forgiveness. Instead of locking sinners in the darkness, he would come to set them free.

The new message of Isaiah was that God loves sinners. The new message said that God would send his Servant, the Messiah, to save the people from sin. Instead of the condemnation and punishment that sinners deserve, there was forgiveness, love, honor, and blessing. There was reason for the people to sing a new song. That same Savior, Jesus Christ, is also our reason to sing.

❦

Lord Jesus, we thank you for your saving love. Amen.

18 *February*

A new song from a new heart

"Jesus loves me, this I know, for the Bible tells me so." That simple song is a very good example of the kind of "new song" that we can sing. It also contains the good news that gives us every reason to sing for joy. God loves us. Jesus came into the world to be our Savior, and we have forgiveness for all our sins. We can't help singing a new song to the Lord when we hear the good news of God's love in Jesus.

But not everyone joins in the new song. Not everyone cares about the good news. Many people don't think the truth that Jesus loves them is good news at all. That's no surprise. The same news is not good to everyone who hears it.

Think about how you would feel if you heard the news that a sudden warm spell is headed your way. All the ice and snow you have will be gone. That would be great news, wouldn't it? No more snow to shovel, no icy roads to drive on, and lower heating bills—wouldn't that make you sing for joy? But what if you like to ski? or skate? What about the snowmobile enthusiast? What about the children of all ages who like to make snowmen and just love to romp around in the snow? What if your basement floods because of the melting snow? What if you have been making a lot of money shoveling or plowing snow? Then the good news becomes bad news. You want to moan and groan instead of sing.

The news is the same, but your attitude is different. It's like that with the old hearts that we sinners have. Such hearts are blinded by sin. People whose hearts stay in that condition may not think their sins are all that serious. They may think that their biggest problems are emotional, physical, social, or economic. The good news they want to hear is that they're going to have plenty of money and be very successful in their businesses. They may want to hear that they'll be popular, that they'll be respected, or that they'll be healthy.

Some people know that sin is the big problem, but they want to be self-righteous. The good news that they want to hear is that they're "okay," that they're "not all that bad." They want to hear that they deserve a reward from God and that anything wrong they do is not their fault.

To sing a new song for the gospel message, we need new hearts. We need hearts that see how bad our sins are and make no excuses for them. We also need hearts made alive by the Holy Spirit, hearts that welcome the good news of Jesus and his forgiving love.

❧

Savior, thank you for my new heart, given by your Spirit. Amen.

19

Into your hands I commit my spirit; redeem me, O LORD, the God of truth. (Psalm 31:5)

God's hands receive my spirit

Do the psalm writer's words have a familiar ring to them? They should. We hear them during Lent, and especially on Good Friday. With these words, Jesus brought a successful end to his humiliation. He had suffered the guilt of the world's sins, had been forsaken by God while on the cross, and now, with these words, was asking his heavenly Father to receive him back to his exalted place at God's right hand. No one took Jesus' spirit from him. Jesus gave his spirit into God's hands, knowing that his Father's hands were reaching down to take him home.

That is God's promise to all who believe in his Son. Because Jesus was exalted, we can follow Jesus into his glory. When we experience our last moments on earth, we can cry out to our heavenly Father, "Into your hands I commit my spirit." We can be sure that God's hands will receive our spirits.

When my daughter was little, she liked to jump off the side of the public swimming pool. She would do it only if I was in the water, holding up my hands to catch her. She would jump only after I repeatedly promised I would catch her and not let her head go under the water. She knew I would save her from that because I said I would. I told her the truth. She put her trust in my word.

Is it any different between us and our heavenly Father? God says in his Word, "The spirit returns to God who gave it" (Ecclesiastes 12:7). God promises that through faith in Jesus Christ, our souls have been declared not guilty of sin. We will live with him forever.

We know this will happen because God says so. Like all human fathers, I have not always kept my word. Although I never let my daughter sink, there were other times I made promises I didn't keep. God our heavenly Father, however, is not like human fathers. He does not go back on his word. God cannot change his mind. God cannot say anything that is not the truth, because he is Truth. God receives my spirit daily as I come to him in humble confession and prayer. At the end of my days, God's hands will receive my spirit as it leaves this earth. God promises it is so. In that trust I go.

❧☙

Heavenly Father, receive my spirit as I come to you in faith. I am not able to save my soul. I have sinned and do not deserve to be called your child. But you have promised to receive me into your eternal home. Let this remain my constant hope. Amen.

Taste and see that the LORD is good; blessed is the man who takes refuge in him. (Psalm 34:8)

Taste and see

Have you ever been in a grocery store that has sampling tables at the end of every aisle? Salespeople are trying to sell their products. They offer you coupons. They give you a big story about how great their products are. But they know the best way to get you to buy the product is to let the aroma overwhelm you and then give you an actual sample to taste. Who can possibly resist when it tastes and looks so good?

The psalmist David invites us to "taste and see that the LORD is good." He invites Christians to actually experience what God has done for them.

It is easy to see what God has done. Every day we open our eyes in the morning and begin again to view the wonders of his creation. We look up and see the sky and the mountains and the trees. We look down and see our hands and feet. Our whole beings are marvelous testimonies to the power and majesty of God. As we view his creation, it becomes clear that only he could make such a place. His creation impresses us and reveals his goodness.

God, however, does not stop with our sense of sight. He adds the sense of taste. How do we taste God's goodness? We might think of the various foods God has created and how good each of them tastes. But the psalmist does not have physical taste in mind. Rather, he is referring to spiritual tasting. He encourages us to put ourselves into God's hands and to put our trust in him. Perhaps we are in a difficult situation and can't imagine how we are going to get through it. Perhaps we are experiencing spiritual struggles brought on by our sinful flesh or by the enemies of God's church. The psalmist invites us to taste the Lord's wisdom, care, power, and ability to protect us. And we are never disappointed. He soon comes to the rescue and gives us a taste sensation that will never go away.

Take up his invitation. Someday you will say, "I have tasted, and the Lord is good. How blessed I am. I will always take refuge in him. I will always be confident that he is with me."

❦

Lord, let me taste and see your goodness every day and then praise your holy name for all these blessings. When I am lonely, depressed, filled with guilt or doubt, or when problems seem beyond my ability to cope, come to my aid. Enable me to experience what so many others have—that you are good and that your love endures forever. Amen.

21

This is the day the LORD has made; let us rejoice and be glad in it. (Psalm 118:24)

Rejoice and be glad today! The day is the Lord's

Ever have one of those days? Everything that could go wrong does go wrong. Plans fall through. People you counted on let you down. Nothing seems to go the way you had hoped. As long as there is sin in this world, there will be days when everything goes wrong.

Some days it may appear there is no reason for rejoicing and being glad. But even during one of those days, you can say, "This is the day the LORD has made; let us rejoice and be glad in it." It is the Lord who made this day. He is the God of free and faithful grace. He is the God who loves us, cares for us, and does everything for our good.

God controls everything that happens each day. Paul reminds us that God exalted Jesus and "placed all things under his feet and appointed him to be head over everything for the church" (Ephesians 1:22). Jesus runs the whole universe with your well-being in mind. He gives you each day as a gift—a time to enjoy his grace and glorify him with your life. Each day he controls the events of the world to make certain that you will indeed be blessed in all things. When you know this, you can say with the psalmist, "This is the day the LORD has made; let us rejoice and be glad in it."

Yet we also must remember that there will come a time when the Lord will make no more days on this earth. On the Last Day, sin and death will be destroyed. On that day the dead will rise. We will receive perfect glorified bodies like Jesus' glorified body. Finally, God will take us to heaven, where there will be no more days when things go wrong and people hurt us. Then there will be nothing but happiness, glory, and bliss beyond anything we can imagine. And it will last forever. On that day we will sing the psalmist's words as we have never sung them before: "This is the day the LORD has made; let us rejoice and be glad in it."

Rejoice and be glad today! The day is the Lord's!

Dear Lord Jesus, every day you love us and rule the entire universe for our good. Every day we enjoy the blessings of your salvation. Thank you for this day, no matter what it brings. I know you will give me opportunities to glorify you and witness to your name. Help me glorify you with my mind and body by keeping them pure. Help me witness to your name by stepping through doors of evangelism you open for me. Help me glorify you with my time by using it productively. Come quickly, Lord. Take me to be with you in everlasting glory. Amen.

The LORD upholds all those who fall and lifts up all who are bowed down. (Psalm 145:14)

22 February

We praise the Lord; he lifts us up and sustains us

Who has not been bogged down by the burden of the guilt of sin? All have—except for those who have allowed their minds to become deluded by self-righteousness or by a belief that what they do is not sin. About them John says, "If we claim to be without sin, we deceive ourselves and the truth is not in us" (1 John 1:8). We, however, lament with the apostle Paul, "I know that nothing good lives in me, that is, in my sinful nature. For I have the desire to do what is good, but I cannot carry it out. For what I do is not the good I want to do; no, the evil I do not want to do—this I keep on doing" (Romans 7:18,19). With the psalmist David, we cry out, "Day and night your hand was heavy upon me; my strength was sapped as in the heat of summer" (Psalm 32:4).

We confess that at times we have tried to get rid of the guilt by ourselves. We have tried to blame others. We have tried to minimize our guilt by comparing our sins with the crimes of prisoners on death row. Yet we keep coming back to this: We are sinners. Our sins may not be as detrimental to society as the sins of others, yet God does not judge sin on the basis of how detrimental to society it is. God looks on every sin as an offense against him. And he reminds us, "Whoever keeps the whole law and yet stumbles at just one point is guilty of breaking all of it" (James 2:10). God has exposed our sin. We need a Savior.

God does not condone sin; he condemns the sinner to everlasting punishment. His love, however, moved him to do something about sin. Already before the creation of the world, God planned for our salvation. At God's right time, he sent the promised Savior. "We all, like sheep, have gone astray, each of us has turned to his own way; and the LORD has laid on him the iniquity of us all" (Isaiah 53:6).

No matter how often or how grievously we have sinned against our God, he is our gracious God and Lord. "He [Jesus] is the atoning sacrifice for our sins, and not only for ours but also for the sins of the whole world" (1 John 2:2). There is no need to despair. There is no need for anyone to go to hell. God promised, "If we confess our sins, he is faithful and just and will forgive us our sins and purify us from all unrighteousness" (1 John 1:9).

God reaches out to every sinner. He lifts up all who are bogged down under the weight of sin. He upholds all who fall.

⁂

Lord, lift us up when we fall into sin and cleanse us from all unrighteousness so that we may praise you in truth. Amen.

The eyes of all look to you, and you give them their food at the proper time. You open your hand and satisfy the desires of every living thing. (Psalm 145:15,16)

We will praise the Lord; he satisfies our daily needs

How readily we take God's blessing of daily food for granted. Sources reveal that the world population could well exceed ten billion by the year 2020. That is quite a contrast from the two people God placed on the earth at the beginning of time. It takes a lot of food to feed that many people. Less than 12 percent of the earth's land area is arable. Only about 3,580 million acres of land can be devoted to raising crops. Nevertheless, God has been taking care of his world. Productivity has steadily increased.

The verse from Psalms above reminds us how God is able to provide for us, not only by natural means but also by supernatural means. God provided manna from heaven for his people in the wilderness (Exodus 16:12). He sent a raven to feed Elijah (1 Kings 17:4), and he did not allow the flour or the oil to be depleted in the house of the widow in Zarephath (1 Kings 17:16). Our God is willing and able to provide. If "God clothes the grass of the field, which is here today and tomorrow is thrown into the fire, will he not much more clothe" and feed us (Matthew 6:30)?

We confess in Luther's explanation to the First Article of the Apostles' Creed that God still preserves us by richly and daily providing clothing and shoes, food and drink, property and home, spouse and children, land, cattle and all we own, and all we need to keep our bodies and lives. He also defends us against all danger, guards and protects us from all evil. All this God does only because he is our good and merciful Father in heaven and not because we have earned or deserved it. For all this we ought to thank and praise, to serve and obey him.

Not only does God provide for us, he provides for every living creature. While God has given us the privilege and responsibility to "rule over the fish of the sea and the birds of the air and over every living creature that moves on the ground" (Genesis 1:28), we have the assurance that he will provide for their needs too.

The glory of the Lord has shined on us. He richly and daily provides for us and sustains us. He is worthy of our praise.

❧◎◎❧

"Praise the Lord, O my soul; all my inmost being, praise his holy name" (Psalm 103:1). Thank you, Lord, for providing for me and all your creation. Continue to give us our daily bread. Help us never forget to praise you for all your benefits. Amen.

After he had said this, he went on to tell them, "Our friend Lazarus has fallen asleep; but I am going there to wake him up." His disciples replied, "Lord, if he sleeps, he will get better." Jesus had been speaking of his death, but his disciples thought he meant natural sleep. So then he told them plainly, "Lazarus is dead, and for your sake I am glad I was not there, so that you may believe. But let us go to him." (John 11:11-15)

Christ calls death sleep

"When I die, I will just fall asleep and never wake up again." These are the words of an unbeliever. He knows that this life has many troubles and heartaches. He feels that if there is a hell, this world must be it. Anything else has to be an improvement. He is not sure why he came into this world, but he is sure (he thinks) that when he leaves it, everything will be better because he will be asleep and will not feel anything anymore.

With certain modifications, some of the major religions of the world base their hopes for the future on essentially this same kind of reasoning. They strive for some sort of eternal extinction. They want to "sleep forever." The millions who follow after Buddha, for example, have no greater hope than that.

But who are we to criticize? Don't we too say that someone has fallen asleep when we mean he or she has died? Doesn't the Bible several times refer to death as sleep? Doesn't Christ call death sleep?

It is true; we do speak of death as falling asleep. In so doing, we are following the example of the Lord Jesus. We do not, however, mean the same thing the unbeliever does. We are not talking that way to soften the blow of death or to suggest that the dead person will probably sleep forever. We are saying it because we know that when we fall asleep, we expect to awaken again. We are indicating that we hope for a resurrection.

As sleep precedes waking, so death goes before resurrection. Good Friday came before Easter. Christ had to die before he could rise again. Lazarus had to die before Christ could raise him from the dead. We have to die (fall asleep) before we can rise (wake up) to live forever with Christ. We believe we will awaken to eternal life because Jesus, who promises it, demonstrated his power over death—he conquered death for us.

❧

Abide with me; fast falls the eventide.
The darkness deepens; Lord, with me abide.
Heav'n's morning breaks, and earth's vain shadows flee;
In life, in death, O Lord, abide with me! Amen. (CW 588:1,7)

On his arrival, Jesus found that Lazarus had already been in the tomb for four days. When Martha heard that Jesus was coming, she went out to meet him, but Mary stayed at home. "Lord," Martha said to Jesus, "if you had been here, my brother would not have died. But I know that even now God will give you whatever you ask." (John 11:17,20-22)

Learn to rely on Jesus

It is said of sports that timing is everything. A mistake in timing can turn a touchdown into a loss of yardage or a home run into a pop-up.

Suspense in the theater is all a matter of timing. Will the hero arrive in time to save the lady in distress? Timing can affect our real lives quite dramatically too. Much of what the world calls success depends on being in the right place at the right time.

Martha considered timing to be critical in the case of her brother's death. If Jesus had been there, she lamented, Lazarus would not have died. It wasn't that Jesus carried some wonder drug with him to cure diseases. Martha had seen Jesus regularly heal the sick by his divine power, by speaking the Word. She knew (such was her faith) that Jesus would have healed Lazarus if he had arrived sooner.

But now it was too late. The touchdown pass was blocked. The game was over. Lazarus had died. Or was it too late? Martha undoubtedly remembered the message Jesus had sent back when he had heard of Lazarus' illness: "This sickness will not end in death" (John 11:4). Jesus had never lied about anything or deceived anyone. Could that mean he would still work a miracle? Would he raise Lazarus from the dead? He had before raised the dead on two occasions. The body of Lazarus, however, lay decaying in the grave.

Martha was torn between grief and hope, but her faith told her to rely on Jesus. She could not understand it, but she confessed, "I know that even now God will give you whatever you ask." "Even now!" she said. Her brother lay dead; still she trusted in the Lord.

Jesus always stands ready to help those who believe. He does not abandon us. Let us not abandon him. He gave himself into death to redeem us from sin and death. He opened the way to eternal life for us by rising victorious from the dead. No matter how hopeless we might consider matters to be at times, we still have reason to rely on Christ. By his works and his words, we know he will answer our prayers and give us all that we need.

⌒◌◯◌⌒

Blessed Lord Jesus, teach us to trust in you for all things. Amen.

Jesus said to her, "Your brother will rise again." Martha answered, "I know he will rise again in the resurrection at the last day." Jesus said to her, "I am the resurrection and the life. He who believes in me will live, even though he dies; and whoever lives and believes in me will never die. Do you believe this?" "Yes, Lord," she told him, "I believe that you are the Christ, the Son of God, who was to come into the world." (John 11:23-27)

"I am the resurrection!"

An air of mystery surrounds the doctrine of a bodily resurrection. To some it seems like more of a dream than a reality. We think of it as something far off, done at some future time. We have difficulty receiving the comfort we should from it simply because we do not see it take place. We have never seen anyone rise from the dead.

As a result, we can easily slip into a here-and-now way of thinking that can undermine the gospel of Christ. The doctrine of the resurrection can quickly fade away into the background, as though it were something uncertain and of little importance. All the talk about politics, poverty, pollution, peace, and prosperity summons us to social action in response to a social gospel. Most religious leaders today call for a resurrection of society and forget about the resurrection of bodies.

It is certainly true that Christianity, properly taught, is a here-and-now religion. But the resurrection adds the most important dimension. It makes Christianity a here-and-now-and-forever religion. It carries us beyond today into eternity.

This is so only because of Christ. His words to us today illustrate the point. "I am the resurrection and the life," he says. With these words he directs our thoughts to eternity and to the everlasting life that he alone is able to give.

We don't have to dream about the resurrection. We have it in our possession through faith in Jesus. He who once died for our sins is alive again. Through faith in him we have new life, new hope. In him we have our resurrection and our life. Concerning the bodily resurrection, we conclude with Martha: "Yes, Lord, I believe."

This does not mean that we do not have anything more to do in this life on earth. The very opposite is true. Besides our other responsibilities, we have the supreme task and privilege of bringing this resurrection life to others.

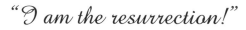

Dear Lord God, grant that we may live by the power of Christ's resurrection. Keep us in the way of truth until we enjoy the blessings of life after death in the glories of heaven. We ask this in Jesus' name. Amen.

When Mary reached the place where Jesus was and saw him, she fell at his feet and said, "Lord, if you had been here, my brother would not have died." When Jesus saw her weeping, and the Jews who had come along with her also weeping, he was deeply moved in spirit and troubled. "Where have you laid him?" he asked. "Come and see, Lord," they replied. Jesus wept. Then the Jews said, "See how he loved him!" (John 11:32-36)

Why did Christ weep?

There are certain events in life during which we expect to see people crying—sometimes for joy, sometimes for sorrow. People may cry at baptisms, at confirmations, at graduations, at weddings, at funerals. The tears we shed at funerals, however, are in a class by themselves, because death is in a class by itself. Who can begin to explain the emotions one feels at the graveside of a loved one?

Some think that maybe we should not cry at a time like that. We can understand why unbelievers might weep, because they have no hope in a resurrection and no assurance of a merciful God. Yet it is not wrong for a Christian to cry at a funeral. In fact, if anything should move us to cry, certainly it would be death. Death is the fullest expression of everything that is wrong with the world. Death brings into focus all the terrible consequences of sin. If ever a person ought to see the need for a Savior, it is when death strikes. Death is a heartrending experience.

The next time you are moved to cry at a funeral, however, remember one thing. You have someone who sympathizes deeply with you, whose sympathy is not forced. He is the one who knows better than you how horrible death is. It is the Lord Jesus. He himself wept openly at the grave of Lazarus. He knows what you feel in your sorrow. He shares your feelings. And he has done something to bring you comfort.

In his sympathy for Mary and Martha, Jesus shed tears and prepared to raise Lazarus from the dead. In his sympathy for all of us, Jesus himself passed through death and came to life again, to prepare to raise us from the dead. He has promised that we and all who believe in him will follow him through death to life. He has taken the stinger out of death so that we might rise victorious to live with him in glory. Christ, by dying and rising again, has opened the way to eternal joy with him in heaven. There God will wipe away all tears from our eyes.

❧

Lord, "even though I walk through the valley of the shadow of death, I will fear no evil, for you are with me; your rod and your staff, they comfort me" (Psalm 23:4). Amen.

So they took away the stone. Then Jesus looked up and said, "Father, I thank you that you have heard me. I knew that you always hear me, but I said this for the benefit of the people standing here, that they may believe that you sent me." (John 11:41,42)

"Father, I thank you!"

Who is Jesus? What can he do for us as we stand by the freshly dug grave of a loved one? In the face of death, the issue of who Jesus is and what powers he has becomes critical. Those who were at the graveside of Lazarus needed some convincing and some instructing on this score. Even the most faithful still registered some doubts.

As a preface to his miracle of raising Lazarus, therefore, Jesus responded to the onlookers' apprehensions by praying, "Father, I thank you that you have heard me." He did this in order to impress on the bystanders exactly who he was and to build up their faith. With these words, Jesus made sure that all glory would go to God for the miracle that followed.

What did Jesus reveal about himself with his words of thanks? His own explanation was "that they may believe" that God the Father had sent him. By introducing the miracle in this way, Jesus presented himself as the heaven-sent Savior of mankind. He is the Son of God in perfect unity with God the Father. He is the Seed of the woman who would crush the power of Satan. He is the Christ, the God-man, the hope of all people for life eternal. He is the one who deserves our faith and trust.

Indeed, were Jesus anything less, his presence at the grave would have given no more comfort than that of a well-meaning neighbor. But he is all of what Peter confessed him to be. His power over death proves it beyond a doubt. Jesus directs us beyond the grave to the heavenly Father and the joyful life at his throne. We don't look upon the grave as an ending but as a beginning. When we have Jesus with us, we have God with us, and he can do everything for us.

We who believe that God sent Jesus know that the grave cannot keep us or any who have died in him from his side. We know that God sent Jesus for our eternal welfare and will send him again to receive us to himself and bring us to our eternal home. We know the meaning of the prayer "Father, I thank you!"

❦

Our Father, we thank you that you sent your Son, our Lord and Savior, into the world and accepted his work for our eternal salvation. Keep us to the end, we pray, through faith in Christ so that we may be with him at his right hand on the Last Day and live in his presence forever. Amen.

When he had said this, Jesus called in a loud voice, "Lazarus, come out!" The dead man came out, his hands and feet wrapped with strips of linen, and a cloth around his face. Jesus said to them, "Take off the grave clothes and let him go." Therefore many of the Jews who had come to visit Mary, and had seen what Jesus did, put their faith in him. (John 11:43-45)

"Lazarus, come out!"

"If Jesus had not called Lazarus by name," an elderly gentleman is quoted as saying, "the whole graveyard at Bethany would have emptied its tombs." Such is the power of a word from Jesus. He speaks, and the grip of death is broken. At the Last Day, say the Scriptures, "all who are in their graves will hear his voice and come out" (John 5:28,29).

Think of the scene at Bethany when, at the command of the Lord Jesus, Lazarus came walking out of a tomb that had held his dead, decaying body for four days. It's an astounding picture—Lazarus, the corpse, wrapped in grave clothes, stepping out of his tomb. Then transfer the picture to the day of judgment and imagine, if you can, the billions of graves in the world opening at one time and all the bodies coming out alive. From the small cemetery next to your church to the depths of the ocean, the dead will rise and will come before Jesus for judgment, summoned by his voice.

There is at least one important difference between our rising on the Last Day and the raising of Lazarus. Lazarus was raised from the dead to continue his earthly life until the natural processes of death took over again. We will be raised in glorified bodies that cannot die again. We see something of that difference indicated by the references to the grave clothes in the resurrections of Lazarus and of Jesus. Lazarus, still in his earthly body, came out of the tomb struggling with the clothes still wrapped around him. Jesus, in his glorified body, rose free from the grave clothes, which remained in place where his body had been lying. Our glorified bodies will not be hindered by earthly things as our earthly bodies are. We will have glorified bodies eternally free of death and decay and disease.

We will be like the Lord, who will call us from the grave. We will "see him as he is" (1 John 3:2). We will be caught up to meet him in the clouds of heaven and will live with him forever. Joy and thanksgiving will fill our hearts. For us and all who believe in Christ, it will be a wonderful day when the Lord commands all the dead to come forth.

⁓⊙⊙⊙⁓

Come quickly, Lord Jesus. Amen.

Then one of them, named Caiaphas, who was high priest that year, spoke up, "You know nothing at all! You do not realize that it is better for you that one man die for the people than that the whole nation perish." He did not say this on his own, but as high priest that year he prophesied that Jesus would die for the Jewish nation, and not only for that nation but also for the scattered children of God, to bring them together and make them one. (John 11:49-52)

Christ will die that all may live!

When we hear or read about murders being committed, we feel shock and anger. As the details of a premeditated murder unfold, we react with disgust and indignation. Everyone knows that murder is wrong and that cold-blooded killers are wicked people. Caiaphas, the high priest of Israel, plotted to murder Jesus. Caiaphas was a ruthless man, brazen and clever. As high priest and head of the Jewish Sanhedrin, he held a position of great power. As he took the lead in planning Jesus' death, he ridiculed his fellow council members for their indecision and told them, "You don't know anything. The solution to our problems is simple. Jesus must die!" He appealed to patriotism, saying the death of Jesus would save the whole nation from reprisals by the ruling Roman government. He gained the council's support for his plan.

What Caiaphas and his cronies were planning was murder, pure and simple—very bad news. Yet today we Christians call the crucifixion of Jesus the heart of the gospel, that is, good news. We see some sacred irony in the scene before us. Caiaphas meant bad news for Jesus and his followers. But God used Caiaphas to proclaim good news. Caiaphas was a villain. Yet God forced him to prophesy. Caiaphas predicted salvation for the nation from Rome. God made his prediction of salvation come true for all nations—salvation from sin and eternal death in hell. Caiaphas said, "Jesus must die that others may live!" Although he did not mean to do so, Caiaphas revealed God's purpose in the death of Christ.

We, therefore, can look back at this horrible plot and thank God for making it bow to his will and serve his purposes. That is not contradictory. Christ came into this world to die the death Caiaphas urged. Christ had to die to conquer sin. Christ had to die in order to rise again and assure us of eternal life. His death and his resurrection go together as twin truths.

❧⦿❧

Heavenly Father, help us understand and believe the true meaning of Christ's death so that we may share the benefits of his resurrection. Amen.

Your attitude should be the same as that of Christ Jesus: Who, being in very nature God, did not consider equality with God something to be grasped, but made himself nothing, taking the very nature of a servant, being made in human likeness. And being found in appearance as a man, he humbled himself and became obedient to death— even death on a cross! Therefore God exalted him to the highest place and gave him the name that is above every name, that at the name of Jesus every knee should bow, in heaven and on earth and under the earth, and every tongue confess that Jesus Christ is Lord, to the glory of God the Father. (Philippians 2:5-11)

The mind of Christ

Paul presents one of the most sublime and wonderful mysteries in all of God's Word: the humiliation of Christ. This is the heart of "the mystery that has been kept hidden for ages and generations, but is now disclosed to the saints" (Colossians 1:26). This is the mystery concerning the incarnation and the atoning death of our Lord Jesus. He is "the only Son of God, eternally begotten of the Father, God from God, Light from Light, true God from true God, begotten, not made, of one being with the Father. Through him all things were made. For us and for our salvation, he came down from heaven, was incarnate of the Holy Spirit and the virgin Mary, and became fully human" (the Nicene Creed). This is the mystery of his humiliation, which in no other portion of Scripture is so eloquently, so clearly, so fully expressed and taught as in our text for today's devotion.

Christ's mind is just the opposite of man's. Sinful humans are devoted solely to self. This causes all evil in the world. Nervous disorders in personality may often be traced to self-pity. Family strife often arises because of selfishness. All areas of political and economic life are saturated with self-advancement. Triumph over self is a critical need achieved solely through the mind of Christ.

This Christ who left his heavenly home and came to earth 20 centuries ago is none less than God himself. This is the one in whom Paul says "are hidden all the treasures of wisdom and knowledge," in whom "the fullness of the Deity lives in bodily form" (Colossians 2:3,9). He is none other than Christ, "who is God over all, forever praised!" (Romans 9:5).

◈◈◈

O Lord Jesus Christ, Son of the living God, who for our salvation came down from heaven, became man, and died on the cross, give us true humbleness in heart and mind to serve you and our neighbors. All praise to your glorious name! Amen.

[Jesus], being in very nature God, did not consider equality with God something to be grasped, but made himself nothing, taking the very nature of a servant, being made in human likeness. And being found in appearance as a man, he humbled himself. (Philippians 2:6-8)

Christ's poverty

The pure and holy love that drew Christ to sinners is seen in the depths to which he was willing to stoop for our sakes. Christ possesses all things as our Creator and Preserver. How amazing, then, that the hunted fox of the field has a hole as a home for its young and the humble little bird in the trees has a nest that it can call its own but this Jesus owned no house or field during his stay on earth.

He, who is the Bread of Life, who opens his hand and satisfies the needs of every living thing, began his public ministry by hungering in the wilderness. He, who was able to provide over five thousand people with sufficient food from five loaves and two fishes, refused to turn the stones of the desert into food when tempted by the devil to do so and went on hungering. He, who is the Water of Life and refreshes the souls of all who come to him, cried out in terrible agony on the cross of pain, "I am thirsty" (John 19:28)

He, who is the King of kings and before whom all must bow their knees and render honor, dutifully paid his taxes and tribute to the government of his land. He, who was able to cast out devils with a word, demonstrating his complete authority over them, was insulted by being told that he was possessed by a devil. He, who hears and answers prayers, himself prayed fervently to his Father and still intercedes for us at the throne of grace as our Savior. With his lifeblood he paid such a precious ransom price that all the sons and daughters of men could be set free from sin, yet he was worth only 30 pieces of silver when Judas betrayed him.

All this humiliation and sorrow he suffered for us. Surely the love of Christ should move us to even deeper love and devotion.

⌀

Christ Jesus, with our whole hearts we thank you for your love that moved you to have compassion on us, to become obedient unto death, even the death of the cross, for our salvation. Help us love, praise, and glorify you for your great mercy. Amen.

[He] made himself nothing, taking the very nature of a servant, being made in human likeness. (Philippians 2:7)

He pleads for us

When Christ became human, he emptied himself of that fullness of glory that was his as eternal God. We might say that Christ stripped himself of his divine glory. He set his powers aside and did not use them.

Yes, he continues to be God, but for his divine glory he substituted the role of a servant. God's Son became a slave. Instead of being served, he did the serving himself. Instead of having his feet washed, he washed the feet of his disciples. He never gave up his divinity, but he assumed our human nature as the God-man. In this way, as the God-man, he took "the very nature of a servant."

From day to day we earnestly try to heed the Savior's call to follow him. Yet we are also painfully aware of the fact that we so often slip and fall along the way. In the awareness of our weakness, there is the danger that we might begin to despair. When we think of the majesty of God, his almighty power, and his holiness that can bear no sin, God seems far away. He is so different from the faltering, wavering people who live on the earth. That God should be concerned about us seems unlikely, if not impossible. Such feelings come when a person begins to think about God in his majesty apart from Christ.

In such a time of temptation, we should remember that Christ came from the throne of God, hid his power and glory as true God, and became a man, made under the law. He was in every way tempted as we are. Satan approached him in the wilderness and tempted him with an offer of worldly power, pomp, and prestige; Satan attacked him through the scribes and Pharisees as they dogged his steps and tried to catch him in his teachings. Satan offered him kingship, glory, and honor so that he might turn aside from his battle against Satan and sin. He was tempted more deeply than any of us, yet he resisted to the end.

It is this Christ who pleads our cause with the Father. He is a friend who understands us better than we know ourselves. He held his hand out to Judas and Peter when Satan set out to entrap them. He understood. But Judas did not want a Savior from sin. He wanted money. But Peter came to Jesus in repentance and found forgiveness. Christ understands our trouble, the trouble of sin, the weakness of our flesh. He has the only answer for our needs: cleansing and pardon. Let Christ handle our cause. Let us throw ourselves completely on his mercy, and our cause will succeed.

Thank you, heavenly Father, for sending us a Savior who understands our needs and our temptations and is able to deliver us from them. Amen.

And being found in appearance as a man, he humbled himself and became obedient to death—even death on a cross! (Philippians 2:8)

Obedient even to death

It was a great act of humility for Christ to become a human. But he did far more. For over 30 years on earth, he was "found in appearance as a man." His contemporaries knew him merely as the son of a Hebrew carpenter who grew to manhood in the village of Nazareth. Few knew him as God. Most thought him just another Galilean. In fact, during his public ministry, the Jews tried to stone and kill him because he said that God was his father.

But he was not merely a man living among sinful men; he made himself lower than the lowest of men. He became despised and rejected. People saw him stricken, smitten, and afflicted, and they thought that he suffered in such ways because of the sins that he had committed. Actually, these were marks not of sin but of Christ's perfect obedience. He came down from heaven not to do his own will but the will of his heavenly Father who sent him.

He obeyed, even to the point of dying the horrible death his Father had ordained for him. His death was like that of a lamb that is led to the slaughter, like that of the wicked with whom they intended to give him a grave. When he died by crucifixion, when he was compelled to hang on a cross, that was the supreme act of his being made a curse for sinful mankind.

And by his suffering and death, he did what no other person on earth could even begin to do. He satisfied God's wrath against sinful mankind. In this respect, what Christ did was not an example for us. It was the ultimate gift of God's unfathomable love. God loved the world so much that he gave his only begotten Son. Whoever believes in him will not perish, but have eternal life. How, then, can we show our love to him in return? By following his example of love and obedience. We can encourage and console one another as Christ did. We can demonstrate the same kind of affection and sympathy that he had, especially for the troubled. We can honor his name by doing what is right for our fellow people and by showing mercy, as he showed mercy to us.

⋘◎◎⋙

Lord Jesus, may your love for us move us to praise your glorious name in the way that we live. Amen.

Therefore God exalted him to the highest place and gave him the name that is above every name. (Philippians 2:9)

A name above every name

The story of Jesus does not end with Calvary and the cross. There is a glorious sequel. The sequel includes his resurrection from the dead, his ascension, his sitting at the right hand of the Father, and his ruling as King of kings and Lord of lords over all things. The obedience of Christ did not remain unrecognized. The Father acknowledged it with a reward. Because Christ poured himself out in death, the Father advances him to a place of honor. Death must let go.

"Therefore," Paul says, he who had "made himself nothing" (verse 7), God now has "exalted him to the highest place" and has given him a name and reputation second to none. The Old Testament had known him as the Servant, but in the New Testament, God himself gave him the name Jesus, meaning "the Lord is Savior." During the Old Testament, the Jews had shown great awe and respect for the name the LORD; in the New Testament, God the Father gave him a name that emphasized his work of salvation. Jesus is the eternal Son of the Father—the one who is, and was, and ever will be—the glorious God himself. That is why his name is above every name.

It is no accident that our Lord was called by the name Jesus. That name sums up all he came on earth to do, the work that he alone could do. He came as the God-man Savior to deliver us from the grip of sin. He came as the heaven-sent Physician to heal the bodies and souls of sinners. God sent his Son to keep the law for us all and to destroy the power of death and Satan by dying and rising again. Our Lord Jesus is the very Son of God.

In this name there is the assurance of sins forgiven. There is evidence of God's peace and mercy and the sure hope of eternal life. Is there any better reason to exalt that glorious name?

❦

The name of Jesus calms our fears
And bids our sorrows cease.
'Tis music in the sinner's ears;
'Tis life and health and peace.
Glory to God and praise and love
Be ever, ever giv'n
By saints below and saints above,
The Church in earth and heav'n. Amen. (CW 340:3,6)

That at the name of Jesus every knee should bow, in heaven and on earth and under the earth, and every tongue confess that Jesus Christ is Lord, to the glory of God the Father. (Philippians 2:10,11)

Partakers of his glory

As it had been Jesus' lot to absorb all the evil of this sin-polluted world while he was on earth, so it is now his honor to receive the worship and homage of the entire universe. While the tongues of men once heaped shame, ridicule, and scorn on him, the tongues of men will join in a grand hymn of allegiance to him whom they reviled. Isaiah (66:23) predicted that, in the end, every knee would bow and every tongue would acknowledge that Jesus is the Lord, the Savior-God.

Yes, when Christ returns to take his followers to be with him forever, all contradiction will stop, all denials will end, and all people will have to confess that Jesus Christ is Lord forever. Christian tongues will confess with thankful devotion that the same Jesus who took the form of a slave is indeed Lord of all.

Charles Lamb once said, "If William Shakespeare would appear in the company of men of letters, they would all rise, but if Jesus Christ came into their meeting, they would all kneel." Now there are many who don't agree with Charles Lamb. They refuse to honor Jesus. But the time will come when they too will be forced to confess that Jesus is what the apostle Paul calls him: the Lord of all.

On judgment day the universe of angels and archangels, of all nations and tribes and tongues, shall stand before the throne of Christ and acknowledge his power, majesty, grace, mercy, truth, and wisdom.

Our names too will reflect the glory that we share with Jesus. No longer sinners and slaves, we will be called sons of the living God.

Meanwhile, let us use our tongues to lead others to confess his name. May the Lord Jesus fill us with his Holy Spirit and bring us, at last, into his heavenly kingdom.

⁓

Lord Jesus, you have been exalted over everything in heaven and on earth. Lead us to acknowledge and to confess in word and deed that you are King and Ruler over all. All praise to your glorious name now and forever. Amen.

God . . . gave him the name that is above every name, that at the name of Jesus every knee should bow, in heaven and on earth and under the earth, and every tongue confess that Jesus Christ is Lord, to the glory of God the Father. (Philippians 2:9-11)

Christ is Lord

In his introduction to *Moby Dick*, the author Herman Melville says that a great book requires a great theme. So does a great life. Endless books and paperbacks flow from modern presses. Some achieve best-seller status, but only a very few become the world's great literature. The themes are generally too small. And who can count the years of life that have been given to humans in the course of human history? How many of those years were squandered in meaningless concern? The themes are much too small.

But now focus on the theme, the purpose, and the goal of our lives as Christians. This is no time for us to drape ourselves in black. Jesus has not left us. He has not retreated to a distant throne in the upper layers of the universe. He has not forsaken the human scene of personal dilemma. He has not removed his presence from this present time. He has ascended far above all heavens so he might fulfill his promise to us: "I am with you always, to the very end of the age" (Matthew 28:20).

"Christ is Lord"! This earliest of Christian creeds becomes the theme of our lives—the greatest theme of all. By this confession we say that Jesus has done what he came to do. He has broken the power of Satan, defeated death, and brought us life with God that will never end.

"Christ is Lord"! By this confession we affirm that Christ is on the throne. The control panels of creation and history are manned by him. And he will reign forever. We can live with faith and quiet confidence that his will will prevail. We need not fear that he will lose control of any situation.

"Christ is Lord"! By this confession we press toward the goal. Christ has gone ahead to claim victory. After a little while, the glory we now see by faith we will see in person as we join him in celebrating the victory he won for us on Calvary.

"Christ is Lord"! By this confession we express our purpose for living—to serve as Christ served in a world whose final gasping hours desperately need a Savior's love.

Praise his glorious name! It's our duty and our great joy. We were made to praise him. He brings us forgiveness, reconciliation, and life!

☙☙☙

Lord Jesus, God of our salvation, may we by our thoughts, words, and deeds praise your glorious name both here and hereafter. Amen.

Who has believed our message and to whom has the arm of the LORD been revealed? (Isaiah 53:1)

Who believes it?

About seven hundred years before the birth of Jesus, the prophet Isaiah was inspired by the Holy Spirit to write about the sufferings, death, and resurrection of the promised Messiah. He wrote as if he had stood at the foot of the cross, as if the mission of Jesus to rescue sinners had already been finished. He foretold the victory of the Christ, the Lord's Servant.

The people of Isaiah's nation, Israel, heard the message he proclaimed. He told them bluntly about their sins. He preached to them the good news of the Messiah, who would humble himself to save them from their sins and who would then be raised again to glory. "The arm of the LORD," the salvation that he would work out for them, would be revealed. But who believed Isaiah's message about the Savior, the Lord's servant? Not very many! Many simply would not believe it.

The Lord's servant did come. He "was pierced for our transgressions" (Isaiah 53:5). "He humbled himself and became obedient to death—even death on a cross! Therefore God exalted him to the highest place and gave him the name that is above every name" (Philippians 2:8,9).

But who has believed it? By nature the message of the cross is foolishness to people. It is beyond human understanding. And so when our Lord did come, he was rejected by the majority of the people of his day, even as he is rejected by the majority of the people of our day.

How is it then that we believe and confess Jesus to be the Lord's Servant who has redeemed us from our sins and prepared for us a home in heaven? By nature our hearts are no different than those of the people who rejected the message of Isaiah. Like them we were born dead in transgressions and sins. In this spiritually dead condition, we were not able to believe in the Christ by our own thinking or choosing. We owe our faith to the Holy Spirit. With the good news such as we have in this 53rd chapter of Isaiah, the Spirit has penetrated our stony hearts and has called us to faith in Jesus.

How _____ the prophet Isaiah! So many _____ his message. Do not _____ who in our ears: "Who has believed our message?" The apostle Paul vo_____ plaint and went on to say, "Faith comes from hearing the message, ___ the message is heard through the word of Christ" (Romans 10:17). We have heard the message. By the Spirit's power, we believe. In thankfulness we will share the good news so that others may also believe and live for their victorious Lord and Savior.

❦

O Spirit of God, we thank you for calling us to faith in Jesus. Give us courage and zeal to share what we believe with others. Amen.

He grew up before him like a tender shoot, and like a root out of dry ground. He had no beauty or majesty to attract us to him, nothing in his appearance that we should desire him. He was despised and rejected by men, a man of sorrows, and familiar with suffering. Like one from whom men hide their faces he was despised, and we esteemed him not. (Isaiah 53:2,3)

Appearances are deceiving

Do you remember the story of the rich man and Lazarus? The rich man seemed to have it made. He didn't have to worry about what he could eat or drink or wear. Lazarus, on the other hand, was a pathetic sight, a beggar who longed to eat the crumbs that fell from the rich man's table. Who would have guessed from appearances that the rich man would end up in hell and Lazarus at Abraham's side in heaven?

The one who told the story of the rich man and Lazarus was the Servant of the Lord of whom Isaiah wrote. This servant would grow up "like a tender shoot, and like a root out of dry ground." You don't expect much from a shoot or sapling that is growing out of dry ground. You don't picture such a shoot becoming a tree that will provide shade or bear fruit. The Lord's Servant would be born from the dried-up nation of Israel, from the descendants of David who no longer even resembled a royal family. No one could have dreamt that such a tender shoot would be the Savior of all humankind.

Isaiah foresaw Jesus in all his humility. Outwardly there was nothing about Jesus to attract people to him. He didn't live in a mansion. He didn't mix with the elite. He mingled with ordinary people and at times ate with tax collectors and sinners. He did not appear to be the kind of Christ for which so many had hoped. Many looked for a Messiah who would restore power and glory to Israel.

"He was despised and rejected by men, a man of sorrows, and familiar with suffering." Yes, see the "man of sorrows" weeping over Jerusalem, which had rejected him as its Savior. See his anguish of soul in the Garden of Gethsemane. See him "despised and rejected by men" and "familiar with suffering" as he walked the way of sorrows to Calvary. See him suffering and dying on the cross. Who could bear to look at this pitiful figure? Defeat appeared imminent; victory was out of the question.

Appearances were deceiving. The Lord's Servant humbled himself to bear the guilt of all sinners. The curse and punishment all sinners deserved were laid on him. What appeared to be a defeat turned out to be a victory. It is our victory through faith in him.

❧

Lord Jesus, help us never be ashamed of you. Give us strength of faith to confess your name before others and to live for you. Amen.

Surely he took up our infirmities and carried our sorrows, yet we considered him stricken by God, smitten by him, and afflicted. But he was pierced for our transgressions, he was crushed for our iniquities; the punishment that brought us peace was upon him, and by his wounds we are healed. We all, like sheep, have gone astray, each of us has turned to his own way; and the LORD has laid on him the iniquity of us all. (Isaiah 53:4-6)

He laid down his life for us

There are stories of combat in which individuals not only risked their lives but gave their lives to save their buddies from certain death. Those, indeed, are heroic acts, deeds not to be forgotten, especially by those whose lives were spared.

On the night before he died, Jesus told his disciples, "Greater love has no one than this, that he lay down his life for his friends" (John 15:13). Jesus laid down his life for them, but not only for them—he did so also for us and for all sinners. He served as our substitute.

There are no more beautiful words to describe this than the words of Isaiah. The Lord's Servant was not "stricken by God, smitten by him, and afflicted" because of any wrongs he had committed. Rather, it was for the sins of others. It was for our transgressions and for our iniquities. By nature all of us were like lost, helpless, hopeless sheep headed for the abyss of hell. Like sheep, each of us has "gone astray." Like sheep, "each of us has turned to his own way" and has followed the path of our sinful desires. We would be lost forever if Christ had not become our substitute, if the Lord had not "laid on him the iniquity of us all."

This servant suffered the terrible consequences of our sins. He took upon himself all the grief and misery caused by our sins. He bore our guilt. For us he was pierced and crushed! For our peace he suffered the punishment of hell. Our iniquity was laid on him.

Isaiah was led by the Spirit to emphasize Christ's suffering for us. This leaves no room for us to trust in our own works and might. ... ary death alone can atone for our sins. On its basis alone, God has declared us forgiven.

These words of the prophet Isaiah are precious. They are the very heart of the good news of the Bible. There is no better news! It is the only news by which the Holy Spirit calls sinners to faith. Through it he strengthens us in faith and enables us to live Christian lives. Let us share it with others to save them from eternal death.

◈◈◈

A thousand, thousand thanks to you, Lord Jesus, for laying down your life for us to save us from our sins. Amen.

He was oppressed and afflicted, yet he did not open his mouth; he was led like a lamb to the slaughter, and as a sheep before her shearers is silent, so he did not open his mouth. By oppression and judgment he was taken away. And who can speak of his descendants? For he was cut off from the land of the living; for the transgression of my people he was stricken. (Isaiah 53:7,8)

He suffered meekly

It is a touching scene. Abraham was about to sacrifice his only son as a burnt offering. When Isaac inquired about the lamb for the offering, his father replied, "God himself will provide the lamb" (Genesis 22:8). Isaac asked no more questions. He trusted his father, and without a word of complaint, Isaac allowed himself to be bound and to be placed on the altar. This is an example of meekness and a type of Christ who let himself be "led . . . to the slaughter" as the Lamb of God who would take away the sins of the world.

Isaiah foresaw the meekness of the Christ as he was "oppressed and afflicted." Jesus was shamefully mistreated. He was falsely accused and condemned to death. His enemies mocked him, spit at him, and beat him. He was forced to carry his own cross until he could no longer bear it. The abuse continued on the cross. And no one came to his defense, with the exception of the criminal who repented.

Mistreated as he was, "he did not open his mouth." Willingly and patiently he bore what wicked men did to him. He was meek like a lamb or a sheep that can be led without complaint to its shearing or even to its slaughter. Conscious of his great work of redemption, Jesus never complained. He did not open his mouth to protest his mistreatment or defend himself against his tormentors.

Jesus suffered meekly and patiently because it was God's will for him to be "cut off from the land of the living" and to be stricken for the transgression of his people. Jesus was willing to go the way of the cross to bear the sins of mankind. He did what neither men nor angels could do. He freed all people from the slavery of sin, death, and the devil.

As God's children through faith in Jesus, we are free. Now we want to follow his example when we are wronged, blamed for something another has done, feeling the sting of injury to our good name or reputation, or when we are mistreated or made to suffer for our faith. In a spirit of Christlike meekness, we will have no thought of or make no threat of revenge to those who wrong us. We can do so as we remember how Christ suffered for our salvation.

Holy Spirit, increase our faith in Jesus so that his spirit of meekness may be reflected in our lives. Amen.

He was assigned a grave with the wicked, and with the rich
in his death, though he had done no violence, nor was any
deceit in his mouth. (Isaiah 53:9)

He was given an honorable burial

Many people make plans for their burials years in advance. They purchase cemetery lots and even install headstones on which their names are engraved. Some may even prearrange the vaults and caskets in which their bodies will await the day of resurrection. They plan for an honorable burial.

Isaiah the prophet foretold the burial of Jesus centuries before it happened. Though the intention of Christ's enemies was that he would be "assigned a grave with the wicked," nevertheless, he was buried "with the rich in his death." The Lord's Servant received an honorable burial.

Yes, the enemies of our Lord intended to give him "a grave with the wicked." So intense was their hatred toward him that it did not stop with his death. They considered him for his claim to be the Son of God who was before Abraham (John 8:58) and who is one with the Father (John 10:30). They considered him wicked, "though he had done no violence, nor was any deceit in his mouth." They intimidated Pilate into sentencing Jesus to die by crucifixion. After his death, they wanted him truly removed quickly from the cross and buried with "the wicked," others who had been executed, in a nameless, shallow grave.

The heavenly Father, however, had different plans. His beloved Son was to be given an honorable burial. It wasn't by chance that a wealthy man, Joseph of Arimathea, requested permission to take down the body of Jesus and to give him such a burial. It was the plan and will of God to fulfill what had been written by the prophet.

The burial of Jesus was part of his humiliation as the world's bearer. His honorable burial, however, also touches on his He who was innocent in word and deed would be glorified. not be held in total bliss. He would rise victoriously!

We who believe in the crucified and risen Savior don't have to fear death and the grave. The Lord's Servant suffered, died, and was buried for our sins. Because he rose victoriously, death has lost its sting and the grave its victory. We too may plan for ourselves honorable burials with the assurance of the resurrection to eternal life.

⤫⤬

We thank you, heavenly Father, for the victory you have given
us through our Lord Jesus Christ. Amen.

Yet it was the LORD's will to crush him and cause him to suffer, and though the LORD makes his life a guilt offering, he will see his offspring and prolong his days, and the will of the LORD will prosper in his hand. (Isaiah 53:10)

His mission is a success

There are countless success stories. Some who succeed receive widespread recognition. Television programs often highlight the author of an inspiring book or the notable achievement of some sports figure. But there is no greater success story than the account of Jesus' mission in this world. The favorable results of his mission were predicted by Isaiah seven centuries before they happened.

At first glance the words of the prophet do not appear to portray success, do not appear to portray victory. The Lord's Servant would be crushed and made to suffer. We think of his agony in Gethsemane. His soul was "overwhelmed with sorrow to the point of death" (Matthew 26:38). We picture him on the cross. There he suffered the torments of hell itself. With his life he made a "guilt offering." In the thinking of all who saw him in his humiliation, it appeared to have been a stinging defeat.

All this happened, however, according to the Lord's will and plan from all eternity. He had made a covenant with his people to save them from their sins. In his grace the Lord fulfilled his promise through the mission of his Servant. In obedience to the heavenly Father's will, Jesus took on himself the guilt of all mankind, and with his life he rendered satisfaction for it to God. Willingly he suffered and died on Calvary to pay the wages of sin. All this happened to save all who are lost in sin and condemnation.

The Lord's Servant would, indeed, have success. There was no doubt in the mind of Isaiah. The Lord "will see his offspring and prolong his days, and the will of the LORD will prosper in his hand." These words announce victory. They proclaim a successful mission. They foretell how Christ, the Lord's Servant, would take back the life he laid down in death, how his days are prolonged as he lives and reigns to all eternity. He will rise and live and rule forever.

As a result of his mission, the Lord will have "offspring." They are all the sinners who by God's grace have been called to faith in their Savior. They walk and talk as the children of God.

By God's grace we who were born dead in sin and daily sin much have been called to faith in the Christ. We are the "offspring." In joy and thankfulness for what he has done to save us, we want to live for him in obedience to his commandments.

❧

We thank you, Lord, for your gracious will that set us free from the guilt of our sins. Increase our faith so that we may serve you more and better. Amen.

After the suffering of his soul, he will see the light of life and be satisfied; by his knowledge my righteous servant will justify many, and he will bear their iniquities. Therefore I will give him a portion among the great, and he will divide the spoils with the strong, because he poured out his life unto death, and was numbered with the transgressors. For he bore the sin of many, and made intercession for the transgressors. (Isaiah 53:11,12)

He rejoices in his inheritance

The Lord's Servant suffered, died, and was buried. But that is not the end of the story. He who humbled himself was exalted, as Isaiah foretold. Christ saw "the light of life." He rose victoriously from the grave. He lives and is the source of life for all sinners.

As the victorious servant, he has been given "a portion among the great." He enjoys "the spoils" of his victory. The nations are his inheritance (Psalm 2:8). Many among them will be converted by the power of the Holy Spirit. To the end of time, many will be brought to faith in him as their only Savior.

The "many" are his inheritance because of what he did. "He poured out his life unto death." He did this willingly! He "was numbered with the transgressors." His cross was placed between the crosses of two criminals. "He bore the sin of many, and made intercession for the transgressors." He asked his heavenly Father to forgive those who crucified him.

Because he bore the iniquities of all sinners, all have been justified. All have been declared righteous. Now everyone who believes in Jesus has the gift of forgiveness and is at peace with God. Every sinner who repents brings great joy to our Savior.

By God's grace through faith in Jesus, we are part of his inheritance. By nature we are sinners who deserve nothing but punishment. We fall far short of what God expects of us in our lives. But we thank the Lord for what he has done for us through his Servant. He has fulfilled the words of the prophet on which we have meditated this week. The Lord's Servant poured out his life for our sins; he bore our guilt. His resurrection assures us of the victory. In thankfulness, won't we live godly lives and make known to all the nations what the Lord has done for them? As his inheritance, we and all believers in Christ will rejoice with him forever.

❧⊙⊙☙

We thank you, Lord, for your humiliation to save us from our sins and for your exaltation to assure us of the victory. Amen.

See, your king comes to you . . . gentle and riding on a donkey, on a colt, the foal of a donkey. (Zechariah 9:9)

He came in humility

Early on Good Friday morning, the rulers of the Jews took Jesus to the palace of the Roman governor. They already had sentenced him to death. All they needed now to carry out their murderous intention was the official approval of the Roman governor. "We have found this man subverting our nation," they charged. "He opposes payment of taxes to Caesar and claims to be Christ, a king" (Luke 23:2).

Pilate's examination of Jesus revealed the charges against him had no basis. However, he did not release him. Pilate had been in trouble with the Jews before. He was afraid to offend them. Seeking to appease the Jews and at the same time to release Jesus, Pilate ordered him to be flogged. The soldiers carried out their task with glee. Not only did they whip Jesus, but they also mocked him. They dressed him in a purple robe, crowned him with thorns, and ridiculed him: "Hail, king of the Jews!" (John 19:3).

Bloodied by his wounds, Jesus was led before the mob. Pilate said, "Here is the man!" (John 19:5). "Here is the man you said wanted to be king," Pilate intimated. "Does he look like a king to you now?" Pilate hoped the crowd would pity Jesus. He was wrong. Instead, they shouted, "Crucify him!" (John 19:15).

Jesus was a king. On Palm Sunday the multitudes had welcomed him as their king. They had called him the Son of David. However, Jesus had not entered Jerusalem as an earthly king. Instead of riding on a spirited steed, Jesus had ridden on a lowly beast of burden. He had not come as the head of a mighty army. Instead, he had been followed by a lowly band of disciples. Jesus had come as the prophet Zechariah had foretold, in humility.

Had Jesus come in his glory as the King of kings, it would not have been to save us but to judge us. In order to save us from our sins, Jesus laid aside the privileges that were his and traveled the road to the cross.

As we ponder the meaning of Jesus' suffering and death, let us praise the God of our salvation for sending his Son into the world. Let us marvel at Jesus' love, which moved him to humble himself. Let us behold him and worship him as our King who deserves our praise and adoration forever.

❧☙

The people of the Hebrews with palms before you went;
Our praise and prayer and anthems before you we present.
Amen. (CW 131:3)

See, your king comes to you, righteous. (Zechariah 9:9)

17 March

He came in righteousness

God had intended that the kings of Israel should set a good example for his people. They were to lead the people in the paths of righteousness. Sad to say, this was not the way things went. When the words of our text were written, the people of Israel had not seen a righteous king for a long time. The majority of Israel's kings flagrantly and repeatedly violated God's will. There had been a few godly kings. David was one, but he was not perfect. His adultery and murder cast a shadow over the rest of his godly reign. Hezekiah and Josiah had been good kings, but they also had had their shortcomings. Finally, the kings of Israel and Judah had led their people down a path that ended in destruction and captivity.

The prophet Zechariah wrote at the time when Judah returned from captivity in Babylon. He foretold that God was going to send a truly righteous king to his people. His prophecy was fulfilled when "God sent his Son, born of a woman, born under law, to redeem those under law, that we might receive the full rights of sons" (Galatians 4:4,5).

Jesus did not come merely to set an example for God's people. He came to keep God's will for all people. God himself entered our world in the person of his Son in order to keep the law for us. To atone for our sinful conception and birth, Jesus was conceived and born without sin. As our substitute, Jesus led a holy life in thought, word, and deed. Only he could challenge his critics: "Can any of you prove me guilty of sin?" (John 8:46). From conception to death, Jesus was truly righteous and holy in his every thought, word, and deed.

How thankful we can be that Jesus kept God's law for us. As we examine our lives, we see how often we sin and fail to do God's will. We do not do what God has commanded. But the Lord Jesus came to take our sins away. Through faith in Jesus we stand justified before God, clothed in the righteousness of his Son. Let us praise the God of our salvation!

⚜

Your works, not mine, O Christ,
Speak gladness to this heart.
They tell me all is done;
They bid my fear depart.
To whom but you, who can alone
For sin atone, Lord, shall I flee? Amen. (CW 401:1)

Rejoice greatly, O Daughter of Zion! Shout, Daughter of Jerusalem! See, your king comes to you. (Zechariah 9:9)

He came to bring joy

At the time Zechariah wrote these words, there was little to rejoice about. The people of Judah had recently returned from captivity in Babylon. Work on the temple had been halted by Samaritan opposition. The Jews had fallen into disfavor with the ruling Persian monarchs. God's people had become spiritually lethargic. To rouse his people to action and also to comfort them, the Lord sent the prophets Zechariah and Haggai. In the midst of Judah's gloom, Zechariah cried out, "Rejoice . . . your king comes to you." God would send his Son to rescue his people. This was cause for rejoicing.

The people of Jesus' day also lived in depressing times. They were under the domination of the Roman government. Tax collectors overcharged them and made their lives miserable. The religious leaders of the day misled and oppressed the people. Yet in the midst of this gloom, Christ brought joy. When he was born on Christmas, the angels filled the fields of Bethlehem with their songs of joy. God's Son had become flesh. This was a cause for rejoicing. When the aged Simeon beheld the Christ Child, he joyfully praised the Lord.

Wherever Jesus went, he brought joy into the lives of sinners. Whether they were publicans, like Zacchaeus or Matthew, or a woman caught in adultery, or the blind Bartimaeus, Jesus brought joy into their lives. The joy he brought was not a mere surface emotion that soon left them. Rather, Jesus brought joy based on the forgiveness of sins and the certainty of eternal life.

In our day, people also live in depressing circumstances. People have financial problems, health problems, marital problems, and a host of other problems. People may be victimized by crime, unemployed, or socially disadvantaged. We all can point to a number of things that are perplexing to us. But whatever problems we may have, we still have every reason to be happy and filled with joy. Jesus came to save us from death and hell. We are the children of God through faith in him. Our King makes it possible for us to reign with him in heaven. We will live forever in the presence of our King before his throne. There is no greater joy than this.

❦

"Hosanna in the highest!" that ancient song we sing,
For Christ is our Redeemer, the Lord of heav'n, our King.
Oh, may we ever praise him with heart and life and voice
And in his royal presence eternally rejoice. Amen. (CW 130:3)

His rule will extend from sea to sea and from the River to the ends of the earth. (Zechariah 9:10)

19 *March*

He came to establish his kingdom

As Jesus entered Jerusalem on Palm Sunday, excitement ran high. The multitudes rushed out to meet him. "Hosanna to the Son of David!" (Matthew 21:9), the people shouted. They were looking for a king to come. If only someone would lead them in throwing off the rule of hated Rome! They longed for the day when they would be free and their borders would extend as far as they once did at the time of David and Solomon.

On Good Friday it seemed as if all their hopes hit a dead end. Jesus had been crucified. His disciples had scattered. All their hopes of a messianic kingdom on earth had been dashed to pieces.

Yet Jesus had come to establish a kingdom. The cross was not the end of the road but the means through which his kingdom was established. Jesus' mission was to pay for the sins of the world. When he suffered the wrath of God for our sins, his mission was accomplished.

On Easter Jesus rose from the dead. Before he ascended into heaven, he gave his disciples the directions for establishing his kingdom: "Go and make disciples of all nations, baptizing them in the name of the Father and of the Son and of the Holy Spirit, and teaching them to obey everything I have commanded you" (Matthew 28:19,20).

Jesus' disciples carried out his commission. Beginning in Jerusalem and traveling to Judea and Samaria, they carried the gospel to the ends of the earth. As Paul wrote to the Colossians, "This is the gospel that you heard and that has been proclaimed to every creature under heaven" (1:23). In this way, Christ's kingdom was extended—not by the power of the sword but through the preaching of the message of salvation.

Jesus' kingdom cannot be located geographically on a map. Rather, it is found wherever the gospel is proclaimed. It is located in the hearts of those who believe in Christ.

Today, as we serve as soldiers of our King, as instruments for extending his kingdom, let us proclaim the message, "Behold your King gave his life for you." Let us pray he continues to reign in our hearts. Let us share his gospel so that he may also reign in the hearts of others.

❧

Savior, sprinkle many nations, fruitful let Thy sorrows be;
By Thy pains and consolations draw the Gentiles unto Thee.
Of Thy Cross the wondrous story, be it to the nations told;
Let them see Thee in Thy glory and Thy mercy manifold.
Amen. (TLH 510:1)

See, your king comes to you . . . having salvation. . . .
Because of the blood of my covenant with you, I will free
your prisoners from the waterless pit. (Zechariah 9:9,11)

He came to make salvation sure

The shedding of blood was important in Israel's history. From the time of Abraham through the entire Old Testament, the blood of countless animal sacrifices was shed. The animal blood did not atone for a single sin. Rather, it was a perpetual reminder of the time when the Son of God would shed his blood to pay for the sins of all people.

Blood was often used to seal agreements made between parties. God himself used blood to seal the agreement he made with Israel on Mount Sinai. Moses sprinkled blood on the people and said, "This is the blood of the covenant" (Exodus 24:8). The shedding of blood made it clear that God was serious about the threats and promises he made to Israel in the law.

About 1,500 years later, Jesus met with his disciples in an upper room in Jerusalem. The time was drawing near when he was to shed his blood for the sins of the world. Jesus took the elements at hand in the Passover meal—bread and wine—gave them to his disciples, and said, "This is my body given for you. . . . This cup is the new covenant in my blood, which is poured out for you" (Luke 22:19,20). Our Lord wants his disciples of all ages to know how serious he is about forgiving our sins. To seal in us the forgiveness he secured for us, Christ gives us the very means that he used to redeem us.

Our King still invites us to his table today to receive the forgiveness of our sins and the assurance of eternal life. He knows how weak we are, so he comes to us in the supper he instituted for us. He gives us his body and his blood as a guarantee that we have been delivered from sin. Just as the Lord through Zechariah assured God's people that he would deliver them from danger for the sake of his promises, so our Lord in the supper he instituted assures us of deliverance from this world to life eternal.

As we contemplate the feast our King sets before us, let us praise the God of our salvation for his grace. Let us with repentant and believing hearts partake of the Lord's Supper for the health of our souls so that we may serve our King more zealously in his kingdom.

⁓᷉᷈᷇᷆⁓

Grant that this sacrament may be
A blessed comfort unto me
When living and when dying. Amen. (CW 312:8)

He came to proclaim peace

The scene was anything but peaceful on Good Friday. Early in the morning, the area around Pilate's palace resounded with the shouts of "Crucify him!" (Matthew 27:23). About 9:00 A.M. the Roman soldiers took Jesus out to Golgotha, the place of execution. There they nailed him to the cross. Jesus was placed between two thieves who were also crucified.

As the mob milled below the cross, they taunted Jesus, "He's the King of Israel! Let him come down now from the cross, and we will believe in him" (verse 42). Over Jesus' head was nailed the final insult of Pilate: "THIS IS JESUS, THE KING OF THE JEWS" (verse 37).

From about noon until 3:00 P.M, darkness covered the earth. At the end of that time, Jesus cried out, "My God, my God, why have you forsaken me?" (verse 46). For a king who had come to proclaim peace, the scene was anything but peaceful. Jesus was forsaken by people and by God.

However, as we behold the situation from the prophet Zechariah's perspective, the events of Good Friday do proclaim peace to us. During those hours of agony on the cross, Jesus suffered the torments of hell for us.

God took the sins of all people of all ages and charged them to his Son. He punished him that he might acquit the world.

When Jesus had completed his mission, he said, "It is finished" (John 19:30). Peace had been established between God and people. Jesus had satisfied God's righteous wrath against sin. Full and complete payment had been made.

What peace the payment of Christ proclaims to sinners! To the penitent thief dying next to him, Jesus said, "I tell you the truth, today you will be with me in paradise" (Luke 23:43). To the troubled paralytic, Jesus announced, "Take heart, son; your sins are forgiven" (Matthew 9:2). To all who labor under the burden of sin, Jesus proclaims, "Do not let your hearts be troubled. Trust in God; trust also in me" (John 14:1).

Good Friday does tell us about God's wrath against sin. But its main message is to proclaim to us the grace of a loving God who sacrificed his Son so that we may have peace with him. Behold Jesus, your King, on the cross. His death proclaims to you and all the world God's peace and pardon.

✦✦✦

On my heart imprint your image,
Blessed Jesus, King of grace,
That life's riches, cares, and pleasures
Have no pow'r to hide your face.
This the superscription be:
Jesus, crucified for me,
Is my life, my hope's foundation,
And my glory and salvation. Amen. (CW 319)

22

The LORD their God will save them on that day as the flock of his people. (Zechariah 9:16)

He came to shepherd his flock

Sheep are very helpless animals. They are not intelligent. They cannot outwit their enemies. They do not have sharp hoofs to ward off enemies' attacks. They do not have sharp teeth to tear at the flesh of an attacking animal. They do not have great speed to outrun predators. They really have only one means of defense—their shepherd. If it were not for their faithful shepherd, the sheep would soon perish.

It is no coincidence that Scripture frequently compares us with sheep. We too are helpless. In and of ourselves, we cannot stand against the attacks of the devil, the world, and our own sinful flesh. If it were not for the constant care of our Lord, we also would perish.

It is with good reason that Jesus is called the Good Shepherd. The prophet Ezekiel foretold the fact that the shepherd of God's people would be a king descended from the line of David (Ezekiel 34:23,24). Zechariah prophesied that this shepherd would be struck down (13:7), sold for 30 pieces of silver (11:12), and pierced through (12:10). All of this coincides with the words of Jesus: "I am the good shepherd. The good shepherd lays down his life for the sheep" (John 10:11). Jesus not only cares for his flock's physical needs. He has taken care of his flock's greatest need—the need for forgiveness. He did this by his death on the cross and resurrection from the dead.

Though his lifeless body was in the grave for a brief time, Jesus rose from the dead triumphantly on the third day. We, the members of his flock, have assurance that he lives to preserve us as his own until we stand with him in heaven. There the glorious vision of John will be fulfilled: "For the Lamb at the center of the throne will be their shepherd; he will lead them to springs of living water. And God will wipe away every tear from their eyes" (Revelation 7:17).

When we become frightened by the troubles in our lives and our own frailty, let us turn our eyes to our King, our Good Shepherd. He says to us, "My sheep listen to my voice; I know them, and they follow me. I give them eternal life, and they shall never perish; no one can snatch them out of my hand" (John 10:27,28).

❦

Lord, my Shepherd, take me to Thee.
Thou art mine; I was Thine,
Even ere I knew Thee.
I am Thine, for Thou hast bought me;
Lost I stood, But Thy blood
Free salvation brought me. Amen. (TLH 523:7)

"Father, forgive them, for they do not know what they are doing." (Luke 23:34)

"Forgive them"

These do not sound like the words of a dying man, especially one who is unjustly undergoing unspeakable pain. Even Christians often lose patience when heavy crosses descend upon them. Job, whose sufferings seemed intolerable, cursed the day of his birth; Jeremiah, who thought the burden of his preaching ministry too great, complained against God. These words from the cross reveal Christ's perfect love for sinners. Most people, innocent or guilty, would curse those who were nailing them to a cross.

If anyone had good reason to ask for divine retribution, it was our innocent Savior on the cross. He was hanging there because of a horrible injustice. On the testimony of witnesses bribed to tell falsehoods, Jesus was condemned to die. A frenzied crowd hissed and screamed at him. He was compelled to carry his own cross. Finally, he was nailed to the cross. And then the cruel Romans started in, hissing, beating him, spitting in his face. Surely such a depraved mob deserved to be destroyed.

Yet Christ loved these very people who without cause hated him so much that from the depths of agony he prayed for them. And there were no ifs or buts to his prayer. "Father, forgive them." Can there be greater proof of Christ's love for us?

This prayer was more than a kindhearted plea that may or may not have been heard. It was Christ's intercession for all the world. And it was heard. Christ had a right to pray like that. It was as though he were praying, "Father, I am shedding my blood for sinners, paying the debt that all people owe; therefore, I ask you to forgive them and let them go free." God answered Jesus' prayer, for Scripture says, "We were reconciled to [God] through the death of his Son" (Romans 5:10).

Think what Christ's intercession for you means. Now you have every right to believe: "If anybody does sin, we have one who speaks to the Father in our defense—Jesus Christ, the Righteous One. He is the atoning sacrifice for our sins, and not only for ours but also for the sins of the whole world" (1 John 2:1,2). You do not need dead saints to pray or intercede for you. You have a greater Priest and intercessor, Jesus Christ, the Righteous One.

❧

Jesus, in Thy dying woes,
Even while Thy life-blood flows,
Craving pardon for Thy foes:
Hear us, holy Jesus.

Savior, for our pardon sue
When our sins Thy pangs renew;
For we know not what we do:
Hear us, holy Jesus. Amen. (TLH 180:1,2)

"I tell you the truth, today you will be with me in paradise."
(Luke 23:43)

"In paradise"

Seeing him who called himself King hanging helpless on the cross, the Jewish leaders began to jeer at Jesus, "Come down from the cross and save yourself" (Mark 15:30). Such mockery became contagious. The Roman soldiers took up the chant. Even one of the crucified thieves joined in the mockery. But one man, the criminal at Jesus' right side, saw nothing to laugh at. He knew he was a sinner. He reproved the other thief and confessed that he was receiving the due reward for his deeds. Then he prayed to Jesus, "Remember me when you come into your kingdom" (Luke 23:42).

Who would have expected the thief to offer such a prayer? He had every reason to fear and despair. His whole life had been given over to crime and defiance of God. Now he was facing eternity—with such a record behind him! But in spite of all that, he dared to hope that Jesus would save him.

Jesus answered, "I tell you the truth, today you will be with me in paradise." Such words to such a man show us that there is no one so corrupt or evil that Jesus does not wish to save him. His mercy extends to all sinners, no matter how deeply they are sunken in sin. He loved Saul as much as David, Judas as much as Peter; and today he loves the drunkard, blasphemer, and murderer as much as the most virtuous Christian. "Where sin increased, grace increased all the more" (Romans 5:20).

But Christ's words to the thief reveal something else, namely, that all sinners can be saved only by God's grace. What good works did this thief have to brag about? What had he ever done to earn salvation? His entire life was one of wanton violence, without respect for law or decency—or God. And yet to such a man Christ said with an oath, "Today you will be with me in paradise." Such words to such a person certainly show that salvation comes by God's grace alone.

Dear reader, Christ's words are a sermon to you. They tell you not to let your sins make you despair but to trust humbly in your bleeding, dying Savior. He chooses to save you, as he did that thief, by grace alone, in spite of all your sins. So ask him to remember you with his pardon. He will not, he cannot, refuse your prayer.

❧

Jesus, pitying the sighs
Of the thief who near Thee dies,
Promising him Paradise:
Hear us, holy Jesus.

May we in our guilt and shame
Still Thy love and mercy claim,
Calling humbly on Thy name:
Hear us, holy Jesus. Amen. (TLH 181:1,2)

When Jesus saw his mother there, and the disciple whom he loved standing nearby, he said to his mother, "Dear woman, here is your son," and to the disciple, "Here is your mother." (John 19:26,27)

"Your son . . . Your mother"

We can imagine how the crucifixion must have rent the heart of Mary. All through his life, Jesus had been such a kind and loving son as no other woman had ever had. Even now in his agony he was tenderly providing for her. He gave her a new son, John, the disciple whom he loved.

When the child Jesus was brought to the temple, Simeon had said to Mary, "A sword will pierce your own soul too" (Luke 2:35). Now these words were fulfilled. "She sees him hanging on the cross, but cannot touch him; sees him dripping with blood, but cannot remove it; sees him wounded over his entire body, but cannot bind his wounds; hears him cry, 'I thirst,' but may offer him nothing to drink" (Gerhard).

But let us turn back to Jesus. With this word from the cross, he tells us that we are the objects of his tender concern and care. Do you ask, How can that be found in these words? Only remember that we are his nearest of kin by faith. Recall that he once pointed to his disciples (that is, people who believed in him) and said, "Here are my mother and my brothers" (Matthew 12:49).

These words are also evidence that Jesus was suffering our dying agony perfectly. If there had been any bitterness or rebellion in his heart, he would not have been concerned about others, even his mother. But every sinful thought was absent from his heart. And so he suffered all our penalties with the perfect obedience of perfect love.

Again, did he not demonstrate here that he had fulfilled perfectly the Fourth Commandment: "Honor your father and mother"? Let this stand in our minds as a sample of his perfect fulfillment of all the commandments in our stead.

What will we say, then, when some tell us that Mary, with her suffering, contributed something toward our redemption? We will reject it, saying, "A horrible teaching!" Mary was blessed above all women, yet she was a sinner in need of redemption. Her son, sinless in his conception and birth, in his living and suffering and dying for us alone is the Redeemer. Mary cannot help us, and we do not need her help. Scripture says, "There is one God and one mediator between God and men, the man Christ Jesus" (1 Timothy 2:5).

∎

Lord Jesus, keep us steadfast in this confession
Christ, his cross and resurrection,
Is alone the sinner's plea;
At the throne of God's perfection
Nothing else can set him free. Amen.

"My God, my God, why have you forsaken me?"
(Matthew 27:46)

"Why . . . Forsaken?"

You and I simply cannot understand what it means to be forsaken by God. We have never been forsaken by God. This has never happened to any believer. The very psalm from which Jesus took the words of this lament proves that: "In you our fathers put their trust; they trusted and you delivered them. They cried to you and were saved; in you they trusted and were not disappointed" (Psalm 22:4,5). There are many such assurances in the Bible.

Even the unbeliever is not completely forsaken by God in this life. God may withdraw his grace from the person who persistently rejects God's offer of salvation so that the person can no longer repent and be saved, but as long as God grants the person the breath of life and permits him or her to find even the weakest kind of pleasure or satisfaction in anything, God has not yet forsaken that person completely.

When God fully forsakes a person, he inflicts a punishment that goes beyond this life and this earth. Then he sentences a person to hell. God did just that to his only begotten Son on the cross. The word *forsake,* which Christ uses, means "to forget utterly," "to leave in the lurch," "to surrender to an enemy." God not only handed over his Son to the wrath of the unbelieving Jews and Romans so that they might torment and kill him. No, Christ was forsaken by his Father in the truest sense: He suffered all the pain and agony of eternal death. God charged his Son with all the sins of the world and made him pay for them. Out of the agony of the damned in hell, the innocent, holy Son of God cried, "Why have you forsaken me?"

These words ought to terrify us. They reveal, as nothing else can, the enormity of our sin. The curse over our sin drove those words from Jesus' lips. "What more forcible, more terrible declaration and preaching of God's wrath against sin is there than just the suffering and death of Christ, his Son?" (The Formula of Concord).

But these words should, above all, comfort us. Why was Christ forsaken? "He was pierced for our transgressions, he was crushed for our iniquities . . . by his wounds we are healed. . . . The LORD has laid on him the iniquity of us all" (Isaiah 53:5,6). Because our Redeemer was forsaken by God, we know and believe that God will not, yes, cannot, ever forsake us.

❦

Though no Father seem to hear,
Though no light our spirits cheer,
May we know that God is near:
Hear us, holy Jesus. Amen. (TLH 183:3)

Later, knowing that all was now completed, and so that the Scripture would be fulfilled, Jesus said, "I am thirsty."
(John 19:28)

"I am thirsty"

After Samson had slain a thousand Philistines, he was fatigued and completely overcome with thirst. It was the same with Christ after his victory over sin and the devil. Earlier Jesus had refused to drink because it would have acted as a sedative. Now when there were only moments left in his life, he accepted the drink, which was not a pain-deadening potion but one of wine vinegar that quenched his thirst.

The meaning of this is pointed out in these words: "[Jesus,] knowing that all was now completed, and so that the Scripture would be fulfilled." Before this, Jesus was like a man engaged in a desperate struggle for the very existence of himself and his family. He forgot, or thought he must ignore, the demands of his body for food and rest. So Jesus, locked in mortal combat with Satan—with the souls of all people at stake—had had no thought for his raging thirst. But now he knew that he had suffered the last bitter agony, the godforsakenness; he knew he had reached the goal the Father had set for him: he had endured perfectly all the sufferings set down in the Old Testament as necessary for mankind's redemption. Only then did he ask for the drink. He wanted to rally his strength to proclaim that all had been done with a shout of victory, which we will consider in the next devotion.

So Jesus' physical thirst leads us to think of the blessed thirst in his heart. It is true that the words "I am thirsty" do not express it. But when we consider that he did not want to be spared any of the suffering for our sin by taking a drugging drink, that he wanted to drain that cup, then we cannot but think of his blessed thirst for our salvation. Because he thirsted in his soul, you and I need never thirst. He has promised, "He who believes in me will never be thirsty" (John 6:35).

Learn from these words, "I am thirsty," how terribly Jesus Christ suffered for you, how deeply he loves you, and how earnestly he desires to fill your every need. Then do not vainly thirst for draughts of worldly honor and pleasure. They only set up other raging thirsts. Sing like David to your Lord: "As the deer pants for streams of water, so my soul pants for you, O God. My soul thirsts for God, for the living God" (Psalm 42:1,2). Live in the spirit of this prayer:

ᴄᴏᴏᴏ

May we thirst Thy love to know;
Lead us in our sin and woe
Where the healing waters flow:
Hear us, holy Jesus. Amen. (TLH 184:3)

When he had received the drink, Jesus said, "It is finished."
With that, he bowed his head and gave up his spirit.
(John 19:30)

"It is finished"

To all outward appearances, the death of Christ seems like a tragic miscarriage of justice. Christ seems to be the victim of a vicious plot, helpless to defend himself, and therefore, doomed to suffer and die. But this very suffering, this helplessness, was his victory. By humbling himself and by suffering sin's eternal penalty, Christ paid our debt in full.

Yes, he suffered; he cried out; he seemed defeated. But from this battle against sin and death, he emerged victorious. "It is finished"! Full, complete pardon has been won for every sinner. This meaning of the sixth word from the cross simply cannot be overemphasized.

There is nothing that Satan would rather have us believe than this: Christ has not paid your entire debt; you must add something to it. Fortify yourself with these words: "It is finished"! Neither the number nor the greatness of your sins can alter that fact.

These three words also cast out all self-righteousness. They teach us that everything concerning our salvation has been done for us. Our redemption was finished before we were born. What we could never do, another has done for us. Here too is a rebuke to the hypocrisy of those who say that they are saved only through Christ but then rely on good works to some degree after all. Hearing Christ's words aright, we can only confess: "I believe that Jesus Christ . . . has redeemed me, a lost and condemned creature" (Explanation to the Second Article).

These words give strength against sin. Of course, some think—and say!—that "It is finished" means just the opposite. "You," they charge, "encourage people to think that since God now freely forgives all sins for Christ's sake, one might as well go right on sinning, since God will forgive each time anyway." But Christians, trusting in Christ's perfect payment, do not think that way. For us, "It is finished" is the same as hearing our Lord say, "Your sins are forgiven." Then our ears are quick to hear what follows: "Go and sin no more." For us, this sixth word from the cross is the reason for shunning evil and doing good; in it we also find strength for the fight.

❧

Lord Jesus Christ, teach us to bring all our sins to you so that they may be nailed to the cross with you and to find in your perfect redemption the strength for a closer walk with you. Amen.

Jesus called out with a loud voice, "Father, into your hands I commit my spirit." When he had said this, he breathed his last. (Luke 23:46)

"Into your hands"

"With a loud voice" Christ uttered his last words. This is significant. Crucifixion was no ordinary death. It was long and drawn out; it slowly sapped all the strength from a person. Most crucified people died in a state of unconsciousness. If one did remain conscious to the end, that person scarcely had the strength to utter a sound. Christ, however, did not die of exhaustion. His mind was clear, and at the very end, he cried with a loud, clear voice. This indicates that he did not die as a result of his wounds. He did not die because he had to. He died because he willed it. Death did not come to him, but, uniquely, he came to death. He died as he had foretold: "The reason my Father loves me is that I lay down my life—only to take it up again. No one takes it from me, but I lay it down of my own accord. I have authority to lay it down and authority to take it up again" (John 10:17,18). It is true, the Jews and Romans murdered him. But they could never have touched him if he had not voluntarily surrendered himself to such a death. His was no ordinary death.

And why? Because his was the death of no ordinary man. Notice the first of his dying words, *Father.* He does not call God "Father" in the sense we do. He is the true, eternal, only begotten Son of God, altogether like and equal to the Father. Therefore, he himself is true God. This was his claim all through life, and it was his claim in death.

Christ's death was the death of a man who was also the Son of God. Here we must take off our shoes, because we stand on holy ground. Here an unsearchable mystery faces us. How could Christ, God's Son, who calls himself the life, die? Let us not throw up our hands, as some do, and say: "Impossible! It was only a man who died." We keep our feet on the solid rock of these facts: With Christ's birth, God became man but did not cease to be God, just as surely as God died when "[Christ] breathed his last."

This great truth of the gospel is a rock, the rock of our faith. No mere man "can redeem the life of another or give to God a ransom for him" (Psalm 49:7). Only the death of God can atone for our sins. "The blood of Jesus, his Son, purifies us from all sin" (1 John 1:7).

༺☙◊☙༻

May Thy life and death supply
Grace to live and grace to die,
Grace to reach the home on high:
Hear us, holy Jesus. Amen. (TLH 186:3)

Oh, that my words were recorded, that they were written on a scroll, that they were inscribed with an iron tool on lead, or engraved in rock forever! I know that my Redeemer lives, and that in the end he will stand upon the earth. (Job 19:23-25)

Resurrection faith is founded in the Redeemer

Have you ever seen the Leaning Tower of Pisa in Italy? In the early 1990s, the lean became so great that the tower threatened to fall. The townspeople were deeply concerned because their economic future was linked to that tower. Engineers found that the only way to keep it leaning properly was to strengthen the foundation. They did just that, and the tower still stands (or, rather, leans) today.

How could Job be so hard-pressed yet remain so faithful to the true God? The answer is found in the spiritual foundation of Job's faith. Job's faith was founded in the Redeemer, his Savior, the Messiah yet to come.

"I know that my Redeemer lives." This is probably the best known and most loved passage in the book of Job. It expresses the foundation of Job's faith and his understanding of the Lord in the midst of his terrible situation. At that time in his life, the wages of sin and death threatened to separate Job from God. But Job's faith was founded in the Redeemer, whom God would send to take away the sins of the world. The Redeemer would atone for everyone's sin and then be raised to life.

We are given a glimpse of Christ's second coming in the words of Job: "In the end he will stand upon the earth." Jesus, the Redeemer, will return again and take to heaven all who trust in him as the Savior. Job looked forward to that day. It kept everything in perspective for him. "Challenge my faith, dear friends," he said, "but someday my Redeemer will vindicate me and set me in God's presence."

The resurrection of Jesus keeps our lives in perspective. Wealth is nothing, because it will not last; the resurrection will last. Suffering in this life is temporary; our time with the Redeemer is forever. Satan points to our sins and tries to make us cave in to work-righteousness. But the righteousness of the risen Savior is ours completely. And someday the Lord will vindicate our faith by pointing to our deeds of service done in his name and saying, "Well done, good and faithful servant" (Matthew 25:21).

What a glorious day it will be when we, along with Job, join all the saints in glory. That divine event is our foundation. And even if we lean a bit under the pressures of the world, we will not fall.

⚜

Lord, when life presses me hard, help me remember that my Redeemer lives. Amen.

And after my skin has been destroyed, yet in my flesh I will see God; I myself will see him with my own eyes—I, and not another. How my heart yearns within me! (Job 19:26,27)

Resurrection faith looks forward to the resurrection

Have you ever received a love letter? Love letters express the feelings of people who really care about one another. Some of the finest love letters ever written were written under great stress. The writer poured out his or her deepest feelings. The words often expressed heartfelt yearning to see the loved one again—to be home by his or her side.

In our reading for today, Job expressed a heartfelt yearning to be in his heavenly home. He wanted to see God and be by his side. His life was filled with pain and suffering. His friends continued to accuse him falsely. They offered him no comfort with their foolish counsel. In the midst of this turmoil, Job cried out, "How my heart yearns within me!"

Job was yearning for the day of resurrection from the dead. With his resurrection would come eternity in God's perfect presence. Job didn't have a death wish to end the pain. He had a life wish to begin a glorified life with the triune God. His resurrection faith declared, "And after my skin has been destroyed, yet in my flesh I will see God . . . with my own eyes—I, and not another."

Job knew that he would die. He had no illusions that he might escape death like Enoch and Elijah, who were taken directly to heaven without tasting death. Job faced the full reality that when he died, his skin would be destroyed. However, he didn't despair; rather, he expressed this living hope: "I will see God . . . with my own eyes—I, and not another." The resurrection of his body from death would be so complete that he would see God with his own eyes.

God has written us a love letter, the Holy Bible. There we learn that "the wages of sin is death, but the gift of God is eternal life in Christ Jesus our Lord" (Romans 6:23). Jesus, our Redeemer, is the object of our resurrection faith. In him we have hope and have life. When our final hours come, we can face death with anticipation. Because of Jesus, death is now the door to eternal life. With resurrection faith, we, along with Job, look forward to the day of our resurrection to eternal life.

ꙮ

Heavenly Father, quiet my fears when I face death. My heart yearns for the day when you will come again and raise all believers to life eternal. Come quickly, Lord Jesus, come quickly. Amen.

But Christ has indeed been raised from the dead.
(1 Corinthians 15:20)

Our King came back from the dead

"How can we be sure there is life after death? No one has ever come back to tell us!"

Have you ever heard someone say that? Most of us probably have. It's usually said by people who don't go to church. Maybe they never really heard the Easter gospel. If they had, they would know that someone did come back from the dead and that he assures us of life after death.

Some of the members in Corinth took that unbelieving attitude too. Paul reminded them that if it's impossible for a human being to rise from the dead, then Jesus Christ was not raised either.

Worse yet, if Christ has not been raised, then all our Christian preaching is useless and our faith in Christ is also worthless. If Jesus' grave is not empty, all we believe is a bunch of lies. A dead Savior can't help us, no matter what anyone says.

If Jesus' body is still covered with Judean sand in a forgotten tomb, then we have no Savior and our sins are still counted against us. In other words, we are duped, doomed, and damned without Easter!

"But"—what a difference that little word makes—"Christ has indeed been raised from the dead." He came back to prove to us that he really is God's Son, that we are completely forgiven and at peace with God, and that we too will rise from death one day.

Yes, a man really died. The Roman soldiers made sure of that when they stuck a spear into Jesus' side. And a man—our Lord Jesus Christ— came back from the dead. The apostles made sure it was really him! They were with him for nearly six weeks after he arose. They saw him, walked and talked with him, ate and drank with him, and even touched him. Yes, he was truly risen from death.

At the end of his life, Napoleon said, "Alexander, Caesar, Charlemagne, and myself founded empires. But on what did we rest the creation of our genius? On force. Jesus Christ alone founded his empire on love. And at this hour millions of people would die for him." Jesus is our King. He is the King of love. He is the King of everlasting life! Alleluia!

⌘

Lord Jesus, we crown you the Lord of life because you triumphed over the grave and rose victorious in the strife for those you came to save. Your glories now we sing, who died and rose on high, who died eternal life to bring and lives that death may die. Amen. (from CW 341:3)

But Christ has indeed been raised from the dead,
the firstfruits of those who have fallen asleep.
(1 Corinthians 15:20)

Our joy has only begun

Before a farmer goes out to harvest a whole field of grain, he makes sure it's ready. First, he pulls a few spears of grain from the field and then rubs some kernels of wheat in his hands. If they are ripe, then he knows the whole field is ready for harvest.

Paul calls the resurrection of Jesus "the firstfruits of those who have fallen asleep." His rising proves that a human being can die and come alive again by God's power. His rising is just the beginning of a general resurrection harvest. On the Last Day, all the dead will be raised. All cemeteries will become empty. Those who lived and believed in Christ at the time of their deaths will be raised with new, perfect, immortal bodies. They will be reunited with their souls to live eternally with Christ in heaven.

Those who died without faith in Christ will also be raised on the Last Day. However, they will not receive new, glorified bodies. They will still have all their sin and corruption. They will be raised to be condemned to eternal punishment in hell.

But those who love and trust in our Savior will have perfect bodies and souls, just like Jesus. The Bible says, "[Christ] will transform our lowly bodies so that they will be like his glorious body" (Philippians 3:21).

In Israel the first sheaf of grain at harvesttime was given to God as a thank offering for the harvest that was ready to be gathered. Christ's resurrection is the most amazing miracle in the Bible. It is the greatest tribute to God's grace and power. God sent his eternal Son to die for all sinners. Christ's resurrection proves that he paid for all our sins. He saved us from the wrath of God. He snatched us out of the jaws of hell. He successfully overcame sin, death, and hell for us.

On the Last Day, the Lord Jesus will also present us as "firstfruits" to God—a tribute and thank offering to him. At that time we, his church, will stand at Jesus' right hand, dressed like a beautiful bride. We will wear robes not covered with the filth of our sins but washed pure in the blood of Jesus, the Lamb. Our sinless souls will be clothed with brand-new, holy, deathless bodies. We shall see God face-to-face and will finally be able to enjoy his glorious presence forever.

※

Lord, our hearts are pining to see your shining, dying or living to you are clinging now and forever. Alleluia! Amen. (from CW 346:1)

Since death came through a man, the resurrection of the dead comes also through a man. For as in Adam all die, so in Christ all will be made alive. (1 Corinthians 15:21,22)

Christ is Adam II

Some lands have been ruled by monarchs. King George I was followed by George II. Queen Elizabeth II came to the throne after Elizabeth I.

Adam was the first human being. He was the head of the first family, the first church, and the first government. Adam was the first human ruler on earth. But he disobeyed God. Adam I became a sinner. All people since Adam are born like him, with hearts in rebellion against God, the King of the universe.

This is why all people die. Sadly, even babies die. They too are born with a sinful human nature. "The wages of sin is death" (Romans 6:23).

Yes, everyone is a sinner except Jesus Christ. He was conceived by the power of the Holy Spirit. He resisted every temptation. He was without sin. He never deserved death.

But God sent his one and only Son to save us from Adam's sin. Jesus became a human being to take the place of every sinner. He was the second Adam, sent to undo all the damage done by the first Adam.

The first Adam sinned and brought us death. Adam II, or Jesus Christ, never sinned. He had perfect love for his heavenly Father and was willing to do whatever God asked him to do. He also had perfect love for his neighbors, even his enemies. On the cross he prayed for his executioners.

Because of his sinless life, Jesus did not have to die. He laid down his life in the place of Adam and all of us. Because he was God's Son, his blood atoned for all our sins. In place of guilt, we have peace. In place of punishment, we have heavenly glory. In place of death, there is eternal life. As death came by a man, so life has also come by a man.

Because Christ conquered sin, death, and hell, all who are connected to him by faith share in that victory. At death the believer's body dies, but that body will be raised to eternal life on the Last Day.

The believer's soul, however, never dies. It simply changes places. It moves from life here to life in heaven—to be with King Jesus, Adam II, the King of life!

❦

Oh, sweet and blessed country, the home of God's elect!
Oh, sweet and blessed country that eager hearts expect!
Jesus, in mercy bring us to that dear land of rest;
You are with God the Father and Spirit ever blest. Amen.
(CW 214:4)

But each in his own turn: Christ, the firstfruits; then, when he comes, those who belong to him. (1 Corinthians 15:23)

We are VIPs

Have you ever seen the excitement when a president of the United States comes to town? After his plane lands, he receives a police escort. There are several long black limousines with motorcycles all around. Lights are flashing everywhere. It is very exciting.

Imagine how much more exciting it would be if you were in the president's company. Because you were part of his entourage, you would get the same special treatment he does. You would be a VIP—a Very Important Person.

The Bible says all believers in Christ are VIPs. We belong to him. We are part of his company. We surely don't deserve such a wonderful position. We should be separated from God and eternal life because of our sins. But through his death and resurrection, Christ has reconciled us to God. Through the cleansing power of his blood, we have been made fit for his company.

Jesus has risen from the grave and so will we. But we must wait our turn. Jesus' resurrection came first but guarantees ours one day too. When he comes back on the Last Day, we will receive VIP treatment. He will send a heavenly escort of angels. "With a loud command, with the voice of the archangel and with the trumpet call of God, and the dead in Christ will rise first" (1 Thessalonians 4:16). In a most spectacular sight, he will raise us up with glorified bodies and take us with him into heavenly glory. There we will sit on thrones with him, ruling over all our enemies, including death and the devil.

In the meantime we are content to suffer whatever troubles God sends us, knowing that they are only temporary. He is our dear Savior, ruling over everything. He won't let the troubles be more than we can bear. He will end them at the right time and in the right way. The fact that we belong to Christ guarantees that we have everlasting life. The best is yet to come. Heaven will more than make up for whatever we have suffered or lost here.

By his amazing grace, we are very important to him. He made us with his own hands; he redeemed us with his own blood; he sanctified us with his own Spirit. Nothing can change the fact that through Jesus we are VIPs to God!

⚬⚬⚬⚬

Heavenly Father, praise and thanks be to you for making us your own dear children and heirs of eternal life through Jesus Christ, your Son, our Lord. Amen.

Then the end will come, when he hands over the kingdom to God the Father after he has destroyed all dominion, authority and power. (1 Corinthians 15:24)

Trophies of victory

Some people like to hunt or fish. If they shoot a special animal or catch a prize fish, they might have a taxidermist mount it. It is a trophy of victory.

Our Lord Jesus was sent into this world to destroy all God's enemies. Some are the fallen angels of hell. Some are immoral authorities in government. Some are ungodly authorities in the arts and entertainment worlds, the business world, and even the church.

Though these enemies may boast great gains against Christ and his church now, one day they will be stripped of all authority and cast down to the lowest hell. God always has the last word. On judgment day all will bow before Jesus our King, some to their everlasting shame and some to their everlasting glory.

David looked as if he would lose as he went out to meet Goliath. But when he lifted up the giant's severed head, all knew he was victorious. Jesus also looked as if he lost when he was crucified, died, and was buried. But when he was lifted up on Easter morning, all knew he had crushed the head of Satan and the authority of his ungodly followers.

We too are often overpowered by the ungodly of this world. Maybe an atheistic teacher in school belittles the Bible. Maybe an employer refuses to promote us because we don't agree with his immoral practices. Maybe we lose some friends because we dislike their ungodly entertainment.

We pray that God changes their hearts. We lovingly admonish them to do right. We strive to set a good example. But when Christ returns, all unbelieving powers will be destroyed. It will be this world's final curtain. Its godless, sinful rule will end. The unbelievers will be raised to life. Then they will be consigned to eternal damnation.

On that day Christ will turn over his kingdom to his heavenly Father. His mission will be accomplished. When this world ends, he will offer to God his Father the trophies of his victory—the spoils of war. Every enemy, including death, will be conquered and put under his feet. Then he will reign with the Father and the Holy Spirit, one God for ever and ever.

Until then we continue to confess our faith boldly, because we know how all history ends. We are on the side of him who will finally win.

୧⊙⊙୬

O Jesus Christ, do not delay, but hasten our salvation;
We often tremble on our way in fear and tribulation. Amen.
(CW 207:6)

Total victory

The United States withdrew from South Vietnam after many years of war. It was the only time in modern history that the United States was not able to claim victory. Though our military forces fought long and hard, the enemy proved to be too stubborn.

Jesus, our King, totally defeated all our enemies. He used no army. He went into combat alone against sin, death, and the devil and won complete victory.

Jesus was pure and holy. Because he took the world's sins on himself, he was assaulted and nailed to a cross. It was as if he had sinned and had brought death on himself. But they were our sins, not his. His holiness was so great that death could not keep him. Sin attacked him, but it could not defeat him. Rather, Jesus defeated sin.

Sin's great ally is death. Just as Jesus defeated sin, so he defeated death. Yes, death took hold of Jesus. It appeared to have conquered him. For three days he was cold and lifeless in the tomb. But Easter revealed that he had, in fact, defeated death. In Christ death had to die and lose all its power.

The devil also tried to prove his power over Christ. He tried everything to defeat Jesus. According to God's promise, Satan struck the heel of Christ, but that was no victory. Satan met a higher power that he could not overcome. Christ descended into hell and returned. Satan's power was completely defeated.

Jesus is our Savior-King. After being cast down, he has been lifted up on high. His powerful enemies—sin, death, and the devil—now lie beneath his feet.

Celebrate Jesus' total victory. Take this truth to heart. Count on it, and live the victorious life in Christ. Sin, death, and the devil may still inflict harm upon us here, but the final, ultimate, and glorious victory is ours through Christ.

ᘓᕲᕬᕲᘒ

I am trusting you, Lord Jesus; never let me fall.
I am trusting you forever and for all. Amen. (CW 446:6)

The last enemy to be destroyed is death.
(1 Corinthians 15:26)

Even death dies

When death strikes, fatalists try to find comfort in the fact that death is inevitable. It comes to all sooner or later, they reason. It is part of life. It is natural.

All honest, feeling people, however, realize that death is completely unnatural. That is why it is so hard to accept. Everything a person worked so hard to achieve is gone in a moment. A person may be warm and loving one day and the next, cold and lifeless.

Death fills us with fear. The first disciples locked themselves in a house after Jesus died. They were afraid of death. Why? Because they knew they were sinners. Death is the punishment for sin. If Jesus died, they wondered if they were next. Without the assurance of Jesus' resurrection, they would have remained in fear and anguish.

But when we cry out to God in such fear, he always hears and helps. Christ came quickly to his disciples, saying, "Peace be with you. Cheer up; don't be afraid." So when we are afraid, God comes and reminds us of his gospel. He assures us that all our sins have been wiped away and that we are on the way to heavenly glory.

When he returns at the end of time, our poor mortal bodies will be raised to new life and we will meet the Lord in the air. We will be with the Lord forever.

Sin has been canceled. Satan has been defeated. One day death will die. Death is the last enemy to be destroyed, for good.

How can we be sure? Easter proves it. Jesus conquered death for himself and for us. We now live between two resurrections—Christ's and the final, great resurrection of all flesh.

Knowing this by faith, we dismiss all fear and worry. Christ has conquered even our worst enemy. He is our comfort and our joy! Jesus is our King of life!

⁂

Lord Jesus, help me live every day with the confidence that you have conquered all my enemies, including the last enemy, death itself. Amen.

Now Thomas (called Didymus), one of the Twelve, was not with the disciples when Jesus came. So the other disciples told him, "We have seen the Lord!" But he said to them, "Unless I see the nail marks in his hands and put my finger where the nails were, and put my hand into his side, I will not believe it." (John 20:24,25)

Give me proof

The little three-year-old boy came bounding into his father's workroom, exclaiming, "Daddy, Daddy, an airplane just landed on the highway!" Of course the father knew airplanes don't land on busy four-lane highways, but he also knew the imagination of a young child. There was a logical explanation—perhaps a low-flying plane on the horizon. To stop the pleading, to play along with the child, the father went outside. There it was, large as life—an airplane parked in the middle of the highway.

The father didn't believe it until he saw it. Isn't that the way things are with us? The human mind cries out constantly, "Give me proof," especially when a claim goes beyond our normal experiences or what our minds deem possible.

The disciple Thomas was brought face-to-face with the supernatural. The ten disciples told him they had seen the Lord. Yet Thomas knew that Christ had been crucified, pierced in his side. There was no doubt that Christ had died. He was buried. But now the disciples said they saw him alive. The reaction of Thomas was, "Impossible! That goes beyond the realm of experience. I don't believe it!"

Thomas had seen Jesus raise Lazarus and others from the dead, but this was something completely unheard of. So he said, "Unless I see the nail marks in his hands and put my finger where the nails were, and put my hand into his side, I will not believe it." He was demanding personal proof. His faith and his God were limited by his mind and experience.

But God isn't limited by what humans conceive as possible. Our God is the God of the impossible. He can accomplish works that go completely beyond our human experiences. He is the God of the supernatural, as well as of the natural. How blessed we are that our God isn't limited by the confines of human experience. How wondrous our God is, because he isn't bounded by what we conceive as possible.

❧

O Lord, help us resist every temptation to doubt your Word. Forgive our sins, and enable us to believe the wondrous historical accounts you have revealed. Lead us to see that nothing is impossible with you. Help us on our pilgrimage through this world, and strengthen our faith in you, for Jesus' sake. Amen.

A week later his disciples were in the house again, and Thomas was with them. Though the doors were locked, Jesus came and stood among them and said, "Peace be with you!" Then he said to Thomas, "Put your finger here; see my hands. Reach out your hand and put it into my side. Stop doubting and believe." (John 20:26,27)

Proof that is real

One can only imagine what went through the mind of Thomas from the time the other apostles told him of Jesus on Easter until the Sunday evening a week later. During that week the ten must have spoken frequently of Jesus' words and of that wondrous Easter night of his appearing. Nevertheless, Thomas remained unconvinced. He demanded real proof.

On the Sunday after Easter, all eleven apostles were together in a house. Even though the doors were secure, suddenly Jesus was standing among them. Thomas' eyes must have practically popped out of his head. His mind must have been reeling as he tried to comprehend what he saw. Right there, as real as could be, stood Jesus. It wasn't a dream! It wasn't just the moon shining through the window. It wasn't just an intense longing in his heart that somehow had fooled the mind. Jesus was really alive.

Jesus greeted them. Then, going directly to Thomas, he spoke, not harshly, not sarcastically, not with a demeaning voice, but lovingly. Jesus' disciples needed to be convinced and strengthened. Jesus freely gave Thomas the proof he requested. Jesus said, "Put your finger here; see my hands. Reach out your hand and put it into my side."

Thomas' beloved master really did physically come back to life. Thomas didn't even have to touch the wounded hands or pierced side. His ears heard Jesus' voice. His eyes saw Christ's body. Thomas was convinced.

How comforting it is to see how our Lord dealt with Thomas. Jesus is so loving and patient. Have we had doubts about some teachings of Scripture in the past? Do we still struggle with some concepts? Do we find ourselves questioning God's wisdom or love in the ordering of our lives? God doesn't abandon us to our doubts or struggles. He comes to us again and again through his Word and lovingly shows us the truth. He patiently seeks to convince us through the power of his Word. While we may not understand everything in Scripture with our limited minds, he has given us real proof in the testimony of many reliable witnesses so that we can believe what he tells us, even something as fantastic as life after death.

❦

O Lord, continue to be patient with us, as you were with Thomas. Amen.

Proof that convinces

"It will take a lot of convincing to make me believe that!" That was the reaction of Thomas when he heard the news that Jesus was alive. It would take an awful lot of convincing to persuade Thomas to believe in the resurrection.

But now Thomas had his proof that it was not a hallucination. It wasn't a magical act with mirrors or some other sleight-of-hand trick. Jesus was standing right in front of them. He was obviously real. He was clearly alive—the same Jesus that Thomas had walked and talked with almost daily for three years.

A quivering voice said, "My Lord and my God!" Thomas was a believer. His mind, which had tried to limit God's work, was shattered by a whole new realm of thought. Yes, it was possible to rise from the dead. Jesus had performed his greatest supernatural act of all. The only words that came out of Thomas' mouth were, "My Lord and my God!" Thomas called Jesus his Lord. Jesus had suffered, died, and risen again for him. Although at first passionately opposed to the thought, Thomas now freely confessed Jesus as his risen Savior.

There is a great deal of comfort for our own faith in this account about Thomas. We don't want to honor his unbelief or his standing in judgment of God's power. Yet here is a man who was not easily convinced. Thomas relied on the scientific method, which informed him that the other disciples had to be wrong. But in the final analysis, even this Thomas was persuaded. The risen Christ himself convinced Thomas. So even a famous skeptic is compelled to join the ranks of witnesses to the resurrection of Christ.

The proof of Christ's resurrection is overwhelming. The Bible records the many historical accounts of his appearances to his disciples and gives us "many convincing proofs that he was alive" (Acts 1:3). More than five hundred eyewitnesses confront us with the truth of his greatest miracle of all. Thanks be to God for this testimony, by which the Holy Spirit has led us to confess that Jesus is indeed our risen Lord and God.

> He lives, all glory to his name!
> He lives, my Jesus, still the same.
> Oh, the sweet joy this sentence gives:
> "I know that my Redeemer lives!" (CW 152:8)

Dear Lord Jesus, you have led me to believe in your resurrection. Strengthen my faith, and help me see in your resurrection my own glorious rising through your divine power. Amen.

Though the doors were locked, Jesus came and stood among them and said, "Peace be with you!" (John 20:26)

Proof of peace

A Christian's peace with God is as old as his baptism. Harmony with God is as much a part of us as our name. At the same time, we still are sinners and have known the terror, or at least the uneasiness, of uncertainty. Our sinful flesh does not, and never will, believe God's promises or know what it is to be at peace with God.

The biggest problem is that people, by nature, are always striving to do something to make peace with God. But even the best efforts leave a person in doubt. Who can, without a sign from God himself, be sure? The Christian can be sure. We have a sign from God in the person of his Son, Jesus Christ, who gave us every assurance that his sacrifice for our sins was accepted. This assurance came on Easter morning.

Jesus brought that thought to his disciples when he appeared to them. He said, "Peace be with you!" This peace wasn't coming from them but to them. Peter would later say to Cornelius, a Gentile, "You know the message God sent to the people of Israel, telling the good news of peace through Jesus Christ, who is Lord of all" (Acts 10:36). Paul would later write, "Therefore, since we have been justified through faith, we have peace with God through our Lord Jesus Christ" (Romans 5:1). Jesus could announce to Thomas and to us, "Peace be with you!" because he accomplished peace through his own life, death, and resurrection.

That peace, coming through Jesus Christ, completely changes our lives. Life is no longer a mad scramble to try to make peace with God through religious activity and outward moral obedience. We already are at peace through Christ. We don't have to try to achieve it. All who believe in Christ can call God their Father.

That gives us a calmness, a peace that does surpass all human understanding. It is peace and joy that illness, disaster, heartache, even death cannot take away from us—a calm that fills our hearts, our souls, our lives.

What is the proof that this peace with God is real? What assurance do we have? We have God's own word on it. The risen Christ to his disciples spoke those comforting words: "Peace be with you!"

❦

Through Jesus' blood and merit
I am at peace with God;
What, then, can daunt my spirit,
However dark my road?
My courage shall not fail me,
For God is on my side;
Though hell itself assail me,
Its rage I may deride. Amen. (CW 445:1)

Then Jesus told him, "Because you have seen me, you have believed; blessed are those who have not seen and yet have believed." (John 20:29)

Proof not seen—yet believed

In an age that elevates reason and logic, it could be easy to fall into Thomas' way of thinking. He believed in only what he could see and touch. Once he saw the risen Christ, he believed. But Jesus then told him, "Because you have seen me, you have believed; blessed are those who have not seen and yet have believed." Jesus accepted Thomas' confession of faith. He didn't put Thomas down for his former weakness, but Jesus made a point for every generation of believers who lived before and who would live after the time when he walked this earth.

Christians in the future would believe in the risen Christ even though they would not see him with their eyes or touch him with their hands. Faith is based on the words and promises of God. It believes the miracles and anticipates the fulfillment of prophecies. Christians believe, not because they have seen the Lord but because the Holy Spirit has convinced them that Jesus is the Son of God and their Savior from sin.

Who was Jesus talking about when he referred to the future members of the Christian church? We think of the Greeks and Romans who came to faith through the preaching of Paul, of the martyrs who joined in singing joyous hymns of praise even as fire consumed their bodies, of the faithful witnesses who withstood heretics and framed our timeless confessions of faith.

The long list of New Testament saints also includes us. It includes the people of the Pacific Rim, Europe, Latin America, Africa, Asia, and all around the world who believe the gospel message.

And the Word of Christ still stands: "Blessed are those who have not seen and yet have believed."

How firm a foundation, O saints of the Lord,
Is laid for your faith in his excellent Word!
What more can he say than to you he has said
Who unto the Savior for refuge have fled? (CW 416:1)

⸎

O Lord, I believe your Word of salvation. Your Holy Spirit has convinced me of it. Thank you for leading me to this conviction, and give me the strength and courage to confess your name boldly. Amen.

These are written that you may believe that Jesus is the Christ, the Son of God. (John 20:31)

Proof for a purpose—believe!

There are 1,189 chapters in the Bible: 929 in the Old Testament and 260 in the New Testament. My Bible has 1,635 pages of text. The Bible is a good-sized book. It contains a wealth of knowledge. What do all of those chapters—those historical accounts of Adam, Abraham, Ruth, David, Esther, Jesus, Paul, and John—have in common? Are they just interesting historical accounts? Are they a source of lessons in morality? They are much more than that.

The whole Old Testament sets the stage for the coming of Christ. It recounts for us God's promise of a Savior through a nation that was often rebellious and stubborn. The New Testament recounts for us God's promises fulfilled in Jesus. John really summarizes the point of the whole Bible with his words: "But these are written that you may believe that Jesus is the Christ, the Son of God."

The whole Bible, including John's gospel, wasn't written simply to document that a person by the name of Jesus once existed. God caused this record of Jesus to be written in order to confirm that "Jesus is the Christ." He is the message of the shepherds outside Bethlehem: "A Savior has been born to you; he is Christ the Lord" (Luke 2:11). The Bible confirms that Jesus is the Son of God. Read all of John's gospel, and a central theme will stand out. John is seeking to establish one point beyond everything else: Jesus is the Son of God.

Why is this thought so important? Jesus' divinity is the focal point of Christianity. If Christ isn't God's Son, he isn't the Savior. The Scriptures are written to convince us absolutely about Jesus' identity, to remove every lingering doubt of his divinity. Through the power of that Word, the Holy Spirit leads us to believe that "Jesus is the Christ, the Son of God."

Believe this truth with all your heart. Meditate on the divine record to keep your focus on Jesus and who he is and what his purpose is. Jesus, the Son of God, is the very center and focal point of your life as a child of God.

さ◎◎◎つ

Heavenly Father, let me always believe your Word that Jesus is the Christ, your Son, my Savior from sin, death, and hell. Amen.

Christ's love compels us, because we are convinced that one died for all, and therefore all died. (2 Corinthians 5:14)

14 *April*

A new motive

If you ask someone, "Why did you do that?" you're likely to hear the answer, "Because I felt like it." It's an answer that many would give when questioned about some of their most important decisions in life. We are living in a climate of "do your own thing" and "go with your feelings." The motivation considered most convincing to many is that "it feels right." How can something that feels good be wrong?

Paul speaks to us about what makes Christians do what they do and what makes them think the way they think. Their motivation is not their own feelings; it's not getting their own way; it's not being comfortable with their emotions. The lives of Christians are so new and different that these old motivations have gone away into past history and a completely new motive compels them.

This new motive, one of the basic building blocks of our brand new lives in Christ, makes its impact on Christians from outside their own personal emotions and feelings. It is Christ's love that compels us. His love for us moves us to think and to act differently than before. His love exerts its power and influence on us. Christ's love—that's what makes Christians new and different.

Just exactly what is this love of Christ that has such a powerful impact on us? He died for all. He died for you and for me. He died for those who crucified him and for those who mourned his death. He died for his enemies and for those who couldn't care less. That is a special kind of love, isn't it? That's love so special and so unusual that the Bible gives it a special name: grace. That's a love so special that it motivates our entire lives, our whole way of thinking and acting.

Christ's love didn't ask, "What will they do for me?" He said he came to serve, not to be served. He didn't go to the cross because he felt like it or because it felt good or because it made him feel comfortable with his emotions. He did it because he loves us.

And he doesn't stop loving us either. He still invites us to trust in him, to be cleansed by his death, to live forever with him in his kingdom. All because he loves us. Now that's a motive that's compelling!

৸৩৶

Lord Jesus, fill us with your love so that it guides us, controls us, and motivates us in all we think and do. Amen.

He died for all, that those who live should no longer live for themselves but for him who died for them and was raised again. (2 Corinthians 5:15)

A new view of death

What is death? Most definitions view death as an end, the end of life, the end of biological functions, when it's all over and done.

Christ our Savior died and changed our view of death. He didn't change the scientific or physical nature of death but radically changed the spiritual aspect of death. The original cause of death was removed when Christ died. And because he died for all, death has been conquered for all.

Dying started when sin entered the world, and since sin passes from one generation to the next, so does dying. Christ came and broke this deadly cycle. When he died, he took everyone's place and experienced once and for all the death that is sin's just punishment. He carried the sins of the world and paid for them by dying not only physically but by suffering all the wrath of a holy God against sin. That's what changed everything and gave us a brand new life and a new view of death.

The old and natural view of death is that it is an awful and dreadful experience. Before Jesus conquered death for us, it hung over our heads as a menacing reality. Worst of all, it brought to mind the problem of finding ourselves face-to-face with God, whom we offend in so many ways.

Now we have a new view of death. It still is frightening to us even though it has been conquered, but now we know that when we die, we aren't being punished. The death of Christ took care of that kind of death for us. Now we can see death as the way to a new life. Our death, thanks to the death and resurrection of Christ, is nothing more than a sleep from which we will awaken totally refreshed and glorified to live in the eternal mansions that Jesus went to prepare for us.

When Christ died, he rose again and so did we. We died with him as far as sin is concerned; when we were baptized, we were buried with him and also rose with him to a new life. Now we don't live to ourselves. Why should I live to myself? What have I ever done or what could I ever do to deserve being the center of my life? Jesus did far more than we could ever have hoped or imagined. He conquered sin, death, and hell for us. Let's live for him!

❧☙

Jesus, thank you for conquering death for me. I will live for you. Amen.

*So from now on we regard no one from a worldly point
of view. Though we once regarded Christ in this way, we
do so no longer. Therefore, if anyone is in Christ, he is
a new creation; the old has gone, the new has come!
(2 Corinthians 5:16,17)*

A new view of other people

"The eyes of both of them were opened, and they realized they were naked; so they sewed fig leaves together and made coverings for themselves" (Genesis 3:7). So began mankind's worldly point of view. By inheriting the sinful nature of our first parents, we have inherited their way of seeing themselves in relationship to others. Before sin they didn't feel any need to cover or protect themselves; they didn't realize they were naked. They weren't ignorant; it's just that they didn't view anyone or anything as a threat.

The worldly point of view sees others as possible threats or opportunities for personal gain. The salesperson sees everyone as a possible customer; the politician sees others as votes. How do we see people? As potential enemies who can make life miserable for us? As possible friends who can make our lives more enjoyable? How do we see Jesus? As a self-taught religious fanatic who got himself into trouble with the authorities? That's how Paul once saw him.

Paul says we no longer see Christ from this point of view. Now we see him as our Savior, as true God and true man, who redeemed us from sin, death, and the power of the devil. We see him as our Prophet, Priest, and King who bought us to be his own and to live under him in his kingdom and to serve him in everlasting righteousness, innocence, and blessedness. We see him as the source of life who has made us completely new creatures, who gives us peace and joy and security.

With this security we have a new point of view toward others. As new creatures we will see people as Christ saw them. When he saw the multitudes, he was filled with compassion for them because they were like sheep without a shepherd. When he dealt with individuals, he dealt with each one according to his or her spiritual needs. When he spoke to the hardened sinner, he wasn't afraid to get to the point. When he met a sinner in despair, he offered forgiveness, not criticism.

Let us also see people as souls for whom Christ died, as sheep who need Christ as their Good Shepherd. We're new creatures; we don't regard anyone from a worldly point of view any longer.

༄ා◎ᕗ

**Lord, teach us how to show compassion and give us the courage
to treat people according to their needs and not our own. Amen.**

17

*All this is from God, who reconciled us to himself
through Christ and gave us the ministry of reconciliation.
(2 Corinthians 5:18)*

A new relationship with God

Our new life in Christ comes from God. He did it all; we did nothing. He reconciled us to himself through Christ. He entrusts us with getting the message out that this reconciliation is an accomplished fact.

The entire process began with what God did in Christ. We didn't start anything, nor did we participate in the plans. We weren't even in agreement with God's plan; we were his enemies. We opposed his plan, but God did it anyhow in spite of us. He brought about a complete and radical change in our relationship with him. In Christ, God made his enemies his friends.

This change didn't occur in God or in us but in our status before him. By nature we are still the same people we were before, with our sinful nature and our sinful ways. God also is the same. He is still holy in every way; he still hates sin. But now we have been made his friends by the redemptive work of his Son. Jesus' suffering and death brought this all about.

This is the basis of our new life in Christ and the basis of our ministry. We can offer the world a message without conditions that need to be fulfilled. Christ has reconciled the world to God—that's our message. It's a historical fact, not something God might consider doing if we are good enough to deserve it. The ministry of reconciliation is not changing or reforming people; it's telling them and inviting them to live in and enjoy the reconciliation that Christ himself brought about. What a privilege to be able to participate in this ministry!

What a privilege and what a joy to live in and enjoy this reconciliation by faith! We don't need to hide from God or run away from him. Now we can tell him our problems, as well as share our joys with him. Now we can look forward to the moments we spend listening to his Word. Now we can take comfort in the fact that he's almighty, all knowing, and present everywhere. He's not our enemy; he's our friend, our loving Father.

And "all this is from God, who reconciled us to himself through Christ."

⚜

To that dear Redeemer's praise,
Who the cov'nant sealed with blood.
Let our hearts and voices raise
Loud thanksgivings to our God. Amen. (TLH 51:3)

God was reconciling the world to himself in Christ, not counting men's sins against them. And he has committed to us the message of reconciliation. (2 Corinthians 5:19)

A new and clean record

The idea of God sitting before an open book, making note of people's sins and recording sins in columns under each individual's name, is a common way that people picture him. People were created with a sense of moral responsibility: the conscience. Even atheists recognize that they are accountable for what they do. The Bible too presents God in his function as a judge to whom we must give an account. Several of Jesus' parables make this same point: The servant comes before his master and must give an account of his service, of his stewardship and of his wrongdoing.

When we think of ourselves on trial before God, our natural inclination is to think of two possible results: approval or disapproval, praise or condemnation. But wait! The apostle tells us of a different outcome. God doesn't praise us for our record, but he says, "I do not count your sins against you." This is the way God deals with our sins. He doesn't excuse them, nor does he let us defend ourselves by explaining how difficult it was for us. No, he says, "Since Jesus paid for your sins, I do not charge them on your record."

This process is called by various names in the Bible. Sometimes it's called justification, sometimes forgiveness, pardon, or remission of sins. Here in 2 Corinthians it's called "not counting men's sins against them." The result is the same. God has said to the whole world, "I forgive you." That's the message of reconciliation.

When the Holy Spirit convinces us that it's true and leads us to trust in this forgiveness, then it's ours. Our brand new life in Christ is new every day. We begin and end every day with a clean record because God's message is the same every day. By faith we receive it, enjoy it, and live in it.

Some people think it's dangerous to preach this message. "If we tell people that God forgives the whole world, what will keep people from sinning even more?" they ask. God forgives, and the person who trusts his forgiveness will not try to ignore or excuse his sins. This is the message that God wants to be heard. Let's proclaim it to the world exactly as God has given it: a new, clean record for everyone.

৵৵৶৶

Thank you, Lord, for not counting my sins against me. Help me teach this truth to others. Amen.

*We are therefore Christ's ambassadors, as though God were
making his appeal through us. We implore you on Christ's
behalf: Be reconciled to God. (2 Corinthians 5:20)*

A new position in the world

Our new life in Christ is one of many privileges, most of which have
to do with our new relationship with God. We have forgiveness of sin;
we have the privilege of prayer as God's dear children. We enjoy peace
with God, his protection, and many other blessings. Today we learn of a
privilege that has to do with our standing with other people. God
appointed us as his ambassadors.

Ambassadors are people who represent their nation in other parts
of the world. They receive honors and special treatment when there are
good relations between two countries, but sometimes they also have to
bear insults and anger when the relations between their own country
and the other are not good. It is a position of responsibility and importance. An ambassador is the official representative of those who send
him, and he must be careful to speak and act in a way that is consistent
with his own country's purpose in sending him.

Paul was such an ambassador, as were all of the missionaries in the
first-century church. Christ has appointed more than one ambassador or
representative in the world. The Bible speaks clearly of a priesthood that
belongs to all believers. All Christians are really representatives of
Christ in this world.

How will we speak and act as his ambassadors? What appeal does
God make through us? What was the appeal that God made through the
apostle Paul? Be reconciled to God. That's our message, and that's our
mission as ambassadors of Christ no matter where we live or what we
do for a living. We are Christ's spokesmen, his ambassadors.

Isn't it risky speaking to people about their relationship with God?
Sometimes, perhaps. But let's not feel sorry for ourselves. After all, it
isn't anything more than any ambassador risks, even those who represent earthly governments. We represent the King of kings, and if someone gets upset over our message, that person is actually rejecting Christ
and not us. Whoever listens to Christ's ambassadors listens to Christ.
Whoever rejects Christ's ambassadors and their message rejects Christ.

⤷◎◉◐↩

*Jesus, we feel weak and worthless when we consider our position
as your ambassadors. Fill us with courage and strength to be
faithful in making your appeal to others. Amen.*

God made him who had no sin to be sin for us, so
that in him we might become the righteousness of God.
(2 Corinthians 5:21)

A new and perfect righteousness

Jesus had no sin. He was born without sin, and he lived without sin. When he was put on trial, he was declared innocent of all charges by Pontius Pilate. God the Father also had declared him to be innocent when he said from heaven, "This is my Son, whom I love; with him I am well pleased" (Matthew 3:17).

For us, God made him to be sin. God charged the sins of all mankind against Jesus. Jesus suffered the curse of sin and endured its just punishment. This is one part of the great exchange. God took the guilt of all the world and laid it on his own sinless Son.

The other part of this great exchange is that the perfect holiness of Jesus is ours by faith. In Christ we have a new and perfect righteousness. It is a holiness just as genuine as the sinless life of Christ. It is a holiness that God himself accepts as perfect; after all, it comes from him. Through faith in Christ we are saints—holy people—in God's sight. That's what God has made us, and that's how God treats us because of what Jesus has done.

The righteousness that is ours by faith in Christ is complete. It doesn't need additives or any final touches. It's not like instant coffee or soup to which you need to add water. It's compared in the Bible to a garment that's already sewn and ready to wear. By faith we put it on and appear before God looking beautiful and impeccably dressed.

Let's remember this when we feel depressed. This perfect righteousness takes away our guilt and our fears. It takes away our tendencies to look at ourselves as mere faces lost in the crowd, as run-of-the-mill human beings. We're saints. God made us holy; God treats us as though we had never sinned. That makes our lives brand new in Christ.

The more we can see ourselves as God sees us, the more we will grow in our own personal holiness as well. I'm a child of God, a saint. I'm not going to follow anyone and everyone who invites me or encourages me to play in the garbage of sin. My brand-new, sparkling-white robe of righteousness in Christ makes me want to stay far away from the dirt.

♰

Jesus, your blood and righteousness
My beauty are, my glorious dress;
Mid flaming worlds, in these arrayed,
With joy shall I lift up my head. Amen. (CW 376:1)

The Shepherd knows his sheep

"The LORD is my shepherd, I shall not be in want" (Psalm 23:1). These familiar words create a vivid picture of a shepherd protecting his lambs from harm, tracking down wandering sheep, and leading the flock to water, food, and safety. For centuries these words helped Old Testament believers understand that their God cared for them as no one else.

From the gospel of John, we see that Jesus applied these words to himself when he said, "I am the good shepherd" (John 10:14). With these words, Jesus taught that he, along with the Father, provides the caring, protection, and comfort promised in Psalm 23.

In today's Bible verse, Jesus expands this thought. He says of his sheep, "I know them." Those who care for animals realize that each animal is unique. A visitor may see a flock, but a shepherd sees one sheep as a fighter, another as an outstanding mother, and yet another as the one that never sits still.

Jesus knows us in the same way a shepherd understands his sheep. If we are easily frustrated, if we are so talkative that we frequently put our feet into our mouths, if we are timid, or if we get lazy, Jesus knows it all. And when these and other tendencies of our sinful flesh lead us into sin, Jesus knows that too.

That's why Jesus, the Good Shepherd, laid down his life for us, his sheep. He knew that we couldn't undo our wrongs. He knew too that we deserved the same punishment for sin that the devil received—hell.

That's why Jesus stepped in to lay down his life for the sheep. He agreed with his heavenly Father that he should receive the punishment we deserved for our sin. That's the punishment he felt when he cried from the cross, "My God, my God, why have you forsaken me?" (Mark 15:34). With this sacrifice for sin, Jesus paid for the sins of his sheep and for the sins of the whole world.

Jesus' sheep are those who trust in him as their risen Savior from sin, eternal death, and hell. To us who believe in him, he gives eternal life in heaven. This is the pledge our Good Shepherd makes to us. No one cares for us more. No one gives us better care.

৵৵৩৫৬৶

Dearest Jesus, my Shepherd, thank you for knowing me, for calling me, and for gathering me into your sheepfold. Amen.

"My sheep listen to my voice." (John 10:27)

The Shepherd's sheep listen to him

A frustrated grandmother once said, "There is something wrong with Grandpa's glasses. Every time he puts them on to read the paper, he can't hear a thing."

Of course, the glasses weren't the problem. Grandpa was just practicing selective listening. Selective listening is an important skill to have in the information age. So many messages compete for our attention that we have to choose what we will listen to. However, we dare not practice selective listening when it comes to hearing the Word of God.

That's what Jesus' enemies did. To them God's law and judgment was for "sinners"—prostitutes, robbers, and the embezzling tax collectors. Jesus' enemies were quick to condemn those people. They were also quick to condemn Jesus because he violated their traditions and healed people on the Sabbath Day.

Jesus' enemies were practicing selective listening. Jesus told them, "If you had known what these words mean, 'I desire mercy, not sacrifice,' you would not have condemned the innocent" (Matthew 12:7). When God's Word told them to have compassion, they didn't hear it.

Selective listening is our problem too. We feel we are justified to strike out when we are angry instead of listening to what God says in Ephesians 4:26: "In your anger do not sin." We feel we are justified in holding grudges because the other person "started it" instead of listening to God: "Do not let the sun go down while you are still angry" (Ephesians 4:26).

The solution comes from listening to what Jesus has to say: "If you hold to my teaching, you are really my disciples" (John 8:31) and, again, "Blessed rather are those who hear the word of God and obey it" (Luke 11:28). When we listen to Jesus, he leads us to the "godly sorrow [that] brings repentance" (2 Corinthians 7:10).

Then we listen further. Jesus announces, "Friend, your sins are forgiven" (Luke 5:20). We listen when we take the Lord's Supper. In it Jesus assures us, "This is my blood of the covenant, which is poured out . . . for the forgiveness of sins" (Matthew 26:28).

Yes, as Jesus' disciples we listen. We know it's for our good when his law humbles us, and we are glad when his gospel promises assure us of his forgiveness and eternal life.

꧁꧂

Dear Savior, bless me as I listen to your voice. Help me hear all of it, both your condemnation and your salvation. Amen.

"I give them eternal life, and they shall never perish."
(John 10:28)

The Shepherd gives his sheep eternal life

"You have already won!" Such words grab our attention on sweepstakes entry forms. They get us excited. But when we read the fine print, we find out that we have won if, and only if, we have the winning number. That's when we feel let down.

Maybe that's why we have a hard time taking Jesus' statement "I give them eternal life" literally. That sounds too good to be true. We think, "Jesus is talking about heaven, in the future. He means that eternal life is something his sheep will have eventually."

But Jesus consistently teaches that his believers have eternal life right now. In John 5:25 he says, "I tell you the truth, a time is coming and has now come when the dead will hear the voice of the Son of God and those who hear will live." All who trust in Jesus as Savior are raised from spiritual death and have eternal life today!

To be sure, eternal life will be ours in all its fullness when our souls and bodies are united again in heaven. Then we will see God in his glory. Then we will receive glorified bodies that are free from all aches and pains, from all sin and death.

But eternal life is also ours right now through faith in Christ. When we were brought to faith in Christ, we began enjoying Christ's life-giving blessings for our souls, blessings that will never end. Those blessings include having God's forgiveness for our sins, having consciences at peace with God for Jesus' sake, and having God's promise that we will never be separated from his love for us. As the apostle Paul tells us in Romans 8:39, nothing "will be able to separate us from the love of God that is in Christ Jesus our Lord." Not even death itself can rob us of life with Jesus as our Savior. He makes physical death serve his saving plans for his sheep. For as we walk through death's dark valley, Christ, our Good Shepherd, is not only with us but is leading us to the eternal pastures of heaven.

You already have eternal life! It's the life we live in fellowship with God now by faith and forever in heaven. This is true of every person who puts his or her faith in Jesus. Eternal life with God is yours right now.

❧

Dear Savior, I thank you for giving me eternal life right now.
Help me live every day with the blessed assurance that you will
never let me perish. Amen.

"No one can snatch them out of my hand. My Father, who has given them to me, is greater than all; no one can snatch them out of my Father's hand." (John 10:28,29)

The Shepherd preserves his sheep

Every Christian can say, "I'm sure that if I die today, I will go to heaven because Jesus lived for me, died for me, and rose to give me eternal life with him." But many Christians wonder, "How can I be sure that I won't fall away from my faith in Jesus before I die?"

The question has a two-part answer.

No thing or person can force us away from God. Jesus says, "No one can snatch [my sheep] out of my hand." The truth is that no person, power, or situation can tear us from God's loving arms.

But does that mean we can never fall away from faith? No. So again we ask, How can we be sure we won't fall away from our faith in Jesus before we die? How can we be sure our faith won't become so weak that we reject Jesus when times get rough? How can we be sure our faith won't be swallowed up with the cares of this life?

The apostle Peter provides an answer: "In [the Father's] great mercy he has given us new birth into a living hope . . . kept in heaven for you, who through faith are shielded by God's power until the coming of the salvation that is ready to be revealed in the last time" (1 Peter 1:3-5). Peter assures us that we are kept in the faith, shielded by the power of God.

But what is this power of God? Paul tells us in Romans 1:16, "I am not ashamed of the gospel, because it is the power of God for the salvation of everyone who believes." God uses the gospel, the good news of our forgiveness in Christ, to keep us in faith. The gospel is our assurance. As we hear and learn the Word of God and as we receive the Lord's Supper, God will strengthen our faith and keep us in faith. That being the case, neither anything nor anyone—not even the devil himself—can take us from God's loving hands.

ᴄᴏ⊚ᴏ

Dear Jesus, I thank you for leading me to trust in your promises. Keep me in the faith as I hear and learn your Word. Continue to strengthen my trust in you until you call me home. Amen.

April 25

The Shepherd is one with his Father

When Jesus identified himself as the loving Shepherd, he made some wonderful promises. He said, "I give [my sheep] eternal life, and they shall never perish; no one can snatch them out of my hand" (John 10:28). But how can he give us eternal life? How can he preserve us in the faith? How can we be sure he will deliver?

Jesus tells us how. He says he is one with the Father. With these words he assures us that he is true God. We confess this truth in the Nicene Creed when we describe Jesus as "one being with the Father." This is not saying he is the same person as the Father. The Bible describes him as the only begotten Son of the Father. But the Bible also teaches us that Jesus, the Son, and the Father and the Holy Spirit are one God—three persons but only one God.

Jesus' deity is the power behind his promises. Because he is God, his perfect obedience means he is "the LORD Our Righteousness" (Jeremiah 23:6). The Father credits his Son's perfection to us. Because the man Jesus is God, he could lay down his life for the sheep and be the sin offering that truly took away the sin of the world (John 1:29). Because he is God, he could take up his life again, rising from the dead (John 10:17). Because he is God, we can trust him when he says, "I am the resurrection and the life. He who believes in me will live, even though he dies" (John 11:25). Finally, because he is God, we can be sure he will be our judge on the Last Day. He will judge us based on his life and death for us.

As God, there is one thing he won't ever do. Paul assures us, "God . . . does not lie" (Titus 1:2). God keeps every one of his promises, pledges, and vows. Most certainly that includes his promise to his dear sheep who follow him in faith: "I give them eternal life, and they shall never perish; no one can snatch them out of my hand. My Father, who has given them to me, is greater than all; no one can snatch them out of my Father's hand. I and the Father are one" (John 10:28-30).

✎⎨⎬✎

Jesus, my Savior and God, I praise you because your promises have made me sure of my eternal salvation. As you assure me of your promises in your Word, teach me too that you will keep them all. Amen.

"I am the true vine, and my Father is the gardener. I am the vine; you are the branches." (John 15:1,5)

26 April

Christ the vine

Do you know your family's roots? If you don't, there are many people who want you to know. It's their business. For a fee, they'll mail you a copy of your family tree; it has already been researched. For a smaller fee, a person at a shopping mall will search a computer database for your genealogy.

Family trees are interesting. They show the relationships that exist among relatives, and they're often filled with surprises.

Christians, however, don't have to research their spiritual family trees. Jesus said, "I am the vine." He said that his followers are "the branches." Those titles describe a close relationship between the Lord and his followers.

As the vine, Jesus is the source of our life. The Christian family tree begins with him. Our genealogical relations with Jesus are not physical; he is the source of spiritual and eternal life. When people are led to look to Jesus as their Savior, they enjoy full and free forgiveness of all sins and heaven is theirs.

As the vine, Jesus not only gives life, he nourishes life. As a vine sends nourishment and strength to all the branches, so Jesus sends nourishment to each of his followers. He uses his gospel—a nourishment that sustains life and increases their faith.

As a vine produces more branches, so Jesus adds branches to himself. This happens when the Holy Spirit brings more people to the conviction that Jesus is the Christ, the promised Savior. That's the reason why it can be said that Christianity is branching out.

The entire relationship of vine and branches is summed up by the titles "Christ" and "Christian." A Christian is a follower of Christ, someone who trusts in him as Savior. As a Christian, you are closely joined to Christ. In Christ you have life and salvation. What a blessing to be a Christian, to be united with Christ now and forever, to be able to say with the hymnwriter, "As the branch is to the vine, I am his and he is mine!" (from CW 385:1).

❧☙

Christ Jesus, may my title "Christian" always remind me of how greatly you have blessed me. May it remind me of the genealogy of which I am a part—one that stretches from eternity past to eternity future. Finally, may it lead me to serve you and to live my life your way. Amen.

"Remain in me, and I will remain in you. No branch can bear fruit by itself; it must remain in the vine. Neither can you bear fruit unless you remain in me. . . . If a man remains in me and I in him, he will bear much fruit; apart from me you can do nothing." (John 15:4,5)

Fruitfulness only in Christ

A well-known religious personality sat all alone on a stool at center stage. The isolated seating arrangement reflected how his ideas stood apart from everyone else's. He had been giving a defense of Christianity before a hostile crowd and an intimidating host.

As the show came to an end, the host fired out one last question: "You mean to tell me that if a guy runs into a burning house and rescues the people inside, it doesn't mean anything to God just because the person is not a Christian?" "That's right," came the answer.

If there had been tar and feathers available in that studio, you wouldn't have recognized the person being interviewed. The crowd booed and jeered, and the host rejected the answer.

As unpopular as that answer was, it was true. Jesus tells people, "Apart from me you can do nothing." Apart from Jesus there is nothing good. There's no salvation; there's no peace with God; there's nothing but sin. Apart from Jesus people can't do anything that is good in God's sight. The inspired writer to the Hebrews wrote, "Without faith it is impossible to please God" (Hebrews 11:6).

What all this means is that many people are doing outwardly good things in life, but from a spiritual standpoint, these deeds have no spiritual value. Christians thank God for good neighbors and law-abiding citizens. These are wonderful gifts of the Lord, and he will reward such people in this life for their acts of kindness. But Christians who are concerned for souls must make it clear that that's not enough. It's not enough that people simply do good. What's needed is that people confess their inability to do the good God requires in his law. They need to realize that what they do with their hands is not generated by love for God.

Only God can change the heart. He does this by leading a person to know his sin and to confess the Savior. Once God joins a person to the vine, good works—works that flow from a heart that loves God—are there. Thank God for your faith. Pray that he would use you to lead others to know Jesus in faith and to produce fruit acceptable in God's sight.

⌘

Lord God, chase away the shades of unbelief and bring many more people into your family through your cleansing Word. Amen.

"If you remain in me and my words remain in you, ask whatever you wish, and it will be given you." (John 15:7)

Blessings of attachment

Back in the days when security at the White House was lax, a soldier cut across the grounds hoping to see President Abraham Lincoln. Instead, he met Thomas "Tad" Lincoln, the president's son. The soldier explained his predicament. He needed a pass to visit an ailing family member. Military officers had denied the request, so in despair he decided to go all the way to the commander in chief.

Young Lincoln took the soldier into the White House and introduced him to his father, who promptly granted the request. That was quite a lesson for the soldier. He found out that the president's child, as little as he was, had access to the most important person in the country and could speak to him at all times about anything he wanted.

Jesus says that that's the kind of access Christians have to God because of their attachment to him in faith. One of the great blessings of being attached to Jesus, as a branch to a vine, is that Christians are able to communicate with God in prayer.

The Christian, however, has more than just the ability to speak to God in prayer. In our reading, Jesus speaks of the effectiveness of prayer: "Ask whatever you wish, and it will be given you."

This does not mean that God will answer every one of your prayers with an automatic yes. Jesus' promise still allows for the wisdom of God to determine what is best and when it is the right time for him to act in your life.

Still, you can be confident that God will give you what you truly need. The Bible says, "He who did not spare his own Son, but gave him up for us all—how will he not also, along with him, graciously give us all things?" (Romans 8:32). The God who has given you his greatest gift, Jesus your Savior, will surely give you everything else necessary for your body and soul.

What blessing there is in being attached to Jesus in faith. You have around-the-clock access to God through prayer. And you know that he will give you the best answer possible. Treasure that privilege by using it throughout each day.

৩৯৩৯

Heavenly Father, what a great gift you have given me in prayer. May your Word continue to remain in me so that I have confidence to come to you in prayer. Train me to be evermore faithful in praying to you. Hear and answer all my prayers for Jesus' sake. Amen.

"Greater love has no one than this, that he lay down his life for his friends." (John 15:13)

Christ showed us the greatest love

Many of the greatest sacrifices people make come in wartime. A person may be wounded and literally give part of his body to protect the freedom we enjoy. One of the most noble pictures of an unselfish sacrifice is that of a soldier throwing himself on a grenade to save his fellow soldiers. One man dies, but many others are spared death or serious injury and live to fight on because their friend gave his life for them.

Many times Jesus told his disciples that he would suffer and die for the sins of the world. In John chapter 10, the Good Shepherd chapter, Jesus said, "The reason my Father loves me is that I lay down my life—only to take it up again. No one takes it from me, but I lay it down of my own accord. I have authority to lay it down and authority to take it up again" (verses 17,18).

Love led Jesus to leave heaven and live on earth. Love led him to become a man and to "carr[y] our sorrows," as Isaiah wrote in Isaiah 53:4. Love led him to obligate himself to keep God's commandments for us. Love led him to the cross and led him to suffer hell for us there. Love led him to be the substitute for every person who has ever lived.

Jesus' love for us has covered over all our sins. It has covered over the ones we know about and the ones we don't even remember doing. It covers over our big sins and our small sins. It covers sins we don't realize are sins, as well as the sins we commit deliberately. It covers over the sins that we continue to struggle with and sins of the past that still haunt us.

There are no conditions to Jesus' love. As Paul says, "God demonstrates his own love for us in this: While we were still sinners, Christ died for us" (Romans 5:8). He has forgiven our sins as a free gift. This love is the greatest love that exists. Nothing has ever topped it, and nothing ever will.

Love divine, all love excelling,
Joy of heav'n, to earth come down,
Fix in us your humble dwelling,
All your faithful mercies crown.
Jesus, you are all compassion,
Boundless mercy from above.
Visit us with benediction;
Comfort us with heav'nly love. Amen. (CW 365:1)

"My command is this: Love each other as I have loved you.
This is my command: Love each other." (John 15:12,17)

30 *April*

Love one another as Christ has loved you

An old tradition says that when the apostle John had grown old and feeble, he had to be carried by his followers into the meeting place of the congregation at Ephesus. Since he was no longer able to speak to his congregation for very long, it was his custom to stretch out his arms to them and say, "Little children, love one another." Eventually, his hearers grew somewhat weary with hearing the same words. One reverently asked, "Why do you always speak this way?" John's reply was, "It is the Lord's command, and if only this be done, it is enough."

We have no way of knowing whether this story is true. Still, it gives us good food for thought. Our Savior has commanded us to love one another. On Maundy Thursday evening, he said, "A new command I give you: Love one another. As I have loved you, so you must love one another. By this all men will know that you are my disciples, if you love one another" (John 13:34,35).

Our Savior, who loves us, tells us to imitate that love. This does not mean merely to be devoted to one another or to be helpful to one another. Even people who are not Christians do that most of the time. Jesus means that we love people with the same kind of love he has for us—love that seeks the eternal good of all.

Martin Luther said that Christians show their love for God in loving one another. He stressed that Christians should have and show special love and faithfulness toward one another because they have one and the same Father and inheritance of heaven and as Christians they enjoy the same faith, heart, and mind.

Paul wrote, "Love is patient, love is kind. It does not envy, it does not boast, it is not proud. It is not rude, it is not self-seeking, it is not easily angered, it keeps no record of wrongs. Love does not delight in evil but rejoices with the truth. It always protects, always trusts, always hopes, always perseveres" (1 Corinthians 13:4-7).

Keep loving one another. Imitate the love of Jesus. He has shown us what real love is with his willingness to live for us and suffer and die for us. Let his unselfishness shine in you.

⸙

Dear Lord Jesus, give me the power and ability to fulfill your command to love my neighbor. Lead me always to your cross, where my sins have been taken away, and help me always love everyone with the same kind of unselfish love you have given me. Amen.

"My prayer is not for them alone. I pray also for those who will believe in me through their message." (John 17:20)

Jesus prays for all who will believe

Jesus prays. What a profound picture! It is the last night of Jesus' life. He knows the cup of suffering he is about to drink. He knows the mission he was sent to complete is now coming to conclusion. He knows of the upcoming trial, the coming desertion of his disciples, and the jeering crowds that would soon taunt him. What does Jesus do as he is about to face such agony, suffering, and heartache? He prays.

Jesus prays for his disciples. He prays for those whom he has gathered and personally taught. He prays that their faith might continue to grow and that they will not fall away during the coming hours and days. He prays that the Word he has planted in them might be spread throughout the world. That Word of the apostles, according to Ephesians 2:20, is the foundation of the church for all time "with Christ Jesus himself as the chief cornerstone." As the Holy Spirit works through that Word, it produces faith. It makes believers. Jesus prays that the Word may be freely proclaimed so that through the message of his forgiveness, souls will be won. He prays that those made weary and filled with burdens because of the load of their sin will find rest for their souls.

Jesus also prays for all those who in the future would come to believe through the working of that Word. He is praying for those who have not yet been formed in their mothers' wombs and yet, nevertheless, are known by him (Jeremiah 1:5). He knows all those who will believe. He knows his children of all generations. He is praying on their behalf.

Jesus is also praying for us. He is praying for our weak faith so that it may grow stronger. He is praying that we do not grieve the Holy Spirit by avoiding the preaching and teaching of God's Word. He is praying that we resist temptation, serve him in all our words and actions, and remain faithful until death.

Jesus prays. What a profound picture. What a comfort to know that right now he is praying for you and for me. In my trials and daily struggles, in the high points of my life, and in the low ones, he is interceding with the heavenly Father on my behalf.

❧

Jesus, comfort me with the knowledge that you are right now pleading to the Father on my behalf. Forgive my sins, and allow me to serve you anew. Amen.

"That all of them may be one, Father, just as you are in me and I am in you." (John 17:21)

Jesus prays for unity

Isn't it a shame there are many different churches in the world? In our country alone, there are literally hundreds of denominations. At times many of them appear to fight and strive more against one another than against the unbelieving world. Is this the will of our God?

No. Jesus wants unity. He prays for unity. What is the basis for this unity he desires? It is the Word of God. Before Jesus ascended into heaven, he told his disciples, "Go and make disciples of all nations, baptizing them in the name of the Father and of the Son and of the Holy Spirit, and teaching them to obey everything I have commanded you" (Matthew 28:19,20). Jesus makes it clear that we are to teach and obey every word that he has given us in order to make disciples.

Unfortunately, in this sinful world, many rebel against the Word of Christ. Some, for instance, do not baptize infants because they claim that God would not expect infants to believe something they cannot understand. Others say that Jesus is not present with his body and blood in the Holy Supper because that's not reasonable, even though Jesus says, "This is my body. . . . This is my blood" (Matthew 26:26,28).

The Lord wants us to be united in his Word. The great and perfect model for unity he gives is that of the triune God. The Father and the Son and the Holy Spirit are one in nature, essence, operation, and mission.

The Lord wants us always to strive toward such perfect unity. It is true that even the smallest spark of faith joins us to God and unites us to his church. Yet this is only the beginning. Through the power of the Spirit, we seek to bring our every thought, word, and action in subjection to the Word. Our knowledge and the range and power of our faith is to grow. As we grow in faith and knowledge, our oneness with God and with Christ and our oneness with one another becomes more and more what Jesus wants it to be.

Jesus prays that as the Word goes out, there might be unity, that people might believe the unadulterated Word and be saved through the good news of forgiveness and eternal salvation.

⟡⟡⟡

Lord of the church, allow all the members of your church to be fully united in faith, love, and service to you. Amen.

"May they also be in us so that the world may believe that you have sent me." (John 17:21)

Jesus prays that the world may believe

The best example of the beauty and attraction of spiritual unity can be seen in the description of the early Christian church: "They devoted themselves to the apostles' teaching and to the fellowship, to the breaking of bread and to prayer. All the believers were together and had everything in common. Selling their possessions and goods, they gave to anyone as he had need. Every day they continued to meet together in the temple courts. They broke bread in their homes and ate together with glad and sincere hearts, praising God and enjoying the favor of all the people" (Acts 2:42,44-47).

Those first Christians did not cause quarrel and strife; rather, they brought peace, love, and harmony. The unbelieving world took note of such believers. They were different and unique. They were a blessing to their families, friends, and communities.

The unity of Christians in love and charity on the basis of God's Word is a beautiful thing. Such unity and love invites others to join them. This is one of the great purposes of spiritual unity for which Jesus has been praying.

Jesus also prays that the world may believe. His reason for this prayer is pure grace. The world is the object of Jesus' love. His saving efforts extend to it. That is the reason he took on human form, lived a perfect life, and died for the sins of the world. Jesus wants all nations to be saved and to come to the knowledge of the truth.

An insight that we dare not overlook is that all nations includes our nation! This is both an opportunity and a challenge. It is an opportunity because no matter where we live, there are people who are mission prospects, people who do not know Jesus as their Savior. It is a challenge because our society has become increasingly secular and pluralistic.

Jesus wants all the world to believe and trust in him. Let us engage the world with the gospel, not just on foreign shores but where we live and work. There also we meet an unbelieving world head-to-head and heart-to-heart. Continue to reach out so that all the world might believe.

⋘◐◑⋙

Jesus, you have commanded your church to preach the gospel to all nations. Use me as your servant in this great endeavor to help in proclaiming the good news of salvation to people everywhere. Amen.

"I have given them the glory that you gave me, that they may be one as we are one: I in them and you in me. May they be brought to complete unity to let the world know that you sent me and have loved them even as you have loved me." (John 17:22,23)

Jesus prays that the world may know the Father's love

A number of years ago, the young son of two of our church's members accidentally drowned. The parents were devastated. Who can understand the pain of losing a son prematurely in death? Only one who has actually experienced the hurt and grief can begin to sympathize. In the funeral sermon, the grieving parents were reminded of the great sacrifice of God the Father. He willingly gave his Son to die for each of us. What incomprehensible love!

Those parents now have a stronger understanding of this great truth: "God so loved the world that he gave his one and only Son, that whoever believes in him shall not perish but have eternal life" (John 3:16). God the Father so loved the world that he sent his Son to die for it. We can rightly deduce that if God loved the world so much that Jesus died for it, then God also loves me. What a great comfort!

You know this great love of the Father. You know the Lord Jesus Christ as your Savior. You know his gospel promises: "Come to me, all you who are weary and burdened, and I will give you rest" (Matthew 11:28) and "Take heart . . . your sins are forgiven" (Matthew 9:2). Our Lord wants all in this world to know the profound love that drove Christ to the cross. Jesus knows the love of his Father, and he wants the world to know this great love.

Such love goes beyond all description and human reason. So great is his love for us that Jesus "made himself nothing, taking the very nature of a servant, being made in human likeness. And being found in appearance as a man, he humbled himself and became obedient to death—even death on a cross!" (Philippians 2:7,8). Jesus prays that the world might know this love.

 ✺

Lord, give me a caring heart to love and seek all who are lost in sin. Overcome the fear in my heart, and give me courage to share the message of your love to all those who have no hope. Amen.

"Father, I want those you have given me to be with me where I am, and to see my glory, the glory you have given me because you loved me before the creation of the world." (John 17:24)

Jesus prays for his believers to be with him

Elderly believers often tell of their desire to leave this world and be with their Lord in heaven. Their bodies have aged; friends, spouses, and relatives have gone on before them; and they are ready to be with their Savior.

Jesus here prays that all believers would come to him. This prayer of Jesus reaches back into all eternity to the eternal love of God and, at the same time, reaches forward to all eternity to the blessedness that will be ours. He wants us to experience his glory in the bliss of heaven. His glory is the brightness of heaven.

Now we know the grace of God through his Word, but in heaven we will behold the glory of our Savior with our own eyes. The veil of sin will be fully removed. Job said, "In my flesh I will see God; I myself will see him with my own eyes" (Job 19:26,27). We will then see and understand more fully Jesus' glorious mission to save all sinners. We will behold the streams of love that emanate from the glorious Son. We will view the glory that has been part of Christ since before the creation of the world.

Jesus prays with confidence. We can be sure that we will experience this heavenly glory because of the work of Christ. It is his will that we join him. His vicarious work is sufficient for all people. He has paid the price for our sins. Jesus holds his elect safe against all enemies. Christ's own happiness will be complete when his elect join him in the unending glory of paradise. The consummation of our Christian hope and joy, according to this prayer, will be when we see the glory of our Redeemer. When we enter heaven, we will behold the head that once was crowned with thorns and is now adorned with everlasting honor. We will serve the eternal Son of God in power. That is the final goal of our faith—eternal life, eternal glory in and with Christ.

✦✦✦

Dearest Jesus, you have prepared a beautiful home for me in heaven. Keep me close to you in faith until you finally take me to be with you. Amen.

"Righteous Father, though the world does not know you, I know you, and they know that you have sent me. I have made you known to them, and will continue to make you known in order that the love you have for me may be in them and that I myself may be in them." (John 17:25,26)

Jesus prays to his righteous Father

Aleksandr Solzhenitsyn, a famous Russian novelist, returned to Russia after saying the United States suffers from sloppiness, indifference, and a corruption of the heart. William Bennett, former education secretary and drug czar, reminds us, "There is a coarseness, a callousness, a cynicism, a banality and a vulgarity to our time." Our society has gone astray. Children are old before their time, and people suffer from "atrocity overload." A book by Charles Sykes says American character has decayed because it is easier to say we are victims of something than to take individual responsibility for our actions.

Now we read that Jesus prays to the righteous Father. *Righteous* is not a well-known or popularly used word today. However, *righteous* describes the Father's character and nature. This is the Father who is holy and perfect. This is the God who will not tolerate sin in his presence. Sin is a reproach to God. He hates it. He condemns it and promises to punish all who transgress his ways. Scripture says, "Be perfect, therefore, as your heavenly Father is perfect" (Matthew 5:48).

Jesus understands righteousness, which is the central message in all the Bible. Jesus came to fulfill righteousness for us. He exchanged his perfect life and innocent death for our sinfulness. What an exchange! What a Savior!

Many today are ignorant about God and his message of righteousness. The world does not know about this righteous Father and his great demands. All people by nature are ignorant of this righteousness. The consciences of all bear witness to the law of God, yet they leave people feeling guilty and in despair. The law tells us we are sinners, deserving eternal punishment.

But thanks be to God! Jesus has come and fulfilled all the righteous demands of the righteous Father. His blood cleanses us from the guilt of all our sins. Now we too can pray to our righteous Father and know that we are heard because of all Jesus has done for us.

❧❧❧❧

Loving Savior, forgive all my sins and empower me through your gospel to serve you in all my thoughts, words, and actions. Amen.

"I have made you known to them, and will continue to make you known in order that the love you have for me may be in them and that I myself may be in them." (John 17:26)

Jesus prays that his love be in us

Two gang members beat up a teenage girl at a local high school. "Why did you do it?" the police officer asked. "Because she was wearing the tattoo of a rival gang," the boys answered. "She deserved what she got. We hate them all!" Today there is much hatred in our world. Everyday we see, hear, or read about senseless acts of violence and brutality bred by hatred.

Hatred is a result of sin. It is part of our sinful nature. When left unchecked, hatred will continue to grow. It can all too easily fill up our lives and destroy us physically and spiritually. Our world is filled with countless examples of the destructive power of hatred.

Jesus prays for his love to be in us. We are to be his lights in this dark and hate-filled world. Jesus says, "Love your neighbor as yourself" (Matthew 22:39).

God's love for us is so great that it can conquer all hatred. The Bible says, "God demonstrates his own love for us in this: While we were still sinners, Christ died for us" (Romans 5:8) and "The blood of Jesus, his Son, purifies us from all sin" (1 John 1:7). Christ came from heaven, took on human flesh, and died a painful death amidst hate-filled crowds to pay for all our sins of hatred and callousness. He did these things so that we might not be punished for our sins but rather have God as our Father and heaven as our home. Such is God's powerful love for us!

Jesus now prays for his love to be in us. He prays that his conquering love may touch our lives and make us beacons of his gospel light and peacemakers in this sin-sick world. May you be the hands, the feet, the tongue, and the heart of God to all around you. May you be a bastion of his love as you feed the hungry, befriend the stranger, care for the sick and dying, and visit those in prison. As you do, remember Jesus' promise: "Whatever you did for one of [these] . . . you did for me" (Matthew 25:40).

❧☙

Jesus, you welcomed all who came to you, even the outcasts and the despised. Give me such a faith that trusts only in your love. Allow me to accept others as you have accepted me. Amen.

"When the Counselor comes, whom I will send to you from the Father, the Spirit of truth who goes out from the Father, he will testify about me." (John 15:26)

The Spirit testifies about Christ

Ever since man fell into sin and his natural knowledge of God became clouded, he has searched long and hard for the meaning and purpose of his existence. This intense search has led people in many different directions. Some, like Darwin, have searched land and sea for clues that could eventually lead to answers about the origin of man. Others, hoping to discover deep within themselves the mystery of man's existence, have followed the Eastern practices of meditation. But whatever methods people may choose to follow, they always lead to the same dead end. After all their activity, people are still left wondering about their origin, for what purpose they are here, and what the end of all things will be.

If we truly are to please God and to lead useful and meaningful lives, we must know our situation and why we were put here. Because no one could possibly have discovered the answers on his own, God sent his "Spirit of truth" to this earth to reveal it to us. It was this sending that Jesus foretold in our text.

The fulfillment occurred on Pentecost. On that day, amid the sound of a mighty rushing wind and cloven tongues of fire, the Holy Spirit was poured out upon Jesus' disciples. That day marked the beginning of the New Testament church, to which the Holy Spirit revealed the answers to the most vital human questions. The Holy Spirit moved the evangelists and apostles to speak the absolute truth and eventually to confirm it in writing. On that first Pentecost, three thousand people listened to the message and, through the working of the Spirit, believed it.

The Spirit of truth is still active among us today wherever God's Word is preached. Through it, God has convinced us of our origin in Adam and of the sinful condition we inherited from him. But he has also convinced us that we have a Savior from sin in the second Adam, Jesus Christ, by whom and for whom and to whom all things were made. In Christ our lives have purpose and direction—the purpose of leading others to the knowledge of the truth and the direction of eternal life in heaven.

❦

Holy Spirit, Light divine,
Shine upon this heart of mine;
Chase the gloom of night away;
Turn the darkness into day. Amen. (CW 183:1)

"When the Counselor comes, whom I will send to you from the Father . . . he will testify about me." (John 15:26)

Someone to comfort you

In India, along the winding roads, especially in the hill countries, there are little resting places for travelers. They are similar to our waysides in appearance, and they are called *samatanga*. Here a person may rest his weary feet, lay down his burden, and pause to talk with other travelers like himself. Then, rested, refreshed, and encouraged, he may resume his journey.

How well we could use such places of rest as we travel the road called life! Along the way we encounter and must shoulder many sorrows that weigh us down. We grieve over the loved ones who have died, leaving empty places in our lives that no one else can fill. We wrestle with discouraging and painful personal and family problems that seem to gnaw away at our hearts night and day, robbing us of peace and joy in life. We fall to our knees under the crosses that our Lord in his wisdom allows us to bear from time to time. We grow weary under the burden of our guilt and sins. How we long for a spiritual *samatanga*, a place where we can find a moment's peace, breathe a sigh of relief, and find at least some refreshment for our souls.

Our Lord has provided us with just such a place. You know where it is—at the foot of the cross of Jesus. There we find the assurance that all is well between God and us, no matter how rough the road of life might become. And in case we have trouble finding this place when we need it and, blinded by grief and sorrow, lose our way, Jesus has sent his Comforter, the Holy Spirit, to be our guide. It is this Comforter who takes us by the hand and leads us back to Calvary. There we are reminded that God is no longer angry with us, that he poured out on his Son the wrath we deserve. There he gave us righteousness, and hope, and life. And no man or devil can take it away from us!

So if the cares and worries of life are threatening to overwhelm you, if you feel yourself sinking under a tremendous load, then go back to the promises of God in Christ. In them you will find not only a passing *samatanga* but eternal rest and comfort for your souls.

❧❧❧

Come, Holy Ghost, in love
Shed on us from above
Thine own bright ray.
Divinely good Thou art;
Thy sacred gifts impart
To gladden each sad heart.
Oh, come today! Amen. (TLH 227:1)

"When the Counselor comes . . . he will testify about me. And you also must testify." (John 15:26,27)

The Counselor enables us to testify of Christ

When the disciples first learned the size of the task that the Lord was laying before them, they must have been terrified. Jesus said, "You will be my witnesses in Jerusalem, and in all Judea and Samaria, and to the ends of the earth" (Acts 1:8). Witnesses of Christ and of his sacred Word before the whole world! Were these not the same men who deserted Jesus in the Garden of Gethsemane when they saw the mob and the soldiers? Were they not the cowards who huddled behind locked doors afraid that the Jews might also do to them what they had done to Jesus?

But what is this we hear? Jesus tells those same men that they will not only carry on his work but that they will gladly suffer for the honor of being able to do it. Impossible! You would have a better chance telling someone who is afraid of heights to become a sky diver for a living. How could people as weak and frightened as these disciples ever hope to get the job done? They must have asked themselves the same question. But in our text, Jesus gives them and us an answer.

When the disciples would be brought before the most powerful men on the earth, the Holy Spirit would be with them to give them the courage to preach the truth. And if they should become so frightened that they felt their voices would fail them, the Holy Spirit would supply words for their trembling lips to speak. The disciples did not have to worry about bearing witness to the truth, even in the most awesome surroundings. The Counselor would do the witnessing through them.

That same Holy Spirit still offers us wisdom, comfort, and help today. Bearing witness to the truth in this sinful world will always be an awesome and frightening task. And there are many times when we seriously wonder how stubborn, selfish, sinful, and often-fearful people like ourselves can ever hope to give a clear testimony of our faith.

But it is in the midst of such fears that the Holy Spirit encourages us and calls to mind those portions of God's Word that apply. He gives us the strength to overcome our weakness and to live our faith. He who has testified of Christ to us is able to continue his work through us.

***

Dear Lord Jesus, thank you for sending us your Holy Spirit with his comfort, help, and encouragement. Give us the strength to fight every temptation to despair along life's way. Make us faithful witnesses to the glory of your name. Amen.

"I tell you the truth: It is for your good that I am going away. Unless I go away, the Counselor will not come to you; but if I go, I will send him to you." (John 16:7)

The Spirit is sent by Christ

Imagine what it would be like to have Jesus as our pastor, to hear him preach and teach, to receive his comfort in times of trouble, to have him counsel us with his wisdom, to have him guide us in our day-to-day living. This was the case for the disciples. What he had told them was true: "Blessed are the eyes that see what you see. For I tell you that many prophets and kings wanted to see what you see but did not see it, and to hear what you hear but did not hear it" (Luke 10:23,24).

But now Jesus announces that he is going away. We can understand the disciples' reaction of sorrow.

But Jesus says, "It is for your good." If the intimate personal association that his disciples enjoyed with Jesus would go on indefinitely, the very purpose of Jesus' mission would not have been achieved. His going away, his ascension, would lead to his "sitting at the right hand of the Mighty One" (Matthew 26:64). As Luther stated it, the right hand of God is everywhere. In other words, it was necessary for us that Jesus should exchange his presence in Judea and Galilee for his throne in heaven so that he might be present with his entire church everywhere. Instead of having us all move into the land of Israel to be with him, he left the land of Israel to come and live with us.

His disciples would not be left alone in a world of evil, injustice, sorrow, and pain. Not at all. Jesus would send the Holy Spirit, as he promised, "If I go, I will send him to you." The Holy Spirit would come into this world to be to the disciples what Jesus had been to them during the days of his personal companionship with them.

The Spirit still comes through the preaching of the gospel. He comes to be our intimate and personal friend. He comes not only to replace the presence of Christ but also to complete the presence of Christ, to continue God's work in our lives. The presence of the Holy Spirit is the secret to a life of fullness, joy, freedom, and power. To have the Holy Spirit as our ever-present friend and to live according to the Word of God, which he has given us, is true Christian living.

❧⦿❧

O Spirit of our Lord Jesus Christ, hear our prayers and make our hearts your home. Descend with all your gracious power so that we may love what you love and do what you would have us do. Amen.

"When he comes, he will convict the world of guilt in regard to sin . . . because men do not believe in me." (John 16:8,9)

The Holy Spirit and sin

The Spirit is holy. The Spirit is God. And we are not. We do not stand on an equal footing with God.

The word *holy* isn't heard much today. There isn't much that is considered to be holy. The word seems almost to be something out of another age. Nothing is sacred; nothing is perfect; nothing is holy. And when we consider our own lives, the word *holy* seems to be out of place.

But it is not. First of all, God's command to us is to be holy, even as he is holy. *Holy* means "without sin." When we fail to hit the mark that God sets for us, we sin. And we know how often we fail to hit the mark. All this is proof of the biblical teaching that we all are sinners from birth. God created us to be his children, but by nature we refuse to live as his children. Instead of trust in him, there is doubt. Instead of humility, there is arrogance. We do not love God as we should, nor do we love our neighbors as ourselves. We are sinners.

It is the Holy Spirit who convinces us we are sinners. The Spirit shows us where we have failed. Jesus said, "When he comes, he will convict the world of guilt in regard to sin." The Spirit comes to convince us of the deadliness of sin, to prevent us from thinking that sin is something not so bad or something that God will disregard.

The world does not deny the existence of sin. It will admit that murder, adultery, and theft are wrong. It will admit that such sins should be avoided. But the world is still mistaken about sin, because it does not realize sin's power to damn, to separate a person from God eternally. It only sees sin as diminishing the quality of life on earth.

The world does not realize that the worst sin of all is that of not believing in Christ. When the jailer at Philippi anxiously asked, "Sirs, what must I do to be saved?" the apostle did not tell him to live better or to refrain from sinning. He urged him rather, "Believe in the Lord Jesus, and you will be saved" (Acts 16:30,31). Faith in Jesus Christ saves. Rejecting him in unbelief damns. Unbelief says no to the forgiveness of sins that Jesus won for all by his death on the cross.

The Holy Spirit gives us understanding of God's holiness. The other side of that coin is sinfulness. The fact that Christ, the innocent Lamb of God, had to die for sin demonstrates that in the eyes of God, sin is terrible indeed.

⁂

We ask forgiveness, O God, for Jesus' sake, and we pray that by the power of your Holy Spirit you would strengthen our faith in him. Amen.

"When he comes, he will convict the world of guilt . . . in regard to righteousness, because I am going to the Father, where you can see me no longer." (John 16:8,10)

The Spirit and righteousness

People have tried strange things to make themselves acceptable to God. They have invented for themselves works that they were sure God would see and approve of and credit to their accounts. They went out into the desert and lived in caves. They climbed up on pillars to live several years of their lives isolated on a platform. They spent enough hours on their knees in prayer to make their knees knobby and deformed. All this with the hope that they might be counted as righteous in the eyes of God!

But all of these are vain, human efforts, which, according to the Bible, cannot earn a single ounce of righteousness before God. If we had to choose a word from Scripture that describes God, that word might be *righteous.* When Adam and Eve fell into sin and away from God, they lost every trace of righteousness, not only for themselves but for the whole human race. The basic purpose for which God gave his one and only Son was that he might bestow his righteousness on us. God is the sum total of goodness, of righteousness. To be truly good, one must be like God. Jesus taught, "Seek first [God's] kingdom and his righteousness" (Matthew 6:33).

The Holy Spirit, who comes to us at the command of Christ, teaches as Jesus did with regard to righteousness. Jesus said the Holy Spirit would "convict the world of guilt . . . in regard to righteousness." This is necessary because sinful humans set for themselves a standard of righteousness that is a delusion. They see righteousness as nothing more than being civic-minded or giving dollars to charity or doing some praiseworthy deed.

The Spirit teaches a far higher righteousness. It is the righteousness connected with Jesus' going to the Father. Keep in mind that Jesus spoke these words on Maundy Thursday as he was about to be betrayed to his enemies. He was about to be crucified like the worst of criminals. But the death he died was our death, the wages of our sin. It was a substitutionary death that paid the sinner's debt. It provided the righteousness that we ourselves could not provide. And the clearest indication that this righteousness was accepted by God is seen in the fact that the Father raised his Son from death. That Jesus is risen and ascended, that we "see [him] no longer," is the Bible's proof that Jesus has provided the righteousness that we need before God.

❦

Come, Holy Spirit. Enable us to know the mighty acts of God in Jesus Christ. May we see in the substitutionary death of Jesus Christ the instrument of our salvation. Amen.

"When he comes, he will convict the world of guilt . . . in regard to judgment, because the prince of this world now stands condemned." (John 16:8,11)

The Spirit and judgment

The Spirit comes to bear testimony to the world, and the Spirit's testimony also includes the fact of judgment. The word *judgment* means "the sentence of a judge that is pronounced in court." We know that our Lord Jesus Christ will pronounce his judgment upon all people publicly when he returns on the Last Day. But as the unbelieving world tries to deny its sin and its need of righteousness, so it tries to deny that it will stand accountable to God on the day of judgment.

Everyone is ready to pass the buck as far as sin is concerned. People blame society for the evils in their lives. They blame the environment. They blame the schools. They blame parents. They blame circumstances. Underneath it all, they are really blaming God for letting everything go to pieces.

But on the day of judgment, there will be no buck left to pass. On that day people will be declared either children of light or children of darkness. They will hear either, "Come, you who are blessed by my Father," or "Depart from me, you who are cursed" (Matthew 25:34,41). It is the Holy Spirit who convinces us that this is the truth.

In elaborating on the fact of the judgment, Jesus makes reference to Satan. Satan already has been judged and condemned. His power over sinners has been broken by Christ's victorious death and resurrection. And God's judgment will fall on all who despise the righteousness that God alone gives and offers us in his Son.

It is the Holy Spirit's work to convince the world of this truth. There is no escaping God's wrath. We can crawl into the deepest cave; God is there. We can climb the highest mountain; God is there. If we attempt to flee to a faraway place, God is there.

The Spirit of the living God, however, comes to people through the preaching of the gospel. Through the gospel he draws them to the Lamb of God, who takes away the sin of the world and gives them eternal life. Therefore, we should gladly support and take part in the work of bringing people the good news that Satan is defeated and that they have been set free from death and hell by the Son of God.

⚛

Dear Lord Jesus, cause your Word of judgment and life to be proclaimed with all zeal throughout the world. Amen.

"When he, the Spirit of truth, comes, he will guide you into all truth. He will not speak on his own; he will speak only what he hears, and he will tell you what is yet to come."
(John 16:13)

The Spirit of truth

It is important to know the truth. It is even more important to live it. Jesus is the incarnation of truth. He said, "I am the way and the truth and the life" (John 14:6). Truth is wrapped up in the person of Jesus Christ. All that he said and did was true, sure, and dependable. And now in our text, he announces his departure to his disciples. Did that mean a vacuum of truth, that they would soon be deprived of the truth on which they were building their faith and their lives?

Not at all. Jesus was about to send them his Spirit, the Spirit of truth. The Spirit's words, like the words of Jesus, would be worthy of absolute confidence and trust. The Spirit would guide the disciples into all truth. When Peter preached at Pentecost or when Paul picked up his pen and papyrus to write to Corinth or Ephesus, the Spirit was guiding their very words and thoughts. Their messages came from the councils of the triune God.

The Spirit's Word of truth stands in opposition to Satan's lies. Here are some of the lies Satan is spreading today: People can make it on their own—they don't need God; money and position are the things that satisfy and are the primary goals of life; immorality brings pleasure, so do your own thing; humans have simply evolved, so we are accountable to no one.

Opposition to the truth, however, cannot silence it. The Spirit's truth stands because it is the Word of God. The Spirit teaches us the truth about ourselves, the truth we are not always anxious to hear or believe. But the Spirit's Word pierces our souls and brings to light the sin that we have tried so hard to hide from others, that we have hidden from ourselves as well. The Spirit's Word likewise teaches us of God's grace—that God is for us, that Jesus died for us, rose for us, reigns for us, and prays for us. The Spirit teaches also of "what is yet to come." He guides us to the throne of God and lets us see "a great multitude that no one could count, from every nation . . . standing before the throne and in front of the Lamb. They were wearing white robes and were holding palm branches in their hands. And they cried out in a loud voice: 'Salvation belongs to our God, who sits on the throne, and to the Lamb'" (Revelation 7:9,10).

O Spirit of God, continue to come to us and to lead us into truth. Amen.

"When he, the Spirit of truth, comes . . . he will bring glory to me." (John 16:13,14)

The Spirit glorifies Christ

In fulfillment of Jesus' words, the Spirit came on the day of Pentecost. The Spirit came; the apostles spoke in languages that all the people of Israel assembled in Jerusalem that day could understand. And in each language, Jesus was glorified. Peter preached the mighty works of God. Each of these mighty works was done by Jesus, who is both Lord and Christ. Jesus was stamped with the seal of God's approval. Jesus was taken by wicked men. Jesus was put to death on the cross. Jesus was raised from the dead by God the Father.

From Peter's sermon on Pentecost, it becomes obvious that the Spirit does not draw attention so much to himself but to Christ. It's important to remember this in a day when many feel that receiving the Spirit is an end in itself. Many people emphasize the emotional experience of being "filled with the Spirit." Do you *feel* the love of God in you? Do you *feel* the power of the Almighty? Do you *feel* that you are saved? They base their assurance of salvation on human feelings. Everything is fine while they are experiencing good times; they can feel God is for them. But what happens when they are fired from a job, when their child becomes sick, when serious depression hits the family? What do they feel about God then? Has he forsaken them? Is God angry with them? Are they sure of going to heaven at their deaths?

The Spirit still comes to us as he came to the disciples at Pentecost— to glorify Christ, to throw the spotlight on the Word made flesh. He traces the steps of Jesus as he went up to Jerusalem and then carried his cross to the place of the skull. The Spirit brings light to our minds and enables us to understand what we are supposed to understand: The Lord Jesus laid down his life to pay for our sins.

When the Spirit comes to us, he also leads us to glorify Christ. We glorify Christ when we live for him—by trusting, loving, and obeying him. Is Christ becoming more and more evident in our lives? Are people seeing more of him and less of us? If not, Christ is not receiving the glory that is rightfully his. If not, we are hindering the sanctifying work of the Holy Spirit in our lives. The answer is to confess our sin and to ask, seek, and knock at the door of the heart of God to seek a greater measure of the Spirit.

That prayer is answered with a yes, and the answer is found in the study of God's Word.

Lord, we thank you that your Spirit has enlightened us through the gospel. Amen.

May the grace of the Lord Jesus Christ . . . be with you all.
(2 Corinthians 13:14)

United through the blessing of grace

We tend to spend time with people who share our interests and ideas. We feel a connection with and a closeness to those who think and act the same way we do. The same holds true for those who follow the same sports teams or belong to the same church—in each case a common cause unites them.

How are we united with God? We are united through the blessing of God's grace. Paul reminds us of that blessing in his closing benediction.

Instead of being united with God, at one time we were separated from him. Sin does that. Our sin did that. It totally destroyed our connection with God. But God did something about our ruined relationship with him. He sent Jesus. And Jesus, whose name means "savior," lived up to his name. He saved us. He was the one who God promised would come to take our place. Jesus lived a perfect life for us, took our sin on himself, and died for us on the cross. His resurrection three days later assures us that he accomplished a most amazing miracle. He reunites us with God.

That is a perfect illustration of God's grace—his undeserved love for us in Christ. In fact, God gave us the very opposite of what we deserved. Instead of hell, we have heaven. Instead of eternal death, we have eternal life. Paul spoke of those riches earlier in this same letter to the Corinthians. He summarized Jesus' work this way: "You know the grace of our Lord Jesus Christ, that though he was rich, yet for your sakes he became poor, so that you through his poverty might become rich" (8:9). Through Christ we are rich. God has forgiven our sins, removed our guilt, and given us heavenly treasures in an eternal home.

While we finish our time on this earth, Jesus rules over us. He does not rule over us as a cruel dictator or merciless tyrant, making unreasonable commands and unfair demands. He lovingly controls all things for us and for our good. We have nothing to worry about—because of his grace.

What a wonderful blessing is the gift of God's grace, which unites us with God and with one another. May the grace of the Lord Jesus Christ be with us all!

⸎⸎⸎

Lord Jesus Christ, we thank you that you love us and gave yourself for us. We praise you that you rescued us from the devil and made us your own. Amen.

May . . . the love of God . . . be with you all.
(2 Corinthians 13:14)

United with a blessing of love

I love you. Husbands speak those words to their wives, and parents speak them to their children. Those words express people's devotion to and affection for one another. Their love for one another is one of the important elements that unite them.

How are we united with God? We are united through the blessing of God's love for us. Paul makes that clear as he reminds us of God's love in his closing benediction.

We know what true love is only because we know God's love for us. The kind of love the Scriptures attribute to God—and that we are to reflect—is not merely a feeling; it is an attitude that is reflected in action. A father does not merely say "I love you" to his wife and children. He expresses his love for them without conditions and without limits by caring for them and giving them what they need. That is the way our heavenly Father loves us. His love is expressed by action. The clearest example of his love is shown by his gift of Christ. In his letter to the Roman Christians, the apostle Paul describes God's love best when he writes, "God demonstrates his own love for us in this: While we were still sinners, Christ died for us" (5:8). He gave us a Savior to free us from sin even when we didn't deserve it. We grow in appreciation for that love every time we bring our sins to God and he fully forgives us in Jesus. It is that love for us that we will enjoy forever by his side in heaven.

We experience God's love in many other ways. We experience his love in the way he provides for us. He blesses us with all that we need and all that we have. We don't have to look very long before we realize that we can't even begin to count his blessings—so great is his love for us. We also experience God's love in the way he protects us. He is by our side, and he keeps us safe. That is his promise.

Just a quick glance at the expressions of his love shows us that there is no reason to grumble and complain ever again. Instead, may we praise and thank God for the great things he has done.

How wonderful is this blessing of love that unites us with God and with one another. May the love of God be with us all!

❧☙

O God, our heavenly Father, keep us from ungratefulness and teach us true thankfulness. Amen.

May . . . the fellowship of the Holy Spirit be with you all.
(2 Corinthians 13:14)

United with a blessing of fellowship

Many of us from time to time need to spend some quiet moments alone to think or to rest. But after some time passes, we need to be with others again. That is the way God has created us. We are social creatures. We need company and companionship, living relationships with others. But even greater is our need for a living relationship with our heavenly Father.

How is it that we have such a relationship with God? We have such a relationship with God through the fellowship of the Holy Spirit. Paul makes that clear in his last words to the Corinthians.

We would not know about the grace of our Lord Jesus Christ or the love of God if it were not for the work of the Holy Spirit. We could not believe in the true God, who has revealed himself as triune. In his first letter to the Corinthians, Paul wrote, "No one can say, 'Jesus is Lord,' except by the Holy Spirit" (12:3). The fact that we have faith in God is entirely the work of the Spirit. He is the one who has brought us into a relationship with God and has united us with God.

Through the means of grace, the gospel in Word and sacrament, the Holy Spirit entered our hopeless, helpless, and hate-filled hearts and embraced us with the gift of faith. Through the water of Baptism, God washed our sin away and adopted us into his family. In his Word, God tells the story of his love as he reveals the way of salvation. With the gift of Christ's body and blood in the Lord's Supper, God personally assures us of his forgiveness and gives us the desire to follow him and love one another. Through those same means of grace, the Spirit continues to keep us in fellowship with God and allows our faith to grow.

This special fellowship continues to grow. Through faith we are united with all the others the Holy Spirit has called and gathered into God's family—with all others who know that Jesus is their Savior. Whenever we are together with others who share the same faith, we enjoy the unity and fellowship that the Holy Spirit has created.

What a wonderful blessing this fellowship is that unites us with God and with one another. May the fellowship of the Holy Spirit be with us all!

⌘

O Holy Spirit, strengthen our faith and hope, and increase our love and trust in God. Amen.

Praise be to the God and Father of our Lord Jesus Christ,
who has blessed us in the heavenly realms with every
spiritual blessing in Christ. . . . Having believed, you were
marked in him with a seal, the promised Holy Spirit.
(Ephesians 1:3,13)

Praise the triune God, the source of every blessing

The church needs a day like Trinity Sunday. During the first of half of the church year—the festival half—our hearts and minds feast on the great works of God in our behalf. Then comes Trinity Sunday. This offers Christians a good time to stop and ask a couple of questions. Just who is this God who gives blessings? And what are the blessings that he gives?

The opening verses of Paul's letter to the Ephesians present God to us as do many other sections of Scripture. They present him to us as Father, Son, and Holy Spirit. Our God is one God, yet three distinct persons. God is our God who gave us life to start with, and he is the Father of all who believe in Christ. The Lord Jesus Christ is our Redeemer. The Holy Spirit seals in us the assurance of our salvation in Christ.

We have a mystery here that defies comprehension by our limited minds. To define the true God, the church has, since the third century, used the word *Trinity:* "one God in three distinct persons." I wonder if we would really want God's revelation of his being to be more comprehensible for us than it is. If God were someone I could comprehend with my finite mind, he would be no bigger than my mind and capable of no more than my mind is capable. If God were no bigger than my mind, he could give no more peace to my conscience or no more comfort and joy to my heart than I am able to give to my spiritually impoverished self.

We could more easily absorb with our minds all the attainable knowledge in the universe than comprehend the being of God. The fact that the being of God is way, way beyond our ability to comprehend tells us that God is able to do for us what he says he can. The trust that the Holy Spirit gives to us will never be changed to disappointment, because the blessings we have in Christ Jesus are the gifts of a gracious, omnipotent God.

Oh, there's another voice that wants to be heard: "The fool says in his heart, 'There is no God'" (Psalm 14:1). But the manifold blessings of God in Christ are so evident in our lives that this other voice is drowned out. And left to stand alone is the gentle whisper of the triune God: Be still, and know that I am God.

⌘

Holy and gracious God, through your Word and its blessings,
make our faith in you always stronger. Amen.

He chose us in him before the creation of the world to be holy and blameless in his sight. In love he predestined us to be adopted as his sons through Jesus Christ, in accordance with his pleasure and will. . . . In him we were also chosen, having been predestined according to the plan of him who works out everything in conformity with the purpose of his will. (Ephesians 1:4,5,11)

Praise God for the blessing of election

The doctrine of election. Here it is—a teaching of Holy Scripture that can prove so troublesome to the mind of man. Every positive thought in the world has its negative side. Building on that reasonable assumption, we would be inclined to say that if God has elected some persons to eternal salvation, it must follow that he has elected other persons to eternal damnation. But that conclusion is not found in these verses. If you search the whole Bible, nowhere will you find that conclusion. It doesn't exist because the doctrine of election is a positive teaching of the triune God. God's Word says only that God has from eternity elected his people to eternal salvation. If we are looking for a negative here, it would have to be on man's part: If we are not saved, it's our own fault.

The doctrine of election is not to be the object of our research and speculation. God gave it to us for our comfort and salvation. It is the perfect medicine for souls that are trembling and afraid. It is the answer to Satan's charge that our sins are so great that God has rejected us. The answer is simply this: God has not abandoned us but has chosen us to be his adopted children. The proof of it lies in the fact of our baptisms and in our conviction that Jesus is the Christ, the Son of God and our Savior from sin.

Therefore, we can boldly confess the Third Article of the Apostles' Creed. "On the Last Day [the Holy Spirit] will raise me and all the dead and give eternal life to me and all believers in Christ."

Human reason wants to have its say. It wants to go beyond what God himself says in order to explain God's will and action. Therefore, there are those who contend that God in eternity looked into the future and saw those people who would believe and elected them because of their faith. But in Isaiah chapter 40 and Romans chapter 11, God clearly forbids such conclusions. They are not supported in his Word. God did not choose us because he saw anything at all in us but because he saw our sins laid on Jesus Christ, who died and rose again for us.

It is enough to see ourselves in this statement: He chose us.

❦

Dear Lord, we thank you for making us sure of our salvation by your doctrine of election. Amen.

He predestined us . . . to the praise of his glorious grace, which he has freely given us in the One he loves. (Ephesians 1:5,6)

The blessing of acceptance

"His glorious grace, which he has freely given us in the One he loves"—we can approach these words with this understanding: his grace by which he has accepted us in Christ Jesus. It's a simple repeat of what we already know so well: the triune God accepts us for eternal salvation because of what Jesus Christ has done for us.

When we think about being accepted by someone who has it in his power to give us what we need and want but can't get by ourselves, we think about getting the person's approval. The list of our spiritual needs is obvious. We need the forgiveness of sins, a clean heart, a clear conscience, strength to replace our weakness, deliverance from death, and eternal life. We can only look to God for these good things, because it is he who gave us life to begin with and it is he who continues to give us all that we need in this life. But how can we win his approval and gain his acceptance?

Being reasoning people, we would expect God to lay down requirements to which he would expect us to measure up. He did lay down requirements, and they are presented neatly in this statement: "Be holy because I, the LORD your God, am holy" (Leviticus 19:2). That statement is the spotlight of God's holy law. Being placed under that spotlight, we find ourselves to be cringing, miserable creatures. There is no way that we can escape God's just condemnation. We might try to convince God that there is some good in us. But we know that God wouldn't be impressed. His Word lets us know that our boasting in itself is a sin against God.

Our pride can only work against us and make us fall all the harder. It will shut us out of paradise. It will get us thrown out of the Lord's wedding feast. It will seal our separation from God.

The opposite of pride is humility. Humility is not a quality of good in us but something done to us. When the law declares us to be sinners, it humbles us. All that is left is the confession of the prodigal son: We are not worthy to be called the children of God. At this point God himself lifts us up—by leading us to the cross, where Christ was humbled and crucified for us. For Jesus' sake, God accepts us as his own—"to the praise of his glorious grace."

❧

O Lord, let us praise you forever for your acceptance of us, in Jesus' name. Amen.

In him we have redemption through his blood, the forgiveness of sins, in accordance with the riches of God's grace that he lavished on us with all wisdom and understanding. (Ephesians 1:7,8)

The blessing of redemption

It's not possible to improve on words like *redemption* and *forgiveness of sins.* God conveys to us his greatest blessings in simple and understandable language. He tells us our needs and what he has done to provide for them.

Our relationship with God should be of prime concern to us. We are answerable to him. At Mount Sinai he gave us the Ten Commandments, in which he tells us what he wants us to do and what he wants us to keep from doing. And this law of God convinces us that we are sinners. We have not done God's will. Therefore, we are under God's curse. The law of God holds out not one ounce of hope for us. It demands absolute perfection and condemns the sinner.

How comforting, then, are the words of our devotional text that lead us away from Mount Sinai and bring us to the foot of Calvary. There the apostle Paul points to Christ crucified and says, "In him we have redemption through his blood, the forgiveness of sins, in accordance with the riches of God's grace that he lavished on us with all wisdom and understanding."

Redemption. The forgiveness of sin. Some are tempted to say that that kind of teaching deprives God of his justness and pictures him as being arbitrary and indulgent. But that isn't true. God does not say one thing about the consequences of sin at one time and then at another time change his mind and say the opposite. He has said that sin must be punished. But in his wisdom and understanding and love for us, he transferred our sins to another who was punished in our place.

Now because Christ has taken our place, we can say, "I will praise you, O LORD. Although you were angry with me, your anger has turned away and you have comforted me. Surely God is my salvation" (Isaiah 12:1,2).

The forgiveness of our sins is based completely on Jesus' suffering and death on the cross. There is never a conditional "if" set up by God—if you do this or if you will submit to some correction, your sins will be forgiven. Jesus' answer to our need for forgiveness is a gift of God's grace. He tells us, "Take heart, son; your sins are forgiven" (Matthew 9:2).

❧◉◉☙

Holy Lord God, lead us always to appreciate your great love and the price you paid for our redemption. Amen.

He made known to us the mystery of his will according to his good pleasure, which he purposed in Christ. . . . And you also were included in Christ when you heard the word of truth, the gospel of your salvation. (Ephesians 1:9,13)

The blessing of the gospel

Among the ancient Greeks and, later, the Romans, there were secret religious assemblies known as mystery cults. No uninitiated person was allowed to enter. Some of these assemblies finally became so immoral in character that they were forbidden as injurious to public peace and morals.

How beautifully different is the mystery about which Paul is speaking to the Ephesians and to us! Paul's mystery is of divine origin. It is a mystery that God has revealed to us in the person of the Son of God, Jesus Christ. Through the gospel of Christ, God makes known his great love for us. It is a mystery not of iniquity but of righteousness—the righteousness that belongs to all who believe in Christ and look to him for their salvation.

There is a religious knowledge that we do possess by nature. Human laws are based on the natural knowledge of God's law. Our consciences tell us that we're in deep trouble if we steal or commit adultery or some other sin. But what we know about God's law cannot help us in the least to gain God's favor. Only the sacrifice of God's Son is able to cover our sins and give us a good conscience. That is what Paul's mystery, the gospel of Jesus Christ, is all about. It is the mystery of God's love.

A story comes to mind that impresses on us how we ought to treasure the gospel. A minister was given permission to conduct religious services in a state penitentiary. He planned with his first two services to acquaint his audience with the two great teachings of the Bible: the law and the gospel. The first Sunday he gave his hearers a powerful message on the Ten Commandments to remind them that they were sinners. The next Sunday he was prepared to tell them about Jesus, who had died so that sinners might live. But a sad note struck the minister's ear when he learned that two of the convicts who had heard him speak about the condemning power of the law had died during the week.

The message of God's wrath against sin must be preached, but as soon as it has done its work of opening the wound, the healing message of God's love in Christ must be applied. Only the gospel has the power to save.

❦

Lord Jesus, let us ever appreciate and faithfully proclaim the message of your salvation. Amen.

He made known to us the mystery of his will . . . to be put into effect when the times will have reached their fulfillment—to bring all things in heaven and on earth together under one head, even Christ. . . . And you also were included in Christ. (Ephesians 1:9,10,13)

The blessing of Christ's eternal rule

"You made him ruler over the works of your hands; you put everything under his feet" (Psalm 8:6). The ultimate fulfillment of that psalm passage rests in Jesus Christ. Our Bible text for today says as much as that. In another statement, in his first letter to the Corinthian Christians, Paul again quotes the psalm and reminds his readers that God has put everything under Jesus' feet. It is obvious that everything always has been under the control of the Son of God. That now also holds true of Jesus according to his human nature.

"When the times . . . reached their fulfillment," the Father put everything under the governance, the administration, of Jesus Christ. In yet another passage, we read that "when the time had fully come, God sent his Son" (Galatians 4:4). The time of fulfillment includes much more than just the day of Jesus' birth. It includes the realization of every promise dealing with the redemptive ministry of Christ, including the testimony given by his followers after his ascension into heaven.

Jesus himself lays down the truth of his all-inclusive rule when he states, "All authority in heaven and on earth has been given to me" (Matthew 28:18). These words were, indeed, the introduction to the Great Commission that Christ gave his disciples. But they stand clearly all by themselves as powerful evidence of the administrative office of Christ. They remind us of the continuing activity of Christ as our High Priest, Prophet, and King. And they signify his absolute rule over all things. Nothing exists outside of Christ's rule. Without his consent, nothing can possibly touch your life from the moment that you are born till the moment you die. The settlement of all matters in heaven and earth rests with the administration of Christ.

The miracles of the apostles were performed in the name of Jesus of Nazareth. They testify loudly regarding the effectiveness of Christ's rule. And we today are the happy recipients of all the gifts that are his to administer. For this we owe him our eternal allegiance and gratitude.

⁓◦◉◦⁓

Lord Jesus, we give you thanks for administering all things for our good. Amen.

In [Christ] we were also chosen, having been predestined according to the plan of him who works out everything in conformity with the purpose of his will. (Ephesians 1:11)

The blessing of our eternal inheritance

One 12th-century Christian is known to us by three hymns that he wrote and that are contained in *The Lutheran Hymnal*. His name was Bernard of Morlas, and the subject matter of his hymns is heaven. All three hymns share the same closing verse. It is obvious that this saint of long ago spent much time meditating on God's great and final blessing, the blessing of eternal life.

This is really the blessing beyond all other blessings because it will celebrate the final victory over sin, Satan, death, and hell. All the results of sin will be gone forever. There will be no more crying, no more tears, no more pain or heartache.

Here on earth we now have pain and trouble. Only with labor and sorrow are we able to sit down to eat our daily bread. Yet God gives us a joy even now—a peace that we can't fully understand or explain because it comes from the unfathomable depths of God's love and grace and wisdom. We have hope.

Our future is very much a known quantity to us because our Savior Jesus won our pardon on the cross on Calvary. By faith in him we are the children of God. And this we know because it is written in words that nothing can erase: "Now if we are children, then we are heirs—heirs of God and co-heirs with Christ, if indeed we share in his sufferings in order that we may also share in his glory" (Romans 8:17).

A respected older Christian woman whose life and living hadn't been all that easy once said to her pastor, "When I come to our church, I feel that much closer to heaven." The message she heard there was a message of peace, hope, and reconciliation. The earthly blessings we enjoy now will eventually be taken away from us in death. But all of God's spiritual blessings in Christ will culminate for us in the blessing of eternal life.

We also speak of God's final blessing to us as our eternal inheritance because the words "we were also chosen" are just as correctly understood with the words "we were made heirs." God alone has determined when he will say, "You have come to full age; accept now your inheritance of eternal life." Mindful of God's love and grace in Christ, we truly can make the poet's words our own: The best is yet to be.

❧☙

Jesus, in mercy bring us to that dear land of rest. Amen.

Oh, the depth of the riches of the wisdom and knowledge of God! (Romans 11:33)

Plumbing the depths

Most of our knowledge about the sea bottom has been gained over the years by the use of special instruments. For many years, the depth of water was measured with a sounding lead. A ball of lead was attached to a wire rope. The lead was dropped into the ocean, and the rope was let out until the lead touched the bottom. The rope went over a wheel that measured the length of rope paid out. Sometimes it took several hours to make one sounding in deep water.

In recent years a new method called sonic sounding was developed. Sound waves sent down from the ship are reflected from the bottom so that an accurate measurement of the depth becomes possible. In this way it has been learned, for example, that the Pacific Ocean off Mindanao is over six-and-a-half miles deep!

How does one plumb the depths of God? Is there a wire long enough to measure the greatness of God? Can we somehow measure reflected sound waves to learn about God? How does one begin to fathom the knowledge of One who knows absolutely everything there is to know? How does one measure infinite wisdom? Can the creature plumb the depths of the Creator? The fact is that if all the greatest minds in the history of the world were to use their combined intelligence and learning, they still could not even begin to plumb the depths of God's wisdom.

That does not mean that we are totally ignorant of God's wisdom and knowledge. The works of God all around us—the universe, the earth, the creatures, our own bodies—lead us to join the psalmist in saying, "In wisdom you made them all" (Psalm 104:24).

Paul certainly was aware of the greatness of the wisdom of God revealed in creation. But in our text Paul sings a song praising the greatness of God's wisdom revealed to us in the gospel of Christ. From eternity God determined to send his Son into the world to die on the cross for the sins of all mankind. No human being ever conceived such a wise plan. In fact, to the mind of sinful man, it seems like nothing but foolishness. Only to the one in whom the Spirit has worked is it true wisdom. "Oh, the depth of the riches of the wisdom and knowledge of God!" Let us join Paul in falling on our knees in worshiping the God of our salvation.

⟶☙◍❧⟵

Lord, help me always to realize that knowing you as my Savior is true wisdom. Amen.

Out of the labyrinth

There is a story from Greek mythology about a labyrinth that was built to confine the minotaur, a creature that was half bull and half human. Once inside the labyrinth, one would go endlessly along its twisting paths without ever finding the exit. There was no possible way to escape. In whatever direction a person ran, he might be running straight to the monster. If he stood still, the monster might at any moment emerge from the maze.

Once a young man named Theseus entered the labyrinth with a ball of thread. He fastened the end of it inside the door at the entrance, and he unwound it as he went in. After slaying the minotaur, Theseus was able to find his way out of the labyrinth by following the thread to the entrance.

All of man's own efforts to search out God's decisions, all of man's attempts to trace the ways of God have led him into a hopeless labyrinth. If he tries to enter the mysteries of the Trinity, he finds himself in a mental maze from which there is no escape. How can there be three divine persons and yet only one God? How can each person of the Godhead be entirely God without multiplication or division? There are other labyrinths, equally tempting to enter, that leave man searching and groping for a clear path. How did evil come into existence? Why are some saved but others not?

God has given us a string that leads us out of the labyrinth. It is the good news of salvation from sin in Christ Jesus. If we take hold of this string and follow it, we safely will be brought through any and every labyrinth. Are we in the labyrinth of the Trinity? The gospel guides us through by telling us that God the Father sent his Son who is revealed as the Savior by the work of the Holy Spirit. Are we in the labyrinth of the origin of evil? The gospel steers us in the right direction by revealing how God destroyed the power of evil for all mankind when he sent his Son to the cross. Are we in the labyrinth of why some are saved and others are not? The gospel escorts us down the right path by assuring us that Christ died for all mankind, that God wants all to be saved, and that it is only unbelief that damns.

We can't trace his ways, but we can know the truth that sets us free and praise him for it. That's enough!

❧

Lord, help me always praise the glories of your grace in Christ Jesus. Amen.

Who has known the mind of the Lord? (Romans 11:34)

A mind-bending mind!

What an amazing creation of God is the human mind! However, most attention these days is given to computers. How much information can the computer store? How fast can it operate? We often tend to forget that each of us has a mind that puts even the most powerful computers to shame.

It has been said that we use only a small portion of our brains. Even at that our minds are capable of some astounding things. Consider the speed of the brain in eye-hand coordination. The eye sees a ball speeding our way and in an instant sends a message to the brain, which in turn sends a message to the hand to reach up to catch it. We think our home computers have an amazing amount of memory capacity, but just consider the memory capacity of the human brain. It has been said that everything we have ever known or experienced is in our minds somewhere. Consider the human mind's ability to reason and to make decisions. Show me a computer that can do these things as well or do them at all for that matter. Even though more is being learned about the human mind all the time, we still don't understand its many-faceted complexities, intricacies, and abilities.

How then can we expect to understand the mind of the Lord?

How can we ever hope to investigate the mind of him who knows absolutely everything? How can we, whose minds are corrupted by sin, expect to comprehend the mind of the holy and righteous God? Isn't that completely presumptuous? Yes, for humans, by nature, it is.

"But we have the mind of Christ," Paul says in 1 Corinthians 2:16. That means that by God's Word, the Spirit reveals the mind of the Lord to us. As believers we know that God thinks thoughts of love and kindness toward us in Christ Jesus. We learn that because of Christ's death on the cross there is no longer in God's mind any wrath or hatred toward us. We understand that God has only our best interests in mind, that he wants only what is best for us in our lives now, and that he wants us with him in heaven forever. In God's Word we come to know the mind of the Lord in another sense. We understand the way God wants us to think and speak and live.

"Who has known the mind of the Lord?" No computer ever built will be able to know God's mind. The greatest minds of humans never have nor will they ever discover the mind of the Lord by their own powers. Only believers know the mind of God because he has revealed it to them in his Word.

Lord, help me know your mind ever better through the daily study of your Word. Amen.

Who has been his counselor? (Romans 11:34)

Some good advice

Downcast and dejected, the man stepped into the counselor's office. "What seems to be the trouble?" the counselor asked. "I don't know exactly. All I know is that I'm not happy. Is there anything you can suggest to help me?" The counselor looked at the man for a moment, and then he said, "I hear a famous comedian is in town playing to a packed house every evening. They say people come away from his performance holding their sides from laughing so hard. Why don't you go to his performance tonight and forget your troubles." The man looked down at the floor for a moment and then he said, "Sir, I am that comedian."

That counselor's advice was as wrong and foolish as the kind of advice people sometimes like to give God. Some would like to advise God that he doesn't really understand human nature or the times in which we live when he forbids marital unfaithfulness, perversion, and fornication. They suggest that God's words are impractical and out-of-date. They would like to tell God that sin isn't as serious as he has said it is and that the punishment for sin surely shouldn't be something as severe as eternal punishment in hell. God ought to relax his standards today, they insist.

Then too they would like to advise God that he has made the way to heaven too restrictive. Anyone who is sincere and honest and tries to do what is right ought to be able to go to heaven, they feel. "Can't we be considered Christians without believing everything the Bible says?" they ask. "How important is belief in the Bible's account of creation or the virgin birth of Christ or the resurrection from the dead?" As ridiculous as it sounds, they suppose that they can counsel the almighty God!

But that's turning things completely around. It is God who is our Counselor. On the night of his betrayal, Jesus promised to send his disciples another Counselor who would be with them forever. That Counselor is the Holy Spirit, who advises and counsels us by means of the Scriptures. He informs us that our sins are many, that they are serious, and that they indeed deserve eternal punishment. But he also assures us that God has declared us righteous for the sake of the innocent suffering and death of the Savior. He comforts us with the knowledge that God will make everything in life serve a good purpose for us and that he will take us to heaven. That is good counsel—the kind of counsel that the comedian needed too!

☙◌◯◌❧

Lord, help me always listen attentively to the counsel of your holy Word. Amen.

Who has ever given to God, that God should repay him?
(Romans 11:35)

What's the pay?

Suppose you lived in ancient times and owned a servant. One day you sent him out to plow the fields. When he came in from the fields, would you say to him, "Relax for a while and have something to eat"? (Remember, he's your servant and is required to wait on you hand and foot all the time.) Wouldn't you rather say to him, "Prepare my supper, get yourself ready, and wait on me while I eat and drink. After that you may eat and drink"? Would you thank your servant simply because he did what he was told to do?

We don't live in a time or place where slavery is practiced anymore, so it may be somewhat difficult for us to put ourselves into the picture above. But we need to try because Jesus told this story to teach us a lesson about our relationship with God. He concluded the story by saying, "So you also, when you have done everything you were told to do, should say, 'We are unworthy servants; we have only done our duty'" (Luke 17:10).

People normally don't see themselves this way. They do something they think is good in God's sight and feel God must be so pleased that he has to reward them. They give a couple hours of their time to some good cause. They give a few dollars to a charitable organization. They see their relationship with God as a business arrangement, as though God has received so much work from them that he has to make some payments to them.

How easy it is to forget that by nature we are unworthy servants. By nature we are evil in God's sight.

Suppose we are able to keep God's will perfectly throughout our lives. That still wouldn't deserve any special reward from God. We would simply be doing what we are obligated to do. No one has ever given anything to God that compels God to repay him.

The amazing thing is that God has anything at all to do with us. The only payment we deserved was eternal damnation. But God, in love, gave his Son to become one of us, to keep the law perfectly in our place, and to endure the curse of our sins when he suffered and died on the cross. God has given us eternal salvation.

We can never repay him for what he has done. But we can give him ourselves. We can devote all we are and have to him as our offerings of praise and thanksgiving.

⁂

Father, remove all thoughts of work-righteousness from my heart. Help me cling to your grace in Christ Jesus alone. Amen.

From him and through him and to him are all things.
(Romans 11:36)

A blank check

Charles Steinmetz, the great electrical engineer and inventor, never received a fixed salary from those who sponsored him. From time to time, his backers would give him a book of blank checks. Whatever he needed, great or small, he only had to fill in the amount on a check, sign his name, and present it to the bank.

Not too bad an arrangement! It surely would help at bill-paying time if one never had to worry about the checkbook balance.

Steinmetz's backers could have eventually run out of money, however. Surely Steinmetz's friends were helpless in keeping him from getting sick. They couldn't give him the strength, knowledge, and ability he needed to do his work.

We have an infinitely better arrangement with God. God provides for the needs of all people. God is the origin of all things. From his creating hand came the universe, the earth, and all creatures. From him comes all we need for our bodies and lives. Rain, sunshine, crops, food, drink, and shelter all come from God. If God were to withdraw his sustaining hand for even an instant, we would have nothing and could not live.

Through him you and I and all creatures continue to exist. "In him we live and move and have our being" (Acts 17:28). If it weren't for God, we couldn't take breaths, our hearts couldn't beat, and we couldn't put one foot in front of the other. He is not only present in our world but in our very beings.

From him alone also comes our salvation. It is the work of his grace in Christ Jesus. Through him alone come all our spiritual blessings.

In a sense God has given us a blank check. It is made out to us, and it is signed in Jesus' blood. We can fill in the amount. Do we desire a stronger faith? We can write it in, and he will give it. Do we wish to see more fruits of faith in our lives? They are ours. Are there things we need for our bodies and lives? We can fill them in, and he will give them to us as he knows best. "From him and through him and to him are all things."

Also "to him are all things." He is the final goal of the universe and all created things. All have been created to give praise and glory to his name.

❧☙

Lord, help me remember that everything I am and everything I need comes from you. Help me praise you with my whole being. Amen.

To him be the glory forever! Amen. (Romans 11:36)

Loving God a lot

Susan was late getting home from volleyball practice, and her parents were concerned. When she finally walked through the doorway, her mother said with relief, "Susan, where have you been?" "Oh, I walked by the church on the way home, so I stopped in for a little while." "But today is Saturday," her mother replied, "there aren't any services today." "I know," Susan responded, "I just stopped by to love God a little."

We can learn a lesson from Susan. Loving God is not something to be reserved for one hour, one day a week. God does not love us only occasionally. He does not love us only one out of the 168 hours in a week. He loves us all the time. From all eternity he has loved us and has chosen us to be his own. When the time had fully come, he sent his Son to be the Savior from sin. He loved all people so much that he sent Jesus to die for us all. He loved us so much that he called us to faith by the gospel. He has kept us in the faith. He has given the Holy Spirit to work in us, and he even dwells in us. He loves us so much that he speaks to us in his Word and listens to us as we bring our prayers to him. He loves us so much that he provides for all our daily wants and needs. He loves us so much that he wants us with him in the mansions of heaven forever and has arranged for that to happen.

How much do we love God? Enough to stop by on a Saturday when no one else is in church and to spend some time showing him our love? Do we love him enough to remember to thank and praise him for all his blessings to us each and every day? Do we love him enough to eat and drink and do all things to his glory? Do we love him enough to devote a generous amount of time to serve him in some special way in the work of his kingdom? Do we love him enough to tell others about him? Do we love him enough to return to him regularly the firstfruits of all the material blessings he has showered upon us? Do we love him enough to recognize the talents and abilities he has entrusted to us and to use them for the welfare of his kingdom?

We will be privileged to give God glory forever in the mansions of heaven. Wouldn't it be good to start now? God doesn't just love us a lot. He loves us with an infinite love in Christ Jesus. Realizing that, we surely cannot be satisfied with loving God only a little. We want to love him a lot.

~*∞*~

Lord, help me love you always and forever, beginning now. Amen.

You are all sons of God through faith in Christ Jesus, for all of you who were baptized into Christ have clothed yourselves with Christ. There is neither Jew nor Greek, slave nor free, male nor female, for you are all one in Christ Jesus. If you belong to Christ, then you are Abraham's seed, and heirs according to the promise. (Galatians 3:26-29)

United in God's family as his children

The mouthwatering scent of Mom's apple pie fills the kitchen. In the backyard the old tree fort still stands—a reminder of the battles and fun of years gone by. At the dinner table, the conversation turns to memories of camping trips in the rain and birthday parties at the skating rink. Shared experiences and memories like these bind a family together.

Belonging to a family can bring great joy and happy memories. Family ties create a bond that is difficult to break. That's why Paul's words, which we will consider this week, bring such great comfort. Paul tells us that when we trust in Jesus as our Savior, we all belong to the same family—the family of God. Members of God's family share unique blessings, especially God's gift of life.

God alone can give the wonderful gift of life to his children. Consider what a great miracle it is when a family is blessed with the gift of a new son or daughter! Where better can we recognize God's hand at work than in his gift of bringing a new life into a family? As we reflect on God's gift of life, we cannot help but exclaim with David, "You created my inmost being; you knit me together in my mother's womb. I praise you because I am fearfully and wonderfully made; your works are wonderful, I know that full well" (Psalm 139:13,14). As God's children, we are united in receiving this gracious gift of life from the hand of our heavenly Father.

But God gives an even greater gift of life to his children. Our Savior proclaims, "I have come that they may have life, and have it to the full" (John 10:10). A life "to the full" can only come through God's gift of faith. The Holy Spirit gives us life when he leads us to believe and trust in Jesus as the only source of forgiveness and eternal life. God's gift of faith unites Christians with a tie that is even thicker than blood. We share the same Savior! We share the same forgiveness! We are brothers and sisters, the children of God, united in God's family!

❦

Lord Jesus, thank you for giving me the gift of life and making me a member of your family. Amen.

You are all sons of God through faith in Christ Jesus.
(Galatians 3:26)

United through faith

"Prove it to me!" Joe said as he tossed the basketball to his brother. Bill had boasted that he could shoot 25 free throws without missing one. But Joe doubted that his brother could really make that many free throws in a row. He would have to see it to believe it.

We live in a world where seeing is believing. We want visible proof of the claims we hear others make. Unless we see proof with our own two eyes, we hesitate to believe the claims of others.

How different is God's gift of faith! It is that wonderful faith that unites us as his children! In his Word our Lord describes faith as believing even when we cannot see. "Now faith is being sure of what we hope for and certain of what we do not see" (Hebrews 11:1). Believing without seeing requires trust. Only God can work such trust in our hearts, which normally are filled only with doubt.

Thank God that he takes the doubts out of our sin-filled hearts and replaces our doubts with his gift of faith! The Holy Spirit works a miracle in the heart of every Christian. As we hear God's Word, the Holy Spirit is hard at work. He uses God's message of the law to show us that something is missing in our lives. We lack the holiness and complete dedication that our Lord requires for members of his family. Once we feel the emptiness that sin brings to our lives, the Holy Spirit follows with the gospel. He shows us how Jesus fills the emptiness in our hearts. Jesus took away the sin that clogs our hearts by taking our punishment for us on the cross. Only as we recognize our sin and trust Jesus' forgiveness do we believe. Only the Holy Spirit working through God's Word can work such recognition and trust in our hearts.

We call this gift from the Holy Spirit faith. Faith alone unites us as members of God's family. Such faith, which enables us to believe in Jesus even though we haven't seen him with our own two eyes, comes only from God. Our sinful human hearts cannot make sense of what God does. We understand God's grace in Jesus only by the work of the Holy Spirit. For every member of God's family, hearing is believing as the Holy Spirit blesses us with faith through God's saving message.

༺☙◉❧༻

We thank you, then, O God of heav'n,
That you to us this faith have giv'n
Through mighty Word and sacrament
To trust the one whom you have sent. Amen. (CW 404:4)

All of you who were baptized into Christ have clothed yourselves with Christ. (Galatians 3:27)

United through Baptism

You have to dress for success. Many of us undoubtedly have heard this proverb. If someone wants to be a success in the business world today, appearance is often an important consideration. Job applicants need to look professional to make a good impression with their potential employers. Sloppy clothes or uncombed hair could easily send a message that the applicants are careless or unconcerned about what others think of them.

With what will we clothe ourselves when we come into God's presence? We are not applying for a job or seeking some favor from God. We come as beggars, pleading for eternal life. We certainly cannot come before the Lord clothed in our own works. They can never be good enough for God's standard of perfection. With the prophet Isaiah, we must confess, "All our righteous acts are like filthy rags" (Isaiah 64:6). We dare not stand before God on our own merits, because our works will never meet his absolute requirement of purity!

How, then, can we ever come into God's presence? Paul gives us the answer: "All of you who were baptized into Christ have clothed yourselves with Christ." Baptism unites us as members of God's family. When we were baptized, God took off our old, dirty garments of sin and replaced them with his gift of clean, pure garments of faith. Our baptisms were not just church ceremonies when we were young or when we were brought to faith. Baptism is the power of God that washes away sin, brings us into God's family, and strengthens us to walk in the path of our Lord. As Paul writes, "Christ loved the church and gave himself up for her to make her holy, cleansing her by the washing with water through the word, and to present her to himself as a radiant church, without stain or wrinkle or any other blemish, but holy and blameless" (Ephesians 5:25-27).

What a gift God gives through the washing of Baptism! Every member of God's family is equally dressed for success—through Baptism we are all clothed with Christ!

⚜

Baptized into your name most holy,
O Father, Son, and Holy Ghost,
I claim a place, though weak and lowly,
Among your saints, your chosen host,
Buried with Christ and dead to sin.
Your Spirit now shall live within. Amen. (CW 294:1)

There is neither Jew nor Greek, slave nor free, male nor female, for you are all one in Christ Jesus. (Galatians 3:28)

United as equals

Playing favorites can destroy a family. If parents show more love and concern for one child than for their other children, the other children can easily become jealous of the favored child. The child who is favored could be tempted to look down on his or her brothers and sisters. Parents need to love their children equally, because favoritism has no place in a family!

God does not play favorites. He treats every member of his family the same. God isn't concerned with where his children come from, whether they are male or female, or what kind of work they do. All are equal in God's sight—equally sinful and equally forgiven!

God's children all share the same need. "All have sinned and fall short of the glory of God" (Romans 3:23). Every Christian comes before God as a sinner—one who deserves nothing but eternal punishment from our just and holy Lord. No Christian can brag that he or she is better or more deserving of God's grace than any other member of God's family. None of us deserves God's grace!

God's children all share the same forgiveness. John the Baptist described our Savior and his mission in these words: "Look, the Lamb of God, who takes away the sin of the world!" (John 1:29). Jesus went to the cross for all people of all time. As he suffered in agony, he was satisfying his Father's demand that every sin must be punished. Jesus paid the price for every sin ever committed and ever to be committed in the entire history of the world. No sin or sinner is left out. Through the Holy Spirit's gift of faith, this forgiveness becomes our own. We are all equal members of God's family, because we are all equally forgiven!

Because we share forgiveness as members of God's family, we also share a common purpose. God wants us to extend his family as we share the good news of Jesus with others in our neighborhoods and throughout the world. Even though our talents and roles in the Lord's church may differ, our goal remains the same. We want to grow in love for our Father, who loves all people equally. We want to share his Word with others in order to win more brothers and sisters for God's family for all eternity!

❧

Lord Jesus, give me faith to speak of your love to others. Then work through my simple witness to draw others into your church. Amen.

If you belong to Christ, then you are Abraham's seed.
(Galatians 3:29)

United as Abraham's seed

"He looks just like his father!" New parents quickly grow accustomed to hearing comments like this. It's only natural that a child will bear some resemblance to the parents who gave him life. As parents raise their children, the similarities often grow. If Dad likes football, it's a good bet that Junior will too. As we grow older, we begin to realize how much we are like our parents, who gave us life and raised us.

In God's Word today, Paul tells us that all who belong to Christ share the same spiritual father. We are all Abraham's seed. In many ways God wants us to be just like our father Abraham, especially where our faith is concerned!

How are we like Abraham, our spiritual father? First of all, remember that Abraham did not seek out or choose God. Instead, God sought and chose Abraham to be his child and an ancestor of our Savior. The Lord handpicked Abraham to bless him, even though Abraham was no better than any of the other wandering shepherds of his day.

We are just like our father! We did not seek out or choose God. Just as with Abraham, God saw nothing inside us that would lead him to choose us to be his children. He chose us out of his amazing grace—the love he chose to pour down on us—even though we do not deserve it. Our faith and eternal life come entirely from our Lord without any effort or merit on our part.

When God called Abraham, God told him simply to go. He didn't tell Abraham how far to go or where he was going. Abraham had to believe his Lord and take him at his word. We call such God-given belief *faith*. Even though Abraham could not see where God was leading him, he trusted that his heavenly Father would always keep his word and do what was best for him.

God calls us to have a faith just like our father's, just like Abraham's. We may not always see how God is working through the events in our lives. We may not understand how challenges and problems will work out for our good. But we have God's word that he will work out all things for our benefit! May God grant us a faith just like our father's—a faith that marvels at God's grace and trusts that God will keep every promise!

୧ଓ⑤ର

Lord, give us such a faith as this,
And then, whate'er may come,
We'll taste e'en now the hallowed bliss
Of an eternal home. Amen. (CW 405:6)

If you belong to Christ, then you are Abraham's seed, and heirs according to the promise. (Galatians 3:29)

United as heirs

In my library I have a set of books written by Martin Luther that I enjoy using. These books are special not only because of the information they contain but because of how I received them. I received them from my father, who in turn had received them from my grandfather some time ago. Lord willing, I will someday pass them along to someone else in our family. Knowing that these books have been passed down from generation to generation makes them even more special.

Many families love to pass down heirlooms from one generation to the next. The treasure may be Grandpa's pocket watch, Grandma's solid oak kitchen table, or something else filled with precious memories of a family member who had lived before. These heirlooms have great value, not only because of what they are but because of who used them and cared for them before they were handed down to the next generation.

As members of God's family, we share a wonderful inheritance from our heavenly Father. Because we share a Savior who was willing to give up his life on the cross for us, we share God's gift of eternal life. What a glorious inheritance belongs to us as children of God! Jesus himself assures us: "God so loved the world that he gave his one and only Son, that whoever believes in him shall not perish but have eternal life" (John 3:16). Through the faith he has worked in our hearts, our Father has passed on to us an inheritance that will last forever. Our heavenly inheritance will not rust or spoil. It will never grow old or out-of-date. We will spend eternity with our Savior!

And there's even more! God's gift of eternal life is not only for the future. Our inheritance brings us blessings for today too! Our lives now have new meaning and purpose. We now live to give glory to our Father, who has given eternal glory to us. Paul reminds us that our new lives, for now and for eternity, come from our crucified and risen Savior: "[Christ] died for all, that those who live should no longer live for themselves but for him who died for them and was raised again" (2 Corinthians 5:15). By God's grace and strength, we can live our inheritance of life today as we look forward to its fulfillment in the future.

❧⊚⊚☙

Abide, O dear Redeemer,
Among us with your Word
And thus now and hereafter
True peace and joy afford. Amen. (CW 333:2)

You are all sons of God through faith in Christ Jesus, for all of you who were baptized into Christ have clothed yourselves with Christ. There is neither Jew nor Greek, slave nor free, male nor female, for you are all one in Christ Jesus. If you belong to Christ, then you are Abraham's seed, and heirs according to the promise. (Galatians 3:26-29)

United around the promise

"But, Dad, you promised!" Little Joey was wiping tears from his eyes as he spoke. His father had promised that he would go watch Joey pitch in his first Little League game. In spite of his plans, suddenly Dad's job made it impossible for him to watch his son pitch that day. Sadly, Joey's dad broke the promise he had made to his son.

Sometimes fathers have to break the promises they have made to their children, even if they do not want to. Thank God our heavenly Father is different! When he makes a promise, he keeps it! Think of all the promises God made in the Old Testament. He promised Jesus would come, and Jesus did. He promised that his Son would be born in Bethlehem, and Jesus was. Our Father carried out every promise he made concerning the coming of Jesus, our Savior.

God has given us, his children, many wonderful promises. "Never will I leave you; never will I forsake you" (Hebrews 13:5). "In all things God works for the good of those who love him" (Romans 8:28). "In my Father's house are many rooms. . . . I am going there to prepare a place for you" (John 14:2). We can count on each of these promises and on every other promise our Lord has ever uttered. We have a Father who will not and cannot go back on his word. When he makes a promise, he carries it out, every time! What a tremendous blessing to trust our Father fully in every situation!

As we are united in God's family, we come together as children of the promise. Because we belong to Christ, we need not fear the future. Our Father has promised that all things remain in his control. Because we belong to Christ, we live for our Lord as we help one another today and every day. We walk together as joyous children in God's family as we share John's assurance: "How great is the love the Father has lavished on us, that we should be called children of God! And that is what we are!" (1 John 3:1).

❧☙

I am trusting you for power;
You can never fail.
Words which you yourself shall give me
Must prevail. Amen. (CW 446:5)

"I praise you, Father, Lord of heaven and earth, because you have hidden these things from the wise and learned."
(Matthew 11:25)

God has revealed what was hidden

How could the Lord of heaven and earth be hidden? How could anyone fail to recognize that the Creator and Ruler of the universe exists? You would think God's awesome power and grandeur would be obvious to everyone. Every day he causes the sun to shine, warming the earth and giving it light. Every day the infinite variety of birds, flowers, trees, and animals gives evidence of his goodness.

What do we find, however? In our parks we are told how the forces of nature formed the mountains and carved the canyons. We are told of the evolutionary changes that brought into being the living creatures. The wise and learned of our world say with straight faces, "It all just happened by accident." The Bible's teachings regarding the almighty Creator and Ruler of the universe are openly attacked and ridiculed.

The explanation for this lies in the fact that we are sinners. The truths of God are taught clearly in the Bible. They were taught openly and plainly by Jesus too. But these truths aren't what the world wants to hear. Man wants to be his own god. In judgment, therefore, God gives people what they desire. They do not want to see. They want to walk by the light of their own wisdom. Okay, so be it! They shall not see. And the light of God's wisdom shall be hidden from them.

Such is our condition from birth. We are like the child who took great pleasure in his ability to draw amusing little sketches. One day in a museum he noticed a blank piece of canvas and sketched a picture on it. When he stepped back to admire his cleverness, he saw that the canvas was part of a huge painting of tremendous worth. The painting, which had been done by one of the masters, was so large that the child hadn't even noticed it when he scribbled in its corner. In his foolishness he had marred it.

In the same way, the wisest and greatest people of this world stand on top of God's masterpiece without recognizing what it is or who made it.

And to all who continue to trust in their own wisdom, the truths of God remain hidden.

The correct perspective on life is to be found only in God's Word. And the way to know God's heart is only through his Son, Jesus Christ.

⌾

We praise you, O God, for revealing your love and wisdom to us through Jesus our Savior. Amen.

"I praise you, Father, Lord of heaven and earth, because you have hidden these things from the wise and learned, and revealed them to little children." (Matthew 11:25)

God revealed it to little children

There's an arrogance in every new generation. We, as people of the new generation, are inclined to feel certain superiority over those who have gone before us. It's easy for people to say, "We are modern, 21st-century Americans. Look at all the advancements we have made in science and technology. We really have come a long way since the days of the prophets and apostles. Isn't it obvious that we know more now and see more clearly than they did? How can we be expected to take seriously the beliefs of 21 centuries ago?"

Jesus rejects this kind of thinking. As much as man has discovered in this world, he still has not been able to find the true God who remains hidden behind his creation. Each new discovery, in fact, is simply another testimony to the wisdom of the God who created the universe. But the question still remains unanswered as to who this God is and how he feels toward us.

The Father has chosen instead to reveal his heart to "little children" through the gospel. The Father comes to babes who lack everything and realize the smallness of their understanding. He comes to those who have nothing so that he can fill them with everything. God chose to do it like this so that all can be included in his blessings. No one is so small that God doesn't want him.

What a marvel that the eternal Father, to whom all heaven and earth must bow in submission, should love us and redeem us, who do not deserve any of his blessings. God's love reaches out to all, even to the lowliest and most helpless. For this Jesus praised his Father. It's the reason we praise him too!

Jesus commends a childlike faith. A small child doesn't question or doubt what his parents tell him; instead, he believes and puts his confidence in all they say. A small child is fully dependent on his parents for all his needs, yet he doesn't worry about whether they will feed him or care for him. A small child wants to be near his parents and doesn't enjoy long separations. He feels safe when Father and Mother are near.

This is the kind of faith God wants in his people. He wants us to put full trust and confidence in all he says. He seeks our complete reliance on his protection and salvation in Christ.

⌀⌀⌀

Thank you, Lord, for revealing the Savior to us children. Amen.

"Yes, Father, for this was your good pleasure."
(Matthew 11:26)

God revealed his good pleasure

God has an unexpected way of dealing with mankind. It is a seemingly backwards way. He hides his truth and his blessing from the wise and learned—the ones we would be inclined to favor. He reveals these things instead to the little children—those we would expect him to shun.

All of this is no accident. No matter how it may seem to our reason, God's dealings are not arbitrary or capricious. They are based on a definite and well-thought-out plan. There is a clear and simple purpose behind the way in which God acts. It is the inevitable result of the way God is. "God is love," the Bible tells us (1 John 4:16). Because he is love, God wills what is good for his creatures.

Because he is love, God sent his only begotten Son into the world so that all who believe in him will not perish but have eternal life.

God could do no greater good than to give people the forgiveness of sins and eternal life. This is precisely what God wants. He "wants all men to be saved and to come to a knowledge of the truth," Paul says (1 Timothy 2:4).

To assure that this is possible, God calls all people through the gospel. No one is excluded. The gospel message is to be proclaimed even to the humblest and simplest. And the message is simple: "It is by grace you have been saved, through faith—and this not from yourselves, it is the gift of God" (Ephesians 2:8).

We are saved due to God's good pleasure. He wanted to rescue us from our sins. In Christ he did. He wants us to praise him for his goodness. In his Word he reveals it to us. He wants us to believe it. Through his Holy Spirit he brings us to faith.

The more we comprehend this good and gracious purpose of God, the more we will praise him. We praise him with our lips in our personal devotions and our public worship. Even more, we are to praise him with our entire lives. We view each day as another opportunity to live for him and to bring glory to his name. That is God's good purpose for us too, and it is a miracle of his grace. "It is God who works in you to will and to act according to his good purpose" (Philippians 2:13).

⋘◎◎⋙

We praise you, O God, for making us the objects of your good and gracious purpose through our Savior Jesus Christ. Help us praise you with our lives this day and always. Amen.

"No one knows the Son except the Father, and no one knows the Father except the Son and those to whom the Son chooses to reveal him." (Matthew 11:27)

The Son revealed the Father

There are many who spend long hours tracing their family trees and take pleasure in every long-lost cousin found along the way. There is something in us that desires to know our roots. The people of Israel took great pride in their ability to trace their roots back to Abraham.

As Christians, we are especially concerned with our spiritual roots. By faith we have become members of God's family. By nature we had no spiritual roots but were outside of God's family and under the curse of death. Sin had separated us from God. But the Lord Jesus came into the world and was born of the virgin Mary in order to give us new life—to make us acceptable to God so that we might know him and be able to call him our Father.

There is no way of knowing God without knowing Jesus. "I am the way and the truth and the life," Jesus said. "No one comes to the Father except through me" (John 14:6).

The Son who knows the Father perfectly reveals him to us. There is no other way. Only by the Son's revelation can anyone really know the Father. As Luther once wrote, "Here the bottom falls out of all merit, all powers and abilities of reason, or the free will men dream of, and it all counts nothing before God. Christ must do and must give everything."

By nature we know the law of God. We look around us and stand in awe of God's creation. Our consciences also remind us of the fact that God is the judge of all. But this bare knowledge of the fact that there is a God only leads us to be uncertain and afraid.

That is where the Son of God steps in to reveal to us who the true God is and what he has done for us. "No one has ever seen God, but God the One and Only, who is at the Father's side, has made him known" (John 1:18). Jesus reveals the Father's heart to us—a heart that loves us so much that the Father gave his only begotten Son so that all who believe in him will not perish but have eternal life.

Praise be to Jesus for revealing the Father to us! Now we have roots—and wonderful roots at that! We are the children of God through faith in our Savior, Jesus Christ. The Father sent the Savior to us so that we might be his own and live under him in his kingdom and serve him in everlasting righteousness, innocence, and blessedness.

❧◉◈◉☙

Thank you, dear Father, for revealing your love to us in your Son. Amen.

"Come to me, all you who are weary and burdened, and I will give you rest. . . . Learn from me, for I am gentle and humble in heart, and you will find rest for your souls." (Matthew 11:28,29)

Rest for the weary

Every Friday evening at 6:00, quiet spread across the land of Israel. The Sabbath was beginning. For 24 hours the land and its people enjoyed rest. This day of rest gave the people a weekly opportunity to reflect on the spiritual rest God promised to give them. That rest would come through the promised Messiah, the rest-giver.

The message God reveals to us in the New Testament is that this rest has now come! Jesus invites us to come and receive it for ourselves.

Isaiah said the Messiah would use his authority and power to bring rest to his people. Seven hundred years before Christ entered the world as a child, he spoke through Isaiah and said, "Come, all you who are thirsty, come to the waters; and you who have no money, come, buy and eat! Come, buy wine and milk without money and without cost. . . . Listen, listen to me, and eat what is good, and your soul will delight in the richest of fare. Give ear and come to me; hear me, that your soul may live. I will make an everlasting covenant with you, my faithful love promised to David" (Isaiah 55:1-3).

The invitation that Jesus extends in Matthew chapter 11 is the fulfillment of Isaiah's prophecy. Jesus invites us to come. It is the powerful gospel invitation that in itself has the power to place those heavenly gifts into our hearts and lives.

To those weary with their futile attempts to save themselves, it offers rest. To those heavily burdened with a guilty conscience, it speaks of grace. It tells us of God's rich treasures of mercy, pardon, and peace, now and for all eternity.

In North Africa, Augustine struggled to find happiness and contentment. He was wild and reckless as a young man. When he found no happiness in a life of dissipation, he dabbled in one of the religious cults in vogue at that time. After years of searching in vain, he finally heard the sweet gospel of Christ, and it struck his heart. He wrote of the difference that it made for him: "You, God, made us for yourself, and our hearts are restless until they rest in you." The sweet gospel of God's mercy in Christ has made the same difference for all of us who have been baptized in his name.

✦

We praise you, God, for giving rest to our weary souls. Amen.

"Take my yoke upon you and learn from me, for I am gentle and humble in heart, and you will find rest for your souls. For my yoke is easy." (Matthew 11:29,30)

A yoke made easy

There are really only two religions in this world: the Christian religion and all others. These two are complete opposites. According to all of natural man's thinking and all man-made religions, blessings from God are on a pay-for-services-rendered basis. If you do something good, they say, God will reward you. If you do something bad, God will punish you. In actuality, God does it backwards, however—or so it seems to our human reason. Instead of demanding works from us, God carries our yoke for us. That is Jesus' promise in today's Scripture reading.

A Jew hearing Jesus' words "Take my yoke upon you," would be reminded of the yoke of the law under which his people labored and groaned. This was a heavy and burdensome load that was made even more oppressive by the interpretations and additions that hundreds of years of Jewish tradition had added.

The oppressive nature of the law's yoke shows itself in the Pharisees' attempt to condemn Jesus for healing a man on the Sabbath. According to the letter of the law, no work was to be done on the Sabbath. But the law also commanded that works of love should be done whenever possible. The letter of the law posed a frustrating and oppressive burden.

Christ stepped in, however, and did what the law could not do. As Lord of the Sabbath, he ruled over the law and at the same time kept it perfectly for us. "Christ is the end of the law so that there may be righteousness for everyone who believes" (Romans 10:4). He fulfilled the law for us and credited his righteousness as a free gift to all who believe in him.

Christ set us free from the oppressive yoke of the law. But that does not mean we are free to go into spiritual sleep or hibernation until judgment day.

As Christians, we find the law to be a light yoke. It is a yoke of love that we want to bear because Christ loved us first.

Apart from Christ the yoke of the law is a deadly weight around our necks. Without Christ we cannot have a clear conscience. Without Christ there is nothing but fear and uncertainty, sin, death, judgment, and hell.

But with Christ there is freedom from fear; there is righteousness, hope, life, and peace with God. The yoke that remains for Christians is a light and pleasant yoke—the opportunity to show our gratitude for all that God has done for us in Christ.

❦

We praise you, O God, for removing the oppressive yoke of the law and for enabling us to serve you joyfully out of a clear conscience, for Jesus' sake. Amen.

"My yoke is easy and my burden is light." (Matthew 11:30)

A burden made light

Christ has already carried the heavy burdens for us. Isaiah writes, "Surely he took up our infirmities and carried our sorrows. . . . The punishment that brought us peace was upon him, and by his wounds we are healed. We all, like sheep, have gone astray, each of us has turned to his own way; and the LORD has laid on him the iniquity of us all" (53:4-6). The crushing load of sin and guilt has been lifted from us. Jesus Christ took upon himself the sins of the world.

No longer are we the slaves of sin and Satan. Now we serve a new master, our Savior Jesus Christ. He did not come to fill the shoes of Moses or to put us under a new yoke of the law. He was not like the scribes and Pharisees who heartlessly piled burden on top of burden and regulation on top of regulation.

Jesus came instead to remove the oppressive burden of the law from us in two ways.

First of all, he fulfilled the requirements of the law for us. Since it was impossible for us to keep the law from the heart, he kept it in our stead. He willingly placed himself under the law's requirements. He was circumcised on the eighth day. He submitted himself in obedience to his parents. He went about doing nothing but good and useful works for those who were in need. He prayed for his enemies, respected those in positions of authority, and the like.

Second, he endured the curse and condemnation of the law for us, as we confess in the Apostles' Creed: "[He] suffered under Pontius Pilate, was crucified, died, and was buried."

Now since the burden of fear and condemnation and the compulsion and threats of the law have been removed by Christ, there is nothing left for us to do but thank and praise him for his mercy and for his unspeakable love.

This, then, is the light and easy burden that remains—the joyful opportunity we have to say thank you to God by showing love to others.

In the early 1970s, there was a popular song with the lyrics, "He ain't heavy, he's my brother." Now that we have been freed from our sins, we have become brothers and sisters through faith in Christ. What a wonderful thing it is that the crashing burden has been removed. And what a wonderful thing that God has enabled us to thank him by helping our brothers and sisters carry the little burdens that remain in this life. They're not heavy.

❧❦❧

Dear Lord Jesus, fill our hearts with that kind of unselfish love that you have shown, and continue to show, to us. Amen.

Do not merely listen to the word, and so deceive yourselves.
Do what it says. (James 1:22)

Doing without hearing is impossible

Someone who sees you going to church on Sundays but does not follow you there may reason, "I don't have to go to church. I can still be just as good a Christian as those who run to church every Sunday. I believe that the important thing is to live your religion. Deeds are much more important than creeds." This dangerous and perplexing line of reasoning appears to be very common in our society. Many still wish to be called Christian, but few are interested in what Christ has to say.

In our text James surely emphasizes the doing of God's Word, but we note that he does not speak of deeds alone. He speaks of both doing and hearing. He reminds us that doing God's Word without hearing it is impossible. We cannot obey God without first hearing what he wants us to do.

Jesus tells us, "I am the vine; you are the branches. If a man remains in me and I in him, he will bear much fruit; apart from me you can do nothing" (John 15:5). Jesus comes to us in his Word, the Bible. We abide in him, and he in us, as we hear and believe what he tells us there. Only in this way can we produce fruit that is acceptable to him.

We can no more do God's Word without hearing it than a branch cut off from the vine can continue to produce grapes.

Martin Luther reminds us of this fact when he tells us that obedience to any of God's commandments begins with fearing and loving God. This attitude of reverence and love for God is not something that we produce by ourselves. It exists in us only as a response to the love of God in Christ, which is revealed and conveyed to us in the Bible.

What would you think of a worker who never listens to orders yet claims that he can do the job as well as those who listen to their orders carefully? Or what about the athlete who wants to perform his own way and insists that he does not need to listen to the coach of the team? They surely speak foolishly. What they claim or promise is clearly impossible. In the same way, it is impossible to do God's Word without hearing it or to keep on doing it unless we keep on hearing it. "He who belongs to God hears what God says" (John 8:47), Jesus said. If we refuse to hear God's Word, we cannot be or remain God's children. Doing God's Word without hearing it is impossible.

❧

Make us faithful hearers of your Word, dear Lord, that we may both understand and obey your holy will in our lives. Amen.

Do not merely listen to the word, and so deceive yourselves. Do what it says. (James 1:22)

Do not deceive yourself!

If a person only hears God's Word and does not obey it, he may be able to deceive others. But in the end he is only deceiving himself, because he cannot deceive God.

Out of love James gives us this very serious reminder. The full five chapters of his letter, in fact, rise up to warn us and admonish us to live as true followers of Christ. This type of instruction is vital—especially for those of us who are not novices or recent converts and have had a good beginning in faith.

There is a very real temptation to lean back in lazy self-satisfaction and to say, "Oh well, I have been born into a Christian family, baptized, instructed, confirmed, and classified as a solid church member. I attend services regularly. I consider myself a pretty good Christian." But it is this attitude that James condemns when he says, "Do not merely listen to the word, and so deceive yourselves. Do what it says."

It is easy for a person to have his name on the church membership roll, show up for services, recite the liturgy, sing the hymns, and listen to the sermon. But if the Word that is spoken there does not sink into his heart, if he neglects to believe and obey it, he is not a Christian. He may be able to deceive the pastor and the rest of the congregation (and that requires very little skill since love believes all things), but he cannot escape the penetrating eyes of the almighty God.

By his admonition, James is saying, "Wake up! Repent of your sins, and believe the gospel. Arm yourself with the Word of God, and go into battle against the sinful desires of your flesh. Adorn your life with good works. Be honest and active doers of the Word. Hear it, believe it, and live according to it."

In a world that is characterized by lovelessness, pride, impatience, boastfulness, selfishness, and oppression, we have more than an occasional opportunity to make an active confession of our faith. To be sure, our creeds exalt Christ and condemn all ungodliness. But our creeds are worth nothing if we oppose them by our deeds.

May we your precepts, Lord, fulfill
And do on earth our Father's will
As angels do above,
Still walk in Christ, the living way,
With all your children, and obey
The law of Christian love. Amen. (CW 458:1)

Anyone who listens to the word but does not do what it says is like a man who looks at his face in a mirror and, after looking at himself, goes away and immediately forgets what he looks like. (James 1:23,24)

The forgetful hearer

Those who do something dishonest usually expect to gain some personal advantage by their deceit. And often they seem to accomplish their purpose. For example, even by the deception of hearing God's Word without doing it, a person may gain the social approval of others, may increase his business in the community, or may be able to avoid family criticism. By his presence in church on Sunday morning, he may please everyone, including the pastor. But by his failure to do what he heard there, he may please his worldly associates during the rest of the week.

James compares this kind of person to a man who walks past a mirror, catches a glimpse of himself in it, and immediately forgets what he saw. He might say, "I saw myself in the mirror," but it did him no good. It was of no service to him. Likewise, all the benefits of the gospel are lost on anyone who hears the Word of God and then walks off to do exactly as he pleases, forgetting what he has learned from it. He might say, "Oh yes, I went to church this morning," but for all that he brought back with him, he could have stayed at home.

This kind of forgetful hearing is not only useless and a waste of time but is also dishonest and disobedient and merits the wrath and punishment of God. Furthermore, anyone who hears and then forgets about God's words bears a greater guilt than one who never heard it at all.

This does not mean that we should hear God's Word less in order to lessen our guilt. God forbid! It is only by means of that Word that God brings us forgiveness and removes our guilt. So we should listen to it attentively, believe it, remember it, and do it.

We ought to cultivate the attitude of the psalmist who wrote, "I meditate on your precepts and consider your ways. I delight in your decrees; I will not neglect your word" (Psalm 119:15,16).

ↄℓ⊙ℭↄ

Dear Lord Jesus, we ask that you would continue to bless us with the opportunity to hear your Word. Send your Holy Spirit to us in rich measure. Increase our understanding of your promises. Awaken and sustain in us the memory of your commandments so that we may follow them all our days. Amen.

June 20

The man who looks intently into the perfect law that gives freedom, and continues to do this, not forgetting what he has heard, but doing it—he will be blessed in what he does.
(James 1:25)

The perfect law of liberty

When God tells us to obey his Word, it is not his intention to make slaves of us but to make us members of his family. He wants to bless us and to bring blessings to others through us. He wants us all to appear with him at last in heaven. That is why he reveals his will to us in the Holy Scriptures.

We need to do a better job of looking into God's Word than the person who briefly glances at a mirror, goes his way, and forgets what he saw in it. We should look carefully into "the perfect law that gives freedom" and adjust our lives according to it. "The perfect law that gives freedom" is the gospel of Christ, which offers and gives us genuine liberty. Those who describe the Bible as a useless book full of outdated laws and restrictions are only describing their own great ignorance. They have not looked into "the perfect law that gives freedom" at all. Sacred Scripture was not given to make slaves out of free people but to make free people out of slaves— for all of us by nature and birth were in bondage to sin and Satan.

So we need to take a good look at the entire message of Holy Scripture. We need to understand that there are two basic doctrines in the Bible: the law and the gospel. Both of these doctrines require our close attention.

We must first look into the mirror of God's law to see ourselves as we really are. And what do we see? Complete sinfulness and unworthiness. We see daily disobedience to his commandments in thought, word, and deed. We see that we are sinners and learn that "the wages of sin is death" (Romans 6:23).

But the gospel of Christ reveals that Jesus took our place, suffered our punishment, died to atone for all our sins, and rose again that we might live with him in eternity. The gospel not only tells us to have faith in Jesus but also brings to us the Holy Spirit, who works that saving faith in our hearts.

Having been brought to faith in Christ, we want to do his will. We are able to experience the pleasure of doing what pleases our heavenly Father. We are led to look even more earnestly into "the perfect law that gives freedom" and to live by it.

⟡

Thank you, dear Lord, for your sacred Word. Bless us as we continue to gaze into your "perfect law that gives freedom" so that we may be and remain your disciples indeed. Amen.

If anyone considers himself religious and yet does not keep a tight rein on his tongue, he deceives himself and his religion is worthless. (James 1:26)

Our speech is revealing

Just before he ascended into heaven, Jesus told his disciples, "You will be my witnesses . . . to the ends of the earth" (Acts 1:8). He wants to speak to the world through us who know him personally and who realize how desperately all other sinners need to know him too. This is a God-pleasing way for us to use our tongues. This is the main purpose for which God has given us the ability to communicate with spoken words, so this should be the prime subject of our conversation.

We are to use our tongues to glorify God, to sing his praises, to make his Word known to others. When we use our tongues to express God's love for us in Christ, our love for God, and our concern for our neighbor, this is pleasing to our ascended Lord. When we use our tongues for the common purpose of expressing our feelings and desires, to share information with one another, or to make an honest living, this is also God-pleasing and ultimately glorifies him.

When we put our thoughts down on paper, we are generally cautious and measure our words carefully. But how carefully do we guard our tongues? Since the tongue is the most convenient tool of communication that a person has, Satan is all too ready to ignite it with the fires of hell. Who can tame the tongue? How little effort it takes to curse, to lash out in anger, to spread malicious gossip, or to repeat indecent stories and filthy jokes!

A person may profess to be a Christian. He may even perform fine and outstanding deeds. But if he does not put a bridle on his tongue and treat it like an untamed animal—if he gives it free rein to gallop ahead in producing angry, blasphemous, or filthy words—then, James tells us, this person's faith and deeds are worthless. His religion is vain. He is no Christian at all.

In order to bridle our tongues, we first need to realize that the real issue is in the heart and not on the tongue. The tongue merely reveals what the heart contains. Therefore, we need to ask our God daily to cleanse our hearts through the recollection of his Word. It is only through the gospel that the Holy Spirit enters our hearts, cleanses them, and makes them fitting places for Christ to dwell. And when Christ dwells in our hearts by faith, how can our tongues do anything but glorify God!

❦

Create in me a clean heart, O God. Amen.

Religion that God our Father accepts as pure and faultless is this: to look after orphans and widows in their distress. (James 1:27)

Practicing our faith

In the devotions for today and tomorrow, James gives us a concrete example of "pure and faultless" Christianity. If our religion is the genuine article, he says, we will want to be active in producing genuine works of love. We will want to press our hearts, tongues, and hands into the service of the heavenly Father by serving our fellow members of the household of faith and by doing good to all people.

The "orphans and widows" in this passage represent all who require our personal attention, advice, and help. This list certainly includes those who are among the poor, the lonely, the bereaved, the sick, and the dying.

Here, in a single breath, the Holy Spirit destroys the myth that "pure and faultless" religion is something to be practiced behind closed doors. Nowhere does the Bible instruct anyone to withdraw from society. Nor does it ever advise anyone to separate himself to become a secret and mystical holy man. We know that sacred Scripture urges us to separate ourselves from the world, but not in the sense that we should hide from one another and from our responsibilities. It is true that the apostle Paul separated himself for a time in order to complete his training—but only to emerge again as a missionary and to shed the light of the gospel abroad into the western world.

The members of the first congregation in Jerusalem likewise did not lock themselves in their rooms in order to practice "pure and faultless" religion. But we read that "all the believers were together and had everything in common. Selling their possessions and goods, they gave to anyone as he had need. Every day they continued to meet together in the temple courts. They broke bread in their homes and ate together with glad and sincere hearts, praising God and enjoying the favor of all the people" (Acts 2:44-47). If we are looking for a historical example of "pure and faultless" Christianity, we have a most excellent one in the Jerusalem congregation. And God was pleased to bless this atmosphere of common Christian love and concern. We read, "The Lord added to their number daily those who were being saved" (Acts 2:47).

And God, in his grace, also promises to bless our efforts of love on behalf of the poor, the widows, the orphans, the lonely, the sick, and all who need our help.

⌑⌒⊙⌒⌑

Heavenly Father, renew a right spirit within us, for Jesus' sake. Amen.

*Religion that God our Father accepts as pure and faultless
is this: . . . to keep oneself from being polluted by the world.
(James 1:27)*

Christians in the world but not of the world

We need to be reminded that we are not of this world simply because we are living in this world. We are travelers in a strange land. Our goal is to reach our real home in heaven. That is where we hold citizenship, but our citizenship is constantly threatened and endangered while we are in this sinful world.

This world is not only stained by sin but is completely saturated with sin. Nothing in the world has escaped the corrupting power of sin. In such an environment, it is not easy to love as children of God. Yet James tells us that we, as Christians, are to keep ourselves "from being polluted by the world."

It is vitally necessary for us to beware of the evil attitudes and ideas of this world. This is difficult because sinful thoughts and opinions, when they find expression on the tongue, present themselves as being pious and reasonable. It seems pious, for example, to say that we can be saved on the basis of our good conduct. On the other hand, the doctrine that we are saved by the merits of Christ alone seems to be foolish and irreligious. At the same time, it seems reasonable to say that we may all establish our own moral values—that we can live however we please as long as we do not harm anyone else. But it seems unreasonable to believe that God has established absolute standards of right and wrong in that "old" Book and that we have no right to deviate from them in our modern society.

We also are to recognize and to avoid the evil deeds of this world. Man's natural attitude of defiance and rebellion gives birth to every kind of wicked behavior: lying, cheating, stealing, disobedience, violence, bloodshed, fornication, adultery, and so on.

So we see that it is a full-time occupation for a Christian to keep himself "from being polluted by the world." And we realize that it is necessary for us to come to our God in daily contrition and repentance— confessing that we have not always kept ourselves clean and firmly believing that the blood of his Son, Jesus Christ, cleanses us from all sin.

❦

*What is the world to me with all its vaunted pleasure
When you, and you alone, Lord Jesus, are my treasure!
You only, dearest Lord, my soul's delight shall be;
You are my peace, my rest. What is the world to me! Amen.
(CW 477:1)*

June 24

When Jesus came to the region of Caesarea Philippi, he asked his disciples, "Who do people say the Son of Man is?" They replied, "Some say John the Baptist; others say Elijah; and still others, Jeremiah or one of the prophets." "But what about you?" he asked. "Who do you say I am?" Simon Peter answered, "You are the Christ, the Son of the living God." (Matthew 16:13-16)

Confess him as the Son of Man

What do you say about Jesus of Nazareth? Who is he? He is your Savior; he is the Son of God; he is the Redeemer of the world; he is the Good Shepherd; he is the key of David. We could go on and on with the many beautiful names of our Savior, all of which tell something true and wonderful about him.

When we call him by these names and when we say what they mean, we are confessing his name. We are making a confession, an admission, to ourselves, to the world around us, and to the Savior himself. We are admitting that he really is who he claims to be and that he really did all that the Bible says he did.

When we confess the name of Jesus, we are also praising him. We cannot tell the truth about Jesus without saying how great he is, and to praise God means to say how great he is. To confess the name of Jesus is our highest duty and our greatest pleasure.

When we admit the truth about Jesus and confess his name, we should also remember the title he applied to himself. Jesus called himself the "Son of Man." This was one of the titles of the promised Savior based on the prophecy of Daniel. It was a title that showed that the promised offspring of David and Abraham would come as an ordinary man. It was one of the humbler titles of the Promised One, because the phrase "Son of Man" describes a man with all the weakness of humanity.

Because it was a humble phrase, it was fitting that our Savior used it in referring to himself. Jesus was born in weakness. He humbly submitted to his parents, just as he humbly placed himself under the law. In weakness and humility, Jesus suffered and died.

Confess Jesus as the Son of Man. As a man he kept the law that you did not keep so that you could have the record of righteousness that you need to come to God. Confess Jesus as the Son of Man, because as a true man he suffered and died for you. Praise the Savior whose life and death earned for you the forgiveness of sins and life everlasting.

✦✦✦

Dear Savior, we praise you for living and dying for us as the Son of Man. By your Spirit, help us confess your name. Amen.

Confess him as the Anointed One

God made many promises to the people of Israel about the coming of the Savior. As soon as sin entered the world, God promised that an off-spring of the woman would come and defeat the evil one. God repeated that promise to Abraham, to Isaac, to Jacob, to Judah, and to David. Isaiah said that the Promised One would be born of a virgin, that he would be the mighty God, and that he would be the Suffering Servant.

God also showed what the Promised One would be like by the institutions he established. The tabernacle and the temple symbolized God's presence with his people. The priests, who were anointed by a special mixture of olive oil and spices, offered sacrifices in those places. Only through the priests ministering in the temple could the people come to God in worship. The priests also prayed for the people, represented the people to God, and taught the people the law.

Also anointed with olive oil were the prophets. They were God's mouthpieces. They let the people know what God wanted from them and for them. They especially called the people to repent of their sins and to trust in God's mercy. They told of the coming of the Promised One, and they called people to live new lives in view of his coming.

The kings were also anointed. Sometimes the anointing signified only their appointment to office, and sometimes it signified the Holy Spirit's equipping them for office. A true king ruled his people with their best interest at heart. He judged justly and fairly. He protected the people from their enemies, even to the point of putting his life on the line. This last point was by far the most important.

Jesus is the Christ, the Messiah, the Anointed One. He was anointed to be our Prophet, Priest, and King. As our Prophet he kept the promise made to Israel. He revealed the will of God in his teaching, and he still reveals that will in his Word. As our Priest he offered the perfect sacrifice that paid for our sins and brings us to God. He prays for us now. As our King he rescued us from sin, death, and hell, giving up his life to do so. He rules us by his Spirit and by his Word.

Confess him as the Anointed One. Accept his sacrifice, and come to God through him. Accept his Word, and follow it completely. Rejoice because he rescued you, and praise him for it.

⌒⌒⌒

Dear Lord Jesus, we praise you as our Prophet, Priest, and King. Amen.

Simon Peter answered, "You are the Christ, the Son of the living God." (Matthew 16:16)

Confess him as the Son of God

". . . the only Son of God, eternally begotten of the Father, God from God, Light from Light, true God from true God, begotten, not made." In these majestic words of the Nicene Creed, we join our hearts and voices with the church of all times and all places. In these wonderful words, we confess the truth about who Jesus of Nazareth really is. In these sublime words, we say what we believe with childlike hearts. Along with these words is the admission that we do not understand this truth any better than the smallest child.

Our minds are not big enough to take this truth in. Jesus is man, and at the very same time, he is God. As the Bible tells us, he is both God and with God from all eternity. As the Bible says, he came into the world that he himself created. The eternal one entered time; the Almighty accepted human weakness; and the Lord of all became a subject of the Roman Empire.

But that is not what is most amazing. The most amazing revelation about him who is true God and true man is that he loves us. He came into the world that he made to get us out of the mess that we made. The judge of the living and the dead let the sentence of condemnation that would have been passed on us be passed on him. The sinless Son of God came into the world so that he could be numbered with the transgressors. He was numbered among us so that we could be numbered among the righteous.

It is important to know, believe, and confess the truth that Jesus really is the Son of God. It is important because that is just what the Bible says. It is also important because of what it means to us. We need a perfect record of righteousness, and we need to have our sins washed away. Jesus lived a perfect life for us, and he died for us. If he were only a man, that would not do us any good. Psalm 49:7 says, "No man can redeem the life of another or give to God a ransom for him."

Because Jesus is really God, what he did in his life on earth counts enough to make up for what all of us do not do. Because he is God, his sufferings and death carry enough weight to pay for our sins and his blood has the power to wash them all away. Praise the name of the Son of God for who he is and what he did for us!

∽༺ঔৣ঺༻∽

Lord Jesus, we confess you as our Savior and praise and bless your holy name. Amen.

Jesus replied, "Blessed are you, Simon son of Jonah, for this was not revealed to you by man, but by my Father in heaven." (Matthew 16:17)

27 June

Confess what God has revealed to you

When the Lord Jesus started this conversation with his disciples, he asked them what the people thought of him. The common opinion was that Jesus was one of the prophets. The people did not recognize Jesus as the promised Messiah, the Son of God, and the Savior of the world.

Speaking for the disciples, Peter confessed the truth of who Jesus really is. Why did Peter and the other disciples recognize him while most of the people did not? Were Peter and the disciples better than the rest of the people? Were they more intelligent than the rest of the people? Had they made a decision that enabled them to know the truth? Were they a little less resistant to the truth than the people around them?

No. They knew the truth because God revealed it to them. The prophets had written about what the Savior would be like. Through them God revealed to all people the truth about Jesus. Through that message, the hearts and minds of the faithful were prepared to receive the Savior when he came. Both the promises that God revealed in the Word and the faith that God created in their hearts were gifts of his mercy and love.

We usually refer to this as the work of the Holy Spirit, and properly so. The Spirit revealed the truth to the writers of the Bible, and the Spirit reveals that truth to us personally and leads us to believe it. Jesus tells Peter that the Father led him to recognize who Jesus really is. Jesus also speaks of the fact that he himself reveals the Father to whomever he chooses to reveal him. The Father, Son, and Holy Spirit are one. They cannot be divided, nor can their activity toward us and the rest of creation. They work as one God in creation, in preservation, and in deeds of grace and judgment. They also work as one in revealing the truth about Jesus to us. There are three persons in the Godhead, yet they are only one God. This is a mystery that we accept by faith.

If God did not let us know who Jesus is, we would not know either. That we know Jesus as the Son of God who became a man to save us is a great gift of God's love. God has spoken to us through the Bible. Let us thank and praise him for letting us know who Jesus really is! And let us confess Jesus to be everything that the Bible says he is!

❦

Dear Lord Jesus, thank you for letting us know you as you are. Help us boldly confess your name and all the truths of your Word. Amen.

"I tell you that you are Peter, and on this rock I will build my church, and the gates of Hades will not overcome it."
(Matthew 16:18)

Confess him as the sure foundation

Our verse for today has been as argued about as any verse in the Bible. Its Latin translation is inscribed in the dome of Saint Peter's Basilica in Rome. The pope uses it and its following verse as part of the basis of his claim to rule the church as the successor of Peter. But those who claim to honor the apostle Peter should read and believe Peter's own commentary on these words. In 1 Peter 2:4,5 he writes, "As you come to him, the living Stone—rejected by men but chosen by God and precious to him—you also, like living stones, are being built into a spiritual house to be a holy priesthood, offering spiritual sacrifices acceptable to God through Jesus Christ."

As Peter himself explains it, the living stone that is the foundation of the church is Christ himself. Peter, whose name means "stone," is not the foundation of the church. He would rather die than have such a claim made about him. It is true that Peter is one of the building blocks of the church. His confession of faith in the Savior showed that he was built on the foundation, who is none other than Christ, the Son of the living God.

In this respect, we are like Peter. No, we cannot be apostles. Jesus only called a few men to that specific office. But we have the truth that was revealed to the apostles. That truth is written in the New Testament. All who share Peter's confession of faith are, like Peter, built on the foundation, which is Jesus Christ.

If you believe that Jesus is true God and true man, if you believe that he is your Savior from sin, if you believe that God has accepted you on the basis of what Jesus did for you, then you are part of that building that is the church. All who have based their hopes on Jesus will not be disappointed.

The "gates of Hades" cannot overcome you. *Hades,* the ancient Greek word for the "underworld" or "the realm of the dead," is used in the New Testament to refer to sin, death, and hell. From the gates of the city come the armed forces as they march to war. The forces of sin, death, and hell—the devil and all the demons—cannot overcome us. Jesus beat the devil, beat him soundly, and beat him permanently. He did that on the cross. He also freed us from sin with his blood and from death with his death. Praise him for the victory he won for us! Confess his name, and rest securely on the true foundation!

❧◉☙

Savior, we thank you that we may rest securely on you. Amen.

*"I will give you the keys of the kingdom of heaven;
whatever you bind on earth will be bound in heaven,
and whatever you loose on earth will be loosed in heaven."
(Matthew 16:19)*

Confess him to the church

Our confession of Jesus as our one and only Savior from sin shows that we are founded on him. We are members of his church. "We are God's house of living stones," as the old hymn says (CW 529:3). The gates of hell cannot overcome us.

Our faith is the cement that holds us to the foundation, and it holds us to our fellow Christians of all times and all places as well. You cannot see the faith of your fellow Christians, and they cannot see what is in your heart. But they can hear what you say and see what you do, and you can hear and see them.

Your confession of faith in word and action unites you with the members of your congregation, and their confession makes them one with you. A common confession of our faith in the Savior and in all the truths of his Word binds you and your congregation to the other members of our synod and its sister churches.

Together we confess the name of our Savior. We praise him for coming into the world to rescue us from sin, death, and hell. We rejoice together in the forgiveness and life that we have because the Son of God died for us.

As you confess your faith with your fellow Christians, you also confess to them. You help strengthen their faith, and they help strengthen yours.

We have a special obligation to admonish a fellow Christian who begins to fall away and pursue a sinful way of life. If what he is doing goes against what the Bible says, he is not confessing but denying the name of the Savior.

You have an obligation to make a confession to such a person. If you truly confess the name of Jesus, you must also walk in love. Love includes Christian admonition, as our Lord Jesus describes it in Matthew chapter 18. It is not an option but an obligation we have to warn those who have wandered onto the pathway that leads to destruction. If we were to wander from the road that leads to eternal life, we would want our fellow Christians to show that same love toward us—to confess the truth in love.

∞⊙⊙∞

Lord Jesus, may we always speak and act as your Word directs. Amen.

"I will give you the keys of the kingdom of heaven; whatever you bind on earth will be bound in heaven, and whatever you loose on earth will be loosed in heaven." Then he warned his disciples not to tell anyone that he was the Christ. (Matthew 16:19,20)

Confess him to all the world

We frequently hear Jesus telling someone not to tell. He told people he healed not to tell anyone. He told his disciples not to tell anyone that he was the Christ. He told Peter, James, and John not to tell anyone what happened on the Mount of Transfiguration.

Why? Why did Jesus act as if he had something to hide? Because he did. He wanted to hide his divine glory and majesty. He wanted to emphasize his main reason for coming into the world—to suffer and die for us.

He had not come to glorify himself on earth. Everything Jesus did on earth was for the glory of the heavenly Father. This is very important for us, because it was an important part of our Savior's obedience. He kept the First Commandment perfectly so that we could have that obedience on our record.

Now the situation has changed. Jesus no longer tells us to keep quiet about him, even if Christians sometimes may act as if he does. Jesus wants us to confess his name to as many people as we possibly can.

He wants us to talk to the members of our family, to our friends, to our neighbors, to our coworkers. He wants us to confess him whenever he gives us an opportunity to do so.

Our Savior wants us to confess his name in any way we can. It may be in the informal contacts we make. It may be in the organized evangelism efforts of our congregations. We may find ourselves slow of wit and thick of tongue. Still, we ought to speak and trust the Holy Spirit to bless our words.

But we can also confess the Savior in other ways. We can help others confess the name of Jesus. An evangelism committee needs visitors, door knockers, and people to talk on the phone. But it also needs people to write and type materials, to stuff and lick envelopes, and to distribute flyers. Your prayers are important, both for the success of your congregation's confession and for that of the missionaries who are working in your name. Do not forget the importance of generous offerings that enable us to confess the Savior's name around the world.

❦

Dear Savior, we praise you for the greatness of your love, the wonder of your sacrifice, the majesty of your person, and the beauty of your gifts. Help us confess your name to all the world. Amen.

Then he said to them, "Give to Caesar what is Caesar's, and to God what is God's." (Matthew 22:21)

Rightly dividing our double citizenship

"To Caesar . . . to God." Jesus' answer to the Pharisees points out that each area of our double citizenship has its own specific purposes and responsibilities that are ordained by God.

To bless us through his representative, the government, God has placed certain things into the government's hands: matters concerning our temporal welfare, the protection of life and property, and the protection and defense of its citizens.

Whatever involves the name and the Word of God, our spiritual lives and blessings, our prayers and our worship, the will of God for us as revealed in the Bible, our Christian faith is not the business of the civil government. These things are God's and God's alone.

There is a God-ordained separation, then, between what is God's and what is Caesar's. One of the things we can be most thankful for as citizens of both kingdoms is that our country still recognizes this separation between church and state. Although, it is true that this distinction between the purposes and functions of the two kingdoms is often clouded today by government intervention in the affairs of the church and also by some churches' attempts to intervene in the affairs of the government.

May God help us recognize that we are, first and foremost, citizens of God's heavenly kingdom through faith in Christ Jesus as our Savior and Redeemer. There is our first loyalty. But may he also help us recognize that it is our Christian responsibility to respect and obey the government as citizens of an earthly kingdom.

How richly blessed we are as American Christians! We have the best of both worlds in our double citizenship. We have so many earthly blessings through God's representative, the government. And we have all the spiritual blessings of faith, forgiveness, life, and salvation as citizens of God's kingdom and heirs of heaven.

"Give to Caesar what is Caesar's, and to God what is God's."

⋘◉◉◈⋙

Dear Lord, you have showered both temporal and spiritual blessings upon us through our double citizenship. Through the government and through your church, continue to provide us with every need of body and of soul. Hear our prayer for Jesus' sake. Amen.

Everyone must submit himself to the governing authorities, for there is no authority except that which God has established. The authorities that exist have been established by God. Consequently, he who rebels against the authority is rebelling against what God has instituted. (Romans 13:1,2)

God himself instituted government

"Be thankful we're not getting all the government we're paying for." Humorist Will Rogers used to get a laugh every time with that line back in the 1920s.

Unfortunately, things haven't changed much since then about the way people view their government. Today we still joke about the inefficiency, vanity, waste, and favoritism we think we see in the corridors and back rooms of our national and state capitols. We rarely hesitate to blame politicians for inflated prices, energy shortages, and any other social ills we might suffer.

And yet in spite of whatever shortcomings and failures it may have, our government lays claim to the complete allegiance and obedience of all of us. Does that seem arrogant? Paul didn't think so. In his letter to the Romans, he urged Christians of all times to submit to governmental authority. Submission is not a grudging surrender or a humiliating loss of rights. Rather, our submitting is simply an acknowledgement that it was God who put the authority there in the first place and that human governments can demand our obedience only with God's permission. As Paul says, "There is no authority except that which God has established."

The apostle Peter says essentially the same thing in his first letter: "Submit yourselves for the Lord's sake to every authority instituted among men: whether to the king, as the supreme authority, or to governors" (1 Peter 2:13,14). Our God is a God of order. And a society that respects its authorities respects the God who wisely ordained that some should rule over others for the good of all.

All governments—from the heathen pharaohs who enslaved the Israelites to the pagan Roman governor Pontius Pilate—exist by God's command. Our Savior himself told Pilate, "You would have no power over me if it were not given to you from above" (John 19:11). And so long as governmental authorities do not require us to disobey God or his holy Word, we owe them our support out of respect for the God who has established all authority.

❦

The powers ordained by Thee
With heavenly wisdom bless;
May they Thy servants be
And rule in righteousness! Amen. (TLH 580:4)

Do you want to be free from fear of the one in authority?
Then do what is right and he will commend you. For he is
God's servant to do you good. (Romans 13:3,4)

Government is God's servant for our good

We Christians have an obligation to submit to our government's authority since it was God himself who established it. Paul points out a practical reason for supporting our government: It is a servant that God, in his mercy, is using for our good.

One of the eternal mysteries about the way God acts is that he chooses to get his work done through people, ordinary people like you and me. His Word, for example, does not boom forth from the skies but must patiently be preached and taught from one human being to another. In the same way, God does not create law and order by selectively raining fire and brimstone on evildoers, but he chooses, rather, to use senators and police officers, presidents and aldermen as his agents in establishing an orderly society.

People need leaders. A tribe of all chiefs would wrangle ceaselessly, and a tribe with no chiefs would collapse from indecision. Firm, clear-headed governmental leadership is a gift from God to satisfy a society's most basic needs: defense from attack, care for the weak, education of the young, and protection from criminals.

Naturally, political leaders do not always make decisions that help people. Because they too are flawed with sin, Satan will often succeed in corrupting them by enticing them to abuse their God-given powers. Hence there are the Hitlers, Stalins, and Pol Pots of this world. A few years after Paul wrote this letter to the Roman Christians, the Emperor Nero launched a savage and cruel attack on them and reveled in the sport of watching them die slow, agonizing deaths. That was just the start. In the next centuries, tens of thousands of Christians were slaughtered with official encouragement from the rulers of Rome.

Yet Paul urged Christians to obey even such manifestly unjust rulers because God was working his holy will through them. God still was Lord of his creation. "Through rulers everywhere," Paul is saying, "God is working all things together for the good of those who love him, who have been called according to his purpose." No emperor, no king, no dictator, no general will ever succeed in plucking any of the Lord's chosen out of his hand.

❧❧❧

Lord, help us see clearly your mighty hand in human history
so that we might trust confidently in your promise to work all
things together for our good. Amen.

Rulers hold no terror for those who do right, but for those who do wrong. Do you want to be free from fear of the one in authority? Then do what is right and he will commend you. . . . But if you do wrong, be afraid, for he does not bear the sword for nothing. He is God's servant, an agent of wrath to bring punishment on the wrongdoer. (Romans 13:3,4)

Government is God's avenger upon wrongdoers

Obedience and *submission* are not popular words these days. We live in a culture that loudly and aggressively promotes maximum liberty for people to act and speak as they please. We support a legal system that goes to elaborate lengths to guarantee protection of every individual's rights.

Unfortunately, something has been lost along the way. Many modern social theorists denounce life sentences and the death penalty as cruel and unusual punishments and prefer instead to fault our society itself for producing criminal behavior. The concept of punishment for a crime is a barbarous relic from the Middle Ages, they say.

Paul disagreed. The government is God's "agent of wrath to bring punishment on the wrongdoer," he told the Roman Christians. God wants governments to teach people, the hard way if necessary, that lawbreakers will be punished so that people will get the message that God too means what he says in his holy law. The vengeance taken upon criminals here on earth is only a taste of the wrath that God will send down on unbelievers in the final judgment.

By grace, however, God's people will escape that awful day. Although we richly deserve to hear all our sins listed as damning evidence and to receive the verdict of guilty, we can flee for refuge to the cross of Christ. On Calvary the Father blamed the Son for our sins and subjected him to the punishment that we deserved. We are now free!

Consequently, we Christians need not shrink from supporting a government that rewards good and punishes evil. A sinful world needs to hear from Paul that the government does not bear the sword for nothing but, as God's servant, takes vengeance upon evil. The world needs to hear our message that evil also brings God's everlasting vengeance and that the only hope for sinful humans is faith in the atoning work of Christ, the Lamb of God.

❦

Lord, on that day, that wrathful day,
When man to Judgment wakes from clay,
Be Thou the trembling sinner's Stay,
Tho' heav'n and earth shall pass away. Amen. (TLH 612:3)

This is also why you pay taxes, for the authorities are God's servants, who give their full time to governing. Give everyone what you owe him: If you owe taxes, pay taxes; if revenue, then revenue. (Romans 13:6,7)

God's people pay their taxes

It's not always easy to feel grateful for government when April 15 rolls around. Tax time is a rather painful reminder that federal, state, and local services do not come free or even cheap.

Satan finds fertile ground here to plant seeds of resentment. We begrudge our tax dollars to the IRS and the statehouse and city hall because we're sure that taxes are higher than they need to be. We begrudge these areas the money because we're not always in complete sympathy with how it's spent. And we're sure that the citizens at our income level always bear the heaviest tax burden. Then comes the temptation to adjust the figures a little, to omit reporting a little income here and there, and to claim a few deductions that we know aren't completely justified.

Evading our rightful responsibilities as citizens is both unpatriotic and unchristian, whether it involves one dollar or one thousand dollars. The emperors of Rome were hardly models of Christian piety—they even allowed themselves to be worshiped as gods.

Yet Jesus himself obeyed them to the letter of their law.

"'Show me the coin used for paying the tax. . . . Whose portrait is this? And whose inscription?'

"'Caesar's,' they replied.

"Then [Jesus] said to them, 'Give to Caesar what is Caesar's, and to God what is God's'" (Matthew 22:19-21). Jesus submitted to the Roman government, even though he knew that within one generation the Roman legions would destroy the holy city of Jerusalem.

From his Word it becomes clear that God wants us to submit without grumbling to all the laws of our government, no matter how unpopular they might be. That means submitting to tax laws, highway-speed laws, the local age of majority, and the draft and the drug laws, whether or not we think that these laws are wise. It is not the mark of a Christian to obey only those laws with which he is in agreement or which he thinks apply to him. In humility we will follow Christ's lead in preferring to suffer what might seem an injustice now while setting our hearts on the glories of the life to come.

Dear Lord, help us assume the duties of our citizenship without complaining. Lead us always to give to Caesar what is Caesar's and to give to you what belongs to you. Amen.

Give everyone what you owe him: If you owe taxes, pay taxes; if revenue, then revenue; if respect, then respect; if honor, then honor. (Romans 13:7)

God's people honor their rulers

"Authority is entitled to the respect it earns, and not a whit more." So wrote historian Arthur Schlesinger, and there is some truth to that observation. Political leaders, for example, ought to feel accountable to their people. They ought to prove themselves worthy of the people's trust and not use their privileged positions to take advantage of people.

Nevertheless, we Christians will still respect all our rulers regardless of how competent we think they are. Paul reminded the Romans in his letter that besides taxes, they also owed the government their respect and honor, remembering who established its authority in the first place. We may disagree with policies, criticize decisions, and argue about platforms all we want, but we, as Christians, will never mock or seek to subvert the authority of those who govern us.

We in America certainly have less to complain about than the rest of the world. The Lord has not only favored us with genuine freedoms, such as the freedoms of assembly, speech, and the press, but he has given us unparalleled material blessings as well. Americans seem to have two chickens in every pot and two cars in every garage. We ought to acknowledge cheerfully that this prosperity can be traced in large measure to good government, which in turn is a blessing from God himself.

The one exception that God permits to the honor we owe the government is when it requires its citizens to oppose or deny God's Word. For instance, when the Jewish Supreme Council in Jerusalem forbade the apostles to preach the good news, Peter stoutly replied, "We must obey God rather than men!" (Acts 5:29). Here the government had forfeited the honor and obedience that was normally its due.

Fortunately, the freedom of worship guaranteed by the First Amendment means that few Americans will ever have to face that dilemma. Our concern, rather, is how we can best support our country's leaders. Paul wrote to Timothy, "I urge, then, first of all, that requests, prayers, intercession and thanksgiving be made for everyone—for kings and all those in authority" (1 Timothy 2:1,2). Let us all, then, out of gratitude for God's great kindness, pray regularly for the wisdom and health of those in authority over us.

✺

O Lord, stretch forth Thy mighty hand
And guard and bless our Fatherland. Amen. (TLH 580:Refrain)

*You are a chosen people, a royal priesthood, a holy
nation, a people belonging to God. . . . Once you were
not a people, but now you are the people of God; once
you had not received mercy, but now you have received
mercy. (1 Peter 2:9,10)*

We are God's chosen people

What makes an article valuable? Sometimes it is valuable because of the person who owned it. If I held in my hand the Bible that Martin Luther used when he carried out the Reformation and offered it for sale, I am sure that I could easily get a huge sum of money for it. That Bible would be no different from many other Bibles as far as the text goes. Similar Bibles could be bought for much lower prices. The difference is that Martin Luther once possessed the Bible.

Peter drives home a similar point in today's Bible text. You and I may not be very valuable on the world's value scale. We may not be high on the social ladder, famous, or very wealthy, but in the eyes of God we are precious because we belong to him. We may look like many other people, but we are different because we are God's possessions.

This was not always the case. Gentiles were formerly excluded from God's kingdom. Our ancestors worshiped pagan idols. But God has adopted us into his family and made us his chosen people.

God's grace and mercy brought this about. God paid a terrific price so that we would be his. "You were bought at a price," declares the Lord (1 Corinthians 7:23). God sacrificed his dearest treasure, his Son, to purchase us for himself. Because of Christ's work of salvation and the shedding of his blood, God can say to us, "You are my people, and I am your God."

We are called a "holy nation." We are holy and blameless in the eyes of God because Jesus' blood washed away our sins. The God who saved us sends the Spirit so that we grow in righteousness and holiness. Even though we are full of faults and blemishes, we strive to overcome them by God's power.

A Christian does not act like the unholy world. He does not relish and revel in dirty stories. He defends others when their reputations are tarnished by evil gossip. He maintains his honesty and resists the pressure to cheat. Christians are different.

When we think of God's great love for us and the value he puts on us, let us live as his chosen people and the holy nation he has called and privileged us to be.

O God, help us show in our lives that we belong to you. Amen.

You also, like living stones, are being built into a spiritual house. (1 Peter 2:5)

We are living stones in a temple

You know that your body is the temple of the Holy Spirit. But do you know that all Christians joined together are the temple in which God dwells? Paul makes a beautiful commentary on today's Bible verse when he says in Ephesians 2:19-22, "Consequently, you are no longer foreigners and aliens, but fellow citizens with God's people and members of God's household, built on the foundation of the apostles and prophets, with Christ Jesus himself as the chief cornerstone. In him the whole building is joined together and rises to become a holy temple in the Lord. And in him you too are being built together to become a dwelling in which God lives by his Spirit." The cement that holds us Christians in a group is our faith and love for Christ and our love for one another.

We must readily admit that we do not deserve to be stones in God's temple. By nature we are not fit. We are rugged and jagged boulders with many ugly spots and blotches of sin. But the Holy Spirit hews sinners into shape in the sense that he washes, cleanses, and polishes them with the precious blood of Christ and prepares them for his glorious purposes. How thankful we should be that God has made us part of his church and members of his kingdom!

Each one of us has a place in this spiritual structure. You can't be a Christian by yourself. As long as a brick lies by itself it is useless. It becomes useful when it is built into the building. To realize his destiny, a Christian must be built into the structure of the whole church. We need one another. We can't stand alone. We need life and support from Christ. We need to share our spiritual experiences with one another and nourish one another's faith.

We are given a place in the church, and we should stay there. We are to be found faithful in whatever we do. Sometimes people complain that others are given greater attention while they themselves are never noticed. They say, "We are not given sufficient prominence." But it is easier to remove a decorative stone than one down near the bottom of the wall. If that is done, the whole structure might collapse. Let us thank God for the privilege of being a stone in his superb temple, irrespective of where he places us.

❧❧❧

O Lord, help us be useful, living stones in your church. Help us form a beautiful temple together with our fellow Christians. May you be pleased to dwell among us. Amen.

You also, like living stones, are being built into a spiritual
house to be a holy priesthood . . . a royal priesthood.
(1 Peter 2:5,9)

We are God's priests

The Old Testament priesthood was a glorious office that only a select few enjoyed. It entailed special clothes and ceremonies. The priests took care of the glorious temple and its religious ceremonies, primarily sacrifices. They approached God for the people. They taught and blessed the Israelites.

Even more glorious is the New Testament priesthood. Ever since the veil was torn in the temple at Jesus' crucifixion, all believers can approach God directly and come boldly before his throne in prayer. Our beautiful garments are the righteous robes washed in the blood of Christ, the Lamb of God. The Holy Spirit has anointed us with his power and spiritual gifts. We have the Bible and its glorious gospel to be a blessing to others. Since Christ, our High Priest, has paid for all of our sins by his perfect sacrifice, no more shedding of blood is necessary or desired. We are royal priests who share in Christ's victory. We are kings overcoming sin, Satan, death, and hell.

"You are talking about my pastor but not about me as a layperson," you may say. The fact is that every baptized Christian is and ought to be called a priest just as Peter and Paul were. The Bible refers to us as priests as surely as it calls us Christians, children of God, or saints. Peter is directing these words to the whole body of believers, not just to a select few. Nowhere does Peter give the hint that he is addressing the clergy and excluding the laity. You are a priest, although for the sake of decency and order the pastor normally preaches and administers the sacraments.

You are beautiful, holy, royal priests. Just the thought of this great privilege boggles the mind. But you are not merely to be ornaments in the church. You have been called to serve as active priests. You have been baptized. Have you brought someone else to be baptized? You have been confirmed in the faith. Have you brought someone else to a knowledge of Christ? You receive Communion. Have you brought someone else to Communion with God?

Yes, we all have been honored and made priests. Let us use our access to God to better our spiritual lives and plead for others!

❧◎◑◍

Lord, give us the confidence to approach your throne for
ourselves and others and to share the blessings of our noble
priesthood. Thank you for making us glorious priests. Amen.

You . . . a holy priesthood, offering spiritual sacrifices acceptable to God through Jesus Christ. (1 Peter 2:5)

We offer up spiritual sacrifices

Sacrificing animals daily for sin was the chief function of the Old Testament priests. This is no longer necessary since Christ by his own suffering and death paid and atoned for all of our sins. Christ did it all. Nothing we could do, including sacrificing animals, could pay for our sins.

Rather, as we learn to appreciate Christ's supreme sacrifice, we offer up spiritual sacrifices. They are spiritual because they are prompted by the Spirit and done out of faith to serve God. They include everything we do as we follow God's will and promote his glory.

First of all, we offer up ourselves. Our hearts, minds, wills, emotions, and bodies with all our talents are to be placed in the service of God. The apostle Paul writes, "Therefore, I urge you, brothers, in view of God's mercy, to offer your bodies as living sacrifices, holy and pleasing to God—this is your spiritual act of worship" (Romans 12:1).

What are some spiritual sacrifices? The Bible says, "Through Jesus, therefore, let us continually offer to God a sacrifice of praise—the fruit of lips that confess his name. And do not forget to do good and to share with others, for with such sacrifices God is pleased" (Hebrews 13:15,16).

You are privileged to offer up spiritual sacrifices when you praise God in church, carry out a family devotion, plan and discuss matters in voters' meetings, and work to extend the gospel outreach here and abroad. You are also offering spiritual sacrifices when you wash your dishes, sweep the floors, are honest and fair in business, offer hospitality, are patient in suffering, and live as children of light.

Our sacrifices are pleasing to God and are a sweet odor to his nostrils. Amazing, isn't it? This is not due to our goodness. We often do our sacrifices with a great deal of unwillingness, indifference, sluggishness, pride, and selfishness. God only desires pure and perfect sacrifices. But for Christ's sake he forgives all the imperfections of our deeds and is pleased to accept them. The sacrifices go through Christ, and he removes all the taint of sin and covers them with his righteousness.

What an incentive to do good works! There are so many God-pleasing sacrifices we can do. Indeed, our lives seem too short to do them all.

⋘◎◉◉⋙

Dear Lord, accept all we do for you for Christ's sake. Amen.

You are a chosen people, a royal priesthood, a holy nation, a people belonging to God, that you may declare the praises of him who called you out of darkness into his wonderful light. (1 Peter 2:9)

We show forth God's praises

Can you imagine being in complete darkness? You may have fine clothes and plenty of food, but if you had no light, life would be miserable. Most people walk without the light of Christ. Mankind gropes in the darkness of sin and shame. God seems distant, remote, and unknowable. Many people have no real guide and live in a bewildering maze.

A person does not know where to go and what to do until the light of God shines into his heart—until he comes to faith in Christ. In Christ the way becomes clear and plain. What an amazing deliverance that is for us!

How can we keep quiet about this? We want to praise God! We do this by telling. If we want to praise someone here on earth, we can do this by telling him to his face of his virtues and the good he has done. We can also praise him by telling others of his goodness. Praising God is no different. We can tell him to his face of his goodness, as we do in worship and in prayer. When we go to church, we witness to the community around us that there is a God who is worthy of our praise. It is so important we spend time doing this.

Perhaps most of our praise will be done by telling others, that is, not by telling God "How great thou art" but by telling others "How great he is." We praise God best by simply setting forth who he is and what he has done. As we present the law and the gospel, the mercy of the Father is recognized and the plan of salvation is understood. Then all those who believe our message will want to praise God and live to his glory.

Telling others about Christ does not come naturally. It takes practice and determination. But we need to try to talk about Jesus as our Lord and Savior over coffee cups, around the watercooler, between classes, walking to the next hole, in the boat, after dinner, and riding in the bus. If you feel uncomfortable and inadequate, talk to your pastor or evangelism committee if your church has one. They will encourage you and give you helpful materials.

What a privilege it is to tell the good news. God chose us to do this. He could have let the angels do it. But he chose us!

Never forget that we need the Holy Spirit to carry out this great privilege. Without him our actions and thoughts would dishonor God. But with the Holy Spirit we can praise God with our lives and voices.

ぐろう

O Holy Spirit, help us praise God with our voices. Amen.

"If anyone loves me, he will obey my teaching. My Father will love him, and we will come to him and make our home with him." (John 14:23)

Jesus' presence in our hearts is a comfort

The Bible tells us that God is present in all places. God asks, "Can anyone hide in secret places so that I cannot see him? . . . Do not I fill heaven and earth?" (Jeremiah 23:24). According to this passage, God is present with unbelievers just as much as he is present with Christians.

But in today's Scripture verse, Jesus is talking about his special presence with his church. He is talking about what we also refer to as the "mystical union." He is telling us that he and the Father actually live in the heart of every believer.

The Savior's presence in the hearts of his people is an unspeakable honor. At the same time, it is a wonderful comfort. Because we are still living in a sinful world, we Christians must face all sorts of problems and troubles, sorrows, and trials. But in the midst of them all, we are never alone. Jesus, our Savior, dwells in our hearts. He will not allow us to suffer any temptation that is greater than we can bear.

And during our lives here, because we are Christians, we are bound to face even more than the usual difficulties that are common to humans. We must put up with the scorn and ridicule that come from unbelievers. In many countries our Christian brothers and sisters still live under the threat of physical persecution. But as terrible as things may seem to be for the church, we have the assurance that we are never alone. Jesus dwells in our hearts. Not a hair can fall from our heads without his permission. Nothing at all can separate us from his love.

With Jesus at our side, we are able to see through the sorrows of this life to the time when we will be forever with God in heaven. There in the presence of God we shall have fullness of joy (Psalm 16:11). There God himself will "wipe every tear from [our] eyes" (Revelation 21:4). But even here on earth, heaven is not that far away from us. As Jesus dwells in our hearts by faith, he gives us a taste of heaven. He reminds us of his suffering, by which he took away our sins, and he puts our conscience at ease.

We cannot see Jesus in our hearts. And our confession of his presence there is bound to invite mockery and opposition. But the words of our Scripture verse are clear. By faith in Christ, our hearts have become God's castle and we are safe in his care.

✦

Redeemer, come! I open wide my heart to Thee;
here, Lord, abide!
Let me Thine inner presence feel,
Thy grace and love in me reveal. Amen. (TLH 73:5)

"You heard me say, 'I am going away and I am coming back to you.' If you loved me, you would be glad that I am going to the Father, for the Father is greater than I. I will not speak with you much longer, for the prince of this world is coming. He has no hold on me, but the world must learn that I love the Father and that I do exactly what my Father has commanded me. Come now; let us leave."
(John 14:28,30,31)

Jesus is able to give us real peace

Jesus' promise to make his home with us would offer us no comfort at all if Jesus were just another human being or if Jesus had failed to accomplish his work as our Savior. Our Scripture verse is, however, a great comfort to us. It tells us that this Jesus who comes to us in his Word and who dwells in our hearts is a mighty victor over our enemies. He is able to give us a real victory and real peace.

Jesus spoke the words of our Scripture verse on the night before his death. Even at that time our Savior knew that he would be successful in his battle against sin, death, and the devil. Here Jesus describes his victory over our enemies in three different statements. Jesus says, first of all, "I am going away and I am coming back to you." The Savior knew that he would be taken from the disciples. He would be arrested and put to death. But he also knew that he would come out of the grave alive on Easter morning and appear to the disciples. Jesus knew that he would be victorious over death.

Jesus also tells his disciples, "The prince of this world is coming. He has no hold on me." The prince of this world is Satan. He rules over the unbelievers in a kingdom of spiritual darkness. The prince of this world would fight against Jesus as he hung on the cross. But Jesus would be the victor! Jesus is without guilt or sin. Therefore, Satan cannot claim Jesus as his own. Satan has nothing on Jesus.

Finally, Jesus tells his disciples, "But the world must learn that I love the Father and that I do exactly what my Father has commanded me. Come now; let us leave." The Savior's walk to Calvary would be a sign to all the world of his obedience to the will of the heavenly Father. It would be a sign even to the unbelievers that Jesus is the victor over sin. Therefore, with full assurance of victory, Jesus leads his disciples out of the upper room to the Garden of Gethsemane with the confident statement, "Come now; let us leave."

The Savior who dwells with us is our conquering hero. His victory is our victory—a real victory that gives us real, everlasting peace.

◈

Dear Savior, may your victory over sin, death, and the devil fill our hearts with joy and gladness. Amen.

"Peace I leave with you; my peace I give you. I do not give to you as the world gives. Do not let your hearts be troubled and do not be afraid. You heard me say, 'I am going away and I am coming back to you.' If you loved me, you would be glad that I am going to the Father, for the Father is greater than I. I have told you now before it happens, so that when it does happen you will believe." (John 14:27-29)

Jesus gives us his peace

Martin Luther found a great deal of comfort in these words of Holy Scripture. Luther knew that he did not deserve eternal life from a holy God. Therefore, when the Savior announced, "Peace I leave with you," these words filled Luther's heart with joy.

Many people today, unfortunately, do not share Luther's attitude toward sin. As far as the world is concerned, sin is only a sickness or a weakness in the human soul. Because the world does not view sin as a real problem, the world does not appreciate the Savior's announcement of real peace. Unless we first learn to confess, "Lord, I am by nature sinful and unclean; I also have sinned against you in thought, word, and deed," the Savior's words will mean nothing to us.

But after God's law has shown us how poor and wretched and needy we really are, the Savior's words of comfort bring great joy to our hearts. "Peace I leave with you; my peace I give you. . . . Do not let your hearts be troubled and do not be afraid." His peace is not another kind of temporary peace such as the world has to offer. It is a peace between God and us. It is a permanent peace, the peace of knowing that God will give us every blessing for Jesus' sake. It is the peace that settled over the disciples once they realized that Jesus had risen from the grave. It is the peace that the Holy Spirit, the Comforter, brought to them and still brings to us through the gospel.

This peace, which is ours in Christ, is the cause for endless joy. Jesus has now returned to the throne of his Father's majesty on high. Jesus did humble himself—even to the extent of dying a shameful death on the cross. And he did it all for us. But now Jesus, having completed his work here on earth, sits in glory at the right hand of the Father. From his exalted position in heaven, Jesus continues to assure us, "My peace I give you"! And he offers it to us again and again through his Word and sacrament.

The peace of this world may be very attractive, but it is also very temporary. The peace that Jesus offers, on the other hand, though it appears much less attractive, even irrelevant, to the eyes of men, is real and eternal.

⁂

Grant us your peace, O Lord! Amen.

If I speak in the tongues of men and of angels, but have not love, I am only a resounding gong or a clanging cymbal. If I have the gift of prophecy and can fathom all mysteries and all knowledge, and if I have a faith that can move mountains, but have not love, I am nothing. If I give all I possess to the poor and surrender my body to the flames, but have not love, I gain nothing. (1 Corinthians 13:1-3)

If we have every spiritual gift but not love, we have nothing

The Corinthian Christians were highly gifted people. But what the Corinthians were sorely lacking was love, agape love, the giving love that seeks to benefit others. The Corinthians had become proud. They believed their special gifts made them superior to those around them, and they began to look down on those who did not have the same gifts they had.

But they were forgetting what spiritual gifts are all about. First of all, spiritual gifts are gifts of grace, which means that we don't earn them and cannot take credit for them. The Holy Spirit distributes his gifts to the members of the body of Christ as he sees fit. Spiritual gifts are not meant to puff us up with sinful pride. Rather, they are to be used to build up the entire body of Christ and to serve one another in love.

Spiritual gifts used in self-centered ways serve no good purpose. That is why Paul says that using spiritual gifts, no matter how valuable they might otherwise be, counts for nothing if love is not present.

The pattern for using our gifts to serve others comes from Christ himself. He came to this world "not . . . to be served, but to serve, and to give his life as a ransom for many" (Mark 10:45). When we see Jesus patiently instructing disciples who often ignored or misunderstood him, when we see Jesus combining his love for truth with his love for souls as he rebuked and sought to win over his enemies, when we see him doing miracles out of mercy for those affected by Satan's kingdom, and, finally, when we see Jesus suffering so horribly for our sins, we see true love in action. Love for us. Love for the world. Love that should guide and shape everything we do. That is Jesus' love for us.

Whatever gifts you have, put them to good use out of love for the benefit of others in your family, in your marriage, in your congregation, and in your community.

⌒⊙⌒

Holy Spirit, help me use my spiritual gifts to honor my Savior and to serve my neighbors in love. Amen.

*Love is patient, love is kind. It does not envy, it does not
boast, it is not proud. It is not rude, it is not self-seeking,
it is not easily angered, it keeps no record of wrongs. Love
does not delight in evil but rejoices with the truth. It always
protects, always trusts, always hopes, always perseveres.*
(1 Corinthians 13:4-7)

The characteristics of love

How would you define the word *love* in this sentence? "I love cake,
ice cream, and cookies." In this context, "love" refers to the good feeling
I get when someone or something pleases me. I love those foods
because of what they do for me. They look good and taste great. Actually, I am the object of my love, and I use those treats simply to satisfy
my desire for something sweet.

Sad to say, some people base their relationships with others on
that kind of love. I will love you and stay with you as long as you meet
all my needs and satisfy my desires. I love you because of what you
can do for me, what you offer me. But if you can't do that anymore,
then I don't love you anymore. That's really the self-centered love
upon which couples who live together outside of marriage base their
relationships. They only pledge to stay together as long as the other
person meets their needs and makes them feel good. And only if
mutual good feelings continue for a long enough period of time are
they willing to make it permanent.

How different is God's love for us! Since God loves us, he did something for us, not something for himself. He gave his one and only Son,
Jesus Christ, to be our Redeemer. In his great love for us, Jesus was even
willing to give up his life on the cross to take away our sins. Yes, God's
love is a sacrificial love that always knows our best interests.

God now wants us to pattern our love for other people after his love
for us. In our Scripture reading today, the apostle Paul doesn't tell us
how love feels. Rather, he tells us what love does. In each example,
Christian love seeks the benefit of others. Christian love seeks to give,
to build up, and to help, rather than to hurt, to destroy, and to take.
Reflect on each of the words Paul uses to describe love. Ask the Lord to
give you a greater measure of the love of Christ. Be a blessing to those
God puts in your path.

**Lord, fill me with your perfect love. Help me demonstrate this
same Christian love to others. Amen.**

Love never fails. But where there are prophecies, they will cease; where there are tongues, they will be stilled; where there is knowledge, it will pass away. And now these three remain: faith, hope and love. But the greatest of these is love. (1 Corinthians 13:8,13)

Love is the greatest gift

Why does Paul call love the greatest gift? Many gifts of God are necessary for this life, but in eternity they will no longer be needed. For example, direct prophecies were important before we received the Bible in its completed form. The Holy Spirit also enabled some early believers to speak in tongues. This gift was a sign to unbelievers and helped confirm the truth of the gospel message. But it too passed out of use after the Lord established the witness of the written Word.

Even faith and hope have their time and place. Faith is being sure of what we hope for and certain of what we do not see. Right now we have faith that through Jesus' blood and righteousness, Jesus will take us to heaven when we die. Our hope right now is a reality, but we still have not received what we hope for. That's why we hope for it.

But when we get to heaven, we won't need to hope any longer in the same sense we hope now. Our hope will be a present reality. We will not need to have faith in God's promises of good things to come because we will be experiencing them all firsthand and forever.

But love will still remain unchanged. God's gracious love for us and our grateful love for him will continue into eternity. It was God's love that caused him to work out our salvation from eternity. It was God's love that sent his Son, Jesus, to be our Savior at the right time in history. It is God's love that also sends the Holy Spirit into our hearts to create faith in Jesus. And it is God's love that we will experience ever more completely for all eternity.

David described the glories of heaven for us in Psalm 16:11: "You have made known to me the path of life; you will fill me with joy in your presence, with eternal pleasures at your right hand." Each of us has already experienced God's love abundantly in this life, but everything now is just a taste of the love he will shower upon us forever in heaven. That's why love is the greatest gift of all!

⌘

Lord, thank you for your great love. Keep me in faith until you take me to the joys of heaven. Amen.

*The L*ORD *is my shepherd, I shall not be in want.*
(Psalm 23:1)

The Lord, my shepherd

Psalm 23 is one of the best known and most loved portions of Holy Scripture. And rightly so.

It speaks directly of our Savior Jesus Christ. Jesus showed that he is our Good Shepherd, who laid down his life for the sheep of his flock and then rose again. Through his death and resurrection, we have the assurance that he is indeed our Savior and that the hope of eternal life with him is certain. What joy is ours!

How great is our comfort that we as believers can express that joy with the conviction of the psalmist: "The LORD is my shepherd"! Yes, the Good Shepherd, who died and rose again, is our Shepherd. He is ours with all his glory and grace, his power and peace, his love and leadership.

"The LORD is my shepherd." These words are the outburst of every confident, faith-filled child of God. They declare what all believers have experienced as adopted members of the family of God. All through their lives they have seen how their Shepherd has tended and cared for them. He has provided them with home, food, clothing, health, and every spiritual need for their temporal and eternal welfare.

Having received his shepherd's continued loving care in the past, each believer looks to the future without any worry or concern whatsoever. With calm conviction, he therefore continues, "I shall not be in want." "My shepherd," he confesses, "will provide me with everything that is good in itself and good for me. He will supply all my needs." Luther says, "In this little word 'shepherd' there are gathered in one all the good and comforting things that we praise in God."

"The LORD is my shepherd, I shall not be in want." This is the dynamic faith of each believer. In the next several days, the devotions in this book will explore many individual blessings our shepherd supplies. As we explore, let it be with the certainty of the hymn writer who sings:

c⟨◎⟩ɔ

The King of love my shepherd is,
Whose goodness fails me never;
I nothing lack if I am his,
And he is mine forever. Amen. (CW 375:1)

He makes me lie down in green pastures, he leads me beside
quiet waters. (Psalm 23:2)

The Lord, my provider

Picture a shepherd taking his sheep from the fold each morning and leading them out to a pasture for their daily food and drink. The prospects do not look good. Much of the land seems uninviting. The weather is hot and dry. The landscape appears scorched and desolate.

The sheep, however, show no worry or concern. They know and trust their shepherd. He has always led them to choice places along the hillsides where lush grass and fresh water abound. They will spend the day eating and drinking and relaxing.

In this attractive scene, we have a delightful picture of the loving care and comfort that the Good Shepherd provides. He leads his sheep to the greenest pastures and the freshest streams, where they may first feast and then relax under his careful eye. His sheep, the believers, can truly say that they lack nothing. Each, indeed, must confess, "My shepherd supplies all my needs from day to day. He gives me food and drink, days of health, and hours of relaxation. He provides family and friends with whom I can share the joys of life. Through Word and sacrament, he nourishes my faith and strengthens me in every stress and strain."

How comforting to know that this Shepherd is mine, especially at times when the horizon seems dark and gloomy and the way appears dreary and hopeless. I didn't get the raise I thought I needed. I was laid off. My savings are dwindling away. Sickness has invaded my family. Death has struck close to home. My faith and my hope seem to be nonexistent.

How Satan loves to tempt us in such cases to look to ourselves for answers! How he tries to get us to question our Shepherd's gracious and continued love!

The answer in such times of doubt and misgivings is not to look to ourselves but to that Shepherd whose love we have experienced daily. Shout in Satan's ears: "The LORD is my shepherd"! Then lie down and relax. The Lord will open his hands and supply your every need.

⁂

**Good Shepherd, continue in your grace to supply what my soul
needs so that my faith and trust remain in you alone. Amen.**

20

He restores my soul. He guides me in paths of righteousness for his name's sake. (Psalm 23:3)

The Lord, my guide

Sheep are not always the docile, obedient animals they appear to be. Sometimes one or more will be distracted by something and stop along the way. Some get tired and want to rest on the spot. Others are tempted to leave the flock to find their own paths. The shepherd gently prods the stragglers and lovingly calls the wanderers back to the flock so that together they may reach and enjoy the pleasant pastures to which he has led them.

So too our Shepherd deals with us. Sometimes we become weary with all the tasks and sufferings of life and want to stop. Our sagging spirits often need to be revived. At times, burdened by the knowledge of our sin, we grow faint in our faith life and are ready to give up. Then again, we decide to go on our own ways and choose those paths that we think will offer greater pleasure. Too late do we realize that those paths were merely mirages—that those tempting paths led us into evil and that we distanced ourselves from both flock and Shepherd.

That's when we really learn to appreciate the loving manner in which our Shepherd deals with us. He restores our souls. He revitalizes us with new life. He revives our feeble faith. He renews our courage with the sure promises of his Word. He brings us back, calling us with the sweet voice of the gospel.

Just as was the Israelite shepherd of old, our Good Shepherd is patient with us. He does not drive us from the rear with angry words or strike at us with cruel blows. He is out front, guiding and calling to us in the well-known voice that we trust, choosing the paths along which we are to go—the paths that are straight and even, where there is little danger of our stumbling. He reminds us that he knows the better destination and will choose the best paths, the paths of righteousness, to get us there.

Though the ways he takes us at times may seem difficult and we don't always understand his choices, as we take him by the hand we find new strength and courage to follow in lives of doing his will.

"The LORD is my shepherd." I need and want no other guide.

⚜

Good Shepherd, gently and patiently lead me so that I may live that life which pleases you and reach the destination you have prepared for me. Amen.

Even though I walk through the valley of the shadow of death, I will fear no evil, for you are with me; your rod and your staff, they comfort me. (Psalm 23:4)

The Lord, my security

Who has not, at one time or another, been afraid of the dark? Who has not desired to flee from gloomy days of trial and trouble and tribulation? Whose weak flesh has not at times cried out in terror at the thought of the final darkness, which is death?

We all experience days of suffering, days when the going gets rough, days when a blanket of darkness seems to descend upon us. We all undergo periods of trial and temptation. We all live through hours when we are confronted by wickedness and sin. And we all know that the last bitter enemy, the final darkness—death—awaits us. How can we stand up to these dark days of adversity?

The child of the world can only cringe at the assaults of evil. He has no real source of help and comfort, no place of refuge. Even the believer's weak flesh cries out fearfully in dark days, "Has the Lord forsaken me?" With trembling heart, he wonders whether God really cares for him.

But these moments of doubt and weakness are short-lived for the child of God. Even in the darkest of valleys, a light will shine through. He remembers his Shepherd-Guide and confidently states, "I will fear no evil, for you are with me." And that isn't just loud talk to bolster his sagging spirits or to quiet his hands that are trembling or his knees that are shaking.

He wonders how he could have ever thought of being forsaken by the Lord who promised, "Fear not, for I have redeemed you; I have summoned you by name; you are mine. . . . I will be with you" (Isaiah 43:1,2). The believer knows that no security force on earth could offer the protection and safety that God's security force of one provides daily and hourly.

The child of God takes his Shepherd by the hand and leans on him for comfort and support. Under the Shepherd's protection, he knows that the worst of troubles that life has to offer cannot really harm him in body or soul. Even death itself no longer creates fear in his heart. He knows that death is just another form of rest and peace that he will experience when the Shepherd returns to gather his sheep into his arms. Then the believer will find eternal rest and security forever.

❧❧❧

Lord, I know that you are always near me. Your rod and your staff offer me comfort in all need. Sustain me in the faith so that in your protecting arms I may rest securely in this life and in the hour of my death. In Jesus' name, I pray. Amen.

You prepare a table before me in the presence of my enemies. You anoint my head with oil; my cup overflows. (Psalm 23:5)

The Lord, my royal host

A king has prepared a royal banquet. Elaborate preparations have been made. Tons of food and delicacies have been ordered. The palace has been decorated throughout. The king himself stands ready to receive his guests personally, ready to welcome them and honor them by anointing them with costly perfumes. And wonder of all wonders, I, a loyal but humble servant, have been invited!

In this verse David subtly changes the picture. The Lord, who had been represented as the Shepherd, now appears as a royal host who has prepared a delicious banquet for his faithful followers. They are to be his guests of honor. A grand occasion indeed!

Though the picture has changed, the message remains the same. The Shepherd is truly a King of love, a royal host at the feast of salvation that he has prepared for his humble subjects—a host who continues to serve his guests with such generosity that their lives overflow with an abundance of joys and blessings.

Each Christian can shout in joyful faith with David: "The Lord has prepared a banquet for me. He welcomes me by pouring sweet perfumes on my head as a sign that I am an especially important guest. He has provided for me in such abundance that I have more than I need. He has filled me with such happiness that my joy is complete. I can desire no more."

This feast, which is a symbol of the eternal banquet that the Lord prepares for those who love and follow him, has really already begun. After times of toil and trouble in life, after seasons of sorrow and suffering, the King of love, our Good Shepherd, refreshes us with everlasting joy. Already in this life, happiness follows sadness according to the Lord's will. Already in this life, the King of love provides for us a taste of that heavenly feast in the Word and sacrament through which he sustains the true life in us. Even now we are participating in our royal host's feast of salvation as we live our lives of faith.

And David says that God has prepared this banquet "in the presence of my enemies." The enemies of the believers—the devil and the world who create much of the hardship and suffering of life—will look on only in shame and defeat. No longer will they be able to prevent or disturb the good fortune of the Savior's royal guests. They will only envy us, who in faith confess, "The Lord is our Shepherd, our royal host, our King of love."

⁓⁓⁓

Lord, feed me with your Word of Life and bring me finally to taste of your heavenly feast above. Amen.

Surely goodness and love will follow me all the days of my life, and I will dwell in the house of the LORD forever. (Psalm 23:6)

23 July

The Lord, my eternal Shepherd

David began his song of praise with this triumphant outburst of faith: "The LORD is my shepherd, I shall not be in want" (verse 1). He then reviewed all the blessings of body and soul he had experienced at the hands of that Shepherd who lent credence to his trust. Now, looking to the future, he speaks with the same exultant faith, asserting that the same Shepherd-love and goodness of the Lord would remain his throughout time and eternity.

This same victorious faith is ours. Our Shepherd-sheep relationship with the Lord began at baptism. In that gracious act, he gave us the forgiveness of sins, life, and eternal salvation. He made us members of his family and assured us that all the benefits of that union were ours. We entered a most holy fellowship with the triune God. Nothing in life or death can now separate us from the love of God in Christ Jesus.

We experience his goodness in this life of faith. We can confess with David: "I was young and now I am old, yet I have never seen the righteous forsaken" (Psalm 37:25). We know God's love as he gathers us around Word and sacrament, always nourishing and strengthening our faith with spiritual food for our souls. His goodness supplies our every need; his love casts out our very sin. We indeed lack nothing.

All these joyous experiences in life are but shadows compared to our lives when we will dwell with our Shepherd-God forever. Our unions with him will be perfect. No more grief or sadness, no more trials or temptations, no more sickness or dying. Nothing that detracts from our joyful fellowship with our Shepherd here on earth will mar that perfect eternal fellowship with him in heaven.

Our Shepherd in life, our Shepherd in death, our Shepherd in eternity. What joy, what comfort, what peace is ours!

Are you troubled and afflicted? Are you weary and burdened? Are you weak and lonely? Then say right now, "The LORD is my shepherd," and keep singing this truth in faith. It will fill your heart and life with the fullness of peace and joy forever.

⊂⊙⊚⊃

Lord, you are my eternal Shepherd. Keep this faith burning brightly in my heart and in my life through your Holy Word. In Jesus' name, I pray. Amen.

Come, let us bow down in worship, let us kneel before the LORD our Maker; for he is our God and we are the people of his pasture, the flock under his care. (Psalm 95:6,7)

The Lord, the object of my praise

Someone has said, "The more a soul knows the greatness of God's glorious mercy, the more it will be stirred up to praise him." Praise is really the theme of faith. A true child of God not only has a heart full of praise but a heart that must express that praise. So it is with us who are the flock of the Lord's pasture, nourished by his Word and guided and protected by his almighty hand. We want to offer the Lord, our Shepherd, the highest praises possible. "How?" you may ask.

We can praise him in our public worship. There we can listen to his voice, confessing our sins and receiving his gracious Word of pardon. There we can join in singing hymns to the glory of his majesty and mercy. There we can offer together our prayers of faith, calling on him in days of trouble and glorifying him for his rapid responses.

We can praise him in our stewardship of his many blessings. As we thankfully receive his gifts in rich measure, we can share the abundance with those less fortunate. We remember his example of giving and want to follow him who gave even his life for us.

We can praise him with lives of service, offering the help of our hands where needed and the aid of our treasures as opportunities are presented to us. But perhaps the best service we can offer is to tell others about our gracious Shepherd.

Recall his words: "I have other sheep that are not of this sheep pen. I must bring them also. They too will listen to my voice, and there shall be one flock and one shepherd" (John 10:16). He has given us the privilege of being his voice to others. We are his undershepherds, to whom he has entrusted his saving gospel. Let us praise him for that honor by sharing his Word of grace with those who have not yet heard it. Let us do this by our personal witness to those in our neighborhoods and communities and by supporting our missionaries who are going to the ends of the earth in our name. Can we who are the sheep of his flock do less? How happy we will be when these "other sheep," brought into the fold by our efforts under God, greet us in the heavenly pasture!

⌇⟲⟳⌇

The Lord is our Shepherd. Praise his holy name! Lord, you are indeed the object of my praise. Let my life be one that glorifies you in every way. Amen.

Create in me a pure heart, O God, and renew a steadfast spirit within me. (Psalm 51:10)

Renew me

We regularly renew subscriptions, vehicle registrations, and prescriptions. We renew acquaintances, relationships, and friendships. These are renewals of outward things. The renewal David seeks in this psalm verse is spiritual. He seeks God's renewal for his heart and soul.

After confessing his sins, David now desires a "pure heart" so that he may serve the Lord with pure motives. He also asks for a "steadfast spirit" that will stand firm in the face of temptation. David asks for nothing less than a new attitude. He wants God to enable him to live a God-pleasing life.

How does this renewal come about? The apostle Paul writes, "Be transformed by the renewing of your mind" (Romans 12:2). Such renewal comes about only when we immerse our hearts and minds in God's Word.

By God's grace, David found renewal for his struggling spirit. Psalm 51 is evidence of this. David was well aware of the fact that he himself could not achieve renewal or a pure heart. He knew that willpower would not accomplish this, so he asked God for those blessings and received them through the Word.

We need the renewal that God gives through his Word. We cannot achieve it ourselves. God gives, and we receive.

For many, renewal is a casual concept, revolving around rest and relaxation. A weekend away brings renewal, as does a day at a spa. For some, renewal is found in a recliner or in vigorous exercise. But these approaches attend only to physical renewal. True renewal of the spirit is something only God gives, and it comes only through God's Word. Renewal takes place when we spend time with Jesus. Worship, Bible study, reception of the Lord's Supper, and scriptural meditative prayer all get us to spend time with Jesus. The renewal that results is both refreshing and resistant. It refreshes us spiritually. It strengthens our resolve to fight temptation and to serve the Lord.

Spiritual renewal is a daily need. As we repent of our sins every day, we seek to amend our lives so that they are in line with God's will. Perfectly pure hearts and sinless, steadfast spirits cannot be achieved this side of heaven since sin will be with us until the grave. But Christ's sacrifice covers our sins and makes us pure in God's sight, even as his Word provides daily, refreshing renewal.

∽⊙⊙∾

Holy Spirit, renew my spirit by your Word. Amen.

Since we have been justified through faith, we have peace with God through our Lord Jesus Christ. (Romans 5:1)

Real peace

After the Iron Curtain fell, many people hoped that we might have peace on earth. Encouraged by successive years of prosperity, the hope of peace grew stronger for some. But peace on earth is elusive and uncertain at best. We were reminded of that when a bomb brought down the federal building in Oklahoma City, when deadly mayhem erupted in Columbine High School, when two US embassies became the targets of terrorist strikes, and when domestic jetliners were crashed into the World Trade Center towers and the Pentagon.

Indeed, world peace is elusive and uncertain. This is not the case for spiritual peace.

The angels who interrupted the quiet of the first Christmas night sang praises to God for bringing peace on earth. Their song spoke of peace between God and man, a peace more important than the peace among the neighborhoods of our world.

But that peace could be suspect too if we focus on our lives. We might well wonder if there can be peace between God and man. Think of the greed that so often robs us of happiness. Observe the obsession with success that causes so much tension. Listen to the harsh words that hurt family members and disrupt our lives. Remember the lost tempers and their victims, countless injured souls. Consider how our families have been weakened by disobedience to parents or perhaps maimed by the struggles of divorce courts. Repeated failure to be what God wants us to be leaves us hanging our heads in shame, wondering how we could possibly expect peace with God.

Yet to people who might well despair of ever living in worldly peace, our loving God gives true peace. In today's verse, the apostle Paul sums up that peace: "Since we have been justified through faith, we have peace with God through our Lord Jesus Christ." In God's courtroom there is no need for long jury deliberations. Our guilt is an undeniable fact. Yet God has declared us to be not guilty through faith in Jesus' sacrifice for our sins. With the eyes of faith, may we see and believe the proof of our peace.

⟞⟝⟞⟝

Lord Jesus, you came into a world that is filled with struggles and torn by strife. You came to bring true peace. Strengthen us through your Holy Spirit so that we may never lose sight of the peace that is beyond our understanding. Amen.

There is now no condemnation for those who are in
Christ Jesus, because through Christ Jesus the law of
the Spirit of life set me free from the law of sin and death.
(Romans 8:1,2)

Free at last!

"Free at last, free at last! Thank God Almighty, we are free at last!" Dr. Martin Luther King Jr. spoke those famous words from the steps of the Lincoln Memorial in 1963. Although his words were aimed more at the heart of the civil rights movement, they convey a sense of spiritual freedom as well—freedom from the bondage and chains, from the terror and tyranny of sin, death, and Satan.

Free at last! That has a nice ring to it, doesn't it? Free at last! But free from what? Are we free from dishes and homework and the daily grind? from hardships and heartaches that boggle the mind? from problems and pressure and not passing the test? from suffering the consequences when we don't do our best?

No, such things are part and parcel of everyday life. As long as we live and breathe and carry on, such challenges naturally come with the territory.

The apostle Paul directs us to the cross and to the crucified. He points us to the sole source of the one freedom that matters most, the only freedom that will truly last. He turns our eyes toward Jesus, to God's one and only Son, who wrote an emancipation proclamation for all of creation with his holy, precious blood and through his innocent sufferings and death. Jesus freed us from the curse of every sinful deed—past, present, and future. We are free from Satan's fire and fear, free from all our guilt and shame, free to follow in Jesus' footsteps and to celebrate his name!

Jesus' work opens for us life in opposition to death as well as freedom in opposition to captivity. He didn't just set us free from sin, but he also set us free to serve. Our Savior didn't just emancipate us from death and damnation, but he also liberated us to life and salvation.

We have freedom without and freedom within. We have freedom from guilt and freedom from sin. We have blessed spiritual freedom to worship the Lord Jesus from the bottom of our hearts, from the back pews at church, and from the tops of our purses and pocketbooks. We sing his praises and praise his name for seeing our sinfulness and saving us all the same. Free at last. Indeed, free forever!

꧁꧂

Heavenly Father, thank you for setting me free in your Son.
Help me share the message of freedom with those I meet. Amen.

"Do not be afraid, little flock, for your Father has been pleased to give you the kingdom." (Luke 12:32)

A gift from your Father

In the midst of the Great Depression, gifts were often meager and rare. That made any gifts received highly treasured. One boy had wanted an electric train set for as long as he could remember, but there just wasn't any money for it. Then one day when he was in the eighth grade, his parents gave him an electric train set. He didn't have the opportunity to play with it much since he headed off to high school soon after, but it meant a lot to him because it was a reflection of his parents' love for him.

Our heavenly Father is pleased to give us a great gift: the kingdom. We are part of our Father's kingdom of grace and salvation because of his good and gracious will. Nothing we could do could earn this kingdom. It makes our Father very happy to give us this kingdom based only on his great love for us in Christ. It costs us nothing. The cost was borne by our heavenly Father, who gave up his one and only Son to be sacrificed on the cross for our sins. The price God paid for our salvation is measured in the blood of Jesus, our Savior.

Since God has demonstrated his great love for us in this way, do we need to be afraid? By comparison to all the forces of evil that oppose the message of God and his Word, what we have and proclaim may seem small indeed. Many people teach and believe many things that are contrary to the Word of God. Verbal ridicule and persecution of God's message of repentance and forgiveness in Jesus are widespread. Those holding to the truth seem few.

Even though we are a small flock, do we need to be afraid? No. Look at what God has given us. He has opened our eyes so we may see our sin and need for a Savior. He has given his Son to pay for our sins. He has given us his Holy Spirit. By bringing us to faith in Christ, God has made us members of his everlasting kingdom. So do not be afraid!

❧⊙⊙❧

Dear heavenly Father, thank you for making us part of your kingdom through your Son's blood. Cause your perfect love to drive fear from our hearts. In your fatherly love, grant that we may always remember that we belong to you. Amen.

"Sell your possessions and give to the poor. Provide purses for yourselves that will not wear out, a treasure in heaven that will not be exhausted, where no thief comes near and no moth destroys." (Luke 12:33)

A treasure that will last forever

What do you have that you will be able to enjoy forever?

Though God has granted us many earthly blessings, happiness is not found in how many possessions we can stack up for ourselves. Jesus reminds us that the same heavenly Father who has given us all we have will also see to it that we will have all we need for as long as he grants us life on earth.

Rather than focus on seeing how many of these blessings we can store up for ourselves, Jesus invites us to sell some of the things we have and give to the poor. As Jesus did not come to be served but to serve and to offer his life as a ransom for many, he invites us to demonstrate that same love. Jesus doesn't require us to sell all our possessions, but he does invite us to consider what we have that we could get by without. Many poor people don't even have adequate food and shelter, while many of us have much more than the necessities of life. What items could we do without to help those with much less than we have?

When we have the same sacrificial attitude that Jesus had when he sacrificed himself for our sins, we are acting on our sure hope of heaven. We know where we will be for eternity. In heaven we will enjoy the glory of God forever. Our earthly possessions are but temporary treasures. What we have in heaven lasts forever. That treasure in heaven is Jesus himself and the bliss of being with him forever.

As we consider this great treasure, Jesus reminds us not to become focused on or attached to our material possessions. These possessions wear out, are stolen at times, or are destroyed by rust or moths. Jesus reminds us that heaven and earth will pass away but not his Word of love and forgiveness and the promise of eternal life.

Since we have Jesus as our greatest possession, he invites us to be willing to use what we have to serve him and others during our lives now. That reflects the treasure we have in heaven, a treasure that will last forever.

✦✦✦

Dear Jesus, as you have sacrificed yourself for us, may we be willing to serve others with the blessings you have freely given us. Amen.

"Where your treasure is, there your heart will be also."
(Luke 12:34)

Where is your heart?

Stop for a moment and consider all the blessings God has given to you. Think about the possessions he has placed under your management and the employment through which he gives you many earthly blessings. Look at the people God has placed in your life: family members, friends, and people who serve you in many ways. Of all these blessings, which is the most valuable?

People usually put their hearts into whatever is most valuable to them. A young man wants his first car, so he'll work and sacrifice and save to get what he wants. A young woman wants to teach and, therefore, studies her lessons well so she will be the best teacher she can be. A beloved spouse lies in a hospital bed, and a husband or wife will do everything possible to help. But do these earthly blessings, no matter how great or rewarding, become the greatest treasures of our hearts? Unfortunately, such earthly blessings may become the most important treasures in our lives. The blessings are not the problem; the problem lies in our hearts when we look at these blessings as the most important treasures.

Jesus invites us today to consider a treasure greater than any temporal blessing. Only Jesus can give us eternal life. Only through Jesus' sacrifice on the cross do we stand forgiven in our Father's eyes. Only Jesus can actually give troubled souls true peace and rest. Jesus is our greatest treasure, in this life and the next. Whatever we do for him is of everlasting value.

Do we seek to share our greatest treasure in life? We give gifts of everlasting value when we bring the children in our family and in our congregations to be baptized in the name of Jesus Christ, when we share with others the Bible lessons we have learned, and when we point troubled neighbors to the peace that comes from sins forgiven. When we share Jesus and the eternal blessings he gives, we reflect where our greatest treasure lies: in heaven.

Where is your heart? Take a look at what you consider most valuable in your life. "Where your treasure is, there your heart will be also."

⁓◉◉⁓

Dear Jesus, often the eyes of our hearts become focused on earthly treasures, which will not last. Teach us that in you we have our greatest treasure, an everlasting one. That which is done for you will last forever. May the desire of our hearts reflect you and your love in all we say and do. Amen.

[God] saved us, not because of righteous things we had done, but because of his mercy. He saved us through the washing of rebirth and renewal by the Holy Spirit, whom he poured out on us generously through Jesus Christ our Savior. (Titus 3:5,6)

Christ's kingdom comes through Holy Baptism

On the Day of Pentecost, Baptism was at center stage. We may quickly pass over the reference to three thousand baptisms, but baptizing that many people didn't happen quickly, especially before the days of running water.

Holy Baptism is still at center stage in Jesus' church and will be until he returns. It is part of the reason why the church will endure.

Sad to say, churches are divided over this teaching. Some hold that Baptism is only a fine and important ceremony. Others see Baptism as a powerful means or tool that the Lord uses to bring us his grace and blessing. Scripture teaches the latter belief.

Our passage today tells us that God saved us through the washing of rebirth (Baptism). Baptism does not merely picture our salvation but actually conveys our salvation to us. In Baptism, God washes us in such a way as to cause rebirth. In biblical terms, death is separation. All of us were born into this world separated from God, which means we were spiritually dead. But God would not have us remain that way. He gives us a special washing that gives us new life, a second birth into his family, where we are joined with him for eternity.

In Baptism, God gives us his Holy Spirit, who renews us. If God would let us see a record of our sins, we would be shocked at how many we have committed. Yet that record of misdeeds is wiped clean through the faith in Christ that the Holy Spirit works in us through Holy Baptism. We are made into new people, filled with the peace that comes from sins forgiven.

In Baptism, Christ has become ours, and we know that Christ is greater than our sins. The apostle Paul tells us in Romans chapter 6 that we are united with Christ through Baptism. What is Christ's is now ours. His righteousness is our righteousness. His power over sin is our power over sin. And so to the baptized in whom Christ lives, Paul says, "Count yourselves dead to sin but alive to God in Christ Jesus. Therefore do not let sin reign in your mortal body so that you obey its evil desires" (Romans 6:11,12). Let the comfort of Baptism give you the power to live for him.

❧

Lord, help me cling to and live in my baptism today and always. Amen.

"I am coming to you now, but I say these things while I am still in the world, so that they may have the full measure of my joy within them." (John 17:13)

Jesus prays for you—to live joyfully

When I worked at the Starlite Outdoor Theatre many years ago, I remember seeing on the soft drink cups the phrase "Enjoy life." I often wondered what was meant by those words.

How can we really "enjoy life"?

It appears the soft drink company felt that taking a swig of cola was a definition of enjoying life. The dictionary says, "Joy is the emotion evoked by well-being, success, or good fortune." I suppose for some the acquisition of a soda is good fortune.

Unfortunately, the joys of life are often short-lived: a drink of cola is good for several seconds of enjoyment, a movie is good for a couple hours, and a new car may be good for several months. But soon the novelty wears off and the car breaks down, the movie ends, and the cola is gone.

We imagine that it would be nice if everyone could always enjoy life, but with sin it is impossible. We cannot always "enjoy life." In fact, real life in this world is marked by bitterness and sorrow.

Still, we can always live joyfully. That is because true, lasting joy is not found in a piece of property or earthly honors. Rather, it is found in a person, a person who prays for us, a person who prays that we have "the full measure" of his joy. That person is the God-man, Jesus Christ. And the joy he brings us is not just here today and tomorrow but forever.

The joy he brings is the full forgiveness and peace with God that he won for us by his life and death. And the resurrection joy he brings makes us able to go to bed at night knowing that "whether we live or die, we belong to the Lord" (Romans 14:8).

The world does not know and cannot give this joy. That is why Jesus is praying for us. He sincerely wants us to have a "full measure" of his joy. He wants us to appreciate what he won for us on the cross. He wants us to enjoy a good conscience and the certainty of God's forgiveness.

❦

Dear Lord Jesus, pray for us. You know we live in a world of sin and trouble. Satan with his accusations tries to rob us of every joy. But we can live joyfully because of you and your salvation. Help us live in the joyful awareness of your eternal love. Amen.

"I have given them your word and the world has hated them, for they are not of the world any more than I am of the world." (John 17:14)

Jesus prays for you—to combat hatred

"If you become a Christian, God promises that you will become prominent and prosperous!" That is the promise some current, high-profile religious leaders hold out to people. Such promises are not only misleading but absolutely false.

For example, if you lived in certain countries today and became a Christian, you would not become wealthy but would become needy. Your job could be in jeopardy; your steps would be watched more closely; your family could even be physically persecuted.

Becoming a Christian does not invite a celebration by the world. It means rejection. The world has no cheers when someone follows Christ, instead it sneers. When a famous pop singer turned to Jesus for forgiveness and salvation, the news media (which previously were his friends) became his enemies. They referred to this converted Christian as a "religious weirdo." The press also attacked another popular musical group for promoting "the hocus-pocus of Christian enlightenment."

Twenty-first-century Christians are not treated any better by the world than Christians were in the past. In fact, historians estimate that there were more Christian martyrs in the 20th century than there were in the previous 19 centuries combined. Jesus knows there is hatred from the world against those who turn to him in faith. That is why he prays for us. As people who are not of the world but of the Word, Jesus wants us to combat hatred. And the weapon he wants us to use is the same one he used against us—love. Before Jesus came into our lives, we were by nature his enemies. But in his love he laid down his life for us, and he made us his friends through the miracle of Baptism. And his love, which moves us to love him, is the force that compels us to love our enemies, to bless those who curse us, and to pray for those who despise and persecute us. Love is the only way to combat hatred.

Now, no one said it would be easy. That is why Jesus is praying for us.

❧❧❧

Dear Lord Jesus, lead us to appreciate your great love for us and move us to love our enemies and to pray for all people. Amen.

"My prayer is not that you take them out of the world but that you protect them from the evil one." (John 17:15)

Jesus prays for you— to protect you from danger

God wants us to stay *in* the world. But as Christians, we are not to be *of* the world.

On the one hand, our sinful flesh wants us to be of the world. We want to do what the world does. Not only because it "feels good" but also because it is the way of least resistance, the pathway to popularity.

On the other hand, our flesh would be pleased if we would not stay in the world to do the work God has called us to do here. As people who cling to the crucified and risen Christ, we know that the world will hate us because of him. In the prayer we are meditating on over these several days—Jesus' High Priestly Prayer—the Lord warns us about that.

In a world that tries to feel good about itself, it is not popular to preach that all people are born sinners and are worthless in God's eyes and that only Jesus can make us acceptable to God.

So one of the temptations we face is to try to remove ourselves as Christians from the world. Who wants to face possible ridicule or mockery? It is so much easier to remain recluse Christians and to isolate ourselves from people around us so they do not know what we believe.

But Jesus does not pray that his Father will take us "out of the world." He wants us to stay in the world. He wants us to be his witnesses and to tell others about the new life he came to give us. How will others hear about him if his followers remain silent, unavailable, and noncommittal?

While we are not to be of the world, we need to stay and do our work in the world. Jesus himself came into our world, and he prays that we remain in the world.

But he also prays that his Father will protect us from the "evil one" while we are doing our work here. He knows the power of Satan. He overcame Satan's temptations in the wilderness, and he conquered Satan for us through his death on the cross.

Jesus prays that we will have the strength to overcome temptation and not fall prey to Satan. Jesus prays for us because he loves us and desires our eternal salvation.

❧◈❧

Dear Lord Jesus, thank you for praying for us. Give us strength to overcome the evil one. Amen.

"They are not of the world, even as I am not of it."
(John 17:16)

Jesus prays for you— to reject the world and remain with him

The world around us—the sun, moon, and stars, the trees, lakes, and flowers—was all perfect when God created it. The material things around us are, in and of themselves, good and not evil. We are to view the earth as a gift of God.

But God's good world has been corrupted by sin. And that is where the problem comes in with the world. So when Jesus speaks of "the world" in his High Priestly Prayer, he is not referring to the world he created but the world Satan corrupted.

To be "of the world" means to leave God and to love ourselves; to make pleasure, power, and possessions our goals in life; to seize the gifts and use them contrary to the will of the giver. To be "of the world" means to seek and to do what is pleasing to the flesh and not what is pleasing to God.

Yes, the natural law of God is written in our hearts. By nature all people know it is wrong to steal or to commit murder or adultery. But sin has clouded and corrupted the natural law written in our hearts. The Bible says that our human minds now have become enemies of God and that our natural reflex is to justify ourselves and to reject the law of God.

By nature a person still knows what is right and wrong. The conscience is still very much alive. But there is no desire to do what is right. That desire is found only in those who have been born again, that is, in those who have been baptized and brought into Christ's kingdom.

Such people are not "of the world" but of God. Jesus is not "of the world" and neither are we, because we are his children. Without Jesus we are nothing. But God, in his mercy, made us much more than just "something" in Christ. For Jesus' sake he adopted us as his very own children, forgave all our sins, freed us from hell, and gave us the hope of eternal life.

Can you think of a better reason to reject the world and to remain with him? That is why the Lord Jesus is praying for us in our text. He wants to strengthen our faith and our resistance to temptation.

❧◉◎❧

Dear Lord Jesus, while we are in the world, prevent us from becoming part of it. Keep our hearts and minds fixed on your cross, and fill our hearts with the desire to do your will. Amen.

"Sanctify them by the truth; your word is truth." (John 17:17)

Jesus prays for you—
to let the Word purify you

How can a young person go to college and stay a Christian? How can one go to work and keep from joining others in their cursing and foolish conversation? How can a couple hold its troubled marriage together? Answer: By hearing and learning God's Word and applying it to their lives.

The Word of God has the power to convince us that we are by nature unacceptable to God and totally depraved in his eyes. The Word of God has the power to comfort us with the assurance of our resurrection from the dead and with the hope of heaven. It surely also has the power to help us live the holy life that Jesus wants us to live.

In addressing young people, the Old Testament psalmist writes, "How can a young man keep his way pure? By living according to your word" (Psalm 119:9). God's Word gives us the wisdom and courage to say no to sin and yes to him. The message of Jesus' unselfish love and sacrifice for us moves us to live for others. "We love because he first loved us" (1 John 4:19).

God's Word has the power to help us be kind, gentle, patient, self-controlled, at peace, and faithful. His Word has the power because it is his Word—the Word of the living God who made all things and is judge and ruler over all.

Many think they have within themselves the power to change their ways. And outwardly some people have changed their habits. But their hearts remain as evil as they ever were. God's Word is the only power that can enter hearts and change them to hearts that love God and desire to live Christian lives.

In Romans 12:3 the apostle Paul tells us, "Do not think of yourself more highly than you ought, but rather think of yourself with sober judgment, in accordance with the measure of faith God has given you."

When you have trouble guarding your tongue, remember Matthew 12:36: "I tell you that men will have to give account on the day of judgment for every careless word they have spoken."

If your marriage is in trouble, remember Ephesians 4:32: "Be kind and compassionate to one another, forgiving each other, just as in Christ God forgave you."

The Bible is available to all of us. In our country we can open it and read it freely, and we should do so while we have that opportunity. If we don't do so, God may take the opportunity away from us and give it to others who will appreciate it.

✦

Dear heavenly Father, guide us according to your Word so that we glorify you in our lives in Jesus' name. Amen.

Jesus prays for you— to love, show, and tell

We are God's witnesses. And the first thing we need in order to be effective witnesses is love—love for people. Christ has taught us the meaning of love. God saw a world of people struggling with sin, alienated from him. He saw people without help and without hope in the world. And he loved them so much that he sent his Son into the world to rescue them from their sins.

What about your irritating neighbor or the unlovable person you work with or that person you know who is behind bars—have you silently removed that person from your love list? God has not removed that person. God has not removed us. He still loves us, and he wants us to love such people. We do not have to go to a seminar or join an evangelism team to do this. All we need to know is Christ's love. His love will help us love others. It's as easy as that and as hard as that—that is why Jesus prays for us. That is why he prayed, "[Father] as you sent me into the world, I have sent them into the world." Loving others is the first step in reaching out to others with Christ's love. An important step.

The second step is to show others that we love them. And we can show our love to others by giving them our time, by praying for them, and by sitting down and listening to their problems. Someone once wrote, "Love sees needs and stops. Love reschedules busy days. Love surrenders to the needs of hurting people. Love gets its hands dirty for others. Love costs." Showing people we love them because Christ first loved us often begins in the simple everyday activities of life. Jesus showed that he loves us by the ultimate sign of love—laying down his life for us. But he also shows it in simple actions every day of his life on earth, like when he washed his disciples' feet.

To be a witness for Jesus, we need to love people, to show them we love them, and finally, to tell them of God's love. We need to tell them of God's judgment against sin but also of the fact that God does not want anyone to perish. We need to tell them how God sent his Son to deliver us from eternal damnation and to give us the sure hope of salvation. We need to tell them that "whoever believes in the Son has eternal life" (John 3:36).

Now we may not be called public workers in the church like pastors and teachers, but we are all witnesses of God's love because we can testify of God's great love for us. And God gives us daily opportunities to show others we love them as God has loved us. And God has given us mouths with which we can tell others about Christ, as God has told us. Witnessing is as easy as that and as hard as that. Jesus is praying for us.

꿍

Dear Lord Jesus, help us be faithful witnesses. Amen.

"For them I sanctify myself, that they too may be truly sanctified." (John 17:19)

Jesus prays for you— to live a holy life

"What did Jesus do for you?" Most Christians would immediately answer, "He died for me." Others would say, "He suffered and died for me." Still others would respond, "He rose for me." All these answers are correct but incomplete.

Besides his suffering, death, and resurrection, Jesus lived a holy life for us. God is holy, and he demands holy lives from us (Matthew 5:48). However, we were unable to pay for our sins and unable to lead holy lives. Therefore, Jesus did both for us. We refer to this as the active and passive obedience of Christ. The active obedience of Christ is the holy life he lived for us; his passive obedience is the death he died for us.

In his High Priestly Prayer, Jesus points to his active obedience. He prays, "For them I sanctify myself." For us Jesus lived a holy life and died a cruel death so that we might "be truly sanctified" and live forever.

All this Jesus did for us. And now we are free to live for him. But our sinful nature has a way of distorting the definition of Christian freedom. "Well, a little sin is okay. After all, Jesus forgives us our sins, and he understands that nobody is perfect, and we can't be saved by our own works, so . . ." says the misguided Christian. "I can indulge myself a little." With that attitude it is not surprising to hear so-called Christians defending pre-marital sex or excusing occasional drunkenness or approving of unwholesome speech or activities.

But that is a terrible abuse of the gospel! Jesus did not live and die for us in order to give us a license to sin. To this attitude the apostle Paul says, "God forbid!" (Romans 6:1,2). Such godless and misguided attitudes are found in the enemy's camp. They are an insult to Christ, and they pose a grave danger to one's soul. Intentional, willful sinning will most certainly lead to rejection by God and eternal punishment in hell. (See Hebrews chapter 10.)

Jesus prayed, "For them I sanctify myself, that they too may be truly sanctified." The Greek word for "sanctified" means "different, set apart, holy." Jesus prays for us to be different from the world, to set ourselves apart from sinful lifestyles, and to live holy lives. Be different. Live for Jesus who lived and died for you. He's praying for you.

❧☙

Dear Lord Jesus, we love you for living and dying for us. Help us live our lives to your glory. Amen.

8
August

By grace the citizens of heaven

"Citizen of heaven" is more than a pious phrase that has a pleasing sound. It describes the great honor that God is pleased to bestow on us for Jesus' sake. Citizenship in Israel was highly prized in Old Testament times. Roman citizenship was highly prized in New Testament times. American citizenship is highly prized in our day. But how can we ever begin to compare any of these with citizenship in heaven!

The kingdoms of this world come to an end. They are constantly vulnerable. Citizens of this world have to switch allegiance as their rulers and governments change. Earthly citizenship is never sure, and its eventual loss is inevitable. But the citizen of heaven belongs to a kingdom that will never end and never change. This kingdom stands firm and sure, because Jesus is defending it and those in it. The citizen of heaven will not have his citizenship taken from him, nor will his citizenship end when he dies. He has an "inheritance that can never perish, spoil or fade—kept in heaven" (1 Peter 1:4).

The heart of the blessing of citizenship in heaven is that the citizens are the redeemed people of God. They are the people to whom God has granted his mercy in Jesus Christ. They are the people who have been delivered from the condemnation and destruction that will belong to the enemies of God. Rather than being separated from God as foreigners and strangers, because of Christ we have become fellow citizens with the saints and members of his family.

We ought to prize our citizenship highly. It is not something humans can achieve or merit by their own efforts but is awarded by the grace of God. We are citizens of heaven because Jesus won a place for us there by his atoning death on the cross. He sealed our citizenship in heaven by his resurrection from the dead. And he ascended into heaven to prepare a place for us there.

Through the gospel invitation, the Holy Spirit leads us to believe these wonderful truths concerning Christ. By the powerful promises of God in the Scriptures, we are assured that we belong to Christ and that heaven belongs to us. People may steal our earthly lives. But no one, no, nothing, can separate us from the love of God in Christ or deprive us of our citizenship in heaven.

❧❦❧

We thank you, Lord, that you have called us into your kingdom of grace and mercy. We rejoice that you have forgiven our sins and written our names in the book of life. Amen.

We eagerly await a Savior from there, the Lord Jesus Christ, who, by the power that enables him to bring everything under his control, will transform our lowly bodies so that they will be like his glorious body. (Philippians 3:20,21)

Look forward to Christ's return!

We live now in a world that wallows in sin and is opposed to God's Word. And it is a constant vexation to us, as it was to righteous Lot while he lived in Sodom. But, like Sodom, our world and society will one day come to a crashing halt. And Christ, the great King and judge, will appear. He will deal righteously with a sinful and rebellious mankind. And only those will escape who have washed their robes in the blood of the Lamb, that is, who believe in Jesus as God's appointed sacrifice for their sins.

To us and to all believers, Jesus will appear, not as a fearful judge but as our Savior and glorious Lord. He will rescue us from this world; he will take us with him to that land that we have never seen but is nonetheless our homeland.

And his deliverance will be complete—a deliverance not only from the evil influences of this world but also from its evil effects. We feel those effects each day we remain here: the quarreling and strife, the disappointments and frustrations, the worries and fears, the sickness and pain and weakness.

But when Jesus comes to deliver us, all that will be changed. The final episode in his plan of salvation will be to bring us out of this place into a marvelous place of joy, happiness, and glory. Even our bodies will be changed for our new lives there. Our present bodies corrupted by sin will be glorified at our resurrection, even as Jesus' body was at his resurrection. They will be cleansed from all weakness, from all sinful inclinations, and from death and corruption.

But for the present we are still on earth. And God has a reason for keeping us here for a while. It is our time of grace, during which God has graciously called us to lives of repentance and faith. It is also a time of opportunity—to bring that same gospel invitation to those still in darkness. But while we work and wait here, let us also turn our thoughts heavenward to our homeland and to the one who will bring us there.

∽◎∾

Our faithful God, continue to assure us of our deliverance through the gospel. Keep us faithful to our heavenly citizenship while here so that we may realize it there forever. Amen.

There is a time for everything, and a season for every activity under heaven. He has made everything beautiful in its time. (Ecclesiastes 3:1,11)

A time for everything

When God created the world, what's the most amazing thing he invented? Let's propose something you may not have considered before: God's invention of time.

Think about it. There was no time before God created the world. God himself is timeless. He lives in an eternal present. There really is no past or future for God.

But when God created our world, he built "seasons and days and years" (Genesis 1:14) into it. As a result, the life of God's world and our lives as individuals take place in time. One moment slips into the next; moments become days; days become years. And as our days and years slip by, we change, as do the circumstances of our lives.

The changes time brings are so profound, says Solomon, that there's a right time and a wrong time to do just about everything. There's a time to plant tomato plants in your garden and a time to pull them up again. Loud laughter is fine at a wedding banquet, but it's completely out of place at a funeral. Even taking a life can be the right thing to do at one time—for example in wartime—when at another time it's a damnable sin. Often whether an action is appropriate or inappropriate depends on the situation.

And the situation, in turn, depends on God. As one Christian explained, we're like the characters in a novel and God is the author. God lives outside our story. We live inside it, and we must play whatever roles in the story the author assigns us. God has the entire story laid out in his mind so that he can see it all at one time. We go through life day by day, turning one page at a time, dealing with whatever arises. And like characters in a story, we're helpless to know or change what's coming next. We are utterly at our author's mercy.

That would be frightening if we didn't know this author the way we do. But through Jesus Christ, we've come to know how deeply he loves us. Through Jesus Christ, God wrote himself into our story to save it— and us—from disaster. And in Christ, God promises to bring our story to an amazing, happy ending.

Our loving Savior-God is in control of the times of our lives. That's what makes them "beautiful"—the whole story and every page along the way.

～⊙⊙⊙～

Lord, my times are in your hands—and that's exactly where I want them. Amen.

I know that there is nothing better for men than to be happy and do good while they live. That everyone may eat and drink, and find satisfaction in all his toil—this is the gift of God. (Ecclesiastes 3:12,13)

A time to enjoy

The story is told about two New England Puritans who were walking down a country road. Suddenly one pointed and exclaimed, "Just look at that lovely flower!"

"I have learned to call nothing lovely in this wicked and sinful world," the other sniffed.

Is that the proper attitude for a child of God? Hardly!

Of course the Puritan had a point. This *is* a wicked and sinful world. This world has been in rebellion against God since shortly after its creation. It's a place of heartache and frustration, and it's doomed to destruction on the day of Jesus' return. We thank God that Jesus' atoning work has saved us from this "present evil age" (Galatians 1:4) and has earned us a place in the better world to come.

But even though this world has fallen, it is still the same world God made. When God first made it, he pronounced this world "very good" (Genesis 1:31). This fallen world still retains unmistakable traces of its original goodness.

Solomon points to some of them here. Think about the happy times of your life. Think of all the good that God has allowed you to see. Think of the ability he's given you to eat and drink and of the satisfaction he gives you in all your toil. For all its faults, this is still a world in which babies are born and children grow up, men and women fall in love, families and friends gather around a table to enjoy a delicious meal, and a weary worker, at the end of the day, can take pleasure in a job well done.

God is not pleased when his children close their eyes to the blessings of this life, as if this will help them concentrate more intently on heaven. The blessings of this life too, Solomon says, are "the gift of God." We cannot despise any gift without insulting the giver.

It would be a mistake to value food and drink or work or fun more than God's spiritual blessings: the forgiveness of our sins, fellowship with Christ, and eternal life. But children of God see God's love in everything good they receive—even the simplest and most humble things. Even here in this world we can hardly open our eyes without seeing yet another reason to thank and praise our gracious God.

❦

Father, thank you for all the rich gifts you have given me. Amen.

I know that everything God does will endure forever; nothing can be added to it and nothing taken from it. God does it so that men will revere him. (Ecclesiastes 3:14)

Time to revere him

Have you noticed that lately the word *irreverent* has become a compliment? For example, when a film critic describes a new comedy as "irreverent," the critic means it's witty, satirical, and a whole lot of fun. *Reverent* to many people means "stuffy," "old-fashioned," and "boring." Our world doesn't seem to revere much of anything.

Sadly, that's not just true of the world. Sometimes it's even true of the church. Much of the talk about God one hears these days exhibits very little reverence and a great deal of casual familiarity. Church workers who plan worship services sometimes feel pressure to make them more informal, more folksy—in other words, less reverent. God is in danger of becoming our heavenly "good buddy," whom we approach as casually as we would our next-door neighbor.

That's not how the Scriptures describe a believer's attitude toward God. The God of Scripture is the almighty and eternal God whose holiness sets him apart from everything he has made. It simply is astounding that this infinite, holy God has entered into relationships with such frail, sinful creatures as you and I—but he has. He has revealed himself to us in Jesus Christ. He has shown us his love, atoned for our sin, and brought us to himself.

Why? Solomon says, "So that men will revere him." The Hebrew word translated "revere" really means "fear"; it's the same word used in the phrase "the fear of the LORD" that occurs so often in the Old Testament. Solomon doesn't mean that we should continue to be afraid that God will punish us for our sins. Our punishment fell on Jesus, who bore it for us. Solomon also doesn't mean that we should at all hesitate to approach God with our prayers or our worship. The "fear of the LORD" is a kind of fear that draws us near to God, not the kind that drives us away.

Solomon does mean that although God loves us and forgives our sins, he does not cease to be God—the holy, infinite God. Casual, buddy-buddy familiarity with this God is completely out of place. David said, "Serve the LORD with fear and rejoice with trembling" (Psalm 2:11), and the writer to the Hebrews said, "Let us be thankful, and so worship God acceptably with reverence and awe" (12:28).

We stand in awe of God because of who he is and what he has done. Let's let the world see our awe and reverence for God in our worship and our lives.

Lord, I stand in awe of you and what you have done for me. Amen.

How great is the love the Father has lavished on us, that we should be called children of God! (1 John 3:1)

We are God's children— dearly loved by him

A teacher once asked her students what was most amazing about God. A child responded, "He knows all about me, and yet he still loves me." Indeed, God's love for us is amazing. He does know all about us. He knows about our defying his commandments, our failing to carry out his will, our unloving thoughts and unkind words. He knows we deserve nothing but his wrath. Yet he still loves us. He loves us so much that he was willing to send his Son to die for our sins.

In our text, John tells us that the Father has lavished his love on us. God loves us very dearly. In fact, we could say that his love for us is so vast that we cannot even begin to measure it.

The fact that we are God's children tells us that God has lavished his love on us. We do not deserve to be God's children. We forfeited this privilege because of our sins. Yet God in his love for us satisfied his justice. He made us acceptable to himself. He brought us to faith in Jesus. Through faith we possess Christ's righteousness. We stand before God, acceptable to him through his Son. We are God's sons and daughters. We will inherit the heavenly kingdom our Father has prepared for us.

What a comfort it is to know God loves us. There are times when our consciences condemn us. We recognize our sinfulness and wonder how God can let us into heaven. When problems arise, we may feel God doesn't care about us anymore. At times such as these, we need to look beyond our feelings and reason. By faith we lay hold of the words and promises of God. It is not how we feel about God that gives us comfort. The fact that God loves us gives us hope.

"How great is the love the Father has lavished on us, that we should be called children of God!" What a joy it is to bask in the radiance of these words. We are sinners; it is true. We deserve nothing but God's wrath. Yet God loves us. Christ paid for our sins. We are God's children. Heaven is ours. This is a fact. Thank God for that!

❧⊙⊙❧

Heavenly Father, thank you for wanting me and loving me as your own dear child. Amen.

You know that he appeared so that he might take away our sins. (1 John 3:5)

14 August

We are God's children— redeemed from sin

If God is love, how can he punish sinners? If God can do anything, why doesn't he do away with all the sin and misery in this world? These are questions that people ask frequently. Behind these questions is the thinking that God is morally responsible for the evil that exists in the world.

Such questions, however, reveal our natural lack of knowledge about God and about sin. God is a holy and just God as well as a loving God. He wills and does only what is right and good. He cannot tolerate what is evil. Sin is evil, for in reality sin is man's attempt to dethrone God and to enthrone himself. Behind every sin is the devil's suggestion to Eve: "You will be like God" (Genesis 3:5). When sinful humans rise up in rebellion against their Creator, God in justice must punish the rebellion and condemn the rebels.

We expect earthly judges to be just. If a judge allowed a guilty criminal to go free, we would condemn the judge for being unjust. How then could it be that the Lord of heaven and earth is unjust? God is a just God. He cannot overlook sin. He will not sweep it under the rug. He must punish the sinner.

Yet God also loves the sinner. He does not want us to be condemned to eternal punishment. He wants us to spend eternity with him in heaven. Thus, in his love for sinners, God provided the way to satisfy his own justice. He sent his Son into this world so that he could take away our sins.

How did Jesus do this? Since we cannot keep God's will, Jesus kept it for us. He passed through every phase of our existence, from birth to death. He did so without any inherited sin or any actual sin. He carried out God's will for us to the last detail. Then he went to the cross to make the payment for our sins. God took our guilt and charged it to Christ. God punished Christ as though our sins were his. The Creator suffered for his creation. God's justice was satisfied. He accepted the payment his Son made on our behalf and declared the world forgiven. Through faith, this forgiveness is our own. Thank God that we are his children! Christ redeemed us from our sins.

✂◉◉✂

Thank you, Lord, for redeeming me from my sins and making me your own dear child. Amen.

And now, dear children, continue in him, so that when he appears we may be confident and unashamed before him at his coming. (1 John 2:28)

We are God's children— eagerly awaiting Christ's coming

Jesus is coming. Are you ready? The thought of Jesus' second coming fills the unbeliever with terror. John saw a picture of that terror, and he recorded it for us in the book of Revelation. He wrote, "Then the kings of the earth, the princes, the generals, the rich, the mighty, and every slave and every free man hid in caves and among the rocks of the mountains. They called to the mountains and the rocks, 'Fall on us and hide us from the face of him who sits on the throne and from the wrath of the Lamb! For the great day of their wrath has come, and who can stand?'" (Revelation 6:15-17).

The unbeliever is right in fearing the coming judgment. What about us? Does the thought of judgment day make us uneasy? It does because we are sinful human beings. We have violated God's will in thought, word, and deed. We deserve nothing but God's wrath and punishment.

Yet listen to the words of John in our text: "Continue in him, so that when he appears we may be confident and unashamed before him at his coming." We are God's children. Through faith in Jesus we possess the forgiveness of all our sins. The Lord has told us, "I, even I, am he who blots out your transgressions, for my own sake, and remembers your sins no more" (Isaiah 43:25).

When the Lord summons us to stand before him for judgment, our sins will not rise up to condemn us. Jesus paid for all of them by his death on the cross. We will not be ashamed to stand before God on that day, because we will be arrayed in the righteousness of our Savior.

It is no wonder that John tells us that we may be confident and unashamed before Christ at his coming. Our confidence is not based on anything we have done. Our confidence is based on all that our God has done for us.

Jesus said, "I am coming soon" (Revelation 22:20). Are you ready? By the grace of God, we are. We believe in Christ. We are God's children, clothed in Christ's righteousness. We pray, "Come, Lord Jesus" (verse 20).

❦

Lord Jesus, thank you for doing everything for my salvation so that I do not need to fear meeting you on the Last Day. Through faith in you I look forward to our glorious union in heaven. Amen.

Dear friends, now we are children of God, and what we will be has not yet been made known. But we know that when he appears, we shall be like him, for we shall see him as he is. (1 John 3:2)

We are God's children— anticipating heavenly joy

What will heaven be like? From what Scripture tells us, heaven is a place of perfect joy and happiness. It is interesting to note, however, that Scripture often speaks of heaven in terms of what will not be there. This is because we are sinful human beings living in a sinful world. We have not experienced perfect joy and happiness and cannot imagine what that will be like. Scripture speaks in terms of sin, with all its sorrows being absent from heaven. This gives us a picture of what our heavenly existence will be.

John received a revelation of the new heaven and the new earth. He described heaven as a place where all sin is removed. Death, mourning, crying, and pain will be things of the past. Believers will live eternally in the presence of their loving Savior. John said of those in heaven, "They are before the throne of God and serve him day and night in his temple; and he who sits on the throne will spread his tent over them. Never again will they hunger; never again will they thirst. The sun will not beat upon them, nor any scorching heat. For the Lamb at the center of the throne will be their shepherd; he will lead them to springs of living water. And God will wipe away every tear from their eyes" (Revelation 7:15-17).

In heaven we will be confirmed in holiness and freed from the corruption of sin so that we may serve our Lord forever in righteousness. We shall have the same bodies, but they will be glorified, patterned after the glorious resurrection body of Jesus.

What glory we have to look forward to! What joy will be ours! Yet this joy also serves us now. In this life our eyes are often clouded with tears. Because we live in a world corrupted by sin, we experience pain and heartache. When we become burdened by the problems of this life, we need to remember the words of John: "Dear friends, now we are children of God. . . . But . . . when he appears, we shall be like him." We have joy that makes life worth living. We have hope that takes the fear out of dying. Praise the God of our salvation for the hope he has given us!

❧◉◈◉❧

Oh, sweet and blessed country, the home of God's elect!
Oh, sweet and blessed country that eager hearts expect!
Jesus, in mercy bring us to that dear land of rest;
You are with God the Father and Spirit ever blest. Amen.
(CW 214:4)

Everyone who has this hope in him purifies himself, just as he is pure. (1 John 3:3)

We are God's children— devoted to his service

Christianity is not a spectator sport. Christianity promotes activity. It is true that we have the assurance of the bliss of heaven. But this does not prompt us to sit around idly watching the world go by. The hope that we have moves us to action. It has an effect on our lives and touches the lives of others.

John tells us that the hope we have moves us to purify ourselves. We are God's children. Yet in this life we still have the old Adam with us. Daily we must fight against the temptations of the devil, the world, and our own sinful flesh. We will never be free from them as long as we live. Yet we will fight against them so they do not overcome us.

Out of love for our Savior, we daily say no to sin. In appreciation for what he has done for us, we say yes to his will. We want to carry out our heavenly Father's commandments. It is our way of saying thank you to him for all he has done for us.

Where do we find the strength to carry on this struggle? We do not find it within ourselves. With the apostle Paul, we all must confess, "I have the desire to do what is good, but I cannot carry it out. For what I do is not the good I want to do; no, the evil I do not want to do—this I keep on doing" (Romans 7:18,19).

We find the strength to fight against the sin in our lives from our Savior alone. It is in the forgiveness of our sins that we have in him that we find the strength to carry out his will. The more we appreciate our forgiveness, the more we will strive to conform to his will.

Thus the hope that we have serves a very practical purpose in our lives. It gives us the motivation and the strength that we need to serve the Lord.

We are God's children. We do not want to serve the desires of our sinful flesh. We do not want to conform to the ways of the world. We live to serve our Savior. May he ever move us in view of his grace to live lives dedicated to his service!

❧◉◔◈

Take my life and let it be
Consecrated, Lord, to thee.
Take my moments and my days;
Let them flow in ceaseless praise. Amen. (CW 469:1)

If you know that he is righteous, you know that everyone who does what is right has been born of him. (1 John 2:29)

18 August

We are God's children— recognized by our actions

Actions speak louder than words. This is especially true of those who claim to be Christians. God's children can be recognized by the lives they lead. Jesus said, "Do people pick grapes from thornbushes, or figs from thistles? Likewise . . . a good tree cannot bear bad fruit, and a bad tree cannot bear good fruit. . . . Thus, by their fruit you will recognize them" (Matthew 7:16-18,20).

What are the actions that characterize God's children? First of all, God's children are faithful to Scripture. When God speaks, we listen. God speaks to us through his Word. We do not subject the Bible to our reason. Rather, we submit our reason to God's Word. We do not want to teach what is contrary to Scripture. When others teach error, we reprove and correct it. If we err, we gladly welcome correction so we may teach only what God's Word teaches.

God's children also desire to carry out his will. We want to avoid whatever our heavenly Father forbids. What he commands, we desire to do. We love God, and we love our neighbors. This love identifies us as God's children.

It is possible for people to pretend to live the Christian life. Outwardly their lives may seem to conform to God's will. We cannot look into people's hearts to see if they really are Christians. Yet there are certain characteristics we may look for. When people deliberately and persistently teach or live contrary to God's Word, we have reason to question if they really are God's children.

God's children are blessings to those around them. As the early Christians gave their lives in the Roman arenas, the pagan Romans had to marvel, "How they love one another!" The Christians' lives led others to want to know more about Jesus. May we always live as God's children. May our lives serve to lead many others to learn about their Savior.

৩৩৩৩

Father in heaven, help us always be what we are—your children through faith in Christ. Amen.

How great is the love the Father has lavished on us, that we should be called children of God! (1 John 3:1)

We are God's children— grateful for his grace

It is always fitting to take inventory of the blessings that are ours as God's children. The verses from 1 John that we have been considering for the last several days help us do that. We know our Lord dearly loves us. Even though we are sinners who deserve nothing but his just condemnation, our Lord still loves us. In order to secure our salvation, God sent his Son into the world to redeem us from sin, death, and the power of the devil. Through faith in Christ we possess his righteousness. Thus we eagerly anticipate the joys of heaven that belong to us in Christ.

Truly the Father has lavished his love on us that we should be called the children of God! How great are the blessings that are ours. With grateful and thankful hearts, we worship him with our lips and our lives. Every time we go to church we have a reason to sing praises to God. We are his children who have been redeemed by him. We have meaning and purpose for our lives. We offer our lives as sacrifices to God, who has so richly blessed us.

The jobs that we have take on new meaning when we do them as a way of saying thank you to the Savior. Whether our position is that of a mother, father, or child; whether it is working in a factory or behind a desk; whether it is serving in a pulpit or a classroom or sitting in a pew, our jobs have meaning when they are done out of thankfulness to the Savior. It does not matter whether other people recognize the work that we do. Our work has meaning for our lives in that we do it to thank Jesus for what he has done for us.

We arc God's children, grateful for his grace. We worship him with our lips and hearts. We worship him with our lives. In view of God's boundless grace, may we respond in thanksgiving and thanks-living to the God of our salvation.

ᴄᴏ◎◎⊚ᴄ

[Lord,] were the whole realm of nature mine, that were a tribute far too small; love so amazing, so divine, demands my soul, my life, my all. Amen. (CW 125:4)

Shout for joy to the LORD, all the earth.
Worship the LORD with gladness;
come before him with joyful songs.
Know that the LORD is God.
It is he who made us, and we are his;
we are his people, the sheep of his pasture.
Enter his gates with thanksgiving
and his courts with praise;
give thanks to him and praise his name.
For the LORD is good and his love endures forever;
his faithfulness continues through all generations. (Psalm 100)

Let the whole world praise the Lord!

The mountain is too tall. You can't see all of it because clouds cover its peak. You can't see across the lake because it is too big. Where is the end of a midwestern prairie? You can't see it because the prairie is too vast. The mountain and the lake and the prairie tell you something. They tell you that God knows everything. He knew exactly how to make the world and everything that is in it. They tell you that God is the strong one, so strong that he created heaven and earth and everything that they contain.

Then what am I compared to a mountain and a lake and a prairie? I am the apple of God's eye. He made the mountain and the lake and the prairie so that I could take care of them. He made them for me. He sent his one and only Son, Jesus, to save me from the terror of everlasting punishment. I looked to Jesus, and he showed me the heart of the Father: big with kindness, warm with love, and full of forgiveness. What can I say?

I can join the mountains, lakes, and prairies in praising our great and glorious God. But I can say more than that, more than any mountain, lake, or prairie can say. I know that "God so loved the world that he gave his one and only Son, that whoever believes in him shall not perish but have eternal life" (John 3:16). Here is good news. God loves me; I am his; nothing can separate us. The blood of Jesus guarantees it.

Come, mountains, lakes, and prairies! You can play the accompaniment, but I am going to sing the solo: Father, you made the world and all that is in it. You made me too, and you take care of me. You sent your Son to save me. So I will see you someday in heaven. Then I can praise you all the time and thank you with endless joy.

❧❧❧

Father, if I have forgotten to praise you for your love today,
forgive me. Make me strong tomorrow to proclaim it. Amen.

Worship the LORD with gladness;
come before him with joyful songs. (Psalm 100:2)

Praise the Lord with life and song!

Fasten your eyes on Jesus! He had before him the toughest life of all. He was going to suffer and die for the sins of the whole world. When he saw what was ahead of him, he did not give up. He forged ahead because he was counting on the victory celebration at his Father's right hand. He obeyed, suffered, endured, and died. Then the Father honored him. He raised Jesus from the dead and set Jesus at his right hand, where Jesus governs the world and the church with his Father. Jesus praised and glorified his Father with his life.

Fasten your eyes on Jesus! If you have a job, work hard at it. Praise the Lord with your life! If you lost your job and are waiting eagerly for news of employment, praise the Lord, pray, wait with patience, and trust in his ability and willingness to help. If you are in good health, take care of your body and take care of your responsibilities while you can. Praise God with your life. Are you sick? Set aside your complaints. Thank God for his new mercies every day. Carry your cross patiently, and wait for the Lord to restore your joy in his own good time. Praise the Lord with your life.

We know that in all things God works for the good of those who love him and who have been called according to his purpose. Now let's add a song to the praise of our everyday lives. Let's choose happy words when we talk about Mother or Father. Let's choose happy words when we talk about the gift of children. Let us say thank you to God for our dear country. If you can sing a hymn at mealtime, do it. If you can sing a hymn when you are at work or at play, do it. Whenever you can join others to sing a hymn, do it.

Doubts want to darken your sky. Questions want to furrow your brow. Worry leads people to despair. Well then, sing! Sing a hymn, and you will chase the devil away. Satan hates Christian hymns. Sing praise to the Father who made you, to the Son who redeemed you, and to the Holy Spirit who will keep you in the one true faith until the day of Jesus Christ. On that great day, you can begin the song that will never end:

❧◉◉☙

Praise and glory and
wisdom and thanks and honor
and power and strength
be to our God for ever and ever. (Revelation 7:12) Amen.

Know that the LORD *is God.*
It is he who made us, and we are his. (Psalm 100:3)

22 *August*

Praise the God who made us!

Jesus is your Lord. He redeemed you, a lost and condemned creature. He sacrificed his life for you on the cross. Now sin has no power over you; your faith says no to it. Death cannot frighten you; you will rise from the dead to be with the Lord Jesus forever. Satan no longer has access to your soul. The Holy Spirit has filled it with faith in every word that comes from the mouth of God.

The Lord Jesus and the Father and the Holy Spirit are your God. Put all your hope and confidence in him. He made heaven and earth and all that is in them. All he did was say the word and all was there—everything we can see and even the things we can't see. The Lord who saved you is your God. Believe in him; trust him. Don't trust your money; it will go up in the smoke of judgment day. Don't trust your house and property; they will crumble in the great earthquake of divine judgment. Know that the Lord is God. He is your helper; run to him. He is your refuge; hide in him. He will see you through every disaster. He will deliver you and take care of you in his own way when the time is right. Know it! Trust him! Praise the God who made you!

The Lord God made you what you are. Know it, and be happy about it. I know a young mother with a large family. She has no money to give her children the nice things they see on TV. But she is content. God has given her one of the highest callings in life; he has made her a mother. She knows that the Lord is God. She knows God gave her what she has and praises him for it.

The Lord gave you all that you have. Know it, and be happy about it. God gave you your body. Thank him for it, and use it to bring him honor. God gave you a mind. You can think big things; you can think little things. You can use it to comprehend his Word and to consider ways to serve him. Thank him for your mind, and use it to bring him honor. God also gave you your soul and redeemed it with the blood of Christ. Ask him to keep it safe until the day when the Lord Jesus returns in glory with all the angels.

∽⟨⟩∾

Praise the LORD, *O my soul;*
all my inmost being, praise his holy name.
Praise the LORD, *O my soul,*
and forget not all his benefits. (Psalm 103:1,2) Amen.

We are his people, the sheep of his pasture. (Psalm 100:3)

Praise the Lord who saved us!

Jesus is our Lord. He is also our Good Shepherd. Now, there are many shepherds, but Jesus is the Good Shepherd. A shepherd is good if he is willing to do his best to secure the safety and welfare of his sheep. Jesus the Good Shepherd gave his life for his sheep. He suffered and died so that everyone who believes in him will not perish but have eternal life.

Now the word is out: "Your sins are forgiven! Come into the pasture where the Good Shepherd is in charge." All had strayed from the pasture and were in desperate need. They were sheep without a shepherd. They were caught in the underbrush of sin and shame. They broke their legs on the rocky soil of rebellion. They had no hope. They were ready to die. But the Good Shepherd went looking for them. He also sent under-shepherds to help gather them in. Slowly, one by one, each lost and dying sheep was brought into the pasture of forgiveness, life, and salvation. Here there is hope and comfort for all. Here there is renewal and restoration in the water of God's Word, in the good news of his free and full forgiveness.

You were baptized in Christ's name. You belong to his flock. It is called the holy Christian church, the communion of saints. The Holy Spirit hands out so many gifts to this community of believers that it is impossible to keep count. He gives a special gift to each believer and encourages him to use it. So we find good technicians, good service personnel, good administrators, good teachers, good pastors. The Holy Spirit feeds his flock with God's Word. He nourishes it with the body and blood of Christ in the Lord's Supper. In this way he leads his sheep to confess their sins, to believe the Word of forgiveness, and to become strong again in the use of their gifts to the glory of God.

No one will steal these sheep from the Good Shepherd. The Holy Spirit will keep them with Jesus Christ in the one true faith. You believe in Christ. You are one of these sheep. You have inherited eternal life. Nothing will be able to separate you from the Good Shepherd, from his flock, and from the hope of eternal life that every sheep possesses. Praise the Lord who saved you! Give him honor and glory! Make his name great in all the world!

⁂

Lord Jesus Christ, you have brought us into your flock.
Strengthen our faith so that we will always listen to your
voice and never give in to the smooth talk of Satan. Our hope
is in you. Keep us with you in the one true faith until we stand
before the Father in heaven to sing his praises forever. Amen.

Praise the Lord in church!

"I rejoiced with those who said to me, 'Let us go to the house of the LORD'" (Psalm 122:1). We went into the house of God with gratitude in our hearts. God had led us safely through another week; we were standing in the courts of the Lord. We were living in a country that allows us to worship God the way he wants us to. We were thankful for the company of fellow believers, for faithful pastors and teachers, for the beautiful gift of music to remind us of the boundless praise of eternity. We were glad we were in church.

As we sat down, we saw the banquet that the Lord had prepared for us. The baptismal font was uncovered. God would bring an infant into the ranks of his believers today. Praise be to God! The books were opened on the altar, lectern, and pulpit. Today our pastor would bring us the Word of God. He had promised to preach God's Word and nothing else. He had done this in the past. Today he would again preach Jesus Christ crucified and risen. A white cloth covered the sacred vessels on the altar. God would again nourish us with the body and blood of his one and only Son, Jesus Christ. We would hear the cherished words, "Your sins are forgiven; go in peace."

So we thanked God and praised his wonderful grace. We could not do otherwise. The glorious gospel of forgiveness through Jesus our Savior compelled us to sing our thanks to the giver of every good and perfect gift. We were not alone in our praise. Hundreds of believers were with us in church. Millions of faithful Christians all over the world were joining us in our praise. Our parents, grandparents, and friends were singing with us around the throne of God. Angels and archangels were in the grand chorus. The creation also added its continuing glory-song. The pastor reminded us of this great thanksgiving chorus when he said, "Therefore, with angels and archangels and all the company of heaven, we laud and magnify your glorious name, evermore praising you and saying . . . Holy, holy, holy, Lord God of Sabbath."

The privilege of worshiping with our fellow believers in God's house is a sign of God's grace and mercy toward us. Let us take every opportunity to go to the house of the Lord and say, "I am glad that I can go to the house of the Lord."

꧁꧂

Lord, show us our sin. Then point us to your house where the streams of forgiveness flow fresh and clear and never dry up. Have mercy on us, gracious Father. Amen.

25

Give thanks to him and praise his name. (Psalm 100:4)

Praise the name of the Lord!

There is a beautiful song in our Sunday order of worship. It is titled "Gloria in Excelsis," "Glory Be to God." When we sing this song on Sunday morning, our hearts and voices and lips deliver to God one of the greatest songs of praise to come from the pen of a Christian poet. This song praises the name of the Lord. The end of this song in particular praises the name of the Lord Jesus. "For you only are holy; you only are the Lord. You only, O Christ, with the Holy Spirit, are most high in the glory of God the Father."

It is indeed proper for us to praise our Savior Jesus Christ with the finest words and expressions that we know. So we say to the Lord Jesus, "You are holy; you are the Lord; you are most high." When we take these words to the hill of crucifixion, the meaning of these words takes on a new splendor. "Jesus, you are holy." Jesus is indeed holy. But Calvary reminds us that Jesus took our shame and guilt on himself and gave us his holiness. He put it on us like a new garment without blemish. Now we can be happy and stand before the Maker of heaven and earth and call him Father.

Jesus, you are my Lord. We know people with important titles. When their presence is announced, everyone jumps. But Jesus did not come to lord it over us. He came to lord it over our enemies, namely, Satan, sin, death, and hell. He came, as Luther says in the Second Article, and "redeemed me, a lost and condemned creature, purchased and won me from all sins, from death, and from the power of the devil, not with gold or silver but with his holy, precious blood and with his innocent suffering and death." Jesus is my Savior.

The Lord Jesus is most high with the Father and the Holy Spirit. Could there be anyone higher, loftier, more worthy to be honored than Jesus? Think of it. He shared the honor, power, majesty, and glory of the Father in the unapproachable light before the worlds were formed. When he saw our hopeless predicament, he laid aside his glory and became one of us, but without sin. He loaded upon himself all the heartaches, the traumas, and all the sins of the world, and died on a cross to gain for us a victory that reaches into eternity. Jesus is most high.

❧

Lord Jesus, we praise you because you saved us from sin and from everlasting punishment in hell. Help us honor you by living a holy life until the day when we shall stand before you. Then the praise we began here on earth will continue without end before you, the Father, and the Holy Spirit. Help us, Lord Jesus. Amen.

*For the LORD is good and his love endures forever;
his faithfulness continues through all generations.
(Psalm 100:5)*

26 *August*

Praise the Lord forever!

"The LORD is good and his love endures forever."

Before the worlds were formed, long before the first man breathed his first breath of life, in eternity, God took counsel with himself. He remembered that his goodness and kindness had no beginning; it never ceases; it never ends. Therefore, he made a plan to redeem us from the power of Satan and from eternal death in hell. He revealed his faithfulness to all humankind and to us in particular when he sent his only begotten Son to suffer and die for our sins. When Jesus' work was done and he said, "It is finished" (John 19:30), the stranglehold that Satan had on each of us was broken.

We know this because we became members of God's family through the washing of Holy Baptism. We get stronger every time we hear God's Word and take it to heart. The body and blood of Jesus in the Holy Supper remind us that nothing can separate us from the love of God because Jesus died for our sins.

Now it is our duty to thank and praise, to serve and obey him. Praise and thanks begin at home. We praise God when we give thanks to him for the food, clothing, and shelter we have. We praise him when we thank him for the gifts of a good spouse, good children, faithful friends, good neighbors. We praise him when we take no credit for any good thing we have but continually point to our Father in heaven as the source of every good and perfect gift. We honor and praise God when we give all glory and honor to Jesus, our Lord and Savior, and strive to serve and obey him by living holy lives.

In this way the goodness, love, and faithfulness of God is published from generation to generation. The children will see the faith and the lives of their parents. They too will follow Jesus, their Lord and Savior. They will speak of his great mercy in saving them from eternal punishment. Their children will believe. In this way the gospel of our Savior Jesus Christ will make its way throughout the world. Great will be the number of those who will stand before the Father and sing:

ॐ

*"Hallelujah! For our Lord God Almighty reigns.
Let us rejoice and be glad and give him glory!
For the wedding of the Lamb has come,
and his bride has made herself ready. . . .
Blessed are those who are invited
to the wedding supper of the Lamb! . . . Come, Lord Jesus"!
(Revelation 19:6,7,9; 22:20) Amen.*

Whether you eat or drink or whatever you do, do it all for the glory of God. (1 Corinthians 10:31)

Here for a reason—to give God glory

Why am I here? That question has been around for as long as the earth itself. Throughout the centuries, the world's best and brightest minds have offered a wide range of answers: "I exist to continue the cycle of life. . . . I am here to accumulate as much wealth as possible. . . . Life has no real meaning or purpose." These answers are quite diverse, but they have one thing in common. They aren't satisfying. Intellectuals may have ideas. Philosophers may offer suggestions. But if there was a definitive answer to that question that human beings could agree on, people wouldn't have to keep asking it.

If you have ever asked yourself this question, I have some good news for you. There is an answer. It is the answer the apostle Paul shared with the Christians at Corinth: "Whether you eat or drink or whatever you do, do it all for the glory of God." The people of Corinth knew how to offer sacrifices to their gods. They knew how to satisfy their sinful desires. Deep down they knew that they deserved to be punished for their sins. What they did not know is that those sins had been forgiven.

Then Paul came. He announced that God had sent his Son into the world to make the ultimate sacrifice. He explained how Jesus had given up his life on the cross to pay for the sins of the world. Paul's presence among the Corinthians demonstrated that God wanted to extend his salvation to all people. This amazing revelation gave the Corinthians a new hope in life and a new reason for living.

The same good news gives all believers a clear purpose in life. You are here for a reason. You exist to give glory to God. Every new day provides new opportunities to give him glory.

As a missionary, Paul dedicated his life to God. He put himself in harm's way. He put the needs of others before his own. Paul serves as a model of Christian commitment, but you don't have to travel overseas or sit in shackles to serve the Lord. Paul said it himself. Christians can give glory to God in everything they do.

ᴄᴏꙅᴏꙅᴏ

Dear Lord, thank you for sending your Son, Jesus, to rescue me from sin. Use me day by day so that, through my words and actions, I may bring glory to your name. Amen.

Let us run with perseverance the race marked out for us. Let us fix our eyes on Jesus. (Hebrews 12:1,2)

28 *August*

Just keep running!

Running is a very strenuous activity. Most athletes never forget those dreaded wind sprints at the ends of daily practices. Marathon runners train year round for the privilege of running in a few races. But more than physical conditioning, running also requires a mental attitude of determination and persistence.

How different it is with our faith-life. So long as we fix our eyes on Jesus, we are able to see that the victory is already ours! By his innocent suffering and death, Jesus paid the price in full for our peace with God in this life and for life eternal after this earthly run is over. Each believer has a victory trophy in his or her possession. It is inscribed with the words "Redeemed by Jesus."

But why, then, is there the admonition to run with perseverance the race marked out for us? The answer is that we have a war going on inside of us. While with the faith God has given us we run joyfully and thankfully through this life on our way to heaven, we nevertheless meet subtle or violent opposition all the way.

Thanks be to God that he has so dearly marked out for us the path we are to travel through this life. In his holy Ten Commandments, he has clearly spelled out for us his unchanging will. And the more we look at that holy Law, the more we see how much our gracious God loves us. In the second table of the Law, he protects all authority, life, marriage, property, and even our good names!

It is a never-ending battle to put God's will into practice as we strive to run our races each day. Our sinful nature is at constant odds with the will of God. It takes the kind of persistence that only our gracious God can give us. He gives us perseverance as we keep our eyes fixed on Jesus our Savior.

What blessings abound in our lives each time we, with grateful hearts, follow our God's gracious will! The light of our faith shines ever more brightly for all to see. The warmth of God's love melts our cold hearts so we point others to the Savior's love. But most of all, our Savior-God, the triune God, is glorified when we follow his will.

৩৩৩৩

Lord, help us run the race of the Christian life you have marked out for us so that we do not become weary and lose heart. Amen.

The peace of God, which transcends all understanding,
will guard your hearts and your minds in Christ Jesus.
(Philippians 4:7)

Peaceful joy in Jesus

One of the most sought-after conditions in the world today is peace—between nations, between peoples, between neighbors, between family members, and just plain peace of mind. Sometimes nations strive for peace by piling up more and more weapons of war. Often we look for personal peace at the expense of others. Peace of mind for many means nostalgia, a turning back to the good old days when things seemingly were slower and easier. The peace that is offered from God transcends all these by far.

The main reason we have no peace, within or without, is sin. Sinful pride, sinful jealousy, sinful greed are all causes of unrest. Sin cannot be ignored. You can't whitewash it or put a Band-Aid over it. You can wait forever, but it will never go away by itself. And it never stays the same. Either it is removed, or it gets worse. Sin must be dealt with.

Throughout the ages people have tried to handle sin in their own ways, and all have failed. It takes more than a mere human. It took the God-man Jesus Christ to deal effectively with sin by removing its curse and threat. This he did by willingly sacrificing himself in our place, giving his sinless body into death, and shedding his holy blood on the shameful cross. He took our place, suffering and dying for us. His resurrection from the dead proved his victory over sin, death, and the devil. We now have nothing to fear. Jesus died for us. He forgives our sins daily. He sends his Holy Spirit to create, nourish, and strengthen our faith so we may receive this forgiveness as our own.

God is now our Father. By faith in Christ we are part of his family of forgiven believers. We are no longer God's enemies; we are at peace with him. Jesus has reconciled us to God and has made peace between God and us by removing the cause of our dissension, our sin, and our guilt. This is real peace from God.

This peace "transcends all understanding." But God's peace is not beyond our comprehension. Scripture tells us at length and in detail how Jesus earned it for us and how the Holy Spirit gives it to us by grace through faith. It "transcends all understanding" in its ability to give us comfort, joy, and peace. It even guards our hearts and minds in Christ Jesus. Nothing can diminish our joy.

Merciful Lord, we thank you for the peace and joy you
continually offer us in your Word. Grant us these gifts for Jesus'
sake. Amen.

God demonstrates his own love for us in this: While we were still sinners, Christ died for us. Since we have now been justified by his blood, how much more shall we be saved from God's wrath through him! For if, when we were God's enemies, we were reconciled to him through the death of his Son, how much more, having been reconciled, shall we be saved through his life! (Romans 5:8-10)

We are secure in the depth of God's love

How great is God's love for us! He saved us from guilt and damnation. He has opened heaven's doors, and he calls us to come in.

But sometimes we wonder whether God really loves us. How can I be sure he wants me to be his child? we ask. How can I be sure if he is at peace with me? we wonder.

Have no fear. Paul anticipated your concerns and answered them in today's reading. Perhaps he had these concerns too.

Follow Paul's logic. He argues from the greater deed to the lesser. In the first verse of our reading, Paul spells out the great deed God did. He showed his love for the world by sending his Son, the Christ, to die for our sins. He did this "while we were still sinners." There was nothing at all good in us. We were disgusting with sin. We had nothing to offer him, nothing that made us the least bit lovable. But he died for us because of his love.

Paul argues that Jesus died for the world—declared the world to be not guilty because of his work—when we were sinners. Now that Christ's work of justification is done, can there be any doubt that on the Last Day we will stand before God in Christ? No.

Paul then repeats what he just said in slightly different terms. He argues that we were God's enemies—not just sinners but people who hated God—and that at that time God reconciled us to himself through the death of his Son. In Christ, God declared himself to be at peace with a world full of enemies. Since this is so, can there be any doubt that we will be saved from his wrath? Since God took the initiative toward his enemies, sent his Son to take away his enemies' sins, and is now at peace with us, can there be any doubt that through faith in this peace we will go to heaven? No. All doubt concerning God's love for us is gone.

⚬⚬⚬

Dear Lord, since you saved us when we were enemies, there is no doubt that our salvation is secure. Amen.

It is by grace you have been saved, through faith—and this not from yourselves, it is the gift of God—not by works, so that no one can boast. For we are God's workmanship, created in Christ Jesus to do good works, which God prepared in advance for us to do. (Ephesians 2:8-10)

The gift of work

This is a well-known passage, one of the foundation passages on which the teaching of salvation by grace stands. It teaches us that we have been saved because God poured out his undeserved kindness on us. Not only has his grace accomplished our salvation, but it also brought our faith into being. Faith is the hand that receives his salvation. Salvation is through faith, worked by a gracious God and not by us; this is the bedrock of our salvation.

Paul, however, says still more. He says to us, "Look at yourself. Do you see what you are? You have been created by God. Just like a craftsman might fashion a beautiful clay pot or a woodworker might fashion an ornately carved box, God, the spiritual craftsman, has fashioned you into something new. He has joined you with Christ and has made you into a person who has dedicated his or her life to God's service."

Yes, you would like to serve the Lord better. Every Christian does, and Paul will encourage us to do that later in his letter to the Ephesians. But for now forget your weaknesses and what you have not done, and think about what you are doing. Think about the ways you are serving your Lord. Don't become proud, but I'm sure you can think of many acts of service—how you serve God at your job, at home with your children, at church, and in your devotional life.

What Paul tells us is that we were "created in Christ Jesus" to do these things. We were chosen to be changed people, people who no longer seek our own glory and pleasure but who seek God's glory and the work of the kingdom. God chose you to come to faith. But he also chose you to do good works.

Don't just look at your shortcomings. Look at what the Lord has given you the power to do, and thank him for it.

Keep us focused, Lord, on your grace. We work because you first worked for us and in us. Amen.

God's grace creates trust

In Walt Disney's adaptation of Rudyard Kipling's *The Jungle Book*, one of the characters, a snake, attempts to induce the feeling of trust within the main character, a young boy, by repetitiously singing in a soothing voice, "Trust in me." If the snake's soothing song had not been interrupted, the young boy would have become the main course of the snake's next meal.

Isn't that true for a lot of what is portrayed as being worthy of our trust today? That old snake in the grass has certainly been applied to doctors, lawyers, car salespeople, insurance agents, and, yes, even pastors—sadly enough, rightly so at times. In fact, no human being is completely trustworthy. The seeds planted in Eve's ear by the serpent's song continue to be planted and bear fruit. A spouse who promised to love, honor, cherish, and be faithful has lapses. Even parents who promise that they won't let anything bad happen to their children don't always come through. So whom can you trust?

Jesus answers, "Trust in God; trust also in me." Think what Jesus means here. The disciples knew the God of grace who promised that the Savior would come through the descendants of Abraham. That promise had been repeated throughout the centuries. The disciples knew the Old Testament Scriptures. They had learned to trust the Lord of Samuel, David, and Isaiah. "Trust in God," Jesus said. "Trust also in me." He is the Lord of promise. He is the Savior promised throughout the Old Testament. When God says something, it happens. Trust every promise. Not one word will fail to come to pass.

Through the gospel, God has given us a place in his kingdom of grace and glory. We can always trust the words of Jesus just as we trust the words of God. There is no difference, because Jesus is God. When Jesus tells us our sins are forgiven, they are. When he tells us he will watch over us day and night, he does. When he tells us that we will rise just as he rose, we will. "Trust in God; trust also in me." We need regular encouragement to trust Jesus, because we struggle in this world of sin, pain, sorrow, and death. The gospel soothes our fearful, doubting, and weary hearts with the assurances of God's love. Trust God. Trust Jesus. Trust his Word.

⁓◎◎⁓

Thank you, God, for being trustworthy. Amen.

September 2

God's grace is wide and deep

Did you know that the Amazon River in South America is about 210 miles wide at its mouth? That would be about 3,080 football fields end-to-end. That's really wide!

Or did you know that the deepest part of the ocean is found east of Guam? It's known as the Marianas Trench and is 6.8 miles deep. To help you visualize just how deep that is, imagine about 25 Sears Towers stacked on top of one another. That's really deep!

The width of the Amazon River and the depth of the Marianas Trench are nothing when compared to how wide and deep God's grace is. When God in his grace looked at what had happened to his perfect creation—it was spoiled by sin—he didn't say, "I see some who are worthy of being saved." He said that he wanted "all men to be saved and to come to a knowledge of the truth" (1 Timothy 2:4). And his wide grace set in motion the plan to save every sinner. The evangelist John wrote, "God so loved the world that he gave his one and only Son" (John 3:16). God's one and only Son, Jesus Christ, "died for all" (2 Corinthians 5:15). And through his death, "God was reconciling the world to himself" (2 Corinthians 5:19). The message of God's wide grace, the gospel, proclaims, "You are all sons of God through faith in Christ Jesus" (Galatians 3:26). And because God's grace is so wide, Jesus tells you, "In my Father's house are many rooms" (John 14:2).

As wide as God's grace is, it is equally as deep. Consider the depths Jesus went to secure salvation for all people. The apostle Paul describes it: "[Jesus] made himself nothing, taking the very nature of a servant. . . . And being found in appearance as a man, he humbled himself and became obedient to death—even death on a cross!" (Philippians 2:7,8). The prophet Isaiah describes the depths even more vividly: "He took up our infirmities and carried our sorrows. . . . He was pierced for our transgressions. . . . The punishment that brought us peace was upon him. . . . The LORD has laid on him the iniquity of us all" (Isaiah 53:4-6).

There truly is no mountain of sin high enough, no valley of despair low enough, and no river of tears wide enough to keep God's grace from you. Jesus' death and resurrection guarantee this.

❧☙

Thank you, Jesus, for your wide grace and deep love for me and all sinners. Amen.

"In my Father's house are many rooms; if it were not so, I would have told you." (John 14:2)

God's grace will bring glory

Clichés are so irritating. Perhaps because you hear them so often, they lose the impact they once had. For example, the only things certain in life are death and taxes. If you've never heard this truism, then undoubtedly it may start you thinking. But since you've no doubt heard it before, it probably just went in one ear and out the other. Another example of an overused cliché is this: Nobody knows what the future holds.

Both of the above clichés deal with the future. The future seems to be something many people dwell on. Many want to know what the future will hold for them, so they call their "psychic" friend or read their horoscopes. Others choose to live their lives as if there will be no tomorrow. Still others are so busy stockpiling for the future that they don't take the time to enjoy today. Some are so terrified of what the future may hold that they refuse to even think about it. How sad!

It's sad because that is not at all the approach the Lord God wants you or any one of his children to take toward the future. The Lord wants you to be confident about the future, not fearful. He wants you to look forward to the future, not dread it. Jesus wants you to live today mindful of what the future holds for you as his child. He promises you that the future is in his hands. With that promise, you don't have to worry about whether you'll have enough money or materials saved up. What is necessary to know about the future God has made known to you in his Word.

Jesus says to you in his Word, "In my Father's house are many rooms; if it were not so, I would have told you." Do you see what he is saying to you about your future? There is a room for you in your heavenly Father's mansion. God's grace will bring you to the glory of heaven, because God's grace has already brought you to saving faith in Jesus Christ as your Savior. If that wasn't the case, he would have told you. But he's telling you your future. What a glorious future God's grace has in store for you! Praise God with your life now as you, through the Word and sacrament, get ready for the kingdom of glory.

❦

My gracious, heavenly Father, I look forward to the glory that you have in store for me. Amen.

"I am going there to prepare a place for you." (John 14:2)

A kingdom of glory is prepared for you

When was the last time you hosted a party? Whether it was just a small gathering of friends or a big blockbuster, undoubtedly you put some time and effort into getting everything prepared. Preparation seems to be a key to having a successful party, although you can't possibly anticipate or be prepared for everything that could happen. Unfortunately, many people find themselves frantic as the party approaches. They may not be as prepared as they'd like to be, or they may be apprehensive about who's coming to the party. With those worries, they have a hard time enjoying themselves.

Being apprehensive, being frantic, and being unable to enjoy oneself are all things that have been deleted by God's grace. When it comes to your place in the kingdom of glory, everything has been done. Jesus has prepared a place for you. Being frantic isn't necessary because Jesus has taken care of the arrangements. Not being able to enjoy oneself doesn't apply because Jesus has taken the worry out of the picture. How?

The sinless Son of God lived a perfect life in your place, suffered in your place, endured the punishment your sins deserved, and died for you. Since he did all this for you and God accepted it as full payment for you, Jesus left your apprehension, anxiety, and worry buried in the grave he rose from. Jesus' time and effort prepared a place for you in his kingdom of glory.

Since he did all this for you, you don't want to be selfish about it. He did the same thing for the entire world. Wouldn't you like to have company at the eternal celebration Jesus has prepared? Wouldn't you like your relatives and friends to come too? Then you'll want to tell about what Jesus has prepared to those who don't know. Share your invitation with others. Jesus encourages you to do just that: "Go and make disciples of all nations" (Matthew 28:19). You can invite the world by remembering the missionaries in your prayers and by supporting called workers at home and abroad with your offerings. And you'll want to do this now, because the time is coming when this important work of preaching and teaching the gospel won't be able to be done any longer. What a great way to say, "Thank you, Jesus, for your time and effort on my behalf."

Keep me prepared, Lord, for your final summons. Amen.

"If I go and prepare a place for you, I will come back and take you to be with me that you also may be where I am."
(John 14:3)

The King of glory will take you home

A number of years ago, John Denver sang this line: "Take me home, country roads." The whole song was about the singer's deep desire to return home, to go back where he was comfortable and felt loved. The song touched a desire we all have. We desire to go home, where we belong.

Do journeys away from home stir up the same longing in you? Does the distance between you and your loved ones cause your heart to grow fonder? Does being separated from where you really want to be cause you to feel anxious? Does a feeling of great anticipation sweep over you when you know that you're going home after having been gone for a while? How would you feel if you found out you couldn't ever go home again? Going home is what Jesus focuses on in the words of today's Bible reading. He was going home, not to Bethlehem or Nazareth or one of the other towns where he lived here on earth. He was returning to his Father's house after having been gone for about 33 years. He was going home because he was about to finish the work his Father had sent him to do. Because he would finish the work he was sent to do, he could make this wonderful promise to us in today's Bible reading: "I will come back and take you to be with me that you also may be where I am."

You are going home, to your real home, to the home Jesus has prepared for you in his kingdom of glory. You don't know when, but the fact remains that you are going home. Jesus' life, death, and resurrection guarantee it. God's grace has created faith in your heart to believe it. Because Jesus, your King, promises it, it's as good as done. All that's left is the waiting—no wondering ifs, no disappointing maybes, just an eager longing to go home.

While you're waiting, don't sit around with your bags packed. Make the most of the time you have left. Share the Word with others so that it will be an even bigger homecoming!

∾⊙⊙∾

Here I am, Lord; take me; take me home! Amen.

"You know the way to the place where I am going."
(John 14:4)

God's grace has revealed the way to glory

Have you ever been lost? Not the "walk out of the shopping mall into the parking lot and can't find your car" type of lost but the "just can't get to where you want to go no matter how hard you try" kind of lost. Maybe that happened to you when you were quite young and somehow got separated from your parents. Perhaps it happened to you recently when you were in a strange place. It's not a good feeling, is it? No one likes to feel helpless. Have you noticed? People who are lost are pretty easy to spot.

By nature we are lost. We are hopelessly lost. Our sinful nature doesn't like to admit that we are lost and that we can't find our way to God. Yet the sinful nature does a very thorough job of demonstrating that we are lost and separated from God. Jesus said, "Out of men's hearts, come evil thoughts, sexual immorality, theft, murder, adultery, greed, malice, deceit, lewdness, envy, slander, arrogance and folly" (Mark 7:21,22). It's worse. No matter how hard we try, we can't find the way to God's grace on our own. We can't even make one right turn onto the path that leads to God. The prophet Isaiah makes that very clear when he writes, "All our righteous acts are like filthy rags" (Isaiah 64:6).

But God's grace has changed all that. God's grace has found us. God's grace has made us children of God. We have become "heirs of God and co-heirs with Christ" (Romans 8:17) through the gift of faith in Christ Jesus. Instead of being lost and bound for hell, we are found and bound for glory. God's grace has shown us the way. God's grace has shown us our Savior. He is "the way and the truth and the life" (John 14:6).

So why would we want to do anything that would give someone the impression that we are still lost? Why would we neglect the very means of grace by which we were found—the gospel? Why wouldn't we want to spend the rest of our time on this earth thanking, praising, and serving God because of his amazing grace, which has revealed the way to eternal glory?

⁓◖◗⁓

Thanks, Lord, for your amazing grace, which will bring me to glory. Amen.

You see, at just the right time, when we were still powerless,
Christ died for the ungodly. (Romans 5:6)

Love for the ungodly

Psychologists agree that people don't really want to see themselves as they truly are. When Queen Elizabeth I ruled England, she was never hailed for her beauty. As she grew older, what little beauty she had disappeared. To spare the queen, her maids had all the mirrors removed from the palace, which prompted one journalist to write, "The queen has not had the heart to look herself in the face for the last twenty years."

When we join the congregation in the act of confession on Sunday morning, we paint a word-picture of ourselves that is far from regal: "poor, miserable sinner." The words may roll easily from our lips after years of use, but they are still the truth. The condition of our hearts is that of a dirty, stained rag. Poisonous words spew out of our mouths. The excuse: "Well, what did you expect? I'm only human!" But that only underscores the fact that we humans are guilty sinners.

Didn't God have a right to expect more from his creation? He had a right to expect perfection. But in return for his love, he received rebellion. Paul accurately summarizes the root of our sin to be ungodliness. We haven't simply missed the mark established by God; we haven't only failed to measure up. By nature we are in every way ungodly, utterly hostile toward God and enemies of God.

Not at all a pretty picture! It is no wonder that we do not care to have the mirror of God's law remind us of what we are—and to what terrible extent we should be punished. But as powerless as the queen was to prevent the deterioration brought on by age, so powerless are we to change the image of our sinfulness. The situation would appear to be hopeless. Unregenerated and helpless, we could not establish a loving relationship with God.

But God in his infinite love and compassion did not allow us to die in our weakness. According to "God's set purpose and foreknowledge" (Acts 2:23), Christ Jesus died in behalf of all people, all of whom were ungodly. What a comforting truth! Just think, Jesus' death was no accident. Motivated only by his own mercy and desire to save us, God reached down in love into the mire and muck of our wretchedness. He did not hesitate to pay the price justly required of us. Truly, was there ever love like this?

୧৩⊚૭৩৬

Dear Lord, in humble awe we bend our knees
Our grateful thanks to pay.
Enable each believing heart
With joy to say,
"My Savior died for me!" Amen.

*Very rarely will anyone die for a righteous man, though
for a good man someone might possibly dare to die.
(Romans 5:7)*

Love's value of a life

"It is a far, far better thing that I do, than I have ever done." So Charles
Dickens concludes his literary classic A *Tale of Two Cities*. Sydney Carton
goes to the guillotine and gives his life in the place of another. It is the
stuff of which good novels are made, but how true is it in real life?

"Very rarely will anyone die for a righteous man," declares Paul in
today's reading. Now and then it will happen. A pilot nose-dives his crippled plane into the woods to avoid a populated area. A soldier is posthu-
mously decorated for suicidal gallantry that spared the lives of the
others in his company. But occurrences like this are extremely rare.
Even then, one life is given for one other life or for a handful of lives.

What is the value of a life? your life? my life? Are we worth dying
for? Would someone else make the supreme sacrifice of his own life to
spare us? Some might say that is hardly a fair question. Yet it is the very
question God himself asks and answers for us.

Unlike the chemist who reduces humans to the basic elements of
their physical bodies and declares their value at the current market
price, God has marked every soul as priceless. He made us and gave us
life. Isaiah rightly declared, "Yet, O LORD, you are our Father. We are the
clay, you are the potter; we are all the work of your hand" (Isaiah 64:8).

Perhaps for a good person someone might give his life. But we were
not good people before God. We weren't even righteous or law-abiding.
We were the ungodly, as yesterday's reading reminded us. We had no
claim upon God's love, no right to look to God for deliverance. Yet—most
improbable event of all—God gave his life to spare the ungodly, not just
any life but his life, the life of his own Son. No momentary, spontaneous
burst of heroism inspired God's sacrifice. Love planned and love carried
out the death of Jesus—not one life for one but the One for all.

> He saw me ruined in the Fall,
> Yet loved me notwithstanding all.
> He saved me from my lost estate—
> His loving-kindness, oh, how great! (TLH 340:2)

※

**Father in heaven, we thank you for the importance your love
placed upon us, unworthy though we were, for Jesus' sake. Amen.**

God demonstrates his own love for us in this: While we were still sinners, Christ died for us. (Romans 5:8)

He loved us first

It is our human nature to do what we enjoy first and postpone the unpleasant tasks. In some instances, it may make no difference in what sequence we do things. At other times, the order may make all the difference in the world.

It may be more pleasant to wash and polish a new car than to mow the lawn we have mowed so many times before. But if later it begins to rain, it would have been better to have mowed the lawn first.

It may not matter whether Tommy plays baseball or does his homework first after school. But if later he doesn't have enough time to finish those studies, the next day in the classroom he will wish he had completed his homework before he picked up his glove to play.

In God's plan of salvation, Christ's death was the basis for any change brought about in us. It could not be otherwise, since "we were still sinners." We could not approach God to sue for peace. The searchlight of God's holiness exposed the corruptness of our lives. We had to admit we had fallen far short of his requirements. His law justly condemned us.

On the other hand, neither could the holy God accept us, the ungodly, until he had dealt with our sin. Forgiveness and acceptance could not come until atonement had been made. Oh blessed and holy day when God's love went into action! Instead of abandoning us to die in our sins, he decreed the death of his own Son on our behalf. When Jesus died on Calvary—the innocent for the guilty—God's justice was satisfied. Our debt was marked "Paid in full." Christ absorbed the sentence of condemnation that had been passed on us. From before the world's foundation, this was God's gracious plan for us.

"Don't tell me you love me! Show me!" we sometimes say to one another. In our devotional text for today, the Holy Spirit is nudging us, urging us to take God at his Word, but not blindly. The gospel is more than a message from God saying, "I love you." The Scriptures present concrete proof of the depths of God's love—in the death of Jesus Christ. By nature we are afraid to meet our Maker. We know what we deserve. But once we have visited the cross, we are no longer afraid. There we see Christ crucified for us. And "we love because he first loved us" (1 John 4:19).

Dear Father in heaven, we thank you for the evidence of your love. We pray that our love for you might never grow cold, in Jesus' name. Amen.

10

Since we have now been justified by his blood, how much more shall we be saved from God's wrath through him!
(Romans 5:9)

Love did more than expected

The Bible tells us that the forgiveness of sins comes only through the shedding of blood. Even before Mount Sinai, where God prescribed specific animal sacrifices, the principle of blood atonement was recognized among his people.

After the first sin in the Garden of Eden, God provided animal skins as coverings for Adam and Eve's nakedness. They had attempted to cover themselves with leaves, but as unavailing as that effort was, so too was their attempt to hide their guilt from God. In clothing them, God provided a temporary, superficial covering for the body of the sinner. Even to do that, however, an innocent creature had to die.

The animal offerings of Abel, Noah, Abraham, and others, as well as the Passover lamb and sin offerings at the temple, required the death of innocent substitutes to cover sinners' guilt. Yet all that ocean of blood did not remove a single sin. The sacrifices merely prefigured the slaying of the innocent Lamb of God for the sin of the world. His was the once-for-all sacrifice God had in mind already in Eden, and long before.

By the blood of Christ, declares Paul, we have been justified. Justification is not our action. God declares sinners pardoned not because we are innocent but because he judged his Son to be guilty in our place. The blood of Jesus covers our shame and protects us from the judgment of God.

Yet love did even more. God credited not only Christ's death to our accounts but the righteousness of Jesus' life. His blood removed our guilt, and God credited his life of perfect obedience to us. In Christ, God has given us the only covering that he will accept. Love gives us more than we could ever expect or have a right to claim.

Paul's words remind us there is a hell. A day will come when the wrath of God will be poured out against all the ungodliness and unrighteousness of men. Yet we who have put our trust in Christ will never experience that wrath. How can we be sure of this? God has given his Word. Our security rests upon the death of Jesus as our Substitute and God's declaration that there is not now, no, nor will there ever be, any condemnation of those who believe in Christ Jesus.

✦

Gracious Lord, we thank you that your love has removed our sin and has clothed us with the righteousness of Jesus, in which we will be able to stand before you. Amen.

Love ended hostility

Over two hundred years ago, a famous New England minister named Jonathan Edwards delivered a sermon entitled "Sinners in the Hands of an Angry God." In the style of that day, he described a scene of God holding sinners over the pit of hell as one might hold a loathsome insect over a fire. Today many would deride such preaching as "fire and brimstone." However, the danger in our permissive age lies in the opposite extreme. Today the awfulness of sin is usually minimized. To offend God is brushed aside as a minor infraction, either because people consider themselves as better than "sinners" or because God is thought of as being a weakling, or at least indulgent.

A prominent bishop recently remarked, "I don't have a God who demands his pound of flesh. I would never ask anyone who owed me anything to pay in this gruesome manner." His reference was to the death of Jesus. He saw only the disgrace of Calvary, not the necessity. He did not appreciate God's wrath against sin. Therefore, he did not appreciate God's love in sending his Son to rescue the sinner and did not glorify God for his mercy.

The whole trouble lies with us, says Paul, not with God. We were the ones who had alienated ourselves from God. We needed to be changed, not God. Yet without any union to bargain in our favor, God's love went into action to change the miserable status of all mankind.

When Christ died, the status of the whole world of sinners was completely changed. No longer is the world under condemnation. It is a world whose debt has been paid in full. It is a world in which the angels of Bethlehem continue to shout, "Peace!"—not the kind of peace the world is looking for but the precious peace of eternal reconciliation with God. Those who are lost are lost only because they have rejected the peace that God purchased for them on the cross.

The cross of Jesus is gruesome evidence of God's wrath against sin, but for that very reason, it is the glorious evidence that our sins have been taken away. The cross of Christ is the evidence of God's love and of our new relationship with him. Knowing this, let us rejoice and eagerly serve our Savior-God who so loves us.

❦

O Father, when we tremble because of our sins, hold the cross of Jesus before us. Remind us that we have been accepted by you through the blood of Jesus Christ, your Son, our Lord. Amen.

12

If, when we were God's enemies, we were reconciled to him through the death of his Son, how much more, having been reconciled, shall we be saved through his life! (Romans 5:10)

Love will follow through

"Daddy, how do you know you are going to heaven?" Becky asked her father. Good question. How can a Christian be sure of salvation? Indeed, isn't it presumptuous to believe that one is saved before that heavenly roll is called? No! In fact, it is arrogant and presumptuous and damnable to doubt it.

In the reassuring words of our lesson, Paul examines the certainty of our salvation. He concludes that Christ died and rose again in order to establish our salvation as a certainty. A courtroom lawyer would appreciate the case Paul presents. Were we not God's enemies? Worse—our whole being was hostile toward God. Yet didn't his Son, when we were still God's enemies, die for us? We know that was so. And didn't his substitutionary death enable God to declare us righteous? Haven't we been brought into fellowship with God, reconciled through Christ? Certainly! The gospel repeatedly declares this. Why, then, would God have done all this except for our eternal salvation? Yes, salvation is the end result of God's reconciling us to himself. And we know this for a fact, since Jesus himself rose from the dead and promised to return and to take us to live with him.

As Paul said to the Corinthians—what good is it all if Christ did not rise from the dead? If we have no hope of eternal life, we are stupid to remain Christians. But eternal life is the center of our hope, through him who died and rose again. And to preserve this hope, our Lord has given his Holy Spirit as "a deposit guaranteeing our inheritance" (Ephesians 1:14). The Spirit has brought us to realize and to acknowledge all Christ has done for us. And he is working to keep us in that faith. Certainly God, who has done so much for us, will not fail to follow through to the goal.

Yes, Christ is not dead but alive. And did he not promise, "Because I live, you also will live" (John 14:19)? Even now he is working to that end, preparing a place for us, and working in us to bring us there.

Yes, to be a Christian is to be certain of salvation, that is, to be certain of God's ability to keep his promises in Christ.

❧◉◉☙

Father, remove all doubt and help us keep our eyes of faith firmly fixed on the cross and the empty tomb of Christ, our Savior. Amen.

Jesus said to [Martha], "I am the resurrection and the life. He who believes in me will live, even though he dies; and whoever lives and believes in me will never die. Do you believe this?" "Yes, Lord," she told him, "I believe that you are the Christ, the Son of God, who was to come into the world." (John 11:25-27)

Faith confesses the resurrection

Jesus' friend Martha was grieving over the death of her brother. The way she dealt with her grief provides a wonderful example for Christians today as they struggle with their own losses.

Martha and her sister, Mary, had tried to get Jesus to come to their home while Lazarus was still sick. But Jesus waited until Lazarus had died. As Jesus approached their home, it was Martha who came running to meet Jesus. This meeting gave Jesus the opportunity to minister to Martha and for her to confess her faith. Jesus said, "Your brother will rise again" (John 11:23). Martha responded that she believed. Jesus went on and told her, "I am the resurrection and the life. He who believes in me will live, even though he dies; and whoever lives and believes in me will never die."

Then Jesus said, "Do you believe this?" He wanted her to confess her faith so she could hear with her own ears where she placed her trust. She confessed, "Yes, Lord, I believe that you are the Christ, the Son of God, who was to come into the world."

It is one thing to sit in church on Easter Sunday and sing "I Know That My Redeemer Lives." But it is quite another to sing that song at the casket or graveside of a family member or friend. Yet that is what Martha did, and that is what every Christian does.

So often when people are faced with going to a Christian funeral, they worry. They think, "I don't know what to say." But that is only half true. You may not know exactly what you should say to comfort the grieving survivors over their loss, but you do know that you can say with Martha about Christian loved ones who have died, "Your loved one will rise and be with Christ, who is the resurrection and the life."

❦

Risen Savior, let me confess your resurrection in my life. When I or those around me must deal with death, empower me to say, "I believe in my Savior and know he is the resurrection and the life!" Amen.

14

"Come, follow me," Jesus said, "and I will make you fishers of men." At once they left their nets and followed him. (Matthew 4:19,20)

Step forward and be a fisher of men!

Fishing is hard work! If you really want to catch a lot of fish, you have to work for it. A good fisherman knows this. He has crawled through brush and over trees to get to that perfect spot on the stream. He has gotten up in the middle of the night and has given up precious sleep so that his boat is in the right spot at the right time. He has stood against the cold wind, and his hands have ached as he has tried different nets and baits. He has also come in after long, hard days with nothing to show for his work.

Fishing for people is just as hard. You, as Christian witnesses, know this. You have to go out at different times and to different locations. Your sleep is interrupted because you have been given an opportunity to reach out and help someone. You try different approaches, and you work hard to be in the right place at the right time to share Jesus with the hurting and brokenhearted. At times people ridicule you and try to keep you from going out and seeking the lost. And, sadly, there are occasions when you return discouraged, sad, and empty-handed.

Why then did the disciples drop everything and leave their occupations to become fishers of men? Why should they have left tough jobs for an even tougher one? The answer is that the disciples had put their faith in Jesus, the Savior of the world. Jesus is the only one who can pull people from the depths of guilt and shame. Jesus is the only one who can snatch people from the rapids and rocks of sin that so easily sweep us away. Jesus is the Son of God who left heaven to seek the lost. When Jesus chose some of his followers to help him reach the lost, they followed him with joy.

How wonderful that God has found us! What a blessing that God has given us the message of Jesus to share! The first disciples stepped forward in faith, and God made them into fishers of men. Brothers and sisters, step forward in faith, and God will give you opportunities to catch people for him!

⌒⊙⌒

Lord Jesus, give us the faith to be fishers of men. Give us the courage and love to go out and speak about our faith in this world. And then, Lord, fill our nets! Amen.

*Be filled with the Spirit. Speak to one another with psalms,
hymns and spiritual songs. Sing and make music in your
heart to the Lord. (Ephesians 5:18,19)*

Sing to the Lord

Luther once said, "Music drives the devil away." He meant Christian music, of course. In his own life he demonstrated this way of expressing Christian faith in song. Music played an important role in his family devotions and friendly get-togethers. His hymns and liturgical arrangements continue to be sources of inspiration in our congregational worship over four hundred years after they were composed. Singing to the Lord was a natural part of his Spirit-filled life.

Being filled with the Spirit is characteristic of every Christian. One of the finest ways of expressing this, as Paul points out in today's text, is to "speak to one another with psalms, hymns and spiritual songs."

"With psalms, hymns" reminds us of our congregational worship. Our Lutheran liturgy contains portions of Scripture beautifully arranged in word and song to help God's children bring their praises to their Savior and receive a message of hope from the God of their salvation. Through the seasons of the church year, Christians are reminded of God's mighty acts of grace as well as of their need to bring joyous response for undeserved blessings.

"With . . . spiritual songs" reminds us of special choral presentations that beautify our church services.

"Spiritual songs" also brings to mind times when groups of Christians would come together informally, gather around a piano, and sing hymns and carols just for the sheer joy of singing to the Lord. Is that still being done? Or has television also managed to relegate this wonderful custom to "days of yore"?

"But I'm not a very good singer," someone might say. Paul answers that excuse immediately. "Make music in your heart," he says. Do it "to the Lord." You're not there to glorify your voice but to praise the God of your salvation. A musical performance in church can be ever so technically perfect, but if it doesn't come from the heart to the Lord, it is only like an empty gong or a clanging cymbal as far as God is concerned.

❦

Grant that your Spirit prompt my praises;
Then shall my singing surely please your ear.
Sweet are the sounds my heart then raises;
My prayer in truth and spirit you will hear.
Then shall your Spirit lift my heart in love
To sing these psalms to you, my God above. Amen. (CW 189:3)

16

Submit to one another out of reverence for Christ.
(Ephesians 5:21)

Be considerate of others

With this verse, Paul concludes a section of his letter in which he gives examples of what it means to be a wise Christian. It means, first of all, to take care how we live. The Christian life is to be different from that of an unbeliever. It means to value our brief time on earth in the light of eternity and to make good use of the hours that bring us closer to our final goal. It means understanding the Lord's good and gracious will for us in the Holy Scriptures. It means finding life's fulfillment not in pleasure seeking or excess but in cultivating spiritual values. It means singing to the Lord with hearts and voices. It means giving thanks to God for everything, always aware that he knows what is best for us.

Paul's closing admonition in today's verse touches on interpersonal relationships. That's finally where Christian wisdom is reflected in this life more than anywhere else. How do we get along with our fellow human beings—at home, at work, at school, wherever we are? What Christian quality should predominate?

"Submit to one another," Paul says. From a worldly standpoint, that's not a very popular thing to do. Worldly wisdom tells us to dominate, not to be submissive. We are told that pride, honor, and ambition are the qualities to be cultivated. Selfish desires and vain conceits are the driving forces in trying to get ahead of others. And who will deny that these forces lie within the nature of every one of us?

But these are the very forces that cause so much grief in this world of sin. At the bottom of those quarrels that take place between husband and wife, employer and employee, neighbors, and the like, there is usually some form of selfishness and conceit. Pride is Satan's most powerful ally.

How do we counteract this evil force within our nature? Paul says, "Submit to one another." Cultivate humility. And do this out of reverence for Christ. In our Savior, we as Christians have a perfect model of what it means to lead a Christian life.

His life was dedicated to serving others. He washed his disciples' feet. He died on a shameful cross in order to accomplish his saving purpose for all mankind. Yet all the world belonged to him. "Your attitude should be the same as that of Christ Jesus," Paul wrote to the Philippians (2:5).

The Christian life shows itself first and foremost in our day-to-day associations with others, in our being considerate of the needs of those whom God has placed next to us in life.

❦

Lord, help us have the mind of Christ in serving others. Amen.

Under the Shepherd's personal care

We normally don't refer to governing officials in a personal way. We might refer to the leader of our country as "the president" or even "our president." But rarely do we refer to him as "my president." Part of the reason lies in the fact that the president is not my president exclusively. He is the president for all citizens of the country. But another reason is that most of us don't have a personal relationship with the president. After all, we often find ourselves using phrases like "I took my car in to my mechanic" or "My hairdresser told me to use this great new product." We realize that these people don't serve us exclusively either, but because we've established some kind of personal relationship with them, we refer to them in this personal way.

Our relationship with God can be viewed in the same way. Certainly he is God of all, so we pray, "Our Father in heaven." And certainly he is worthy of our awe and respect, so we sometimes refer to him as "the Lord God Almighty." But we also have a personal relationship with him that he established for us in Christ Jesus. The Good Shepherd who died and rose again is my Shepherd. He died for my sins. He rose again that I might live. And now, ascended to heavenly glory, he watches over me with his gracious care.

As we look at the text of this beloved and well-known 23rd psalm, we see different aspects of that care. But first and foremost, we see that it is an intensely personal care. King David understood this well. He had been a shepherd in his youth and knew the intense care and personal concern he had had for each sheep in his flock. Since he also knew that by faith he was part of God's flock, he was confident that the Good Shepherd had the same personal care and concern for him.

Such confidence is not reserved for David alone. It is for all believers. Job expressed this when he exclaimed, "I know that my Redeemer lives" (Job 19:25), and the apostle Thomas expressed it when he cried out "My Lord and my God!" (John 20:28). Such confidence belongs to you too because God has called you his own. Express that confidence. Go boldly before your Lord with every outpouring of your heart. Say along with David, "The LORD is my shepherd."

⁓⊙⊙⊙⁓

Dear Lord, thank you for making me your own dear child in Christ Jesus. Through your Word, strengthen my faith, and lead me to express this confidence in everything I say and do. Amen.

18

The LORD is my shepherd, I shall not be in want.
(Psalm 23:1)

Under the Shepherd's lordship

The comfort of knowing that I am under the personal care of my Shepherd heightens when I recognize that my Shepherd is the Lord.

He certainly has every right to be my Lord. "By him all things were created: things in heaven and on earth, visible and invisible, whether thrones or powers or rulers or authorities; all things were created by him and for him" (Colossians 1:16).

This is awesome information! When I look up into the night sky and see thousands upon thousands of celestial bodies, the sight fills me with wonder. But when I realize that my Shepherd called all these things into being with a simple command and that he rules over all of them, that is truly awe-inspiring.

When I pick up a handful of dirt, it may not look very exciting. But when I place it under a microscope and find millions of intricate microorganisms working together in concert, I recognize the Lord's wisdom and the careful design he put into his creation.

With this same wisdom and careful design, the Lord also created me. He gave me abilities and members that all work together in ways more complex than I can imagine. He gave me a soul, which sets me apart from all the rest of his creation.

I am not my own master as I would sometimes like to be. I cannot create anything out of nothing. I cannot sustain life without using something created. I cannot bring something dead back to life. But my Shepherd can, and he has done all of these things.

And so I realize that I am under his lordship. I depend on him just as the rest of his creation does: "In him we live and move and have our being" (Acts 17:28).

Yet my Shepherd, though he is Lord of all, does not lord it over me. He is not a tyrant. Instead, he is loving and compassionate. He is personally concerned about me. He knows me so well that he even assures me that "the very hairs of your head are all numbered" (Luke 12:7).

Most important, he knows my greatest need—my need of forgiveness. His great love and mercy compelled him to do for me what I am unable to do. He rescued me from my worst enemies—sin, death, and the devil. This love that my Shepherd first showed to me motivates me and gives me the confidence to place myself under his lordship. He knows me better than anyone. He knows my deepest need. Why would I want any other lord?

❧◉◗❧

Dear Lord, give me the daily confidence to place myself under your divine lordship, humbly submitting to your will. Amen.

He makes me lie down in green pastures, he leads me beside quiet waters. (Psalm 23:2)

Under the Shepherd's leadership

It is often said that the best leadership is leadership by example. We know what an important role this plays in the parenting process. It is also a concern for those who have leadership roles in the government or the church.

King David, the author of this psalm, understood the important role of being a leader. In his early days, he had been a shepherd. He knew his flocks depended on his ability to lead them to green pastures and cool, clean water. Later in life, when he became the king of Israel, his shepherding skills were once again summoned. He led the nation in battle and in obedience to God.

When David failed by committing adultery and murder, the Lord reminded him through Nathan the prophet, "By doing this you have made the enemies of the LORD show utter contempt" (2 Samuel 12:14). Not only had he injured his personal relationship with the Lord through his sin, but as the leader of Israel, he had set a bad example—a double standard.

The Good Shepherd, however, is a perfect leader. His example is perfect obedience to God's law. But we, his flock, do not reap the benefits of his leadership by following his example. In fact, we are completely unable to do so.

When a sheep falls down an embankment or comes face-to-face with a wild animal, the last thing that sheep needs is a good example to follow. No matter how hard the shepherd might try to teach the poor sheep to climb back up the embankment or to fight off the ferocious predator, the sheep would not be able to do it. Even if the shepherd provided a perfect example, the sheep would still be lost.

In such a situation, the sheep needs a rescuer, or a savior, not a good example. That is what our Good Shepherd provides. He laid down his life for us, his sheep. He leads us by conquering all our enemies for us. He alone gives us peace of mind and soul by assuring us that our most deadly foes can no longer harm us. This gives us confidence to lie down in the green pastures he provides and to follow him beside the quiet waters. This is the comfort David sought when he fell.

God's Word and sacraments provide us the spiritual food and drink we need. They assure us of the peaceful life the Good Shepherd has provided for us. May we ever hold them dear and use them often.

❧◎◑☙

Good Shepherd, thank you for leading me to peace and quietness of soul by providing everything needed for my salvation. Amen.

20

He restores my soul. He guides me in paths of righteousness for his name's sake. (Psalm 23:3)

Under the Shepherd's guidance

Most people wouldn't think about going into a dangerous jungle or wilderness without a guide. That would be foolish. A guide is someone who knows the way and can lead us to our destination in a way that avoids danger.

Yet how often don't we try to go through life without a guide? How often don't we try to find the way on our own by following whatever path seems to be the most pleasurable or easy? Like wandering sheep, we often forget that our Shepherd is a guide who knows the way. Sometimes we feel the path he chooses for us is too difficult. Instead, we follow our own desires for what appear to be greener pastures. Only too late do we realize that we have gotten ourselves into danger and are separated from the flock and from the protection of the Shepherd. We run into this problem when we seek to find our peace and joy from the things of this world.

Sin has marred our souls and perverted our thinking. But sin has done an even greater damage. It has broken our relationship with God. True peace and joy can only be found in Christ, who has restored our relationship to him by his death on the cross. It is Christ himself who "restores my soul" through the gospel. Then the Holy Spirit builds us into the temple of God. He creates in us clean hearts. He renews our faith in his promises. He restores us to the flock. He enables us to follow the guidance of our Good Shepherd.

Life can sometimes feel like a bumpy, rut-filled, dangerous road. We don't know what lies ahead of us. Sometimes just thinking about it sends shivers up our spines. But the sure promise of the psalmist calms our fears. Christ is our Good Shepherd. He knows the way that leads to our eternal rest, and he will guide us safely to that destination.

That doesn't mean the way will always be easy. Like many of the saints who have gone on before us, we may be asked to suffer injustices in this life. We may at times need to shoulder heavy burdens during our earthly sojourns. But the goal is clear. The paths of righteousness lead to our true home with the Good Shepherd. This is his territory, so we can trust fully that he knows the way. We therefore confess with another psalmist, "You hold me by my right hand. You guide me with your counsel, and afterward you will take me into glory" (Psalm 73:23,24).

⌘

Good Shepherd, guide me all the days of my life so that I do not wander away from you. Keep me safe in your protecting care. Amen.

Even though I walk through the valley of the shadow of death, I will fear no evil, for you are with me; your rod and your staff, they comfort me. (Psalm 23:4)

Under the Shepherd's protection

It is common practice among sheep ranchers to take their flocks to summer grazing lands up on the mountain meadows. On higher ground, grazing areas are lush and plentiful during the hot summer months. But getting there often requires traversing some rough terrain. Interestingly enough, the valleys encountered on the way to this higher ground can be the most treacherous. Here the raging mountain streams present dangerous obstacles for the flocks. Here predators come to seek their prey. And here the sunlight rarely reaches, leaving a dark and dreary atmosphere.

Our lives on this earth are filled with many such sojourns through dark valleys. These sojourns are not pleasant, but they are inevitable. We cannot avoid them, and the Good Shepherd does not shield us from them.

Neither does he leave us in the dark valleys to die. David writes that even though we "walk through" these valleys, we don't need to fear. Why not? Because our Good Shepherd is with us. Under his care we are protected. The frustrations, disappointments, and discouragements of this life trouble our souls. The disasters, dilemmas, and depressions of living with a sinful nature darken our spirits. But these are not dead-end roads. The Good Shepherd protects us with daily oversight and uses these experiences to lead us to higher ground. He builds and strengthens our faith through these times of trial and tribulation, because "we know that suffering produces perseverance; perseverance, character; and character, hope" (Romans 5:3,4).

Even when the dark valleys seem to end dead in physical death, our Good Shepherd assures us that there is still nothing to fear. Since he has conquered death, death has lost its sting. He is able to protect us from even this worst of enemies. Death is now simply the door through which we pass to go on to higher ground—to an eternity of glory with our Good Shepherd.

Yes, the dark valleys in life are real, and yes, they are unpleasant. But "our present sufferings are not worth comparing with the glory that will be revealed in us" (Romans 8:18).

꧁◎◎꧂

Dear Lord, protector of my body and soul, be my guard and shield through all my days. And when my sojourn on this earth is over, graciously receive me into your heavenly kingdom. Amen.

22

You prepare a table before me in the presence of my enemies. You anoint my head with oil; my cup overflows. (Psalm 23:5)

Under the Shepherd's richness

A shepherd knows that to provide a rich supply of vegetation for his flock, he must place his flock in areas that are potentially dangerous. He wants to protect his flock from harm but keeping them in the barn all day would not fulfill their needs for exercise, food, and water. So he must take them out to fields and streams.

However, there predators lurk. There dangerous terrain awaits. There poisonous weeds sometimes grow among the beneficial grasses. These are enemies of the sheep. The shepherd wants to protect his flock from these dangers, but in order to expose his flock to the lush abundance of the land, he must allow them to forage in the presence of their enemies.

The Good Shepherd spreads out a table of riches for us, his flock. He gives us all our earthly needs and provides us with the spiritual banquet of his Word and sacrament. All this he does in the presence of our enemies. You see, the Good Shepherd wants to keep us safe too. But before we die, taking us out of the world is not an option. When he was here on this earth, Jesus, our Good Shepherd, prayed to his Father, "My prayer is not that you take them out of the world but that you protect them from the evil one. They are not of the world, even as I am not of it. Sanctify them by the truth; your word is truth" (John 17:15-17).

The evil one is a real threat to our lives. He goes about like a roaring lion, seeking those whom he might devour (1 Peter 5:8). But unlike the wolves who prey on sheep, he is not so obvious. He is crafty and cunning. He prepares a different table before us and tempts us to eat. He takes things that are dangerous to our spiritual welfare and makes them look like tempting treats. He says, "Here, try this too." It worked in the Garden of Eden, and it has been working ever since.

Don't be fooled. Only the Lord prepares a table that is spiritually wholesome and nourishing. And only the Good Shepherd can take us to the final heavenly banquet where our heads will be anointed with the oil of eternal bliss. The richness of his blessings make our cups overflow.

Partake regularly of the rich table the Lord has prepared for you. Read and hear and learn his Word of Truth. Allow it to sanctify you. Partake of the Sacrament he so graciously offers you. See how your cup overflows!

⌘

O Lord, I thank you for the rich offering you provide me. Help me partake of it regularly so that it may strengthen my soul. Amen.

Surely goodness and love will follow me all the days of my life, and I will dwell in the house of the LORD forever. (Psalm 23:6)

Under the Shepherd's love

Through our study of Psalm 23 we have seen how the glory of the Lord has shined on us as we live under the Shepherd's care. Today we see the height of this glory as we live under his love.

Love is perhaps one of the most overused words in our language. Our frivolous and carefree use of the word has robbed it of its true meaning. Even in church settings, the word has taken on a meaning that merely evokes a warm, emotional feeling.

The apostle John helps us understand the true meaning of the word: "This is love: not that we loved God, but that he loved us and sent his Son as an atoning sacrifice for our sins" (1 John 4:10). The Good Shepherd's love for us led him to give up his life for us. He himself assures us, "I am the good shepherd. The good shepherd lays down his life for the sheep" (John 10:11). He laid down his life for us at Calvary so that we might live forever at peace with God.

What makes it even more remarkable is that no one forced our Good Shepherd to do this. Once again he says, "The reason my Father loves me is that I lay down my life—only to take it up again. No one takes it from me, but I lay it down of my own accord" (John 10:17,18). This is true love! This is what will follow me all the days of my life!

You see, when the promise is made in this last part of the psalm that "surely goodness and love will follow me all the days of my life," it does not mean that I will have some kind of warm, fuzzy, emotional high throughout my life. It means that the love God showed me in Christ will never leave me. It means that it doesn't depend upon the outward circumstances of life. God's love for me is a finished and completed act. His Son, my Good Shepherd, laid down his life as a sacrifice for my sin and then rose triumphant from the grave. God's goodness and this love can never fail me because he does not change like my emotions so often do.

The goodness and love of the Good Shepherd assure me that my dwelling in this world is temporary. My real home is in the house of the Lord, and there I will dwell forever. That's his promise. His promise is guaranteed by his love, and his love is displayed in his sacrifice. What a blessing to be under the Shepherd's love!

⋅◦☙◦⋅

Dear Lord, my Good Shepherd, keep me always safe in your loving care until I reach my heavenly home with you. Amen.

24

"Come to me, all you who are weary and burdened, and I will give you rest." (Matthew 11:28)

Divine rest for human restlessness

Can you imagine this? In the 1930s, Congress almost passed a law calling for a 30-hour workweek. Experts in the 1950s predicted that by the end of the century, Americans would work fewer hours and enjoy far more leisure time. Some futurists even predicted we would work Mondays through Thursdays and take three days off every weekend.

Wow! Were they wrong! During the 1990s the average American's work hours actually increased by one full week. Executives in many companies routinely work 55 or more hours a week. In the half-century between those optimistic predictions and our reality, we even found it necessary to invent a new word—*workaholic*—to describe a person who becomes overwhelmed by or addicted to his or her work.

"Weary and burdened" describes many people we know—maybe many of us.

Jesus had more in mind, however, than physical exhaustion, as powerful as that is. Many in the first-century world felt the crushing expectations of the Law of Moses. Their religious teachers, the Pharisees, had created hundreds more "traditions," which regulated even the minutest details of the people's lives. By Jesus' time, the line between Moses' laws and men's traditions had become blurred for many, and the people's whole religion had become a matter of endless rules and regulations.

So many of them found religion to be a great burden. The more pious were weary of the constant effort they had to exert—frustrated because even when they tried their best to obey, their best was not good enough. The less pious were burdened by guilty consciences, because they knew their lives had not been good enough to earn God's favor.

Are these only ancient problems? Many Americans may seem less religious than they were a generation ago, less burdened by rules and laws and expectations. But don't let appearances fool you. Sins committed during careless youth haunt people as they grow older. Though they may not fully comprehend their guilt before God, they feel burdened by shame and regrets.

Where do we go with our burdens? It doesn't work trying to hide them from God, but Jesus invites us, "Bring them to me." Jesus once lived among us as our brother. Still he lives to be our advocate in heaven. His heart is full of mercy for those with guilty consciences and shameful memories.

He brings divine rest for human restlessness.

◈

Father, we bring all our burdens and sins to you. Forgive us. Restore to us the joy of your salvation. Amen.

"Now this is eternal life: that they may know you, the only true God, and Jesus Christ, whom you have sent."
(John 17:3)

Knowing Jesus brings the glory of eternal life

To talk with someone who's dying—even someone who lives in the Lord and is confident of falling asleep in Jesus—can be difficult. No matter what we say, we fear that we'll fail. We would like to say something meaningful in order to hear the person respond, "That's exactly what I needed to hear!"

I read about a man who was hospitalized. Day after day his daughter assured him that he was going to get better, that God was going to heal him. She was positive that this was what her father needed to hear. One day she repeated her assurances in front of her father's pastor. Her father simply smiled at the pastor and made the sign of the cross over his heart.

Her father understood what Jesus was saying in the words of our Bible verse from Jesus' High Priestly Prayer—that to know God is the supreme purpose of one's existence. To know God, to know Jesus Christ as one's Savior from sin, is how people possess eternal life. This is how people live forever.

Eternal life is the greatest of all possible blessings. It begins when we are brought to faith and become new creatures in Christ. We enter into its full realization when God calls us home.

It can be difficult to remember this when we're down in the dumps. Difficulties at work or at home, spats with friends or loved ones, and all our failures—especially our sins—can make us feel as if our futures are anything but secure. It's at these times that Jesus comes and reminds us, "In this world you will have trouble. But take heart! I have overcome the world" (John 16:33).

You know who the true God is. You know who Jesus is. You know how the Father sent him to be you in a very special sense: to take your place under the law, to live a perfect life in obedience to every single law, and to receive the full punishment for every one of your sins—past, present, and future. Jesus tells you all these things plainly in his Word.

You have eternal life. God grant that when our hours come—whether each is an hour of pain or sorrow or loss or even the final hour of death—we may face them with the same quiet and unshakable trust in God.

☙◉◉❧

Lord Jesus, thank you for winning eternal life for me. Amen.

26

"Because I live, you also will live." (John 14:19)

Disciples live with Jesus

There's life and there's life. God blessed us with physical life through our parents. We thank him for it. We also thank him for our spiritual life. We were born spiritually dead (Ephesians 2:1). We remained in that condition until we were born again of water and the Spirit in Holy Baptism. Through Baptism we were given spiritual life. The Holy Spirit called us to faith in Jesus. We were made heirs of eternal life.

We and all disciples of Jesus owe our spiritual life to God's love for the world—a love so amazing that he "did not spare his own Son, but gave him up for us all" (Romans 8:32). The Father gave him up into death as a sacrifice to take away the sins of the world. Jesus was preparing to make that sacrifice even as he assured his disciples that Maundy Thursday evening: "Because I live, you also will live."

Even though Jesus died, really breathed his last, he lives. He is "the life" (John 14:6). Death and the grave could not hold him. His resurrection on the third day after his death assures us of the victory over sin, death, and Satan. Indeed, Jesus is "the life." He lives!

This was good news for the disciples. Because Jesus lives, they would also live. Through faith in him as their Lord and Savior, they were alive—spiritually alive. And their life with Jesus would continue even after his ascension. They would never be orphans. They would never be left alone. After their sojourn on earth was finished, they would live with Jesus eternally in the home that he prepared for them.

Because Jesus lives, we also live. Through faith in Jesus, who died for our sins and was raised again, we are spiritually alive. Our life with Jesus is a blessed life. We are never alone. He is with us in our trials and troubles. Through his Word he assures us that nothing will be able to separate us from the love of God. He comforts us in our bereavements with the promise of eternal life. Even in our own last hours, his words to Martha will sustain us: "I am the resurrection and the life. He who believes in me will live, even though he dies; and whoever lives and believes in me will never die" (John 11:25,26). Who of us can imagine life without Jesus?

❦

Lord Jesus, thank you for giving your life for us so that we might have spiritual life now and eternal life hereafter. Amen.

Jesus answered, "I am the way and the truth and the life. No one comes to the Father except through me." (John 14:6)

27 September

Jesus is the only way to heaven

There is a heaven, and there is a hell. Everyone goes to one or the other. Every Christian believes that. We also know that our eternity will be spent in heaven. What comfort this gives the children of God! But only Christians can talk with such confidence. It isn't bragging. It's pure confidence. Thanks to God's grace, we know Jesus. He is the only way to heaven.

Bragging? Perish the thought! It's downright humbling. It makes us get down on our knees and thank God that we are among the elect. The sad fact is that the vast majority of the billions of people in the world don't know Jesus as their Savior from sin. They don't know that God became incarnate at Bethlehem. They don't know that the Son of Mary and Son of God died on the cross to atone for the sins of the world. They don't know the excitement that Christendom has to remember the empty tomb on Easter morning. They don't know the gospel of Jesus Christ.

There is no other gospel. There is no other way to heaven. It can't be earned by doing good. It can't be obtained by another savior. There is no other savior. Without Jesus, there is no good news. Without Jesus, there is no heaven. Without Jesus, there is no peace or comfort.

That's the truth. However, many people still believe in Satan's lies. He continues to mislead people. He gets people by the masses to break the First Commandment and put their trust in false gods. False gods are dead gods. They don't even exist, except in the minds of people. They can't do anything to help a person in life or in death. They can't do a thing to get a soul out of hell and into heaven.

That can only be done by Christ, who conquered sin and the grave. There is only one true and living God—the triune God, the God of our salvation. Jesus Christ is the only way to heaven—the only way to life, eternal life.

That's pure comfort. But it also stresses upon us the importance of doing mission work. Eternity in hell is a horrible thought. We have the gospel. We have the Great Commission. Tell others that Jesus is the only way to heaven.

⌒⌒⌒

Lord Jesus, thank you for being the way to heaven. Give us the zeal to share this good news with others. Amen.

28

"In my Father's house are many rooms; if it were not so, I would have told you. I am going there to prepare a place for you." (John 14:2)

Jesus has reserved a place in heaven for you

We had called in advance and had reserved a table for four at the restaurant. However, upon our arrival, there was no table reserved for us. In the confusion of the busy night and the packed crowd, our message didn't get through. There were no reservations.

Wouldn't that be disappointing on judgment day? *Disappointing,* of course, isn't the right word for it. It would be sheer terror if our names weren't written in the book of life! But have no fear. Our names are written in God's Book. "Nothing impure will ever enter it, nor will anyone who does what is shameful or deceitful, but only those whose names are written in the Lamb's book of life" (Revelation 21:27).

Jesus made sure of that. He took away our sins. He did everything necessary to accomplish our salvation and make sure our "reservations" were made for us. We won't have to stand in line before God's throne wondering if our names are on God's list. Christ's death and resurrection assure us that God's arms will be opened wide as he welcomes us into the bliss of heaven. There's nothing to keep us out. Thank God for that. Jesus made it possible.

Jesus comforted his disciples with this passage. Had he not prepared them ahead of time, they might have become disillusioned after he ascended into heaven. But he wasn't going to desert them. The fact was that his job on earth was done; his mission was accomplished. The purpose of his departure was to make ready the place where he could welcome them permanently. What pure comfort that gives the children of God—them and us!

Jesus has a room reserved just for us in his Father's house. The Greek word means "dwelling place, room, abode." Personally, I like the King James Version's rendering of "mansion." That leaves a nice picture in my head. The point is that there is a place for us in heaven. Jesus gives us that guarantee. He should know. He purchased it—with his life. That's an expensive price. That's an expensive place—held on reserve just for us! When you think of it in those terms, our home in heaven is the most expensive place anywhere.

Jesus has it all ready. He's just waiting for our arrival.

Lord Jesus, thank you for purchasing and preparing a place for us in heaven. We anxiously await the day when we can move in. Amen.

"Look at the birds of the air; they do not sow or reap or store away in barns, and yet your heavenly Father feeds them. Are you not much more valuable than they?" (Matthew 6:26)

You are more valuable than birds

Did you know that North America is populated by some 150 million house sparrows? That's a lot of little birds chirping, scratching, living, dying. Chances are you and I don't pay a great deal of attention to the care and feeding of even one of these sparrows. And yet what we overlook, God graciously provides for. In love, God is concerned about the life and death of each and every sparrow. As Jesus once said to his disciples, "Not one of them will fall to the ground apart from the will of your Father" (Matthew 10:29).

As Creator and preserver of life, God provides for all of his creatures, even without our knowledge or assistance. Yet there is one creature God regards more highly than all the rest. That creature is man. Think about the special things God has done for man. God created the first man in his own image. He gave him an immortal soul and conferred on him authority over all creation. When man disobeyed God by eating the forbidden fruit, God sent his Son, Jesus, to live and die in man's place and thus bring man into fellowship with God again. And through the means of grace, God the Holy Spirit calls men and women to faith in Jesus and makes them members of God's family.

All these things mean that you are more valuable to God than the sparrow. You are valuable not because of what you have done for God but, rather, because of what he has done for you. In fact, Scripture declares that as a Christian you enjoy a very special relationship with your Creator. Paul wrote, "You are all sons of God through faith in Christ Jesus" (Galatians 3:26). While sparrows may call God their master, only Christians can call God their Father.

Remember that the next time you see a sparrow hopping around looking for food. Be assured that God does love and care for that bird. But that creature can never be more than God's "pet." But you, dear Christian, are more than that. You are God's precious child. And if God cares for the needs of his pets, how much more will he care for the needs of his children?

❦

Jesus, shepherd of the sheep,
Who your Father's flock does keep,
Safe we wake and safe we sleep,
Guarded still by you. Amen. (CW 436:1)

*Blessed is he whose transgressions are forgiven, whose sins are covered. Blessed is the man whose sin the L*ORD *does not count against him and in whose spirit is no deceit. When I kept silent, my bones wasted away through my groaning all day long. For day and night your hand was heavy upon me; my strength was sapped as in the heat of summer. Then I acknowledged my sin to you and did not cover up my iniquity. I said, "I will confess my transgressions to the* LORD*"—and you forgave the guilt of my sin. (Psalm 32:1-5)*

Forgiveness brings the greatest blessing

The people of the world will promise us many things in order to make our lives "blessed" in their estimation: a new sport utility vehicle, a $10,000 bonus, fewer wrinkles, and better thighs. But those blessings are temporary and external. David had everything a man could want, but for a time, he still had a wretched life. Although he did not lose his kingdom, he lost his blessed status before God. He lost it by falling head-long into a string of sins without repentance and forgiveness. For nearly a year, he suffered through sleepless nights and stressful days as his thoughts assailed him with guilt over adultery with Bathsheba and the murder of Uriah.

Yet God loved David. God sent Nathan to restore David to his blessed life. Nathan confronted David, and when David repented, Nathan told him about God's forgiveness. David was restored.

Reread the verses printed above. David wrote them to teach us about true and lasting blessedness—the kind no money can buy. They tell us that through faith in Jesus' victory on the cross, we are blessed. Our very real and heinous sins are forgiven.

What is nagging on your conscience right now? Confess it to God. Be assured that Jesus is in heaven right now. He is sitting at God's right hand praying for you. He is saying, "Father, forgive your child because I paid for all those sins." The Father is accepting Jesus' words because he is pleased with him.

When we know that God has forgiven us, it enables us to be coura-geously humble and honest with others. We can freely admit our sins, even if admitting them causes others to think less of us. We know that even if our admission of guilt brings consequences in this life, the great-est consequence, eternal death, is erased.

✎◦◎◦✎

Lord, thank you for making my life blessed in Jesus. Help me freely admit my sins to you every day so that I may never lose your blessings. Amen.

Start at the beginning

Just how important are the first years of a child's schooling? Many educators would say that early childhood education is of the utmost importance. During the early years of education, the foundation is laid for a child's ability to learn. If children don't learn their numbers or the alphabet, they are going to have a hard time in first grade. If children don't learn to read well, they will struggle in every other subject. A proper foundation is critical for a good education.

However, more important than learning about mathematics or reading or science is learning what it means to fear the Lord. Solomon tells us that "the fear of the LORD is the beginning of knowledge." Without the fear of the Lord, all knowledge becomes self-centered and a source of pride.

What does it mean to fear the Lord? First of all, it means to trust in the Lord as your Savior. The psalmist says, "The LORD delights in those who fear him, who put their hope in his unfailing love" (Psalm 147:11). When I realize that the Lord is the one who made me and saved me from hell and gives me eternal life and when I realize that the Lord has the power to do anything he wants, then I stand in awe of him and bow in humility before him. Scripture says, "Let all the earth fear the LORD; let all the people of the world revere him" (Psalm 33:8). When I fear the Lord, I accept and follow his decisions about what is right and wrong. In fact, what he wants is so important to me that I will hate what he hates. As Solomon says, "To fear the LORD is to hate evil" (Proverbs 8:13). When I fear the Lord, I seek to live the way *he* wants and not the way I want. Again Solomon says, "Fear God and keep his commandments, for this is the whole duty of man" (Ecclesiastes 12:13).

Without the fear of the Lord, science, psychology, history, and all other subjects lack what is most important, namely, God's input and guidance. Without the fear of the Lord, everything you do lacks eternal purpose and is useless in the growth of God's kingdom. But with the fear of the Lord, everything you know and do is of eternal benefit to you and to those around you.

∽⊙⊙∾

Dear Lord, work in my heart so that I fear you above all things. Amen.

Trust in the LORD with all your heart and lean not on your own understanding; in all your ways acknowledge him, and he will make your paths straight. (Proverbs 3:5,6)

Put God above your human intellect

Remember what Jesus said about earthly wealth? "It is easier for a camel to go through the eye of a needle than for a rich man to enter the kingdom of God" (Matthew 19:24). Those with earthly wealth in abundance face many temptations. It is tempting to consider wealth to be the greatest treasure or to count on money to take care of every need. If a wealthy person is not careful, money can rule his or her life.

There is another kind of wealth that can also be a stumbling block: intellectual wealth. A brilliant mind, like money, can be a great blessing. However, just as people can be tempted to let money become their god, they can also be tempted to let their human intellect become their god.

Your intellect becomes your god when you allow it to be the final authority on values, beliefs, and what courses of action to take. When human reason becomes your god, you decide right and wrong according to what makes sense to you or what seems fair to you. How many times don't you hear people say, "I think there's nothing wrong with abortion, living together outside of marriage, or choosing an alternate lifestyle" or say, "I think that it doesn't matter what you believe as long as you are sincere" or say, "You can't prove that Baptism brings babies to faith. You can't prove that Jesus' body and blood are received in the Lord's Supper"?

The single most important quality we need in our lives is humility in the presence of God's Word. Paul says that "we take captive every thought to make it obedient to Christ" (2 Corinthians 10:5). Solomon says here, "Trust in the LORD with all your heart and lean not on your own understanding." Regardless of what our human reason may say, what the Lord says is always right and true. Regardless in what direction our human reason leads us, God's direction is always right and true.

So let go of your intellectual powers, and rely on the Lord. Ask him for guidance, and he will make your paths straight. Ask him for the truth, and he will give that to you as well—in his Word. Rest in his revelation and guidance, and he will enable you to use your intellectual gifts well.

Lord, send your Spirit into my heart to lead me to shape all my thinking around what you say in your Word. Amen.

Every good and perfect gift is from above, coming down
from the Father of the heavenly lights, who does not change
like shifting shadows. He chose to give us birth through the
word of truth, that we might be a kind of firstfruits of all he
created. (James 1:17,18)

We're equipped to keep on sharing

Although 20 centuries have come and gone since the days of the early church, not much has changed. Present-day Christians are not much different from early Christians.

Christians, according to their sinful nature, aren't any different from what they were in the first century. We are still sinners. That means we are selfish by nature. Perfect sharing doesn't come naturally. We need to learn to share. We need to be motivated to share.

How similar we are to the early church in how we receive the grace to share! James tells us that everything that is good, everything that is perfect, comes from God. Nothing that we have that is perfect or good in the truest sense comes from our sinful nature.

God does not change. He is not like a shifting shadow—like the shadow of a window pane moving slowly across the living room floor until it disappears when the sun goes down. In respect to giving his people good gifts, God is like the sun when viewed from outer space. He keeps shining. He never sets. His generosity does not change. He still selects carefully just the right gifts and just the right amount of gifts for all his people.

We show generosity, consideration, kindness, forgiveness, patience, and caring for other people because God gives us his Holy Spirit. God chooses to give us birth through the Word of Truth. He points us to Jesus and convinces us that he is the Son of God who became a human being to save us from our sin. He leads us to believe that someday we will live with him in heaven. He gives us feelings of love and compassion for our fellow Christians who need our help. And God gives us the resources we need to help them.

If you need help sharing, go to God "who gives [wisdom] generously to all without finding fault" (James 1:5). God, who does not change, will answer your prayer.

꘏꘎꘏

Lord Jesus, help us recognize that you are the source of all that is good. You have equipped us to share by giving us your Holy Spirit. Move us to keep on sharing, knowing that you can give us far more than we could ever give away. Amen.

[God] made us alive with Christ even when we were dead in transgressions—it is by grace you have been saved. (Ephesians 2:5)

From death to life

The cars were speeding when they collided. The sound of crunching glass and metal was horrifying. Surely no one would survive. No one could have survived. The rescue crew had to use rescue tools to get the drivers out. The doctors prepared the families for the worst. The victims' lives were hanging by threads. But wonder of wonders, they survived! By a miracle they both eventually walked out of the hospital completely under their own powers.

Miracles do happen. With God all things are possible. Did you realize that Cornelius and the members of his household were miracles? God gave them the light of his Word, spiritual insight into Peter's words, and faith that those words were true.

You are a miracle too—a miracle of God's grace. You are a miracle because you believe in Jesus as your Savior from sin.

The Bible teaches us that we were by nature dead in transgressions and sins. But just what does that mean? It means that we were born without faith in Jesus. We were born spiritually dead, that is, with no spiritual life in us at all. We didn't know God; we didn't love God. In fact, we hated God, despised him, and wanted nothing to do with him. Spiritual corpses—that's what we were.

To make matters worse, we could do nothing by ourselves to change our hopeless condition. No rescue tools could pull us out of our spiritual caskets. Hopeless! Helpless! Lost! Condemned to hell!

But God did the impossible. He breathed spiritual life into our spiritually dead bodies. "[God] made us alive with Christ even when we were dead in transgressions." A miracle! Fantastic!

God used the power of his Word to work this miracle. For most of us, it was the Word connected with the water of Baptism. Or for others it may have been the same Word shared with them later in life. In either case, God performed a miracle.

Why you? Why me? He chose us not because of anything good in us but only because of God's grace. As Paul declared, "It is by grace you have been saved." Grace, pure grace, is the undeserved love of God for guilty sinners like us.

Miracles do happen. Praise God that you, once dead in sin, are a walking miracle now alive in Christ Jesus.

❧◉◎◉❧

Heavenly Father, thank you for giving me new life in Jesus. Amen.

You are all sons of God through faith in Christ Jesus, for all of you who were baptized into Christ have clothed yourselves with Christ. (Galatians 3:26,27)

Clothed with Christ

How often don't we think that everything depends on us? We must do this task or solve that problem. We knock ourselves out worrying about things we have no control over. Our sinful nature has the misguided idea that it can play god and do a pretty good job of it. We forget that we are completely dependent on God.

In light of this rebellious attitude, we really do not deserve to have a Father in heaven looking after us and caring for us. But God's love is different from ours. God's law reminds us that nothing good lives in us. It moves us to confess that we have nothing to offer Jesus for our sin. But at God's invitation, we come anyway, even though we are clothed in the dirty, dark sins of soul and body that separate us from him. Why can we come with confidence? Because he took care of our "dirty laundry" of sin, putting it on his Son, who took it with him to the cross. We come with confidence because we know Jesus died to cleanse the whole world in his holy precious lifeblood. "God made him who had no sin to be sin for us, so that in him we might become the righteousness of God" (2 Corinthians 5:21).

That is the wonderful news God declared at our baptisms. Christ Jesus, his holiness, his perfection, and his life now clothe our wretched flesh. God declares us justified and redeemed to him. God declares us to be his sons and daughters for the sake of his one and only Son, who earned our way into his family. When God looks at us, his love for Jesus keeps no record of our wrongs. All our sins—past, present, and future— are forgiven full and free.

Jesus didn't need our help to save us. He did it alone. And the Lord doesn't need our help to handle our daily problems and temptations. He has promised to work in all things for the good of those who love him. Why not turn your problems and temptations over to him before your feet hit the floor in the morning? We can be sure that's what the man from Ethiopia did.

⌘

Dear Jesus, thank you for humbly handling our problem of sin through your death and resurrection. Remind us that at our baptisms you clothed us with your holiness. Amen.

Christ's love compels us, because we are convinced that one died for all, and therefore all died. (2 Corinthians 5:14)

One died for all

Dustin expressed his weariness: "I'm tired of following Jesus. I'm weary of serving him when everything I do meets with little or no success. What's the use?" No matter how strong we as Christians may think we are, at times we have days of discouragement and nights of frustration. We each question the purpose of our lives. We question the value of following Jesus.

The apostle Paul directs us to the only real solution to weariness and discouragement. He reminds us of what motivated him to serve Jesus with untiring zeal. It was Christ's love for him. Christ's love compelled him to desire to glorify his Savior in thought, word, and deed. Christ's love motivated him to reach out to others with the good news of forgiveness. Christ's love gave purpose and meaning to his life. Christ's love enabled him to make it through the rough days.

But Paul also realized something else—Christ's love reaches out to all people. He states that "one died for all." Jesus went to Calvary's cross for every human being who has lived or ever will live. One died for all! Over and over again the Bible testifies to this truth: "God so loved the world that he gave his one and only Son, that whoever believes in him shall not perish but have eternal life" (John 3:16). Later on in 2 Corinthians chapter 5, Paul says the very same thing: "God was reconciling the world to himself in Christ, not counting men's sins against them" (verse 19). One died for all! Think of what that means! The stubborn neighbor next door is one for whom Christ died. The alcoholic whom we may tend to look down on is one for whom the Savior shed his blood. The husband who abuses his wife is one whose sins have been taken to the cross by Jesus.

Think of what that means for us. We are sinners, all of us. Our hearts so often reveal selfish and jealous thoughts. We lack the zeal and commitment to always put the Lord's work first in our lives. We worry and fret instead of trusting the Lord's care promised to us.

Are you discouraged? Are you downhearted? Are you weary of life and its many problems? Journey to the cross. See your Savior there, dying for you and for the world. There at the foot of Calvary find renewed strength for living and for serving the Lord.

❧

Heavenly Father, thank you for sending Jesus to die for me and for all people. Amen.

He was delivered over to death for our sins and was raised to life for our justification. (Romans 4:25)

His victory is ours

When their team wins, sports fans tend to claim the victory as if they had been on the field themselves. Really, however, only the athletes can claim the victory. At best fans can take credit only for cheering and giving their team moral support. In contrast, when nations go to war and one nation wins, its citizens have some right to claim the victory. They all worked and made sacrifices.

Who gets the credit for the victory over sin and death? Paul gives the credit to Christ and to him alone. He was delivered over to death for our sins. Because our sins were credited to him, he was put to death. You could say that we get the credit for Jesus' death, but only because our sins were what caused it.

He was raised to life for our justification. Because we were justified, that is, declared by God to be free and clear of sin, Jesus rose. God raised his Son to life to announce that he was pleased with his Son's sacrifice. God raised Jesus to life because he had, in fact, done everything necessary to rid the world of the guilt of sin. Where the guilt of sin has been removed, there is life and salvation.

Victory did not appear to be ours at first. It seemed as though Jesus' enemies had won. They had falsely accused him and had succeeded in having him sentenced to death on a cross. No fans stood cheering Jesus on to victory at Calvary. Only the voices of his enemies could be heard as they mocked and ridiculed him. But when he rose, the victory cheer swelled louder and louder until the entire world heard his people singing his praises.

This is reason for a victory celebration. We don't celebrate because of what someone else did out on an athletic field. Nor do we celebrate something we are partially responsible for. We celebrate because the Son of God became the Son of Man and took us into himself. He took all our sin and rebellion and put them to death on the cross. When he rose, we rose also, pure and free from sin. In the fullest sense, his victory is ours.

The victories of earthly kings come and go. But the power of the Word will lead people to sing the praises of our King until the end of time.

❧

Christ, who once for sinners bled, Alleluia! Now the firstborn from the dead, Alleluia! Throned in endless might and pow'r, Alleluia! Lives and reigns forevermore. Alleluia! Amen.
(CW 150:4)

I rejoiced with those who said to me, "Let us go to the house of the LORD." (Psalm 122:1)

God's people love to go to his house

For most believers, just the word *Sunday* is an invitation to worship at God's house on the Lord's Day.

The people of God have always rejoiced at the thought of going to the house of the Lord. The faithful Jews loved to go up to Jerusalem to worship at the temple there. They regularly worshiped in their local synagogues. Also, as many as three times a year, the faithful Jews walked to Jerusalem to participate in one of the special feasts of the Lord. It was a time of great joy made even happier when a fellow worshiper invited you to "go to the house of the LORD."

There are so many good reasons to join our fellow worshipers in God's house for public worship. God knows we need the company of fellow believers who will help us keep the faith and live for Jesus. Thus he encourages, "Let us consider how we may spur one another on toward love and good deeds. Let us not give up meeting together . . . but let us encourage one another—and all the more as you see the Day approaching" (Hebrews 10:24,25).

God blesses us in so many ways. He provides all we need for our bodies and lives. Who of us hasn't received food, clothing, shelter, and much more besides? Grateful people thank him in their worship.

Our gracious and merciful God also blesses us with spiritual gifts. He has redeemed us from sin, death, and hell; brought us to faith in Jesus; and comforted us with the peace of his gospel. He has opened heaven to us, assured us that we will rise from the dead, and promised that he will return to take us to heaven.

"All this," Luther says, "God does only because he is my good and merciful Father in heaven, and not because I have earned or deserved it" (explanation to the First Article of the Apostles' Creed). Thank and praise God that he does not reward us according to our sins but always and only according to his undeserved love.

This Sunday we once again have the opportunity to join our fellow believers in public worship of our God. As we recall the words of the angel, "A Savior has been born to you; he is Christ the Lord" (Luke 2:11) and see that that angel is joined by many more angels in praising God, how can we not join their glorious song? "Glory to God in the highest, and on earth peace to men on whom his favor rests" (Luke 2:14).

❧

Heavenly Father, I am always glad to join my fellow believers in your house to hear your Word, feast on your Son's body and blood, and proclaim your praises. Amen.

God placed all things under his feet and appointed him to be head over everything for the church. (Ephesians 1:22)

Jesus rules over all things for you

When I was a boy, fishing was fun, and it was a real treat to be able to fish off a pier. One time my dad and I got the chance. When the day was over, I asked, "Dad, do you think that man would let us fish off his pier again?" "Sure," said my father. "But how can you be so sure?" I asked. "The man has given me permission to use his pier whenever I want," he replied. To me, my dad looked to be pretty important.

Paul's words about the power and authority of the ascended Lord give his people that same sense of awe. How important Jesus is!

God has put all things under Jesus' feet. In ancient times a victorious soldier would plant his foot on the neck of a defeated soldier. That act symbolized that the enemy was totally under his power. Picture the ascended Lord Jesus with the entire world under his feet. Picture the economic powers, the military powers, and the intellectual powers of this sinful world under his feet. Picture Satan under his feet. Picture death under his feet also.

When a soldier had his foot on the enemy's neck, the enemy couldn't move. It's a little different with Jesus and his power over the world. The world is able to squirm a bit. Satan is able to lash out against God's people with persecution and temptation. Death still seems to have its day. But this does not mean that Jesus does not have his feet on these forces of evil. They may seem to squirm, but even their squirming works together for the good of God's church.

Yes, Christians may suffer for their beliefs, but even in that suffering, Jesus is able to work on behalf of his church. How many unbelievers have not been led to Christ as they watched the patient endurance and calm confession of God's people! How many Christians have not had opportunities to confess their faith when on trial!

Look forward with joy to Jesus' coming for you. But in the meantime, accept the life God has given you today. Jesus is ruling over all things for the church, of which you are a member.

తితిలు

Jesus, ruler over all, continue to bless our lives, faith, and church. Protect us from evil, and strengthen us to do your work. Amen.

"Not everyone who says to me, 'Lord, Lord,' will enter the kingdom of heaven, but only he who does the will of my Father who is in heaven. Many will say to me on that day, 'Lord, Lord, did we not prophesy in your name, and in your name drive out demons and perform many miracles?' Then I will tell them plainly, 'I never knew you. Away from me, you evildoers!'" (Matthew 7:21-23)

Let's take it to heart!

Is Christ really serious when he says that he expects fruits of faith to fill the life of the believer? Does he really mean it when he exhorts us to test the spirits to see whether they are from God and to keep testing our own hearts and lives for the genuineness of our faith and works? Just how serious the Lord is in his expectations and demands is revealed in his warning words in the text before us. Not everyone who has the name of Jesus on his lips or who outwardly leads a respectable life will be admitted to the kingdom of heaven on the Last Day.

There are many, the Savior warns, who are nothing but fakers in their profession of Christianity. They mouth the Lord's name in public; they fold their hands at the proper time; they make a show of piety before the world—but their hearts are not in their actions.

Hypocrisy is the name of the game they are playing. Good impressions before others are the reputation they are seeking. Honor and praise from the world is the motive that drives them. Fakers, hypocrites of the worst kind!

But to no avail. Though they receive the praise of humans and for a time their pretense works, their falsehoods will be revealed one day to their shame and terror. Expecting some kind of gainful reward on the Last Day, they will receive the only reward they deserve—a sentence that is brief but terrible: "Away from me."

Such a dire word of warning ought to move us to a sincere and earnest self-examination. Let us indeed take it to heart! Does our profession of Christianity proceed from a heart of genuine faith, or is our Christianity a sham? May we be counted among those "who [do] the will of [the] Father," those who, having been renewed in Spirit by the Word, bring forth genuine fruits of faith. Then ours will be that gracious invitation: "Come, you who are blessed by my Father; take your inheritance, the kingdom prepared for you since the creation of the world" (Matthew 25:34).

⁂

Search me, O God, and know my heart! Try me, and know my thoughts! See if there be any wicked way in me, and lead me in the way everlasting. Amen.

Rejoice in the Lord always. I will say it again: Rejoice!
(Philippians 4:4)

11 October

Rejoice! He is coming!

"My doctor says my heart is failing. I've been suffering minor strokes each day. My husband's health is failing too. By the way, Pastor, how is Mrs. Schmidt doing?" That's what Gretta, one of my shut-ins, said to me the other day. Amazing! This Christian woman was enduring her own illnesses and watching her husband's health fail, yet she was more concerned about how a fellow Christian was doing. This woman knew Jesus was with her, even by her bed, and would never forget her. In the same way, she refused to forget others in need. Out of sight, but not out of mind.

Jesus' ascension provided the disciples with that same conviction and that same desire to forget about themselves and focus on the spiritual needs of others. As they watched Jesus ascend into heaven, little did they realize the power Jesus would exercise on their behalf. After Pentecost, their lives weren't easy, but they found strength to serve because they knew Jesus was with them. This confidence enabled them to overcome their difficulties and serve their Lord. It led them to look beyond their needs to the needs, especially the spiritual needs, of others. It led them to rejoice in every circumstance in which they found themselves.

Too often people get the idea that Jesus should end all their hardships. For many, their difficulties make them focus on themselves and forget about others. Joy? How can we feel joy?

Joy doesn't mean you will laugh all the time. It doesn't mean you will always feel happy. It means that in spite of whatever problems you have, you can look forward to your Savior's return and trust in his presence and power. And it means you are able to serve the Lord and his people. Confidence in God's presence and love removes the self-pity and self-concern that so easily imprison us. Clinging to the hope of life in heaven encourages us to help others look ahead to the hope of eternal life.

It's one thing to sit in church and confess the hope of eternal life. It is quite another to let that hope impact the way we live. Jesus is in charge! He watches over us! He will take us home! Rejoice always!

❦

Lord Jesus, hear us in our need. Grant us relief according to your will. Remind us of your love so that we continue to trust in you and accept your will. When despair comes, let us rejoice in your ascension and its message of hope. Amen.

To him who loves us and has freed us from our sins by his blood, and has made us to be a kingdom and priests to serve his God and Father—to him be glory and power for ever and ever! Amen. (Revelation 1:5,6)

Kings and priests in Christ's kingdom

We join the voices of God's people from all ages in calling Jesus the King of kings. His grace and power have made for himself a glorious kingdom. Under his gracious rule are souls that are free from sin and that will live with him forever. Even if we had no other blessings except this one, we would consider ourselves rich. Today's reading tells us that God gives even more. He makes us kings and priests in his kingdom.

Often we feel like anything but royalty. The sins that pop up and the troubles of living in a sinful world sometimes make us feel far from Christ, let alone the kings who are ruling along with him. Yet God would not have us judge by appearances. Our prayers are powerful, and the King of kings allows us a voice in how he rules the world. Add to this the fact that Christ has our needs and concerns at heart when he decides what will happen in this world. Sometimes we experience this firsthand. More often we know it is true only by faith.

And the Lord bestows another blessing on us. Not only does he make us kings, but he also makes us priests. In Old Testament times, priests had the privilege of access to God. They served at the temple, where God met his people through his Word and the sacrifices that pointed to Christ. Only the priests could enter the inner rooms of God's house, the Holy Place and the Most Holy Place.

On Good Friday, however, the curtain separating the sinful human race from the holy God was torn in two. Now "we have peace with God through our Lord Jesus Christ, through whom we have gained access by faith into this grace in which we now stand" (Romans 5:1,2). Now our Great High Priest has made us all priests with the privilege of access to God. What's more, we can offer ourselves to him as spiritual sacrifices.

Today you are a king and priest in his kingdom. Pray for his guidance and protection. Go about your daily tasks joyfully, knowing that you serve the Lord Jesus who will bless you.

⟡⟡⟡

Heavenly Father, hear our prayers and accept our praises as your royal priests in the name of Jesus, our Great High Priest. Amen.

Blessed is he whose transgressions are forgiven, whose sins are covered. (Psalm 32:1)

We are forgiven

Do you feel blessed? If someone asked you what your greatest blessing is, what would your answer be? Family? Good health? A good job? Something else that is special to you?

There are many days when we don't feel particularly blessed. Sickness has made our lives miserable, or the company has just moved its plant to a different city, or our job is lost, or nothing seems to be going right. When such things happen, we don't feel blessed.

But our gracious God calls us blessed, nevertheless, and he speaks only the truth. By God's standards, true blessedness consists of more than good health, a good job, a precious family—all of which are, indeed, gifts from a loving God. He tells us through his Word about a far greater blessing that we have: the forgiveness of our transgressions.

Transgressions are not merely flaws in our character; they are *rebellions* in the worst possible sense of the word—rebellions against God and his law. When we rebel against God, we are revolting against the holy will of God and deserve the harshest punishment God can measure out.

Sins, in turn, are every failure on our part to measure up to the demands of God's law. And when we remember that God's law requires perfection, we realize how often we miss the mark. The end result of transgressions and sins is the same. We are guilty before God. We deserve his wrath and punishment. We stand condemned.

Yet God calls us blessed. How can that be? We need only look to Christ. God sent his Son, his one and only beloved Son, to bear the terrible punishment we deserve. Willingly he died on the cross for us, not only for us but for the whole world. "Blessed is he whose transgressions are forgiven."

Now our sins have been covered—not covered up. God's justice would not stand for that—but covered. Others may see that we have completely missed the mark of God's law, but he doesn't. It is because of Christ, through his righteousness, that our sins are covered and have been removed from our Father's sight.

Is there any doubt, then, that we are truly blessed?

⌒◉◉⌒

Dear Lord Jesus, you have given me the greatest gift of all—the forgiveness of my sins. Keep me, I pray, from taking my sins lightly. Strengthen my faith in you as my one and only Redeemer. Amen.

14

O Lord, open my lips, and my mouth will declare your praise. (Psalm 51:15)

A praising heart

Guilt silences us. If you are harboring sin in your heart, it's hard to sing from the heart "Praise God, from whom all blessings flow" (CW 334). Until guilt is nailed to the cross, hymns are joyless and even our attempts at prayer are frustrated.

David knew guilt's impact: "When I kept silent, my bones wasted away through my groaning all day long" (Psalm 32:3). Sin had become a barrier between him and God. God's silence had grown deafening.

Forgiveness has the opposite effect. A change of heart brought about by the gospel message does amazing things. David prayed, "Save me from bloodguilt, O God . . . and my tongue will sing of your righteousness" (Psalm 51:14). He added, "O Lord, open my lips, and my mouth will declare your praise." Forgiveness opens lips. The grace of God frees mouths to declare God's praise.

In the last century, John Newton was a naval deserter involved in slave trade in Africa and an outspoken critic of Christianity when Christ brought him to faith and changed his heart. He began to preach about his newfound freedom. He wrote nearly three hundred hymns, one of which we also use to praise God: "Amazing grace—how sweet the sound—that saved a wretch like me!" (CW 379:1). When, at the age of 80, his poor eyesight led some to urge him to give up preaching, he responded, "What, shall the African blasphemer stop while he can speak?"

Once forgiven lips are open, praise flows. When the Lord called Isaiah to be his prophet, guilt made Isaiah say, "I am a man of unclean lips" (Isaiah 6:5). But when the Lord took away Isaiah's sins, the prophet shouted, "Here am I. Send me!" (Isaiah 6:8).

The Lord has forgiven your sin also. You believe the words of Scripture: "Here is a trustworthy saying that deserves full acceptance: Christ Jesus came into the world to save sinners—of whom I am the worst" (1 Timothy 1:15).

Every Sunday morning church bells ring across our land. Organ music fills the air. How can we not add our hearts and voices to those joyous sounds of praise? Will we stop praising him while we can still speak?

❧☙

Heavenly Father, thank you for taking me back into your arms and forgiving my sin. Your Word tells me my guilt is gone, so it must be true! What can I give you for all you have done for me? I will give you my praise and confess you as the Creator and Lord of all. Amen.

He called a little child and had him stand among them.
And he said: "I tell you the truth, unless you change and
become like little children, you will never enter the kingdom
of heaven." (Matthew 18:2,3)

First things first!

To children playing outside, the call to dinner means only one thing: food! All that playing in the sandbox, on the ball field, or just riding bikes up and down the street wears off a lot of energy. At mealtime, an empty stomach demands attention. The call to dinner is answered by a rush to the table.

That's when the notice comes: "Wait a minute! Go wash your hands first!" These words remind children that they are not always acceptable as they are. Like these children, we sometimes naturally find ourselves unacceptable for special occasions. Something has to happen to us before we can sit down as welcomed members of certain groups.

The kingdom of heaven is such a special group. It is made up of those who are part of the family of God. They live within a circle of love. For them, every prayer is answered and every need is met. It is a marvelous household.

The twelve disciples had been arguing about how they ranked within this group. Jesus led them back to a much more basic question: Are you really a member of this family?

Becoming followers of Jesus demands radical change within us. It isn't enough to clean up our language a little bit or to try harder to be honest and fair and understanding. Washing our hands won't do it either. We must throw away a much-loved part of us: our sense of self-importance.

We must change. We must see how weak and worthless we are. We must recognize that all our power is fading and all our fame is fleeting. We must confess that we are nothing. But our God—he is everything!

We lose nothing of value in this change. Pride, conceit, inflated self-worth—these have no basis in reality. These are only the products of our imaginations. We gain everything with this change. Holiness, fullness of joy, life forever in glory—these are what people would die for.

They don't have to. We don't have to. It wouldn't do us any good if we did.

Jesus did. Jesus died. Jesus arose to glory. Now he invites us to join him.

God sends the Holy Spirit to lead us to understand that the greatest title of all is to be called a child—not just any child but a special child—a child of God.

Lord Jesus, let me be yours forever! Amen.

16

"And whoever welcomes a little child like this in my name welcomes me." (Matthew 18:5)

Come, Lord Jesus!

Disciples of Jesus want Jesus to be with them in life. We pray often that he would attend us with guidance, protection, and blessing. One of our most common prayers asks him to come with his blessings to be our guest. We affirm the sincerity of this request with an *amen.* Yet sometimes when he comes in a form that hides his power and glory, we act as if he isn't even there.

A little child is not Jesus. But there is a connection between how we treat that child and how much we trust the Son of God. To receive a child in Jesus' name is to accept that child in the way that Jesus directs. That child is someone important. Jesus says so.

Do we believe Jesus? Do we trust him enough to put those words into practice?

The reality is that a child's fragile life is not left to the ravages of chance. Jesus cares for this tiny one as much as he cares for a famous head of state. He bids us to do the same.

Reject his request, dismiss his evaluation, and we are saying no to the Lord of glory.

We tend to rate people on the basis of power. Whether their power comes from position or money or skill makes little difference. The more a person is able to hurt us or help us, the higher the needle goes on our built-in power gauges.

A four-year-old is little threat to us. A child is not much help to us. Our boss may be both a threat and a help. For the one who is important to us, we will make sure that everything is done in the best possible way. Our welfare depends upon it. For one who is relatively unimportant, we may only give the leftovers of our time and energy. "It's a matter of priorities!" we explain.

And so it is. But whose priorities—ours or our Savior's?

To feed a child, teach a child, comfort a child—these are not big things. Or are they? To hush away fear and tell a child of his or her best friend—these are small things. Or are they?

Does Jesus bring that child before us so that he might bless both the child and us?

At such times, let us not just say, "Come, Lord Jesus!" but, "Welcome, Lord Jesus!" No matter how little our eyes may see the form of our God, he is there.

⚜

Lord God, remind me that you often come to me by means of people who have need of me. Soften my heart to help them. Awaken my soul to receive you. Amen.

He who dwells in the shelter of the Most High will rest in the shadow of the Almighty. I will say of the LORD, "He is my refuge and my fortress, my God, in whom I trust." (Psalm 91:1,2)

Keeping me in the true faith

"My refuge . . . my fortress, my God." These three "mys" come from the heart and mouth of a believer. The threefold repetition emphasizes the psalmist's confession, "I trust." The real emphasis, though, is on the one in whom he trusts. That is the Lord, the faithful giver of free salvation.

In the desert, a solitary rock or a rock formation can provide a shelter from a storm or a place to hide from enemies. It also offers shade from the glare and heat of the noonday sun. In the physical realm, the Lord provides these things.

In the spiritual realm, the Lord is our shelter, our hiding place, and our shade. He wards off the taunts of the world and the temptations of Satan. He shelters us from doubt and despair.

There are bomb shelters and storm shelters and tax shelters, but only God can keep us eternally secure. With an eye on eternity, people are always devising their own shelters. They determine: "I will do this to satisfy God. I will follow this program in order to conform to his will. I will live up to these principles and gain his favor." Such puny structures are no shelters at all from the devastating results of sin. The Lord himself, however, is our eternally secure fortress.

One of God's names is "the Most High." Such a majestic name cuts you and me and every mortal down to size. It diminishes our most significant achievements and puts the important events in our lives in perspective. Yet this God is our God—not to hide from or resent but to find shelter in and be secure.

How can we dwell and rest in the eternal care of such a God? Jesus is the way. He himself prayed this psalm and expressed this confidence in the Almighty. In our place he kept the First Commandment perfectly—fearing, loving, and trusting God above all things. As our representative, he fulfilled the entire law and then suffered the punishment for our sins. Because of him we can be as confident as the author of this psalm.

My "this" and my "that" will finally disappoint and disappear. Toys break; cars wear out; businesses downsize. My God will never lose interest, never sleep on the job, never decide to move.

∽৩৩৩৩

Lord God, help us order our lives by your wisdom and serve you in willing obedience through Jesus Christ. Amen.

18

Live as children of light (for the fruit of the light consists in all goodness, righteousness and truth). (Ephesians 5:8,9)

The goals of a Christian reflector

It was a Chinese Christian who once remarked, "Becoming a Christian is easy. It's being one that's difficult." I think most of us would agree with that statement. Most of us became Christians through Holy Baptism shortly after we were born. But the struggle to be Christian has been going on ever since we became aware of the difference between sin and obedience to our Lord.

The daily battle against the temptations of the unholy trinity—the devil, the world, and our own sinful selves—sometimes leaves soldiers for Christ battle weary and spiritually weak. We sometimes lose sight of what our goals are to be as followers of Christ in the 21st century. Through Paul, God reminds us of the targets we are to shoot for in our service to Christ out of love for him.

With the help of the Holy Spirit, we are to strive after goodness. Our Savior's love for us prompts us to treat others the way he would treat them. But sometimes the temptation not to be too good comes. We join others in making fun of a schoolmate or fellow worker. We shy away from befriending the people who need a friend more than anything else. We don't want to share or become the object of our group's ridicule. We don't want to lose our place in the group. Reflecting the goodness of Christ can be difficult.

Righteousness is also a fruit, or result, of the light. We are to strive to do that which is right in the eyes of God. We live in a world where everyone is demanding his rights but not many are concerned about righteousness. Some demand the right to have an abortion. Some demand their rights to live as homosexuals. For some, public opinion replaces the unchanging Word of God as the standard of right and wrong. Standing up for what is right in the eyes of God can be both difficult and dangerous.

Truth is another fruit that God produces in our lives. Some people don't like the truth. They don't like to be told that their lives of good works just aren't enough to buy tickets into heaven. For the Christian, the Word of Truth is the standard by which everything is to be judged.

"All goodness, righteousness and truth"—are these the goals of our lives? Do we sometimes lose sight of them? For our failures to bring forth the "fruit of the light," we look to Christ for forgiveness. We also look to the Lord as we strive to be better reflectors of his light.

❦

Lord, help us achieve more consistently the goals you have set for us. Amen.

There is now no condemnation for those who are in Christ Jesus, because through Christ Jesus the law of the Spirit of life set me free from the law of sin and death. (Romans 8:1,2)

Not guilty!

"Not guilty!" These are two words that every defendant in a trial longs to hear. When the judge announces this verdict, the heart of the defendant leaps for joy. These words mean there will be no condemnation, no fine, no prison sentence, no punishment of any kind.

Paul begins this chapter of his letter to the Romans by reminding us that we have received the same kind of favorable judgment from our God. Scripture teaches us that when Adam and Eve fell into sin, the entire world was corrupted. We should be concerned about this fall into sin because it means we also were born sinful and unclean. We were born under the power and control of sin, and there is nothing we can do to free ourselves.

To make matters even worse, sin shows itself in our lives. Our thoughts, words, and actions indicate that we often break God's commandments and transgress against his holy will. Our situations seem to be quite hopeless. All the evidence is stacked up against us. We are headed down the path that leads to everlasting punishment in hell.

Yet there is hope. This hope is found in Christ Jesus. It is clear we need a Savior. We need someone to rescue us from sin and the punishment sin brings. Jesus is that someone.

Note, however, that Paul writes, "There is now no condemnation for those who are in Christ Jesus." The word *in* is a small one, but it is very important as Paul uses it here. It indicates there must be a connection between ourselves and our Lord. This connection is faith.

By faith we have the forgiveness of our sins, which Jesus won for us on the cross. By faith we have the certain hope of everlasting life. But even this faith in Jesus is a gift from our gracious God. The Holy Spirit works through Baptism and the Word of God to create faith in our hearts.

God loves us and sent his Son to be our Savior. Jesus loves us and died for our sins. The Holy Spirit loves us and works faith in our hearts. Because the Holy Spirit works faith in our hearts, we receive this verdict from God: "Not guilty!"

❦

Lord, let us never forget how we sinful beings are able to stand before your throne—through faith in Christ Jesus. Amen.

But Ruth replied, "Don't urge me to leave you or to turn back from you. Where you go I will go, and where you stay I will stay. Your people will be my people and your God my God. Where you die I will die, and there I will be buried. May the LORD *deal with me, be it ever so severely, if anything but death separates you and me." (Ruth 1:16,17)*

Faithfulness

"I . . . promise . . . not to part from you; till death us do part." The traditional wedding vow is taken from the words of Ruth. These words are among the most beautiful expressions of faithfulness ever spoken. But it may be surprising to many that these words were not said to Ruth's husband. They were said to her mother-in-law, Naomi.

After Naomi's husband and two sons had died in the foreign country of Moab, she decided to return to her former home in Israel. She encouraged her sons' widows, Orpah and Ruth, to remain with their families in Moab. But Ruth refused to leave Naomi. Ruth spoke the words in the text to affirm her faithfulness.

If Ruth would have turned back, we could understand it. Her sister-in-law, Orpah, returned home. We could not fault Ruth if she had said, "I will try it for a year, and if it does not work out, I can always go back home." But Ruth affirmed without hesitation that her commitment was permanent.

If only we could be sure of such faithfulness in the people we love. If only we ourselves could demonstrate faithfulness like this to our friends, our relatives, and especially to our spouses. What or who inspired Ruth's faithfulness?

The source is apparent in Ruth's words: "Your people will be my people and your God my God." This young woman did not just love her mother-in-law, she loved the God of her mother-in-law. Ruth had come to know the true God in all his power and mercy through her husband's family. By going to Israel with Naomi, she could dedicate her life to God among God's people and forever forsake the idols of Moab.

Here is also the key to our faithfulness. In our attempts to be true to others, we should be moved initially by the faithfulness that God showed to us. His faithfulness is so great that it cost the life of his one and only Son, Jesus. Such faithfulness we did not and do not deserve. When we appreciate God's faithfulness to us, we are in the position to promise faithfulness to others.

⁓◎⁓

O faithful Lord, help me be faithful to others as you have been faithful to me. Amen.

I consider that our present sufferings are not worth comparing with the glory that will be revealed in us.
(Romans 8:18)

A word about suffering

Suffering is a fact of life. It strikes young and old, rich and poor. Its root cause is sin. We all suffer from sicknesses and diseases because we all live in a sinful world. Who could describe all the forms of physical, mental, and spiritual suffering as they exist in our world today?

Thank God that in his Suffering Servant he gave us an answer to suffering. Our Substitute suffered it all. He suffered trial, temptation, poverty, pain, sorrow, rejection, and death. He was indeed a man who was familiar with suffering. Jesus suffered so that we would not have to suffer the eternal torments of hell.

As God's people, that accomplished fact directly affects our view on suffering. By faith in Christ we know that God is our loving Father. In our Father's hand, suffering is a tool by which he draws us closer to himself, trains us, or gives us an opportunity to witness to his undeserved love.

Many of us have experienced a period of suffering. We learned from that experience that a person's life truly does not consist in the amount of things he possesses. God's promises became even more valuable, and in that way he drew us closer to himself.

We all experience the suffering that our Father sends into our lives as discipline. Scripture says, "God disciplines us for our good, that we may share in his holiness. No discipline seems pleasant at the time, but painful. Later on, however, it produces a harvest of righteousness and peace for those who have been trained by it" (Hebrews 12:10,11).

Sometimes God permits suffering to come upon us so that by faithful patience and endurance we might witness to others. Seldom do we think of suffering as an opportunity, but often that's what it is.

In the middle of suffering, we can at times lose perspective. Today's Bible verse puts all suffering into perspective. When all is said and done, suffering isn't worth comparing with the heavenly glory and joy that awaits us. We have God's Word for that.

❧❦❧

Should your mercy send me
Sorrow, toil, and woe,
Or should pain attend me
On my path below,
Grant that I may never
Fail your cross to view;
Grant that I may ever
Cast my care on you. Amen. (CW 116:3)

Seek first his kingdom and his righteousness, and all these things will be given to you as well. (Matthew 6:33)

A lesson in priorities

God doesn't consider you to be second-rate. With him you are a priority. He has always put you first.

He put you first from eternity. From the foundations of the world, he knew you. He put you first by sending his Son, Jesus, to live the perfect life you could not live and to suffer the wrath you deserved. He brought you to faith through the working of the Holy Spirit. He has made you a citizen of his kingdom.

Our Lord did absolutely everything for you and your salvation. You sinned; he suffered. You rebelled against God; he was faithful unto death. You deserved to die forever; he died instead. You have always been first with God.

When we stand in awe of how God has put us in first place, the place God should have in our lives is self-evident. Our humble purpose in life is to serve the Lord. And we are privileged to serve him with all that we are and all that we have.

How sad it is, then, when so many who call themselves Christian are stingy with their lives for God. They love the world's treasures and pleasures, worry about getting the same, and then hoard what they receive. How pathetic it is to see so many people so richly blessed return tiny bits and pieces for the Lord's service. How it must hurt our Savior to see so few redeemed souls answer his call for faithful stewards.

We need God's Word to put things into perspective. Christ teaches us to seek first the kingdom of God. When through his holy law we realize that we are big zeros and little nothings deserving damnation, only then will we rejoice in our salvation. Only then will unselfish dedication and wise stewardship characterize our lives.

Give God your time, knowing it is well-spent time invested in eternity. Give him your talents, using them gladly for his glory. Give generously, freely, the firstfruits of your money for his work. God and his kingdom should be our priorities. What a privilege to put him who gave his all for us first, that we might enjoy eternity with him!

⚮

Take my life and let it be
Consecrated, Lord, to thee.
Take myself, and I will be
Ever, only, all for thee. Amen. (from CW 469:1,6)

"Therefore I tell you, do not worry about your life, what you will eat or drink; or about your body, what you will wear. Is not life more important than food, and the body more important than clothes? Look at the birds of the air; they do not sow or reap or store away in barns, and yet your heavenly Father feeds them. Are you not much more valuable than they?" (Matthew 6:25,26)

A lesson from little birds

If you ever need some cheering up and you want to hear someone with an optimistic viewpoint, just watch and listen to some birds. Birds by their very nature are carefree, light-spirited, happy creatures. Martin Luther pictured little birds as "live saints" who sing praises to God without the least worry and are fed by him day by day.

God expects us to work for a living, using his gifts wisely for our good. Birds aren't expected to work. For them there is no seedtime or harvest. They have no barns or granaries in which they store food. But their tables are always set. Sometimes they have the choicest food, sometimes just enough to sustain life. But they eat, because God takes care of them!

How foolish we would be not to learn from them! We have the same almighty God, only our relationship is a deeper one because he is our heavenly Father and we are his dear children. He loves us and will give us everything we need. After all, he gave us our bodies. How could he fail to take care of their nourishment?

But as sinful creatures, we many times put our noses to the grindstone and forget to look up to our Provider. We may worry about what we will eat, how long we will keep our jobs, whether or not we can afford our house payments. Such anxiety over our physical necessities shows a lack of trust in the Giver of all things. Worrying indicates that we are trying to make it alone, forgetting that all things come from God. In our sinfulness, Christ comes to us with the example of the little birds and tells us to cast our cares upon him and he will care for us. May we trust in him without hesitation, resting on his providence.

❦

What is the world to me!
My Jesus is my treasure,
My life, my health, my wealth,
My friend, my love, my pleasure,
My joy, my crown, my all,
My bliss eternally.
Once more then I declare:
What is the world to me! Amen. (CW 477:4)

This is love for God: to obey his commands. And his commands are not burdensome, for everyone born of God overcomes the world. (1 John 5:3,4)

Love feels no burden

"Shout for joy to the LORD, all the earth.
   Worship the LORD with gladness;
   come before him with joyful songs" (Psalm 100:1,2).

We all know, don't we, that this is religion as it ought to be? Not something that is forced upon people whether they like it or not. Religion, as it ought to be, comes from a heart in love with God, a thankful heart, a joyful heart, a heart that knows the greatness of God's love for us.

The beauty of the Christian life is that it is lived not under law but under grace. What is the difference? The difference does not always show up on the outside. A person of the world too may serve out of a false faith in God himself. This is the devil's way of deception from the beginning. The difference goes back to the heart, the heart in love with God.

This is what John is getting at when he tells us, "This is love for God: to obey his commands. And his commands are not burdensome." It is not a burden, is it, to serve the one you love? Love delights in such service. To please the one we love is a joy, not a burden. Love feels no burden.

Still today the world is out to confuse us by turning joyful obedience to our God into a duty, a chore, a drudgery, and a burden. "Pity the poor Christian," the world cries out, "there's so much he can't do!" If this is the way the world looks upon religion, it's no wonder that the people of the world are always crying out for freedom from the restrictions God has imposed upon us. And so the confusion multiplies. These are the very tricks the devil used to deceive Adam and Eve in the beginning!

"Everyone born of God overcomes the world," John reminds us. You see, that clears up the confusion. It's not a matter of having restrictions imposed upon us. It's not a matter of submitting to a dictator's demands. It's a heart in love with God that delights to do his Father's will. This is beautiful.

⋙⋘

Create in me a new heart, Lord,
That gladly I obey your Word.
Oh, let your will be my desire
And with new life my soul inspire. Amen. (CW 471:3)

Those who are led by the Spirit of God are sons of God.
(Romans 8:14)

Children by and with the Spirit

"Now that's the spirit!" we say of the person in our club or organization—active, participating, volunteering, helping, and always ready, willing, and able.

But just what spirit is it? Is it a spirit of sincerity that recognizes responsibility? Or maybe it's a spirit of pride that wants recognition, a spirit of work-righteousness that wants to earn merit, a spirit of power-hungry control that wants to be in charge of everything?

Those who function under the control of those kinds of misdirected spirits could also be called children of those spirits. So the young man who abuses alcohol is called a child of his alcoholic father, and those who are led by the spirits of materialism, power, social prestige, and sensuality are called, even by God, children of the world.

Not so with those whom God himself has named his children. They are not led by such spirits. They are led by the Spirit, the Holy Spirit. What a blessing of grace that is! It was this Spirit who led each of us lost souls back to God through Baptism. It was the power of this Spirit, working through water and the Word, that took us out of the realm of the devil and transported us into the household of our heavenly Father. Though we may not be able to remember the actual event, never ever should we forget that on that baptismal day our heavenly Father put his hand upon us and said, "You are my child."

But then he did not leave us alone to stumble our way along the path to our heavenly home. As tourists in a foreign land, we have a guide to lead the way. It is again that Spirit, the Holy Spirit. He leads us past the pitfalls and focuses our eyes and hearts on the things that are really important. Thus God's children are not driven like animals to perform but are led as precious creatures to want to do his will.

Can you see that Spirit? Not really. But you can see the results. You can see and feel the patience and love and kindness and tenderness that are the marks of the children of God. Thank God for what that Spirit has done and for the gifts he still gives! In all of life—that's the Spirit, the Holy Spirit.

༺ઓ྇ૐༀ

Heavenly Father, continue to lead me through life as one of your dear children by your Spirit. Amen.

"I tell you the truth, anyone who will not receive the kingdom of God like a little child will never enter it."
(Luke 18:17)

Jesus wants the children to keep their childlike faith

A little girl snuggles close to her mother on a dark, stormy night and feels safe. With unquestioning trust, a young boy accepts his father's explanation of where he came from. The children wait expectantly when Momma tells them that Daddy will be home in 15 minutes. Even when things are terrible and logic suggests they cannot get better, a little child believes things will get better if his or her parents say so. Children don't worry about logic. They trust. If parents or adults tell them something, that settles it. It's true!

A day comes when this naive approach changes. Trusting children become questioning, doubting adults, and in many ways this is proper. Everyday life will go much better if we use our intellect to analyze the decisions that have to be made and then make sensible ones.

When it comes to our Christianity, however, the old childlike way is better. Simply trust your heavenly Father. Many of Scripture's teachings don't jibe with our human reason. A God who is three distinct persons and yet just one God does not add up. A Savior dying on a cross for the sins of the world is not very logical. The concept that we are saved by grace and not by works seems to be too simple of an idea. How can anyone believe such apparent nonsense? We can because God tells us it is so.

As a bumper sticker claims, "God says it. I believe it. That settles it." We sinful mortals can't expect to have all the answers to explain the actions of an immortal, omniscient, omnipotent, and omnipresent God. A god that we could match wits with, that we could figure out, wouldn't be much of a god.

As our text says, we must have a childlike faith to get to heaven. This doesn't mean that we don't use our intellect. God tells us to grow in grace and to go on to spiritual maturity. Gain as much knowledge as you can about the gospel and the world we live in, but don't use it to question God. If Scripture doesn't have the answer that satisfies human reason, accept that the answer it gives is from God and thus is true. Accept it the way you did as a child.

❧

O Lord, make us all willing to set aside our pride and cling to the cross of Christ with childlike faith. Keep us in our faith as your children forever. Amen.

The love of money is a root of all kinds of evil. Some people, eager for money, have wandered from the faith and pierced themselves with many griefs. (1 Timothy 6:10)

A perpetual problem

It isn't money itself; it isn't necessarily even the use of money that is the problem. The real problem is the love of money. We may well picture in our minds the miser gloating over his stacks of coins, fondling each one with obvious delight. We may picture the financier whose life is centered on his wealth and devoted to nothing but increasing it.

That isn't our problem though, is it? Mostly we struggle to make ends meet. Maybe now and then we may indulge ourselves with some modest luxury, but really our only problem with money is our lack of it.

Let's look a little closer at ourselves. Wouldn't it be nice if that lottery ticket would win the jackpot for us? Don't we wish we were as lucky as that person who just won $100,000 with one sweepstakes ticket? Maybe they're only dreams, but don't they show that the love of money lurks in our hearts too?

It isn't only the wealthy and the miserly whose lives revolve around their money for whom the words of the apostle Paul to Timothy are a warning. Those of moderate means, even the poverty stricken, need to listen to them too. They are meant for us.

"Where your treasure is, there your heart will be also" (Matthew 6:21). "Though your riches increase, do not set your heart on them" (Psalm 62:10). The love of money kills all other love. It takes complete possession of the heart. The heart possessed by the love of money is the most poverty-stricken heart that there can be.

Most tragic of all, as the apostle describes such, those who make money their first love have "wandered from the faith and pierced themselves with many griefs." They have lost God and have sold their souls for gold. With their gold they have bought care, worry, anxiety, and disappointment. Remember poor Lazarus? He inherited heaven. Even in hell the rich man wouldn't admit his error. What a poor man!

Christ paid an immeasurable price for the redemption of every soul. It was not gold or silver but his holy precious blood, his innocent suffering and death. This was the price that his love for the lost sinner compelled him to pay. Here we see love in its highest form. With such love directed toward us, can we let our hearts dwell on something so tawdry by comparison—money?

❦

Lord Jesus, take possession of our hearts and lead us to love what is precious in your sight. Amen.

"I tell you the truth, whoever hears my word and believes him who sent me has eternal life and will not be condemned; he has crossed over from death to life."
(John 5:24)

Eternal blessings in the balance

It almost sounds too good to be true! Who wouldn't follow one who makes a promise such as that?

There are millions who don't. Some have never heard of Jesus. (Forgive me, Lord!) But some have and are not impressed. What's wrong?

Perhaps they haven't really been listening. If they had been listening to that still, small voice within them, the voice we know as the conscience, they would have to say, "I'm lost! I'm one of those who will have to enter into condemnation." Or perhaps they don't understand what *condemnation* means. Then they ought to take to heart Jesus' own description: "There will be weeping and gnashing of teeth" (Matthew 25:30). Where? In the eternal fires. Of those who land there, Isaiah once wrote, "Their worm will not die, nor will their fire be quenched, and they will be loathsome to all mankind" (Isaiah 66:24).

You and I have also deserved death and hell. "The wages of sin is death," and we are sinners. But "the gift of God is eternal life in Christ Jesus our Lord" (Romans 6:23). And that's what these words of Jesus are all about. He seeks to move us to be for him all the way so that we may receive from him blessings that no one else can give.

Listen to him. "I tell you the truth"—that's an oath! Could anything be more certain than an oath spoken by God's own Son? "I tell you the truth"—to me, who is only worthy of death. "Whoever hears my word and believes him who sent me"—I have his Word; I know who sent him. "Has eternal life"—so although I'm getting up there, I still have a lot more years to go, an eternity to enjoy in the presence of my Savior. "And will not be condemned"—Conscience, did you hear that? "He has crossed over from death to life"—yes, I was dead, but now I'm alive and will live forever. Yes, I will die, but I'll be with him, and the grave will not be able to hold my body beyond the resurrection.

That's what is all in the balance. Can there be any question about it? Who wouldn't be for him who can promise that!

⟶◉◐⟵

Lord, as I hear your Word, use it to strengthen my faith so that I may forever cling to you and to him who sent you. Amen.

"No servant can serve two masters. Either he will hate the one and love the other, or he will be devoted to the one and despise the other. You cannot serve both God and Money."
(Luke 16:13)

A reminder we need daily

What are you doing this Friday evening?—Perhaps I'll take the family out for a fish fry. Perhaps we'll go bowling. Perhaps we'll stop in somewhere for a drink.

What are you doing tomorrow?—Well, there are quite a few things to do around the house. Then there is shopping. I've also got some woodworking to finish. Actually, the day will be too short.

What are you doing Sunday?—Well, perhaps I'll sleep late; it's the only day I can do that. Then we'll go out for Sunday brunch.

Where have you left Christ?—What do you mean? I'm a Christian. I may not go to church every Sunday, but I'm not against it. I send my children to Sunday school. Besides, the church is always asking for money. They must think I'm made of it!

Let's stop a moment to analyze the conversation. There's nothing the family does that society would classify as an out-and-out sin. The people are good neighbors. The husband would give you the shirt off his back if you needed it. The wife is always friendly, always ready to listen to all your complaints. They keep their yard neat and their home in good repair. They even have their young grandchildren over every once in a while. Good people—that's what they are.

Are they really? Let's ask once more: Where have they left Christ? Looking at them, we must admit that Christ and his church don't make real dents in their lives. But recreation, their home, eating and drinking, money—those are the things that count.

Jesus was right: "No servant can serve two masters. . . . You cannot serve both God and Money" or the things money can buy. The above conversation also supports Jesus when he said, "Either he will hate the one and love the other, or he will be devoted to the one and despise the other." *Love* and *hate* are the right words.

Analyze the conversation again. Was that family for Christ? Not really. Well, then it was against Christ.

But let's do more than just analyze the conversation. The words of Jesus are reminders that we—yes, we!—need daily. Whose servants are we? Our lives answer that question.

⚬⚬⚬

Dear Lord Jesus, grant me daily repentance, and help me overcome the stranglehold that the things of this world have on my soul. Turn my heart constantly in your direction. Amen.

"Surely I am with you always, to the very end of the age."
(Matthew 28:20)

An ever-present Savior

When Jesus gave his mission command to his followers, he promised them his continued presence. He would be with them, not only while they were alive and preaching the gospel but until the end of the world. That was important. Not only would he strengthen and help them in their work, but he would see to it that the Christian church would survive until the end of time. What a reassuring promise that is. What great care and love he shows for us in that promise. We have that promise in other places in Scripture too. For example, in Psalm 46:4,5 our Lord tells us, "There is a river whose streams make glad the city of God, the holy place where the Most High dwells. God is within her, she will not fall; God will help her at break of day."

When Jesus says that he will be with his followers to the end of the world, he also means that the Father and the Holy Spirit will be present. The three persons of the Trinity cannot be separated, even though each has his own work. The entire Trinity will be present with Christians always. The Father's protection and providence will never be lacking. Jesus, the Son, will continue to be their Savior from sin. The Holy Spirit will always be with them as the "Counselor," which the Scriptures call him in John 14:26. He will continue to preserve them in the true faith and to reassure them that their names are written in the book of heaven.

This text guarantees that the Christian church on earth will never be wiped out. It may suffer persecution and hardship, but it will never disappear. We must remember that the day may come when we may be harshly persecuted for our faith. God has nowhere promised that the lives of his disciples would always be easy. But we should take courage and comfort that if persecution should ever take place, Jesus will be with us also in those hard times.

Since the church will endure, the gospel will continue to be proclaimed. Souls will continue to be saved. Satan will continue to be overcome, because Jesus is with the church. Yes, we do have a God who cares. He cares for us until the end of the world.

෴

Dear Lord Jesus, we thank you for your promise to be with us to the end of the world. With this promise, we can face the future without fear. Help us never to forsake you. Amen.

God is our refuge and strength, an ever-present help in trouble. (Psalm 46:1)

31 October

God always helps us

The men who composed this psalm at God's inspiration were descendants of Korah. This is the same Korah who had rebelled against Moses and had been punished by God. Although faithless Korah had tasted God's fury against sin, his descendants lived to celebrate God's mercy and grace. Our God is one who will not leave the guilty unpunished and yet maintains love to thousands, forgiving wickedness, rebellion, and sin. How can this holy God love and forgive sinners? Look to the cross of Christ! There the Son of God suffered the punishment for the sins of the world. Jesus brings sinners forgiveness and peace with God.

God is a refuge for those who trust in him. In ancient times a portion of a city was enclosed with sturdy walls as a refuge or fortress. Farms and most dwellings lay outside this refuge. When danger threatened, the people would flee to the safety and defense of these fortress walls.

The sons of Korah praised God as their refuge. They had seen the wonderful way God protected and helped his people of Israel, especially at Jerusalem. They realized by faith that it was not the walls of Jerusalem but God himself who gave the people refuge and strength. God provided not only for their physical safety but for their souls as well.

Today God continues to defend and aid his people, those who trust in his Son as their Savior. God is ever with us. He preserves his Word and church despite the constant attack of the devil, the unbelieving world, and false teachers. God provides for all our needs of body and soul, even in times of great need and conflict. God is our refuge. His Word endures forever. His grace and power never fail.

But often we are weak. What can we do when we find ourselves mired down again in sins we hate and try to avoid? Even then God's Word reminds us that our freedom from sin and our place in Christ's kingdom are not the result of how hard we believe or how well we keep his commandments. God himself is our refuge, our Savior. His promise is sure.

The confident spirit and exciting imagery of this psalm moved Martin Luther to compose the battle hymn of the Reformation, "A Mighty Fortress Is Our God." As we remember the Reformation this week, also remember its roots of faith in the comforting Word of our almighty God and Savior.

❧❧❧

Lord God, forgive my sins and assure me of your abiding grace by the gospel. Deepen my trust in your power to help and keep me. Amen.

We will not fear, though the earth give way and the mountains fall into the heart of the sea, though its waters roar and foam and the mountains quake with their surging. (Psalm 46:2,3)

Don't be afraid!

To feel helpless is frightening. To fear for one's life is terrible. This psalm reminds us of such feelings in a striking way: the ground giving way beneath our feet, massive mountains quaking and toppling around us, plunging into the deepest part of the sea as the waters crash and roll together with earth-shattering force. The natural catastrophes of earth—earthquakes, tornadoes, floods—remind us of how easily earthly security can give way to overwhelming disaster.

Even in an otherwise peaceful world, trouble may come—a severe accident, an illness, the loss of a family member, or the loss of our job or home. On our own we are vulnerable and helpless in the face of evil. With dangers and trouble all around us, what hope can the Bible offer?

In this world we will have trouble. But in Christ we have a way through the evils of life, through its troubles and trials. God is our refuge and strength. Even when we walk through the valley of the shadow of death, we fear no evil, because our Good Shepherd is with us, leading the way. His Word sets our hearts at ease as we entrust ourselves and all things into his almighty care. His grace restores our lives.

We best cope with hard times by walking with Jesus every day. We draw courage and comfort from his Word. We call for his help in prayer. We learn to share our burdens with Christian friends and in turn help and encourage others. Together as a church and on our own as individuals, we lay down every care at our Father's throne of grace.

How often God's angels told believers in the past, "Fear not! Don't be afraid!" God is our refuge. The Holy Spirit who first brought us to trust in Jesus preserves our faith through God's Word and sacrament. This heavenly assurance of peace with God sets us free from the shame and frustration of sin. It moves us to trust fearlessly in God even in the midst of trouble. We know that all things work together for the good of those who love God. We fix our eyes on Jesus, through whom we have become citizens of an eternal home that will never be lost or destroyed.

Even when the end of this world arrives and the earth gives way to the fire of the judgment, we need not fear. Out of its destruction, we will arise with joy to live with our faithful Savior forever.

❧☙

Thank you, Lord, for delivering me from every evil. Amen.

There is a river whose streams make glad the city of God, the holy place where the Most High dwells. God is within her, she will not fall; God will help her at break of day. (Psalm 46:4,5)

The favored city of God

The city of Jerusalem had a special importance among the people of Israel. God had made Jerusalem his special dwelling place, just as he had made the Israelites his special people. At the temple in Jerusalem, God revealed his special presence and blessings, and there he received the worship of his people. For the Jews, God's saving presence and Jerusalem always went together, just as government and Washington D.C. go together for Americans.

In the New Testament, the Christian church is called the heavenly Jerusalem, the city of the living God. As the promised Savior was at the heart of Old Testament Israel, the One who fulfilled the promise, Jesus Christ, is the foundation of the New Testament church. Wherever two or more gather in Jesus' name, there is the church and the church's Lord. As Jesus taught, "The kingdom of God is within you" (Luke 17:21). God lives within us through his Holy Spirit. Mountains may crumble and empires may rise and fall, but Christ's invisible church will never fall. God lives within it, within us.

Even the sin, false doctrine, and hypocrisy that ravage the visible churches cannot harm or destroy Christ's kingdom of believers. God protects and preserves our faith.

The psalm's phrase "at break of day," the earliest moment of a day, means the Lord comes to our aid without delay. All things, inside the church and out, are governed by his might.

The sons of Korah also speak here of a river "whose streams make glad the city of God." But the earthly city of Jerusalem received its water from a spring, not a river. That's a reminder that this psalm does not merely refer to an earthly place but a spiritual one. The church is that "city" nourished and preserved by the life-giving streams of God's grace. This fountain was opened by Jesus, who lived and died for our salvation. These waters flow freely among us through his Word and sacrament.

Jesus said, "If anyone is thirsty, let him come to me and drink. Whoever believes in me, as the Scripture has said, streams of living water will flow from within him" (John 7:37,38). The Holy Spirit causes his gifts of love, joy, peace, and the rest to flow from faith. And faith is itself created and preserved by the Holy Spirit's power.

This city will endure forever. By grace through faith, we are that city, the church, the kingdom of God. Believers are God's dwelling place. And if God is for us, who can be against us? "He holds the field forever" (CW 200:2).

❧

God Most High, dwell in me and preserve my life in your kingdom through your grace. Amen.

Nations are in uproar, kingdoms fall; he lifts his voice, the earth melts. (Psalm 46:6)

God's powerful Word

How the geography of our world has changed over the ages! Just as clouds appear and disappear across the sky, the pattern of white on blue always changing, so maps have changed. Nations arise; boundaries move; kingdoms fall. Greed and man's lust for power have kept the world in a constant uproar throughout history.

But the greatest conflict has not been political or economic but spiritual. Satan, the prince of this world, strives to lead mankind deeper into sin and death and away from the grace of God. The world's conflicts only reflect the devil's desire to destroy our hope of salvation.

In ancient times the land of Israel was at the center of a turbulent world, tossed like a tiny boat on a raging sea. All around Israel empires rose and fell. Powers threatened to overwhelm the Jews and to put an end to God's promise to bless all nations through Abraham's seed. But into this world God sent his Son to be our Savior and the Lord of the nations. God's Son established a kingdom unlike any other, a spiritual kingdom that will never fall or pass away. We who trust in Christ as our Savior and Lord are citizens of this kingdom by faith.

Today, maps are still changing. Wars and rumors of wars continue. Satan directs his attacks at the kingdom of God. As we go out to proclaim the good news about Jesus, the devil raises obstacles, strikes at our faith, and tries to keep people apart from Christ. He confronts us with the uproar and unbelief of this world. "Deep guile and great might are his dread arms in fight; on earth is not his equal" (CW 200:1).

But no matter. God's promise survived, and Christ's kingdom thrives—because God is with us. His Word is our shield and weapon. The gospel has in itself the power to move forward through our humble efforts. This Word crushes all opposition raised against it. This Word even breaks through the human heart's stony resistance to God's grace and brings about repentance and faith.

Soon God will lift his voice in judgment. He himself will come down from heaven with a loud command, with the voice of the archangel and the trumpet call of God. The turmoil of this world will give way to eternity. We need not fear. The same voice that speaks through the Bible, the same voice that created and that will end the world, assures us, "Be of good cheer! Your sins are forgiven!"

Savior, guide and comfort me through your powerful Word. Amen.

The LORD Almighty is with us; the God of Jacob is our fortress. (Psalm 46:7)

4 November

The Lord is with us

Our modern world craves progress. As long as man seems to be reaching upward and moving forward, all is well. Never mind the crime, strife, anxiety, and corruption. People dream of perfection—being with God or like God, free from evil and decay.

The Bible tells us both bad news and good news about man's lot. We are sinners and can do nothing to change that condition. But God sent us his Son to redeem us from sin. Since God declares us righteous through faith in Christ, we have peace with God through him. God no longer condemns us. Sin no longer dooms us. We are a new creation in which God dwells through his Spirit. He is our refuge.

This promise of deliverance shines forth in the way God describes himself in the Bible. Just as we write our personal signature on important documents, so God personally signed his covenant promises for the Israelites. His name, *the LORD,* in Hebrew literally means, "I am." Of his own free will, God shows free and faithful grace toward sinners. He does not change. God chose to be with us and to redeem us because of his great love and mercy.

The title "LORD Almighty" reveals him to be the commander of the countless heavenly host. The Lord sends his angels to watch and keep those he has called to eternal life through faith in Christ. God not only reveals his presence but his mercy toward us and his almighty power to keep us.

"Though devils all the world should fill, all eager to devour us, we tremble not, we fear no ill; they shall not overpow'r us" (CW 200:3). God's grace and power shield us.

"The God of Jacob is our fortress." Jacob, Abraham's grandson, was one of the Israelites' early ancestors. The Bible tells how God chastised the crafty Jacob and taught him to trust and follow God's Word instead of his own ambitions. We're also shown how God faithfully delivered Jacob through many perils and hardships.

As Jacob, we are more inclined to rely on our own wiles, right or wrong, than to trust and follow the Lord. We also face many trials on life's way. But the God who guided and protected Jacob also watches over us. Through faith in Christ we share in the blessing promised to Jacob.

Because Jacob has entered eternal life, God is still Jacob's God. Nothing in life or death can separate us from the Savior who has chosen to be with us and to defend us. Today and forever, this God is our Mighty Fortress, our refuge and strength!

⌀⌀⌀

In you, O Lord, I have put my trust. Keep me in your grace forever. Amen.

Come and see the works of the LORD, the desolations he has brought on the earth. He makes wars cease to the ends of the earth; he breaks the bow and shatters the spear, he burns the shields with fire. (Psalm 46:8,9)

Judgment as evidence of grace

If God is loving, why does he punish? The Bible teaches that because God is gracious, he is against evil. The Good Shepherd does not allow wolves to prey on his flock. The Prince of peace wages war against those who threaten the peace of his kingdom. "For us fights the valiant one whom God himself elected" (CW 200:2). There can be no love or peace where evil reigns and the rebellion against God continues.

In wrath God remembers mercy. But wrath also comes so that God's mercy is not thwarted by evil. Think of the great Old Testament example of the Lord's salvation: the exodus of the Israelites from Egypt. Delivering those who were enslaved and mistreated meant opposing their oppressors. The plagues that devastated Egypt not only punished unbelievers but served to bring about the gracious deliverance of the Israelites.

There God also showed that grace does not rule out justice. For the Israelites to survive the final plague, the blood of the Passover lambs was shed. This prefigured the death of the Lamb of God. Christ suffered the punishment of sin in our place for our salvation. The debt of sin had to be paid for God's gracious promise of forgiveness to be fulfilled. The Old Testament prophets also showed "the works of the LORD" in this light. Their words of judgment warn that there is no hope for humans except in the Lord's mercy. The prophets also promised deliverance from everything that wars against our souls and causes oppression. God executes judgment in order to make "wars cease to the ends of the earth." Christ will confirm our peace once and for all.

At this time of year, we remember how God brought about the Reformation. With the sword of the Spirit, God's Word, our Lord broke the stranglehold that false teachers had held on the Christian church and restored the one true light of salvation, the good news of Jesus. God fights for us.

God brought down Babylon to free the Israelites from captivity. God destroyed a wicked world with a flood to spare one righteous family. Likewise, Christ will return to judge the living and the dead, to gather his harvest of believers into heaven, and to burn up the chaff with unquenchable fire. Satan wars against us. But thanks be to God! God gives us the victory over Satan through our Lord Jesus Christ!

⌑⌑⌑

Lord God, help me share the good news of your victory with others so that they too might believe in Christ and share in that final victory on the Last Day. Amen.

Be still, and know that I am God; I will be exalted among the nations, I will be exalted in the earth. (Psalm 46:10)

Be still!

On the Last Day, Jesus will claim the honor and the praise of all people. Willing or unwilling, all will acknowledge on that day that Jesus is the Lord to the glory of the Father. The Lord's command, "Be still," reflects his glory. Like two sides of one coin, these words proclaim both the judgment of the law and the reassurance of the gospel.

Think of when Jesus stilled the storm on the Sea of Galilee. At the sound of his voice, the winds and waves grew still and there was a great calm. He gave his disciples comfort and deliverance from danger. For us, God's power and grace mean salvation. And so we sing, "Be still, my soul; the Lord is on your side" (CW 415:1). God's words herald our deliverance and confirm our faith in God's message. The Lord is what he claims to be: holy, faithful, willing, and able to help us in every need. He is our refuge.

Nothing can resist God's power. Nothing can separate us from his love in Jesus Christ. He is our only Savior and is Lord over all. God makes his glory known chiefly in withholding judgment and forgiving sins. But he also breaks every evil design that Satan has made against us. Through the gospel, he extends his kingdom of grace and preserves it from whatever would prevent its progress. Through his angels, God delivers us from every evil attack of the devil. He provides a way of escape in temptation and a refuge of grace when we have sinned.

The Lord works all things together for our eternal good. He is exalted over all people and all things. All this echoes in his command that the earth be still and acknowledge his power and grace. Our God is a consuming fire against all who do evil. But he is a mighty fortress for all who trust in him.

His precious gospel is our great heritage. God entrusts us with the privilege of spreading its pure light of truth and grace. But by no means is this something we accomplish on our own. "With might of ours can naught be done" (CW 200:2). If the outreach of the gospel or the work of our salvation ever rested on what we could do, all would be lost. Thus God reminds us through the prophet Zechariah that our Savior's glory will fill the earth, not by man's might or power but by God's Holy Spirit. The Lord Almighty stands beside us "with his good gifts and Spirit" (CW 200:4). The victory of salvation is assured. Despite Satan and the battle waged against us, "the kingdom's ours forever."

⤜◎⤛

Lord, you are my refuge and strength; God of Jacob, you are my fortress. Comfort and encourage me as I serve you in this world. Amen.

Let the word of Christ dwell in you richly as you teach and admonish one another with all wisdom, and as you sing psalms, hymns and spiritual songs with gratitude in your hearts to God. (Colossians 3:16)

God preserves life through the Word of Christ

Left to our own devices, we could not and would not remain spiritually alive. The nature we inherited from Adam is so powerfully evil that if left unchecked, it would invariably destroy the lives God has given us. Our sinful flesh would squander the peace God himself has given. Thankfully, God does not leave us to our own devices to preserve the lives he has given us in Christ. Instead, speaking to our hearts through his living Word, our Lord nurtures the faith he created and sustains our spiritual lives.

When we spend time alone with his Word in the privacy of our homes, we are not alone because the Lord is there. He feeds our souls and strengthens our faith. Because the Lord always works through his Word, he earnestly desires that we make his Word a priority in our lives. How often doesn't he earnestly command us to read and hear it. Therefore, when our Bibles gather dust, we lose the power that God imparts through his Word. Because we are content with the knowledge we have and fail to use God's Word, we unintentionally design our own spiritual deaths.

We may have wandered dangerously close to spiritual death through our neglect of his Word on more than one occasion. Yet the Lord graciously intervened. He called us back to himself like the wayward sheep we are. He brought us back so that we might turn again to him. He may have sent a Christian friend to comfort us and encourage us on the long and difficult road to heaven. The Lord sought us and turned us again to his Word because he loves us.

Each Sunday as our called servant of the Word brings us a message from Scripture, the Lord is active, feeding our souls and nurturing our faith. Each Sunday as we join our fellow believers in singing psalms and hymns, the Lord is active, using the words that we speak to encourage one another and to preserve our spiritual lives. Sunday after Sunday and Monday after Monday, let the Word of Christ dwell in us richly, because the Lord is always active in that Word, blessing and sustaining us until he perfects us in heaven.

❧❧❧

Abide with richest blessings among us, bounteous Lord; let us in grace and wisdom grow daily through your Word. Amen. (CW 333:4)

Whatever you do, whether in word or deed, do it all in the name of the Lord Jesus, giving thanks to God the Father through him. (Colossians 3:17)

God gives purpose to our lives in this world

Some people spend their entire lives searching for meaning and purpose. They continually wonder what they are to do with their lives. Those who spend their entire lives searching God's Word come across passages like the one above and know what they are here to do. Whatever the occupation, the child of God has a higher calling; indeed, the child of God has the ultimate vocation—to live to the glory of God and to thank him for the gift of his Son.

In calling us out of darkness and making his light shine in our hearts, the Lord himself gave purpose to our lives. In this passage he states clearly our reason for existence. He put us here to increase God's glory with our every word and action and to demonstrate our thanks to the One who has given us life as his children.

When we use words to proclaim the wonderful works of God in our prayers, praise, and witness, we fulfill our mission. When we speak kind and encouraging words to one another, we live up to our high calling and purpose. Ultimately, every word that comes from our mouths should build others up. Such words fulfill our mission and make proper use of God's gift of language.

Sadly, our words have not all been spoken in the name of the Lord Jesus; they have not all served to increase the Lord's glory or to benefit our neighbor. All too often they have merited God's punishment. But instead of speaking judgment upon us, God has spoken peace to us. He forgives us because of Jesus, assuring us of our status as his dear children.

Inspired to action by his forgiveness, we endeavor to do everything in the name of the Lord Jesus. When we serve those in trouble and help those who are down, we give glory to God and thank him for his blessings. When we take our eyes off our troubles and minister to those whom the Lord has placed around us, we fulfill the greatest mission any human being could have: giving glory to our heavenly Father.

❧❧❧

Praise God, from whom all blessings flow;
Praise him, all creatures here below;
Praise him above, ye heav'nly host;
Praise Father, Son, and Holy Ghost! Amen. (CW 334)

To me, to live is Christ and to die is gain. If I am to go on living in the body, this will mean fruitful labor for me. Yet what shall I choose? I do not know! I am torn between the two: I desire to depart and be with Christ, which is better by far; but it is more necessary for you that I remain in the body. (Philippians 1:21-24)

Live for Christ

When a society loses its moral compass, its members develop strange views about life and death. We witness that in the raging debates over assisted suicide. When life is no longer seen as a double blessing of God—both created and redeemed by him—when people refuse to acknowledge that the times of their lives are in God's hands, when people forget that God has a purpose for their lives, then those who suffer from chronic or painful diseases often see no value in their lives. Those who care for them think they show compassion by helping the sick end their lives. When people refuse to believe that life is a gift from God, their thinking gets turned upside down.

The apostle Paul wanted to die. No, his chronic illness and life-threatening imprisonment hadn't turned his thinking upside down. He hadn't lost sight of God's grace. Just the opposite. He knew the words of the psalmist: "My times are in your hands" (Psalm 31:15). He knew that the ultimate decision about his life was in the hands of God, who operated through his human instrument—the Roman emperor. Paul wanted to die because he knew that the ultimate blessing would be his when he would take his place in God's eternal kingdom of heaven.

But Paul also knew that God had a purpose for him—to share the gospel with others. He knew that was important. He would be able to see God's grace at work if God chose to let him live a while longer.

Since the Garden of Eden, our human problem has been the desire to be in control. When disease or catastrophe reminds us that we are not in control, we become angry or afraid. But we can find great comfort in knowing that God is still the Lord of life and death. As a veteran missionary from a country rife with terrorism once said, "There are no stray bullets." Our lives are in God's hands. Whether we are active and healthy or bedridden and ill doesn't matter. What matters is that in life and in death, we are the Lord's.

Lord, forgive me for wanting control over my life and my death. Continue to nurture me through your promise so that whether I live or die, I am yours. Amen.

Christ gives strength

What bold statements those early Christians made. In Acts chapter 3, Peter addressed the crippled beggar: "In the name of Jesus Christ of Nazareth, walk" (verse 6). When a crowd came running to see the miracle, Peter preached a powerful sermon. He urged the people to see in Jesus the promised Savior. Note how bold his words were: "Moses said, 'The Lord your God will raise up for you a prophet like me from among your own people; you must listen to everything he tells you. Anyone who does not listen to him will be completely cut off from among his people'" (Acts 3:22,23). These were bold words, spoken in love to hard hearts that needed to hear them.

It was tough to proclaim the gospel in those days. The Pharisees who hounded Jesus were still around in Jerusalem to hound the disciples. They seemed to be everywhere, because they dogged Paul's steps wherever he went. Yet Paul could rejoice, "I can do everything through him who gives me strength."

What courage and fearlessness these Christians showed as they faced persecution, danger, and even the loss of their own lives! If only we Christians today could be so bold!

We can! The Savior who instructed and encouraged the early Christians is the same all-powerful Savior who is with us and encourages us in our lives of faith. He has filled his Word with promises—promises he will keep. Consider these additional promises for your comfort:

"God is our refuge and strength, an ever-present help in trouble" (Psalm 46:1).

"God will meet all your needs according to his glorious riches in Christ Jesus" (Philippians 4:19).

"[God] will not let you be tempted beyond what you can bear" (1 Corinthians 10:13).

"Fear not, for I have redeemed you; I have summoned you by name; you are mine" (Isaiah 43:1).

"I am with you always" (Matthew 28:20).

Promise after promise after promise. All rock solid and certain! All backed by the King of heaven and earth, our risen Lord and Savior.

No matter how serious the sin, no matter how perplexing the problem, no matter how daunting the challenge, no matter how tantalizing the temptation, no matter how dark the days, in Christ we can say, "I can do everything through him who gives me strength."

⁓⊙⊚⊙⁓

Lord Jesus, help us rely on your strength in every circumstance of life every day. Your powerful promises sustain us. Lead us to cling to them through your Word. Amen.

I have been crucified with Christ and I no longer live, but Christ lives in me. The life I live in the body, I live by faith in the Son of God, who loved me and gave himself for me. (Galatians 2:20)

Christ lives in me

Get a life! Most often those words are hurled as an insult. They imply that you don't have a life worth living. Not true! Next time someone tosses this insult your way, you can respond, "I've got a life. In fact, I've got two lives."

Two lives? Each of us has a physical life. This is a unique, one-of-a-kind existence that consists of body and soul, family, friends, talents, interests, and a physical life history filled with ups and downs and twists and turns. Each of us also has a spiritual life—a second life, so to speak. This life consists of faith, Christian friends, talents, fruits of the Spirit, gifts of the Spirit, and a spiritual life history filled with more ups and downs and twists and turns.

Our physical lives began when God gave us souls when we were conceived in our mothers' wombs. Our spiritual lives began when Christ himself came to live in us. In our reading, Paul describes his spiritual life. He, the old natural Paul, no longer lives. That old spiritual life was crucified with Christ. And in its place Christ came to live within Paul.

Now Paul lives by faith in God's Son, confident that God's Son will forgive all his sins. He lives with Christ shaping his every thought and action. His ministry is performed at Christ's direction and with Christ's power.

This is the life Peter and John wanted to create in the Jewish people in Jerusalem in the days following Pentecost. The Christ, whom these people had killed, was alive and wanted nothing more than for them to repent of their sin and believe in him. He wanted to live in them.

Christ has come to live in us also, and he makes life truly worth living. His Word gives us direction for daily life. His great love for us gives us the ability to make good spiritual decisions and to live in a God-pleasing way.

Get a life! Is that a put-down? Perhaps, but it doesn't have to be. Consider it an encouragement to be alive in Christ through regular and faithful use of God's Word, daily remembrance of your baptism, and regular attendance at the Lord's Supper.

꿈꿈꿈

Lord, help us give our spiritual lives the attention they deserve. Nourish us through Word and sacrament, and equip us to live the lives to which you have called us. Amen.

"Be faithful, even to the point of death, and I will give you the crown of life." (Revelation 2:10)

They know the outcome

I don't think very many of us will ever wear a crown in our lives. In some societies, people get to wear crowns because they belong to royal families. In our society, we give crowns to the winners of beauty pageants.

A crown is a sign of accomplishment. In ancient athletic games, a crown was given to the winner of a race. He had worked hard, had trained and persevered, and had finally come out ahead. On his head was placed a crown of laurel.

A day is coming when we will receive a crown. Our Savior has a wonderful crown in store for us. It's a gift he earned by his perfect life and innocent death. He worked; he persevered; he came out on top. It was the greatest achievement ever. He won the battle against sin, death, and hell. He is the victor.

We are the ones who reap the benefits. Through faith in him, we will receive the prize, the crown of life. Forgiveness and comfort in this life and the blessedness of heaven for eternity, those things are what our crown is made of. It's ours as a free gift because of what Jesus did.

Next month we will be celebrating the birth of our King. He deserves the crown, both as royalty and as the ultimate champion. He offers that same crown to all people. Through the gospel he invites them to become part of his royal family. Through the message we speak, they can share in all that he accomplished and receive the crown of life along with us.

Let us then be faithful. It will be a challenge. Satan will throw obstacles our way. Our sinful nature will urge us to give up the fight. The people around us will often be very unreceptive, but with the power of the Holy Spirit and by the grace of God, we can and will endure. The outcome is assured. Our crown is waiting for us. Let us continue to hold that good news close to our hearts and boldly and confidently proclaim it so that others also receive the crown of life.

❧✿☙

Praise to you, King of heaven, for your wonderful victory over our enemies. Keep us faithful to your gospel so that we may all receive your crown of everlasting life. May your kingdom come to many who are not yet enjoying its peace and blessing. Open their hearts to believe and to join with us in praising your name. Amen.

13

We believe that Jesus died and rose again and so we believe that God will bring with Jesus those who have fallen asleep in him. (1 Thessalonians 4:14)

Jesus is our hope

The death of a loved one is one of the saddest experiences we can ever endure. This was even true for Jesus during his earthly life. Jesus wept tears of sorrow at the tomb of his friend Lazarus.

Death takes away those who are near and dear to us. It takes a parent from children, a husband from a wife, a wife from a husband, a child from parents. From our earthly perspective, death is final. We cannot expect that those we love who have died will ever truly be with us again in this life. For those who view death as the end, this is a cause for real sadness.

But the joy of our faith is that our loved ones are not separated from us forever. The resurrection of Jesus brings us a message of hope. Jesus said, "Because I live, you also will live" (John 14:19). Jesus does live! On Easter Sunday morning, the tomb was empty. It was empty because Jesus arose in triumph over the power of death. He alone can call himself the Resurrection and the Life.

Death is not the end for us or for our loved ones who fall asleep in Christ. Jesus promises eternal life to all who believe and trust in him. When our eyes close in death, the Lord Jesus takes our souls to be with him in heaven. Our bodies rest in the grave.

Because Jesus did rise, the day is coming when he will also raise our bodies from the grave. He will raise us and our loved ones and give to all who died in Christ the gift of eternal life in heaven.

Our King lives! In him we live in hope. Through faith in our living Savior Jesus, we know that the day is coming when he will give us bodies that are fashioned like his own resurrected body.

✼

Dear Lord, when your people die, keep us from grieving as the rest of the world does. Enable us to sympathize with those left behind over the loss yet concentrate on what the departed Christian has gained. Amen.

*"See that you do not look down on one of these little ones.
For I tell you that their angels in heaven always see the face
of my Father in heaven." (Matthew 18:10,11)*

Angels watch over our little ones

There are many things that can keep us from doing God's will. Some of these are external: other people, involvement in our jobs, other activities. Some obstacles are internal: weak faith, jealousy, stubbornness, lack of dedication. The devil may use any of these things to keep us from doing God's will.

One of the responsibilities God has laid upon parents is the upbringing of their children. God wants parents to be concerned about the health and welfare of their children. God has given parents the responsibility to bring up their children in the right way: to lead them to Christ, to care for them, and to protect them.

But sometimes sincere and dedicated parents carry this protection too far. They begin to worry and become upset about every little thing that might possibly happen to their children. They dread the dangers children are exposed to on their way home from school. They watch them constantly in their play lest they be injured. Their minds become preoccupied with thoughts of their children becoming seriously ill.

The best cure for overprotective parents is to trust the Word of the Lord Jesus that assures us that the angels are watching over our little ones. Children are important to God. Jesus showed this when he rebuked his disciples for trying to keep the mothers from bringing their children to him. Jesus blessed the little children. God sends his angels to watch over them.

However, this promise of God that he is watching over children does not release parents from their responsibility of guarding children from danger. But it does release parents from unnecessary doubts and fears. No parent can always be with his or her child. This is work that only God can do.

When parents are released from worries about their children, they will find more energy to do the things God really wants them to do. They will be more relaxed in showing love, patience, and understanding. They will find time to fulfill some call to service outside the home. They will find more joy in worship. Entrust your children to God's care!

❧⊙⊙❧

*Heavenly Father, guard and keep our little ones from danger.
Free us from unnecessary fears so that we may better serve you
in our lives. Amen.*

15

"The time came when the beggar died and the angels carried him to Abraham's side." (Luke 16:22)

The angels' final service for us

Every ten years the US government undertakes the big task of counting all the people living in the United States. Many people are employed and much money is spent to make the census as accurate as possible. And yet we are told that there are thousands of "lost Americans," or people who don't get counted in the census. No matter how carefully people work to make sure that no one is missed, some individuals are still forgotten.

Nothing like this happens with God. Sometimes it may seem to people that God has forgotten them. Some of the psalms express the anguish that grips a person who feels himself forgotten by God. The poor man Lazarus might easily have been one of those whom we would today miss when taking a census. Lazarus might also have felt that God had forgotten him. But such was not the case at all.

God has a whole army of servants doing this very thing: making sure that no one is forgotten. When Lazarus died, we are told that the angels carried him to "Abraham's side," that is, to his heavenly home. God had not overlooked Lazarus. Though this beggar's only earthly companions were dogs, the divine guardians watched over him. Lazarus was on God's census roll.

A verse in Psalms says, "The righteous cry out, and the LORD hears them; he delivers them from all their troubles" (34:17). God delivers his people not only from earthly dangers and troubles that confront us in our present lives. God delivers us from that last and dreadful terror: death. Not even death is able to separate us from the love of God. Even death cannot hide us so that we will not be found. Even the grave cannot take us out of the protecting hand of God.

As servants of our Lord Jesus, the angels are even now preparing for the great day of the Lord's return when they will fulfill an additional service for us. On that day they will go to the ends of the earth to gather in the elect. No one who has ever trusted in the Lord will be missed on that day. God did not forget the beggar Lazarus. He will not forget us either.

⁓◐◑⁓

Praise and thanks, O Lord, for your great goodness in creating holy angels to watch over us. As we live and when we die, comfort us with the assurance that we are not forgotten. Amen.

After this I looked and there before me was a great multitude that no one could count. (Revelation 7:9)

Behold the host arrayed in white— try to count them

The apostle John had just been told that the servants of God number 144,000 (verse 4). In a vision he saw God's angels put God's seal on their foreheads to identify them as belonging to him for this life and for the life to come.

Does this mean that exactly and only 144,000 people will be saved? We take the Bible in the clear and literal sense, which means that we also recognize legitimate symbols and figures of speech. For example, when Jesus labeled Herod a "fox" (Luke 13:32), he obviously was speaking figuratively. Likewise, the number 144,000 is clearly figurative, or symbolic. It represents the total number of believers in Christ from the beginning to the end of time. It assures us that all of God's elect are known to him and that they will not fail to inherit eternal life.

We know that this number is figurative because John tells us that, after having seen the multitude of God's servants and after having been told that they number 144,000, he saw "a great multitude that no one could count." When it is stated that a multitude of 144,000 people could not be counted, it is obvious the sacred author uses the number in a symbolic sense.

We are reminded of God's promise to Abraham that his descendants would literally be as innumerable as the stars in the heavens or the grains of sand upon the seashore. This was true of his physical descendants, which include both Jews and Arabs and others, and it is true of his spiritual descendants, all who share Abraham's faith. Who of us can count them?

If John could have gotten a close look at all the faces in that multitude, he would have seen Abraham, Isaac, Jacob, and many other Old Testament believers. He would have recognized his fellow apostles, with the exception of Judas Iscariot. And—wonder of wonders!—he would have seen you and me and our faithful Christian friends and neighbors. He would have seen children and grandchildren yet unborn. He would have seen all those whom God graciously chose from eternity, called by the gospel, justified through faith in Christ, and glorified—all faithful believers from the beginning to the end of time.

We will rejoice eternally that this multitude of 144,000 is truly beyond numbering. Yet the symbolic use of an exact number reminds us that our heavenly Father knows each of us by name.

❧◍◍◍☙

Gracious Father in heaven, I am grateful that for Jesus' sake you have called me by name and have counted me to be among your countless saints. Amen.

17

After this I looked and there before me was a great multitude that no one could count, from every nation, tribe, people and language. (Revelation 7:9)

Behold the host arrayed in white— note their nationalities

Since people of many nationalities have become residents of the United States of America, our nation is sometimes called a melting pot. The ideal is that all residents blend together to form one harmonious people who live and work side-by-side and share in the privileges and responsibilities of their common citizenship.

But this social blending remains imperfect because we remember our roots and preserve our ethnic differences. It is imperfect on a deeper level because our sinful nature stubbornly clings to its own personal, selfish interests. Our text presents to us the perfect melting pot. Here we have people of "every nation, tribe, people and language," and we will see later how they all live in perfect harmony.

As we consider the various nationalities, we note that no particular nations are singled out. Being a physical descendant of Abraham is no guarantee of being included—even though many in Jesus' day boasted of their relationship to Abraham. They assumed that this automatically made them God's people for all eternity. Pious Christian parents and grandparents cannot believe for their children. Even church membership is not a ticket that will get anyone through the door into heaven. Everyone has to stand alone before God on judgment day.

This great multitude consists of individuals, not groups. It is made up of individuals "from every nation, tribe, people and language," not of nations or tribes as such. No Christian denomination as such will be transported en masse to the glories of heaven. But each individual who despairs of his own righteousness and trusts in Jesus Christ alone for forgiveness and salvation will be joyfully escorted by God's holy angels to the mansions of heaven.

This innumerable multitude does include members of God's chosen Old Testament people, the Israelites. It includes people from gentile nations of Old Testament times, like Rahab, Ruth, Naaman. It includes Europeans, Americans, Africans, and Asians who are in Christ.

Jesus promised that his gospel would be proclaimed to every nation under heaven, and he gave us a part in this glorious task. This multitude gathered from every nation under heaven is positive proof that the gospel is powerful and effective. It does not return empty.

❧☙

Use my hands and my lips and my gifts, precious Savior, to help proclaim your saving gospel to every nation under heaven. Amen.

After this I looked and there before me was a great multitude that no one could count, from every nation, tribe, people and language, standing before the throne and in front of the Lamb. (Revelation 7:9)

Behold the host arrayed in white— see where they stand

They came from every nation on earth, but now they stand united before the throne of God.

The throne symbolizes God's power and rule. Before he ascended into heaven, Jesus declared that all power in heaven and on earth had been given to him. As true God and true man, he rules the world in the interest of his church. At the time portrayed in this vision, this world has ceased to exist and the fruits of Christ's gracious rule are gathered before the throne in heaven.

The Lamb is, of course, Jesus our Savior. John the Baptist called him "the Lamb of God, who takes away the sin of the world" (John 1:29). The original Passover lambs had to shed their blood so that the Israelites' door-posts could be marked and the firstborn sons would be spared by the angel of death. As the Passover was commemorated every year thereafter, the Passover lamb reminded the people of Israel of their deliverance from Egypt. But it also pointed forward to the Savior, who would come and shed his blood to deliver us from the bondage of sin, death, and hell.

All who stand before the throne and in front of the Lamb in heaven also stood with Christ in this world. Some were staunch and faithful believers all their lives—people such as we would expect to see again in heaven. Some were baptized infants whose earthly lives were brief. Some were recent converts, whose sparks of faith grew into flames and survived until the Lord took them into his presence in heaven. There are those who seemed to have died untimely deaths, but in reality the timing was a special blessing of God's grace.

Some who stand before the Lamb in heaven will be a surprise to us. Like the thief on the cross to Jesus' right, these people were brought to repentance in their final hours. They were like brands plucked from the fire. Now they stand among the saints in heaven.

Some had many obvious troubles in this life, but the Holy Spirit graciously preserved their faith and gave them eternal joy in place of their brief sorrows.

All these are pictured as standing with their Savior in heaven. The Lord Jesus, who is both the Lamb of God and our Good Shepherd, did not let anyone pluck them out of his hand.

✆◎◎☙

O Christ, Lamb of God, have mercy on us and grant us your peace for all eternity. Amen.

19

They were wearing white robes and were holding palm branches in their hands. . . . "They have washed their robes and made them white in the blood of the Lamb."
(Revelation 7:9,14)

Behold the host arrayed in white— admire their white robes

There is a very strict dress code in heaven. Everyone must wear a robe that is perfectly white. Not a single spot or stain will be tolerated.

If there is anything that we have in abundance in today's society, it is soaps and detergents and bleaches, whiteners and spot removers. They are advertised constantly in all the media, and their purveyors make extravagant claims for them. Yet all of them together could never produce the perfect whiteness that God requires.

God had to provide these perfect white robes for us. They are not made of natural fibers like cotton or wool, linen or silk, nor are they made of synthetic materials like nylon or polyester. They are made of righteousness and holiness. The hymn writer taught us to sing, "Jesus, your blood and righteousness my beauty are, my glorious dress" (CW 376:1).

The white robes that confirmands wear are reminders that their Savior has clothed them in his perfect righteousness. They put on Christ and his holiness already in the Sacrament of Holy Baptism, and the Word of God that they studied in preparation for confirmation keeps those robes perfectly white. What a tragedy it is when a person thinks he has outgrown his need for God's Word.

As long as we live in this sinful world, we soil our robes day after day. We get them so spotted and stained with the filth of sin that it seems impossible to make them clean and white again. Yet they must be cleaned and can be cleaned, but in only one way. They must be washed in the blood of the Lamb. This is done when Christ's perfect righteousness is bestowed on us in our baptisms. We should dress up in these robes anew each day. Whenever we come to the Lord's Table, we receive his true body and blood and the forgiveness they earned for us on the cross. The blood of Jesus Christ, God's Son, cleanses us from all sin. We are indeed cleansed from all sin through faith in him.

God's forgiveness is always complete. He never forgives some sins and not others. Even all our secret faults have been forgiven. Repentance is not a formal act or ritual for gaining forgiveness of sins one by one, but it is an attitude that looks to the blood of Christ for cleansing.

❦

Wash me with your blood, precious Savior, and I will be whiter than snow, fitly dressed to join the saints before your throne. Amen.

They cried out in a loud voice: "Salvation belongs to our God, who sits on the throne, and to the Lamb."
(Revelation 7:10)

Behold the host arrayed in white— listen to their song

As John beheld this host arrayed in white, he noticed that the multitude was too large to count. The members of the multitude came from every nation under heaven, and they joined their voices in singing a mighty song of salvation.

Salvation should have top priority in our lives. Do not neglect to consider it simply because you cannot see it or hold it in your hands. It has to do not with this brief earthly life but with our eternal destiny. In this life there is always hope and opportunity for change and improvement, but in eternity there will be either unending happiness or everlasting torment. Nothing is more urgent or important than the matter of salvation. Now is the day of salvation.

So listen to this song of salvation. It is being sung by a great multitude of people who know from experience what they are singing about. They tell us, "Salvation belongs to our God." He is the author and source of salvation. There is no salvation except through faith in God's Son, Jesus Christ, who atoned for the sins of the world.

Most people expect that they will have a chance to be saved. If you ask them why, they might say, "Well, I'm as good as most other people— and that ought to be good enough to suit God." There are many variations, but the theme is the same: "Somehow I hope to do enough good things to save myself. Salvation belongs to me."

But God's Word says that all are sinners and fall short of the glory of God. Everyone needs to know that "salvation belongs to our God." Our salvation is God's doing from beginning to end. He planned it in eternity, and he accomplished it in time. God's Son, the Lamb, paid the price for our salvation when he laid down his life on the cross. God the Holy Spirit created faith in our hearts so that we know and trust Jesus for full forgiveness and eternal salvation. Jesus has returned to heaven to prepare a place for us, and he will take us there in his own good time.

Remember that the God of our salvation "sits on the throne." He rules this world in the interest of his believers. No enemy can separate us from his love or deprive us of our salvation.

❧⊙☙

We thank you, heavenly Father, that you have done everything necessary to redeem us from sin, death, and hell, and have graciously given us the gift of salvation through faith in Christ Jesus. Amen.

All the angels were standing around the throne and around the elders and the four living creatures. They fell down on their faces before the throne and worshiped God, saying: "Amen! Praise and glory and wisdom and thanks and honor and power and strength be to our God for ever and ever. Amen!" (Revelation 7:11,12)

Behold the host arrayed in white— learn from the angels' song

All the holy angels in heaven agreed with the song of the white-robed multitude by beginning their own song with the word *Amen.* They were saying, "We approve, for this is the truth." Then they proceeded to expand upon the song of the saints.

"They fell down on their faces before the throne and worshiped God." These angels were holy creatures of God. Yet they were humble before God, because they realized that he was their Maker and that they owed everything to him. They fell down on their faces to express their humility and their eagerness to serve God in any way he might desire.

Angels are spirits. They are personal beings who take on visible form only when God wants them to be seen. That was the case here. John could see the angels, and he could hear their song. We also consider the source when judging whether a statement is credible or not. When God speaks to us through his Word, there is no doubt about the matter. We too can sing and shout, "Amen!"

The song of the holy angels speaks of praise, glory, wisdom, thanks, honor, power, and strength. Neither we nor the angels can give God power or strength or wisdom. We can only acknowledge that he already possesses almighty power and perfect wisdom. The power and strength of God are demonstrated in the universe he created and in the forces of nature that we can observe but cannot control. We can only try to understand and attempt to live in harmony with the laws and forces of nature.

The wisdom of God is evident in the order and complexity of the matter he has created. We are only beginning to understand the nature and the function of atoms. We can use electricity, but who can explain it? Even the simplest living creature is a miracle of God's wisdom. We have bodies that are fearfully and wonderfully made and, even more amazing, immortal souls. We do well to study the wonders of God's creation. We recognize them as God's handiwork and accept the revelations of his wisdom in matters beyond our comprehension. Let us never doubt the wisdom God reveals to us in Christ.

❧◎❧

God of wisdom, power, and mercy, we give you praise and honor and thanks and look forward to praising you eternally, together with all the saints and holy angels. Amen.

Then one of the elders asked me, "These in white robes—
who are they, and where did they come from?" I answered,
"Sir, you know." And he said, "These are they who have
come out of the great tribulation." (Revelation 7:13,14)

Behold the host arrayed in white— consider their great tribulation

The songs of the saints and angels that we have just considered forcefully remind us that our salvation is God's doing from beginning to end. He does everything necessary to bring all of his elect to eternal glory, but he does not use his almighty power to force people to believe or to transport them like shackled prisoners to the mansions of heaven. If you reject the blessings of God's grace or carelessly cast them aside, it is your own fault. God did everything necessary to save you. Those who choose to go the way of the godless majority and to travel the broad road that leads to eternal damnation have only themselves to blame.

God's grace and our responsibility present us with a mystery that our minds cannot fathom. But is it not presumptuous for us sinners to judge the ways of the all-wise God with our limited wisdom? We do well to remember that our salvation is all God's doing and then to refrain from doing the things that jeopardize that free salvation. Our saving faith needs to be nourished and strengthened by means of the gospel and the sacrament. Otherwise, faith cannot survive and salvation is lost.

Our many sorrows and tribulations keep us mindful of our need to rely upon God for every need of body or soul. This is a general reference to the trials and difficulties that are inescapable in this earthly life. They remind us that God is in control and that he is not answerable to us. He chastens those whom he loves, and no trials will come into our lives unless he also gives us the strength to endure them. In the final analysis, he will make all things work together for the good of those who love him.

God uses our tribulations to keep us on the narrow way that leads to life everlasting. They remind us that we are unworthy sinners and that it is only because of the Lord's mercies that we are not consumed. Whenever we pity ourselves or feel like accusing God of injustice, we need to consider all that Jesus willingly suffered so that we might look forward to eternal joy.

❧◑◐❧

Dear Father in heaven, as we behold the host arrayed in white,
we trust you to keep us as your own until we join them in
singing your praises for all eternity. Amen.

23

He will wipe every tear from their eyes. There will be no more death or mourning or crying or pain, for the old order of things has passed away. (Revelation 21:4)

The old order has passed away— no more misery!

Have you ever planned a trip to some distant and exotic place such as Hawaii or Japan and wondered what it would be like? You were told about its climate, its geography, and the culture of the people, but until you actually arrive there and experience that place yourself, your mind can only imagine what it must be like.

No wonder Christians commonly ask, "What will heaven be like?" Little children just learning about heaven will ask this question. Elderly folks expecting to go there someday soon will ask the same. It is natural for those who know that they will one day live in heaven to ask what it will be like.

John gives us a partial answer to this question by telling us what will not be there: tears, death, mourning, crying, or pain. And why won't these things be there? John explains, "The old order of things has passed away." After God judges everyone and destroys the old heaven and earth, he will introduce believers to his own heaven as their new and permanent home. And yes, in heaven there will be no more misery!

One thing that will be gone and certainly not be missed will be our tears. As we enter our new lives with our God, he lovingly wipes away any tears that are present. It is a touching scene of God's deep love for us. Wiping away our tears means removing all things that cause tears. Looking at our lives here on earth now, we find plenty of reasons for tears. None of them will exist in heaven.

In heaven we will finally be perfect like God. Our emotions and all our thoughts will be in perfect harmony with his. Those things that cause people no end of misery here on earth—death, mourning, crying, and pain—will be totally absent in heaven! We know that all of these distressing things are the result of sin. Because there will be no more sin in heaven, the consequences of sin will also disappear.

Is this hard to imagine? It is for me. How can we even imagine something so wonderful? Who hasn't felt the tragedy and the pain caused by a loved one's death? What believers haven't grieved over the heartache of a broken relationship, suffered the pain of illness and disease, or anguished over the many injustices forced upon them? In this glimpse of heaven, John reveals that all of those things will be behind us. Thank God!

✒☙�

Blessed Savior, when trials and troubles cause stress and pain, remind me of this blessed scene. In heaven there will be no more misery! Amen.

So you also must be ready, because the Son of Man will come at an hour when you do not expect him. (Matthew 24:44)

The hour is his to set

We don't know the day when the Lord will come. We don't know if it will be at night. We don't know the hour either. That time will be determined by God. The hour is his to set.

Why does he seem to be waiting so long? In his second letter, the apostle Peter tells us that some people will scoff and will claim that God's slowness in setting the hour means that he won't come. But Peter answers such unbelief by saying, "The Lord is not slow in keeping his promise, as some understand slowness. He is patient with you, not wanting anyone to perish, but everyone to come to repentance" (3:9).

What love! God has not set the hour without thinking. God will not determine that time in anger. God's love for the world will determine that time. In his love he gave his only begotten Son as the spotless Lamb to be sacrificed to atone for our guilt. In his love he causes this good news to be preached now. In his love he is calling us to repentance for sin and to firmly trust in his forgiveness. In his love he is still calling to us today, still giving us time, until the hour comes that he has set as the right hour.

Because we do not know when that right hour is, Jesus says to us, "So you also must be ready." Don't be unprepared. Don't become weak in faith by neglecting the Word of God, by staying away from the Lord's Supper. Don't fall from faith and into eternal loss. Be ready. Be strengthened and sustained by the power of the Spirit through faithful use of Word and sacrament.

Christmas is coming. We can set the hour for our Christmas service. But what of the time when the Lord will come? That hour is his to set.

What joy awaits us then, what bliss beyond comparison! What glory will be ours because of the Lord who came to save, who comes now through his Word, and who will come again—at the hour he has set—to receive us to himself!

❧✣❧

Heavenly Father, thank you for your love that has given us time, for your Spirit who has moved us to repent and believe, and for your Son in whom we believe. In his name, we ask you to keep us watchful and ready for the hour of his return. Amen.

Praise the LORD, O my soul; all my inmost being, praise his holy name. Praise the LORD, O my soul, and forget not all his benefits—who forgives all your sins and heals all your diseases, who redeems your life from the pit and crowns you with love and compassion, who satisfies your desires with good things so that your youth is renewed like the eagle's. (Psalm 103:1-5)

Now thank we all our God— with our hearts!

For more than three centuries, the Protestant churches of Europe and the United States have resounded to the stirring tune of Martin Rinkart's great hymn of thanksgiving, "Now Thank We All Our God." The opening lines express the thoughts of the truly thankful Christian: "Now thank we all our God with *hearts* and *hands* and *voices*" (CW 610:1). We will take these words as a guide in our Thanksgiving meditations.

The psalm of thanksgiving quoted above leads us to understand the meaning of true gratitude. The psalmist does not suggest that true praise is a mere matter of high-sounding phrases and elegant words. He says rather, "Praise the LORD, O my soul; all my inmost being, praise his holy name. . . . And forget not all his benefits." With our *hearts* let us thank our God, because in our hearts we know that all his benefits include more than outward peace and prosperity, health, and happiness.

The psalmist places this benefit at the head of his list in the words "who forgives all your sins."

Let our thanksgiving begin at the top. Let us remember, and not forget, this greatest goodness of God. For Jesus' sake, he has forgiven all our sins; he regards and treats us as his children; he daily restores us; he leads us heavenward. For this benefit alone, we have reason to thank him always.

When we go down the list to blessings for the body, we see further evidence of undeserved goodness. Our gratitude does not depend on how much or how little God has chosen to give us during this past year. Though it is little, as people usually reckon it, to us it is still much; it is still the evidence of God's grace. Even if we are reduced to poverty, we can still say with Job, "The LORD gave and the LORD has taken away; may the name of the LORD be praised" (Job 1:21).

With a full heart, let us thank God, who has forgiven all our iniquities. We will surely then add our gratitude for all the other gifts with which God has crowned our days on earth.

Lord God, teach us true gratitude for your greatest gift— forgiveness in Christ—and give us grace to thank you with hearts and hands and voices for all the gifts of the body. Amen.

Trust in the LORD with all your heart and lean not on your own understanding; in all your ways acknowledge him, and he will make your paths straight. Do not be wise in your own eyes; fear the LORD and shun evil. This will bring health to your body and nourishment to your bones. Honor the LORD with your wealth, with the firstfruits of all your crops; then your barns will be filled to overflowing, and your vats will brim over with new wine. (Proverbs 3:5-10)

Now thank we all our God— with our hands!

Gratitude for God's gifts can never find true expression with mere words. The stirring words of "Now Thank We All Our God" can be sung lustily even by the hypocrite. The inspired words of Psalm 103:1, "Praise the LORD, O my soul; all my inmost being, praise his holy name," can sound sincere even when they are spoken with an unbelieving and thankless heart. True thankfulness is an attitude of the heart, not a mere expression of the lips. It is an attitude that the believer has. By faith he sees God as the giver of eternal life. Then he also sees God as the giver of all good things.

With this attitude toward God in our hearts, it is only natural that we also express our thanks to God with our hands. "Honor the LORD with your wealth." Such is our desire. We want to honor the "Father of the heavenly lights," from whom we have received "every good and perfect gift" (James 1:17). We want to honor the Son, to whom we sing, "Lord of glory, you have bought us with your lifeblood as the price" (CW 486:1). We want to honor the Holy Spirit, who has taught us to know the Father and the Son.

We desire to honor our God "with the firstfruits of all [our] crops," that is, with the first and best of all that God has put into our hands. If we notice that our old Adam wants us to be stingy in our offerings, let us rebuke him, saying, "Should I give my God so little? No, I will strive to offer more generous gifts to honor the God of my salvation."

If such is the spirit in our hearts, we will also listen to these admonitions in the matter of using our earthly goods: "Do not be wise in your own eyes" and "Lean not on your own understanding." Humbly we will remember that we have something only because God has blessed our labors. We will shrink from the boasting of wicked and godless people, from saying things like "everything I have I got because I worked hard and used my head. I have myself to thank, no one else. I'll do with it as I please." Rather, as we take stock of our blessings, let us gladly give glory to God and earnestly strive to become better stewards of his gifts.

Heavenly Father, grant that with our hands we may give thanks for your countless blessings and that our gifts may truly honor you. Amen.

Give thanks to the LORD, call on his name; make known among the nations what he has done. Sing to him, sing praise to him; tell of all his wonderful acts. Glory in his holy name; let the hearts of those who seek the LORD rejoice. Look to the LORD and his strength; seek his face always. Remember the wonders he has done, his miracles, and the judgments he pronounced. (Psalm 105:1-5)

Now thank we all our God— with our voices!

The terms *pious, holy,* and *religious* are sometimes sneeringly applied to Christians. The sneers suggest that the Christian considers cheerfulness a vice, and there may be some misguided Christians who believe that if you take your religion seriously, you will not permit yourself to indulge in a song or a cheerful smile.

But it is true that there are times when the sincere Christian has good reason to be sad. This is particularly true when he begins his Sunday worship with these words: "I am by nature sinful." But then he hears the pastor say, "I forgive you all your sins." This message of grace is repeated in the Scripture readings and the sermon. And so the Christian responds to the invitation of our psalm to give thanks to the Lord, to sing psalms to him, and to glory in his holy name. The liturgy is a golden chain of praise. It bids us to thank our God with hearts and hands and voices. In the "Glory Be to God," the hymns, and the final "Amen," we are invited to sing our joyful praises to God.

The Christian who on Sunday morning raises his voice in praise of God's mercy and marvelous works ought to carry this joyful refrain into every day of his life. At home or away from home, at work or play, his conversation and his behavior should not conceal the joy in his heart over the wondrous works of a gracious and forgiving God. To him the work of his congregation and the mission program of the synod will be invitations to make known the saving deeds of the only true God among people both near and far.

Not only on Thanksgiving Day but every day remember the message of thanksgiving. Remember to thank God for all his benefits with hearts and hands and voices. Remember the best reason for thanksgiving as you sing, "Create in me a clean heart, O God, and renew a right spirit within me." Remember also the closing words of that song, "Restore unto me the joy of your salvation." That is a joy that he has restored and that prompts us to say with David in Psalm 51:13, "Then I will teach transgressors your ways, and sinners will turn back to you."

༺ঞৎ

Now thank we all our God with hearts and hands and voices! Amen.

Rejoice in the Lord always. I will say it again: Rejoice! Let your gentleness be evident to all. The Lord is near. Do not be anxious about anything, but in everything, by prayer and petition, with thanksgiving, present your requests to God. And the peace of God, which transcends all understanding, will guard your hearts and your minds in Christ Jesus. (Philippians 4:4-7)

The Lord is near

Our ultimate hope, the joyful hope of our Savior's return in glory at the end of the world, is under heavy attack by the world. People in our day and age are obsessed with the idea not of having Christ return and take them to heaven but of building some sort of synthetic heaven on this poor earth of ours through politics, planning, and progress. Believers are being affected. We are in danger of losing sight of our hope of heaven, of forgetting Jesus' promise to come again, of forfeiting our joy in Christ's promise.

In this sacred season, we need to pause in the rush of modern living and listen to the voice of eternity that is reminding us, "The Lord is near." Then we will lift up our heads and hearts with rejoicing in the thought that our redemption is drawing near. Jesus came into this world in humility to serve as the Savior from sin and death, judgment and hell. For us who believe in him, his second coming is not an occasion for regret or terror. For us, the Last Day is the best day, the end of troubles and tears, the beginning of the new and eternal life.

Between Christ's first and final comings, we are strengthened for our tasks and toils and comforted in our troubles and tears by the same coming Lord whom we are praising. He who once came to Bethlehem and who will come again in the heavens comes to us faithfully these days in Word and sacrament. He assures us that our sins are forgiven. He strengthens our faith and love. He awakens in our hearts the joy that eagerly anticipates the last great day.

We do not and cannot know when that day will be. That fact does not mean, however, that we will think and talk and act as though it were never coming. Our watchword remains: "The Lord is near." How much different and better our daily lives would be if we would continually remind ourselves that "The Lord is near"! How stronger and surer our joy would be in season and out of season if we always centered hearts and minds on that blessed promise of the Scriptures: "The Lord is near"!

Teach us in watchfulness and prayer
To wait for your appointed hour,
And fit us by your grace to share
The triumphs of your conqu'ring pow'r. Amen. (CW 9:5)

29

And Mary said: "My soul glorifies the Lord and my spirit rejoices in God my Savior." (Luke 1:46,47)

Magnify the Lord—
for the joy of his salvation

Magnificat is the Latin for the first word of Mary's song of praise, so we call her song the *Magnificat*. In the King James Version of the Bible, Mary says to Elizabeth, "My soul doth magnify the Lord."

A magnifying glass makes an object appear larger. A child may be fascinated by it. An elderly Christian may need one to read his Bible or to look up a phone number. A microscope magnifies tiny invisible organisms and makes them visible to us.

So when we magnify the Lord, he does not become bigger or greater as a result of our efforts. He just looks greater to us because we see him better. We grow in our appreciation of his wondrous works and ways.

Mary's song teaches us to magnify the Lord in this way. We want to follow her example.

Mary's situation was unique. God had singled her out for an honor that no one else would ever receive. She was the virgin mother of the Son of God. But we realize that this honor shown to Mary is a blessing for us all. We, therefore, like to sing this song along with Mary.

Today we want to take a closer look at Mary's rejoicing in God her Savior and join her in that rejoicing.

Mary was happy that she had been chosen to become the mother of the promised Savior, but her greatest joy was in being able to call him "my Savior." Although she was a very pious and godly maiden, she knew herself as a person with a sinful heart whose best efforts were not good enough to meet the demands of God's law. She knew that her only hope of salvation rested on the promise that went way back to the Garden of Eden, where God told Adam and Eve that the offspring of a woman would bruise the head of the serpent, Satan, and free us from his clutches.

The time had come for God to keep his promise and to send the Savior, and that was Mary's greatest reason for rejoicing. That joy is ours too as we next month commemorate the birth of Jesus, the Son of God and Mary's son.

We want to thank God this Advent season for his salvation and also for the joy that it brings to us. It brings us the joy of celebration in this blessed season and the joy of the anticipation of our eternal salvation in heaven.

Heavenly Father, restore to me the joy of your salvation, for Jesus' sake. Amen.

"He has been mindful of the humble state of his servant. From now on all generations will call me blessed." (Luke 1:48)

Magnify the Lord— for the blessedness of the humble

Mary was not boasting when she declared, "All generations will call me blessed." In all humility she was expressing her amazement at the message Gabriel had delivered to her.

Mary's "humble state" was apparent to all who knew her. She was a young peasant girl. She lived in Galilee, the northernmost province of the land of Israel. And her home was not even prominent by Galilean standards. She lived in the small village of Nazareth. She had neither fame nor wealth. She may have wondered who would become the mother of the Savior, but she never expected that she would be the one chosen by God for this high honor.

Why should God have chosen a lowly and obscure young woman like Mary for this great privilege? Would it not have been more appropriate for him to choose the daughter of some prominent and pious family in the capital city of Jerusalem? God could have directed the authorities at Jerusalem to select the right person. They could have considered her family connections, her intelligence, her knowledge of God's Word, her good character, her personal accomplishments, and the like. This would have attracted the attention of the people so that they could be prepared to welcome the Savior as soon as he was born.

That might have been a good plan in man's eyes, but it is not God's way of doing things. The greatest people in God's sight are the humble and the lowly. He tells us, "This is the one I esteem: he who is humble and contrite in spirit, and trembles at my word" (Isaiah 66:2).

This is a difficult lesson for us to learn. Even Jesus' disciples found it difficult. To the very end of Jesus' earthly ministry, they argued among themselves and schemed to gain prominent positions in Jesus' kingdom. Jesus told them, "Deny yourselves, take up your crosses, and follow me; serve the poor and the needy, the sick and the imprisoned, the suffering and the dying, in my name—that is the way to be great in my kingdom."

Without humility, real blessedness is impossible. Only when we recognize our sinfulness and unworthiness can we appreciate the blessings that God offers us in his Son—forgiveness, life, and salvation. Only when we are ourselves as we really are by nature and marvel at God's loving concern for us, only then can we magnify the Lord as Mary did.

❦

Heavenly Father, we magnify you for the blessedness of the humble. Teach us genuine humility, that we may know true blessedness. Amen.

"The Mighty One has done great things for me—holy is his name." (Luke 1:49)

Magnify the Lord— for the holiness of his name

God's name is holy. No angel can make God's name any holier, and no devil can make it unholy. When we pray, "Hallowed be your name," we are asking that God would help us recognize the holiness of his name.

The Second Commandment demands that we use God's name aright by calling upon it in every trouble, praying, praising, and giving thanks to that name. It also demands that we refrain from misusing God's name by cursing, swearing, practicing superstition, or lying and deceiving in his name.

God has many names—Father, Son, Holy Spirit, Creator, Redeemer, Sanctifier, Jehovah, and Lord, to mention just a few. In every name that God applies to himself, he reveals something about himself. A particular name of God may emphasize his power, his mercy, his faithfulness, or his righteousness.

But God has not revealed himself to us only in the names by which he asks us to address him. When Mary reminds us that God's name is holy, she is not only saying that every name of God reveals him perfectly to us but is speaking of all that God has revealed to us about himself in his Holy Word.

We may speak of a person as having a good name or a bad name. By that we refer to a person's reputation, which is based upon what we know, or think we know, about him. Similarly, God's good name depends upon the Scriptures, which tell us about him. His name and his Word finally amount to the same thing. That is why Martin Luther says in his Small Catechism that God's name is hallowed when his Word is taught in its truth and purity and when we believe it and obey it.

"Holy is his name" is more than just an abstract statement of truth. It is a brief and simple way of saying that the Scriptures are perfect, reliable, inerrant. It is a way of confessing that we take God at his Word in all things, that we trust his promises, that we recognize our duty to obey his commandments.

It means that we do not place our human reason in a position to judge God's Word. The holiness of the Word rules out any efforts on our part to explain away its mysteries.

It means that we have the responsibility to proclaim God's truth to the world without apology or reservation. How dare anyone presume to improve upon that which is holy!

◦◦◦

Heavenly Father, your name is holy. Help us keep it holy. Amen.

"His mercy extends to those who fear him, from generation to generation." (Luke 1:50)

Magnify the Lord—
for the permanence of his mercy

God is merciful. That basic truth distinguishes Christianity from all other religions. The almighty, eternal, all-knowing, all-wise, righteous God would be our invincible enemy if he were not also merciful. His mercy is our point of contact with him. That makes it possible for us to rejoice in his power and wisdom and justice. If God were not merciful, we could receive nothing from him but punishment now and forever.

God's mercy is his kindness to the miserable and afflicted, to those who have no claim on any favors from God because their sins have separated them from their Creator. That includes all of us.

Yet Mary reminds us that "his mercy extends to those who fear him." Those who do not fear God cut themselves off from his mercy.

To fear God means to respect him and to recognize his complete authority over us. He has told us how to live and demands perfect obedience. Try as we may, we cannot come close to the perfection he requires. We cannot even take the first step. Our best efforts are totally without merit. We cannot stand in his presence.

But the Scriptures tell us that God is merciful. He loves us in spite of our sins. When sin came into the world, he was right there with his assurance of mercy. He immediately promised that he would send a Savior who would free sinful mankind from the clutches of the old serpent, Satan. And God's mercy extends to people of all generations who trust in the Savior who was promised and who came in due time.

In mercy God made that promise, and in mercy he fulfilled it. Mercy is not an occasional attitude of God; it is a permanent attribute of God. In mercy he chose Abraham to be the father of his special people, the Israelites. In mercy he sustained and protected the people of that nation despite their unfaithfulness to him. In mercy he sent his Son to be born of the virgin Mary and to suffer and die for the sins of the world.

We must rely upon that mercy as long as we live, because even our deeds of God-pleasing service are feeble and imperfect. Our only hope is in God's mercy in Christ.

Thanks be to God that "his mercy extends . . . from generation to generation." God's mercy in Christ Jesus is necessary for our generation and for every generation until the end of time. It will never go out of date, no matter how many people imagine that they don't need it.

God, be merciful to me, a sinner, for Jesus' sake. Amen.

"He has performed mighty deeds with his arm; he has scattered those who are proud in their inmost thoughts. He has brought down rulers from their thrones but has lifted up the humble." (Luke 1:51,52)

Magnify the Lord— for the power of his arm

God's arm has no muscle or flesh, skin or bones because God is a spirit, yet God's arm is almighty. When the Bible describes God in human terms, it reminds us how weak and puny we are compared to him. A man's arm may lift several hundred pounds, but God's arm sustains all of creation. He holds the whole world in his hand.

We cannot see God, but evidence of his power surrounds us constantly. The continuous supply of energy streaming from the sun to the earth is only a tiny fraction of what the sun gives off, and the total energy of the sun is only an infinitesimal fraction of the energy that is at work in the universe. And all that power God put in place by the power of his Word.

So it was no difficult task for God to scatter the proud—those who imagined that they were strong enough to defy God and to do things their own way. Remember how Pharaoh defied God, refusing to let God's people go from Egypt. All the horses and chariots of Egypt and the waters of the Red Sea were no obstacles for God.

King Nebuchadnezzar of Babylon gloried in his personal power until God intervened. God drove him out of his palace into the wide-open spaces. He "ate grass like cattle. . . . his hair grew like the feathers of an eagle and his nails like the claws of a bird" (Daniel 4:33).

When Caesar Augustus enrolled all the people of his empire for taxation, he compelled many people to travel to their hometowns, but the only significant thing he accomplished was to send Mary and Joseph to Bethlehem, where Jesus was to be born according to God's promises.

King Herod was determined to kill the Christ Child at Bethlehem. God used the king's murderous threats to send Mary and Joseph to Egypt with the infant Jesus—also thereby fulfilling a prophecy of the Old Testament Scriptures.

God's power will never be diminished, and the Son of God shares in it fully. He will finally summon all people into his presence. He will divide them as a shepherd divides the sheep from the goats. We could label the two groups as "the proud" and "the humble," "the impenitent" and "the penitent," "the unbelievers" and "the believers." The proud will be dismissed from his presence to be separated from God for all eternity. To those who humbly recognize their sins and trust in Jesus alone for forgiveness and salvation, he will say, "Come, inherit the kingdom prepared for you."

⤜⊚⊚⤏

Dear heavenly Father, yours is the power for ever and ever. Amen.

"He has filled the hungry with good things but has sent the rich away empty." (Luke 1:53)

Magnify the Lord— for the bounty of his providence

World hunger is a problem of staggering proportions. Starvation stalks through many nations of Africa, claiming victims by the thousands, and the same problem exists on a smaller scale all over the world. It is ironic that people in some nations are starving while many farmers in the United States cannot make a profit because they grow too much and cannot sell their crops for enough to cover their costs.

There are other problems associated with hunger and food supplies. Fussy eaters may be malnourished because they think they might not like the food that is set before them and are not even willing to try it. Such problems in childhood may result in health problems later in life as well. In our affluent society, many reject what they need and gorge themselves on what they do not need. They prefer to spoil their appetites rather than to satisfy them. They imagine that their needs are satisfied even when their bodies are suffering from lack of proper nourishment.

The "rich" of whom Mary speaks in our text are those who think they have all they need for their souls' welfare and who proudly reject what God offers them. They go away empty, their needs unfulfilled—and they don't even know it.

Just as children sometimes must be urged to try their food so that they may learn to like what is good for them, so we also must learn to appreciate the food that God provides for our souls.

Some of it is bitter to our taste. Who enjoys being told that he is an unworthy sinner? But only after that bitter food has been tasted and swallowed and inwardly digested can a person appreciate the sweet gospel of Christ, which assures us that Jesus took our sins upon himself and suffered as our substitute.

In the Sermon on the Mount, Jesus speaks of the blessedness of those who hunger and thirst for righteousness. This means recognizing our need for righteousness and strongly desiring it. It means admitting that our own righteousness is like a filthy rag in God's sight. It means trusting in Jesus, who fulfilled all righteousness for us. It means gratefully receiving his righteousness, which is credited to us through faith in him. And then it means hungering and thirsting for righteous deeds in our own lives, not as efforts to gain God's favor but as ways to express our gratitude for the gift of his righteousness in Christ.

❧❧❧

We give thanks to you, O Lord, for satisfying the hunger of our souls and filling us with good things. Amen.

5

"He has helped his servant Israel, remembering to be merciful to Abraham and his descendants forever, even as he said to our fathers." (Luke 1:54,55)

Magnify the Lord— for the constancy of his promises

We may be sincere about making promises and conscientious about trying to keep them, yet many of our promises are broken sooner or later.

There are many reasons for this. We promise too many things, and we simply forget about some of them. We promise too hastily, and we change our minds. We have good intentions, but circumstances beyond our control prevent us from doing as we promised, or temptations overcome us. When confronted with our broken promises, we find all kinds of excuses.

Sponsors at a baptism solemnly promise that they will pray for their godchild and do all that they can to help the parents in the Christian training and education of the child, but too often their words prove to be an empty formality. They fail to keep their promises.

Confirmands solemnly promise that they will be faithful in their use of the means of grace and that, if necessary, they will suffer anything, even death, rather than fall away from their Lord and Savior. Some forget that promise even before a week goes by.

Christian brides and grooms promise to love, honor, cherish, and be faithful to one another as long as they live. Divorce courts and police records attest to the high percentage of broken promises, even of this most sacred of all vows.

Promises of sinful humans are always uncertain, but we can rejoice in the constancy of God's promises as Mary does in our text.

God made the most amazing promises to Abraham. Purely out of grace, God singled him out to become the father of a great nation. He promised to make Abraham's descendants innumerable like the stars in the sky. He promised to give his descendants a land to call their own. And most important of all, he promised to send his Son into this world as a descendant of Abraham to redeem the whole world of sinners.

In spite of Abraham's weaknesses and the gross unfaithfulness of his descendants, God kept all his promises. In his own good time, he sent Jesus our Savior, and Jesus did everything necessary for our salvation. He offered his sinless body and soul on Calvary's cross as the perfect sacrifice to atone for all our sins. Now God promises eternal life for Jesus' sake to us and to all believers in Christ. With Mary we magnify the Lord for the constancy of all his promises.

⁂

As I consider the constancy of your promises, O Lord, make me more faithful in keeping my promises. Amen.

To us a child is born, to us a son is given. . . . And he will be called Wonderful Counselor, Mighty God, Everlasting Father. (Isaiah 9:6)

What child is this?— he is the mighty God

At Christmas the world waxes sentimental over the babe born in Bethlehem. People award him glowing tribute. Yet the honor given to Christ often falls far short of what it should be. As we prepare to celebrate Jesus' birth, let us ask the question, What child is this? Isaiah gives us a very definite answer. The child is not a mere man. He is also the mighty God.

Isaiah did foretell that the Savior would be true man. Indeed, Jesus was truly human. He was born of the virgin Mary with a body and soul like ours. He had human emotions and needs. Jesus' humanity differed from ours in only one area: He had no sin. He was conceived by the Holy Spirit and born of the virgin Mary.

In order to save us, Jesus had to be true man. Had he not been a true man, he could not have submitted to the law for us nor suffered for our sins. However, to save us, Christ had to be more than a man. A mere man could not have redeemed all people of all ages. Only the Creator could substitute for his creation. In his prophecies, Isaiah made it clear that the coming Savior would be more than just a man. He would be God himself. Through the names by which he called this child, Isaiah indicated the babe was true God.

Isaiah called him the "Wonderful Counselor." Mary's son was a wonder in that he was God and man in one person. He was the Counselor in whom all the wisdom of the Godhead dwelled. To carry out his mission as Savior, he needed wisdom and knowledge that no mere man could possess. He was the mighty God who had revealed himself in his saving power to the Israelites throughout the Old Testament era. He was the everlasting Father who had always cared for his children of all ages.

As we prepare to celebrate the birth of Christ, let us herald anew the person of the babe born in Bethlehem. The child who lay in the manger was a human being. He was also the mighty God. What a marvel! The almighty God lay in a manger so that he might save us from sin, death, and hell. Praise the God of our salvation that he became one of us in order to redeem us!

೫ఄఄ

Hosanna to the coming Lord!
Hosanna to the incarnate Word!
To Christ, Creator, Savior, King
Let earth, let heav'n hosanna sing. Amen. (CW 21:1)

The people walking in darkness have seen a great light; on those living in the land of the shadow of death a light has dawned. (Isaiah 9:2)

What child is this?— he is the light of the world

At the time Isaiah penned these words, darkness prevailed in the area of Galilee. Assyrian invaders had deported large segments of the population. The very existence of the kingdom of Israel was threatened. The darkness of despair hung like a cloud over a people whose situation looked hopeless.

Yet there was a deeper darkness that covered the people, one which brought on the darkness of deportation. It was the darkness of sin. This darkness began to cast its shadow over Israel when Solomon allowed his heathen wives to worship their idols at shrines erected outside of Jerusalem. It spread further when Jeroboam instituted calf worship at Dan and Bethel in the Northern Kingdom. Finally, it enveloped the whole land when Ahab and Jezebel made the worship of Baal the state religion.

The people of the Northern Kingdom persisted in their ways and refused to heed the prophets' warnings. Thus God sent his judgment in the form of the Assyrian invaders. In 722 B.C. Samaria fell to the Assyrians, and the Northern Kingdom ceased to exist. But still there was a ray of hope. Isaiah indicated a light would rise in the area that had been shrouded in darkness. This was fulfilled in the person of Christ, who spent much of his public ministry in the northern city of Capernaum. There he preached the good news of salvation, bringing light to the people who sat in darkness (Matthew 4:12-17).

Though we live in an age of great learning and education, there still is need for Christ to bring light into the world today. Computer technology boggles the mind. Medical marvels have become commonplace. Satellites have produced instant communication from the far corners of the world. Yet people are still living in darkness. They are struggling to answer the questions, Who am I? Why am I here? Where am I going? The world has no answers to these questions, but Christ has revealed the answers to us. Through faith in Jesus, we are his children. We find meaning for our lives in service to the Savior. After this life we have the assurance of eternal life. This Advent let us share with others the good news that Jesus is the Light of the world.

এ৩৯৩৩

O Jesus, precious Sun of gladness,
Fill Thou my soul with light, I pray.
Dispel the gloomy night of sadness
And teach Thou me this Christmas Day
How I a child of light may be,
Aglow with light that comes from Thee. Amen. (TLH 88:4)

You have enlarged the nation and increased their joy; they rejoice before you as people rejoice at the harvest, as men rejoice when dividing the plunder. (Isaiah 9:3)

What child is this?— he is the joy of the world

There is a great deal of excitement in the air as people prepare for Christmas. Cookies are baked and shared. Homes and yards are beautified with festive decorations. People do their Christmas shopping in attractively decorated stores. Gifts are given or exchanged in a holiday spirit of good will. Parties and programs occupy people's time. All of these activities can serve a good and beneficial purpose in preparing for celebrating Christ's birth. Yet they are not an end in themselves. Sad to say, too often they may be a mask beneath which a great deal of gloom and despair are hidden. Many times when all the celebrating is over, people are left with an empty feeling of despair. This is because they have missed the real joy in Christmas.

The joy that we have at Christmas is not a mere emotion. It does not surface today only to forsake us tomorrow. Our joy is centered in the person of the babe of Bethlehem. He is our Savior from sin and our assurance of fellowship with his Father. Just as people rejoice when the harvest is gathered or when they divide the spoils of victory, so we rejoice in the Savior-God sent to redeem us from sin. Our joy centers on all that Jesus won for us by his coming: the forgiveness of sins, fellowship with God, and eternal life.

This is real joy that cannot be taken from us. It exists in our hearts though our eyes may be clouded by tears. Our joy does not depend on what our earthly circumstances are. We may be rich or poor, healthy or sickly, influential or unimportant, in the company of our loved ones or separated from them. Yet we have a joy that transcends every situation in this life. Our joy is in our Savior from sin, Jesus Christ. It grows stronger as we draw closer to the goal of our lives—eternal life with the Lord in heaven. We have joy, not just at Christmas but all the days of our lives. Praise God for the joy that is ours through his Son, Jesus Christ!

❧◎◎☙

Oh, come, oh, come, Emmanuel,
And ransom captive Israel
That mourns in lonely exile here
Until the Son of God appear.
Rejoice! Rejoice! Emmanuel
Shall come to you, O Israel! (CW 23:1)

As in the day of Midian's defeat, you have shattered the yoke that burdens them, the bar across their shoulders, the rod of their oppressor. (Isaiah 9:4)

What child is this?—
he is the deliverer from oppression

What is the greatest burden people must bear? Some would say it is oppression at the hands of cruel rulers. Tyrants who oppress their subjects in a cruel and inhuman way are still with us in the world today. Yet there is a far greater form of oppression than that which any of the rulers of this world can give out. It is the oppression of all people by sin and Satan.

In Isaiah's day, both Israel and Judah were oppressed by the Assyrians. The cruelty of the Assyrians to captives is well documented in history. Yet even this oppression paled in comparison to the Israelites' own slavery to sin. The people of Israel and Judah had become slaves to their own appetites. They were held in bondage by the idols through which the devil led them down the road to hell.

However, the situation was not hopeless. The Lord promised to send a deliverer. This person would not be a mere mortal. God himself had to intervene to save his people. Just as with Gideon's 300 men the Lord had rescued the Israelites from the 135,000 Midianites and Amalekites (Judges chapters 6–8), so he would rescue all people from sin through his Son. Jesus Christ, the God-man, would take the field of battle on our behalf. He would keep the commandments of God for us. He would suffer the punishment for our sins. He would be the One through whom God would deliver all people from sin.

What we could not do for ourselves, Christ did for us. Through his suffering and death, we have been freed from the power of sin and Satan. The devil no longer can accuse us of our sins. Christ has paid for them in full. Through faith in Christ, we have been freed from slavery to sin for service to the Lord. As Paul wrote, "The life I live in the body, I live by faith in the Son of God, who loved me and gave himself for me" (Galatians 2:20).

As we prepare to celebrate our Savior's birth, we look to that babe in Bethlehem as our deliverer. He has freed us from sin, death, and Satan. That is something to celebrate!

❧❧❧

Oh, come, O Root of Jesse, free
Your own from Satan's tyranny;
From depths of hell your people save,
And bring them vict'ry o'er the grave.
Rejoice! Rejoice! Emmanuel
Shall come to you, O Israel! (CW 23:2)

Every warrior's boot used in battle and every garment rolled in blood will be destined for burning, will be fuel for the fire. (Isaiah 9:5)

What child is this?— he is the finisher of our faith

What do you think of when you hear the word *Christmas*? You probably think back to the birth of Christ in Bethlehem. This is natural because Christmas commemorates the birth of the Christ Child. Yet *Christmas* has meaning for us because of the rest of the life of Christ. Behind the manger in Bethlehem stands the cross of Calvary and the empty tomb in Joseph's garden. It is in view of the entire life of Christ that *Christmas* has its meaning.

To save us, Jesus kept the will of God for us. He passed through every phase of our existence so that he might truly be our substitute. To atone for our sinful conceptions and births, Christ was conceived and born without sin. To pay for our sins of thought, word, and deed, Christ led a perfect life in our place. To atone for our sins, Christ suffered our punishment for us. To assure us that he had completed the work of redemption, Jesus arose from the dead on Easter morning.

Jesus did not grow up to show us how to achieve our own salvation. Instead, he grew up to accomplish our salvation for us. When he cried out on the cross, "It is finished" (John 19:30), he indicated that his mission was accomplished. His life and death atoned for our sins, and his resurrection certified that God accepted the payment he made. As Paul wrote, "He was delivered over to death for our sins and was raised to life for our justification" (Romans 4:25).

In our text, Isaiah describes a warrior disposing of his garments. So complete is this warrior's victory that he no longer even needs the clothing for warfare. In the same way, Christ has finished all that is necessary for our salvation. We need not and cannot do anything. Salvation is ours as a free gift through faith in Christ Jesus, who has done it all for us. It is with good reason, then, that we celebrate Christmas. It is the birth of the Savior who won redemption for us.

❧

Oh, come, O Key of David, come,
And open wide our heav'nly home.
Make safe the way that leads on high,
And close the path to misery.
Rejoice! Rejoice! Emmanuel
Shall come to you, O Israel! (CW 23:4)

11

To us a child is born, to us a son is given. . . . And he will be called . . . Prince of Peace. (Isaiah 9:6)

What child is this?— he is the Prince of peace

Peace! How people of all ages have longed for it! In Isaiah's day the people of Israel desired peace. The Assyrians were invading their territory, bringing death and destruction. In our day people also long for peace. Unfortunately, political unrest continues. Warfare constantly rages in some parts of the world. It does not surprise us that at this time of year people focus their attention on the message of the angel: "Glory to God in the highest, and on earth peace to men on whom his favor rests" (Luke 2:14). People speak of the birth of Christ in the fond hope that his peaceful life will move people to live in peace on earth.

In the first place, it is a vain hope to expect an end to war in this world. Scripture tells us there will be wars and rumors of war until the end of time. There never will be a time in this present world when people will live in total peace with others. The reason for this is sin. Because people do not love God the way they should, they do not love one another the way they should. Till the end of time, sin will cause people to go to war with others.

Then, if they look to Jesus for earthly peace, people miss the point of the angel's message. Jesus did not come to bring peace on earth but to establish peace between God and men. Adam and Eve did have peace with God, but they lost this blessed state through disobedience. Sin separates all people from God. It places the human race under his just wrath and condemnation.

Yet in his love for sinners, God took it upon himself to establish peace. He did this through his Son, Jesus Christ. As Paul wrote, "God was reconciling the world to himself in Christ, not counting men's sins against them. . . . God made him who had no sin to be sin for us, so that in him we might become the righteousness of God" (2 Corinthians 5:19,21).

Through Jesus Christ we are at peace with God. His righteousness covers all our sins and turns God's anger away from us. During this season, when people speak so fervently of peace, let us share with them the message that Christ is truly the Prince of peace because through him we have peace with God.

❧

Our glad hosannas, Prince of Peace,
Your welcome shall proclaim,
And heav'n's eternal arches ring
With your beloved name. Amen. (CW 12:4)

To us a child is born, to us a son is given, and the government will be on his shoulders. . . . Of the increase of his government and peace there will be no end. He will reign on David's throne and over his kingdom, establishing and upholding it with justice and righteousness from that time on and forever. (Isaiah 9:6,7)

What child is this?—
he is our King

How would you feel if a child were elected head of our government? You would be very uneasy, because a child lacks the maturity and the ability to govern effectively. Early in his book, Isaiah indicated that the Lord would judge his people by making "boys their officials; mere children will govern them" (Isaiah 3:4).

Yet in our text, Isaiah foretold that God would bless his people by sending a child to rule over them. The entire responsibility for good government would rest upon his shoulders. He would rule justly over his people. His kingdom would be an everlasting one. It is clear that this child ruler is no ordinary person. He is the God-man, who became a child for us.

Christ was born to be our King. However, as we view his earthly life, his kingly nature is not readily apparent. He was not born in kingly splendor but in a stable in Bethlehem. He did not grow up in Jerusalem, the city of King David, but in the despised village of Nazareth. During his life he did not live in palaces. Rather, he said, "Foxes have holes and birds of the air have nests, but the Son of Man has no place to lay his head" (Matthew 8:20). The only crown he wore was the crown of thorns that pierced his flesh. During his life he wore no royal purple. Only before his death did he wear the purple robe that the soldiers put on him to mock him.

Nonetheless, Christ is our King. He established his reign through the cross. By giving his life as a sacrifice for sinners, Christ broke the power of Satan over us. Through the good news of our salvation, he establishes his reign in our hearts.

The babe of Bethlehem is indeed our King. He is exalted now, ruling this world in the interest of his church. He will come again to judge the world. May the celebration of his birth move us to serve him faithfully until he takes us to reign with him in heaven.

ॐ

Hail, hosanna, David's Son!
Help, Lord; hear our supplication!
Let your kingdom, scepter, crown
Bring us blessing and salvation
That forever we may sing
Hail, hosanna! to our King. Amen. (CW 8:4)

[John's] father Zechariah was filled with the Holy Spirit and prophesied. (Luke 1:67)

Doubts dispelled

Doubts and questions about his faith bothered the young student. One of his teachers had the reputation of having all the answers, so the student went to him and poured out his troubles. But the teacher replied, "If I were to answer all these questions, it would only lead to others. There is a better way. Look to Jesus, and concentrate on what he has done for your salvation." That student was Merle d'Aubigne, who became a celebrated historian of the Reformation.

A priest named Zechariah could have related to d'Aubigne's experience. While Zechariah was serving in the temple in Jerusalem one day, the angel Gabriel appeared and told him that he and his wife would have a son. Zechariah doubted this could be true. "I am an old man and my wife is well along in years" (Luke 1:18), he said. Because Zechariah doubted, the angel told him he would be unable to speak until after his son was born.

Zechariah's wife, Elizabeth, did give birth to a son. With God nothing is impossible. On the eighth day after the son's birth, when they came together to circumcise the child, the family members were going to name the baby after his father, Zechariah. His mother, however, said, "No! He is to be called John" (Luke 1:60). Zechariah, still unable to speak, asked for a writing tablet and wrote, "His name is John" (Luke 1:63). (The name John means "The Lord is gracious.") This was, of course, the child who would grow up to be John the Baptist, the forerunner of Jesus.

No sooner had Zechariah written these words than he could speak again, and he began to praise God. Filled with the Holy Spirit, he sang a song of praise to the Lord for remembering his gracious promise of a Savior from sin. The Lord dispelled Zechariah's doubts—not by explaining to Zechariah how elderly people could have a baby but by focusing his attention on the Savior for whose coming this John would prepare the people.

When we contemplate the great truths of Christmas, doubts similar to those of Zechariah may arise. Did God really become a man? Was Jesus really born miraculously of a virgin? He did, and he was! The Lord dispels our doubts today too by also directing us to the purpose of it all: Christ was born to die for our sins and to rise again for our salvation.

⁂

Heavenly Father, as we prepare for Christmas, dispel all our doubts by focusing our attention on the purpose of your Son's birth at Bethlehem: to be Savior of the world. Amen.

"Praise be to the Lord, the God of Israel, because he has come and has redeemed his people." (Luke 1:68)

14 December

Paid in full

It was a fine boat. Many hours had gone into fashioning the miniature hull and the little sail. It was time to test it. Ten-year-old Johnny set it carefully into the stream and watched as it was quickly carried by the current around the bend in the river. Before he could catch up with it, it was gone.

Some weeks later Johnny happened to be in a secondhand store, and on one of the shelves was the little boat he had made. But there was nothing to identify it as his own, and the storekeeper wouldn't believe him. "You'll have to pay me five dollars if you want that boat," the storekeeper said. Johnny was willing to do it. As he carried the boat out of the store, he thought to himself, "This boat is twice mine. First I made it, and when it got lost, I bought it back again."

In a similar way, God redeemed us, that is, he bought us back again. The price was the precious blood of his own Son, Jesus Christ. All the silver and gold in the world was not enough to redeem us condemned sinners. It took Christ, "a lamb without blemish or defect" (1 Peter 1:19), to provide for our salvation.

Zechariah understood this and praised God for sending his angel to announce that the day of redemption was at hand. The angel had told Zechariah that his eight-day-old son, John, would be the one who would go before the Lord "in the spirit and power of Elijah . . . to make ready a people prepared for the Lord" (Luke 1:17). God had not forgotten his promise to the Israelites. He was about to send his Son into the world to be the Redeemer of all mankind, to pay the price required for all people's sins. It was this that led Zechariah to sing his song of praise.

It is this same knowledge that inspires our Christmas songs of praise. God's wrath demanded punishment for sin. Satisfaction was required. But the price has been paid in full. The Redeemer came into the world. Let us join Zechariah in praising the Lord.

❦

Now sing we, now rejoice,
Now raise to heav'n our voice;
He from whom joy streameth
Poor in a manger lies;
Not so brightly beameth
The sun in yonder skies.
Thou my Savior art! Thou my Savior art! Amen. (CW 34:1)

15

"He has raised up a horn of salvation for us in the house of his servant David (as he said through his holy prophets of long ago)." (Luke 1:69,70)

How strong are you?

There is an ancient myth about a certain giant named Antaeus who lived in Lybia. His mother, so the myth goes, was Gaea, the earth. Antaeus conquered all until he met Hercules. The two began wrestling, and it appeared Antaeus would win. But Hercules noticed that whenever he lifted Antaeus off his mother earth, the giant's strength left him. So Hercules clasped the giant Antaeus around the waist, lifted him off the ground, and thus defeated him.

How strong are you? Strong enough to wrestle a giant? Do you think you could take on the devil in a wrestling match and defeat him? Are you strong enough to overcome the power of sin? Are you strong enough to climb your way into the mansions of heaven? When it comes to spiritual strength, the Bible teaches that by nature we have no strength at all. We need a champion, someone to be strong for us.

We have such a one. It is his birth we will be celebrating in ten days. As we look into the manger this Christmas, we will see a little baby who looks weak and helpless and must depend upon his mother to care for him and feed him. But that little baby is also the Son of God, the one whom Zechariah refers to as the "horn of salvation" (a "horn" in the Old Testament symbolizes strength). That little baby is the God-man who took on Satan in mortal combat and completely defeated him. He did that as our champion. Satan no longer can claim us as his own. Jesus freed us from the deadly hold that sin had upon us. He endured the wrath of God for us. By his death and resurrection, Jesus brought us to God and assured eternal life in heaven for us and all who believe in him. He is our strong Savior.

He also fills us with his strength so that we can do all things through him. He gives us the courage to tell others about the true meaning of Christmas. He causes our Christmas gift-giving and receiving to reflect God's love in giving his Son for us. He helps us rise above the secular celebration of Christmas.

We have much to celebrate this Christmas, and Zechariah shows us how.

Lord Jesus, thank you for coming to this earth to be my strong Savior and to rescue me from sin, death, and the devil. I look forward to the day when you will return to take me to yourself in heaven. Amen.

". . . salvation from our enemies and from the hand of all who hate us." (Luke 1:71)

16 *December*

The enemy has been defeated

The visitor to the zoo watched with apprehension as the attendant carefully opened the door to the lion's cage. Shivers went up and down the visitor's spine as the attendant walked right up to the lion. "You certainly are a brave man," the visitor ventured. "No, I'm not that brave," the attendant replied. "Well then, that lion must be pretty tame," the visitor said. "No sir, he isn't tame, but he's old and hasn't got any teeth," the attendant answered with a chuckle.

The Bible compares our mortal enemy, the devil, to a lion, a ferocious lion who hates us and would devour us. It speaks of him as a terrifying adversary who would stir up all the forces of evil to conquer us and take us into eternal torment in the fires of hell.

Now you might be wondering what all this has to do with Christmas. We don't normally think about enemies, warfare, and fighting at Christmastime. Christmas is thought of as a time for laying down the weapons of warfare, at least for a day. It is a time for love and forgiveness, for peace and good will.

But why is it that the angels sang, "On earth peace to men" (Luke 2:14)? It is because Christ was born to bring us salvation "from our enemies and from the hand of all who hate us." When Christ was born at Bethlehem, he entered the arena to do battle with Satan. The battle was fierce, hard, and long. All through Jesus' life the warfare raged. The devil tried everything he could to win the battle: face-to-face confrontations, subtle suggestions, appealing temptations. He tried working through the leaders of the Jews and even through Jesus' own disciples. But Jesus parried every blow and avoided every thrust. Just at the moment when it seemed Satan had finally won, Jesus by his death on the cross destroyed the power of Satan.

In a sense, we are living in the lion's cage. "The devil prowls around like a roaring lion looking for someone to devour" (1 Peter 5:8). But thanks to Christ, the enemy no longer has any teeth. This is part of what we celebrate at Christmas. Christ came into this world, and the enemy has been defeated.

∽⊙⊙∾

Lord Jesus, thank you for coming into this world to defeat for us the devil and all the powers of darkness. Help us celebrate Christmas in the right way. Amen.

". . . to show mercy to our fathers and to remember his holy covenant, the oath he swore to our father Abraham."
(Luke 1:72,73)

A promise that lasts forever

In July 1941 President Franklin D. Roosevelt made General Douglas MacArthur commander of the combined US and Filipino forces in the Philippines. Later that year, outmanned and outgunned, MacArthur and his army were forced to leave the Philippines in the wake of a Japanese invasion. Before he left, MacArthur vowed to the people of the Philippines, "I shall return." MacArthur kept his promise. By July of 1945, he had returned and had liberated most of the Philippines.

We appreciate people who keep their promises. But we have come to realize that it's not always going to happen. Unforeseen circumstances, complications, and just plain forgetfulness lead to many broken promises. We may even find ourselves becoming a little cynical when promises are made. We've come to realize that they often aren't kept.

God's promises are different. Whatever he promises comes to pass. No sooner had Adam and Eve sinned in the Garden of Eden than God promised a Savior to deliver them. Down through the centuries, God repeated this promise.

There were times when mankind's behavior was such that, from our point of view, God would have been perfectly just in breaking his promise and wiping all people off the face of the earth. The world of the flood comes to mind. So does the situation at the Tower of Babel. But God continued to remember his promise. In his grace he chose an individual, Abraham, and his descendants to be the bearers of this promise. Though time and again the Israelites were a rebellious and unruly people and brought upon themselves God's judgment, God still did not forget his promise. Generation after generation he repeated it—to David, through the prophets. Then when the fullness of the time had come, God sent his only begotten Son into the world to fulfill the promise of salvation.

It is the fulfillment of God's promise that we will be celebrating in the upcoming days. Christ was born at Bethlehem to be our Savior from sin. And just as Christ came the first time, so he will come again. He will return on judgment day to take all who believe in him to the eternal mansions of heaven. His promises last forever!

❧

Thanks be to you, O Lord, for remembering your promise to send a Savior. Cause my whole life to be a song of praise to you. Amen.

". . . to rescue us from the hand of our enemies, and to enable us to serve him without fear." (Luke 1:74)

Nothing to fear

Inscribed across an old map of Jamaica is the title "Land of Look Behind." The map is from the days when there were slaves in Jamaica. Occasionally slaves escaped from their cruel masters and headed for the mountains. Sometimes the government sent troops after them, so the fleeing slaves frequently looked fearfully over their shoulders. This gave the mountainous area of Jamaica the title "Land of Look Behind."

Perhaps we often find ourselves living in the "Land of Look Behind." We should have done this; we should have done that. Our guilty consciences nag at us. We fear our pasts will catch up with us. We remember that at one time we were slaves of Satan. Will Satan's troops overtake us? Will he take control of our lives again? Time and again we find ourselves casting fearful looks over our shoulders.

But not all our troubles are behind us. Concerns for the present weigh heavily upon us, slow us down, and sometimes even keep us from putting one foot in front of the other. Around the bend or over the next hill, disaster may be waiting or trouble may spring upon us suddenly. Off in the distance, or perhaps even close at hand, the specter of death looms large before us. Fears and dreads abound. Under such conditions, how can we live for our Lord? How can we possibly serve him?

We can. Jesus has made it possible for us. He was born to take away our fears. Satan cannot claim us as his own. Christ has defeated him. Our sins cannot condemn us. Christ has suffered God's wrath upon them. "Neither the present nor the future, nor any powers . . . will be able to separate us from the love of God that is in Christ Jesus" (Romans 8:38,39). We need not fear, because he is with us. We need not be dismayed, because he is our God. He will strengthen us and help us. Even death cannot strike fear into our hearts, because Christ has gained the victory over death.

He has rescued us, and we can serve him without fear. Gazing intently upon him and our heavenly goal, we can give our all for the advancement of his kingdom.

Lord Jesus, remove all fear from my heart and help me serve you with all that I am and have. Amen.

". . . to serve him . . . in holiness and righteousness before him all our days." (Luke 1:74,75)

Wholly holy

Imagine a number of learned scientists going down to the beach of one of the world's oceans and saying, "We are now going to cause the tide to come in." There they would stand with all their vast sums of knowledge, expertise, and the latest inventions of advanced technology, determined by some pneumatic or hydrostatic force to cause the ocean tides to rise. Do you think they would be successful?

I guess they would be about as successful as those who try to make themselves holy before God. All mankind's best efforts, all our learning and discoveries, wonderful as they may be, leave us still as lost and condemned creatures in God's eyes. There is no force in all the world that can move the natural human heart to love and obey God. For humans, as we are by nature, holiness is an impossibility.

Scientists cannot cause the tide to come in, but the moon can. The moon exerts its invisible power upon the oceans, and the result is what we call the rising and falling of the tide. Likewise, it is only God himself who can move our hearts to love and obey him. He does it through the gospel of Jesus Christ, the wonderful Christmas gospel, which tells us that Jesus came into the world to live and die for sinners like you and me.

By God's gracious working, the halo—a symbol of holiness—that artists often have painted over the head of the baby Jesus has now become our halo through faith in Jesus. For the sake of Christ's innocent sufferings and death, God has declared us to be holy and righteous before him. "He saved us, not because of righteous things we had done, but because of his mercy" (Titus 3:5). God looks at us and sees only Christ's holiness. He sees us as completely holy for the Savior's sake.

By the same powerful gospel, God inspires us to serve him in holiness and righteousness. As he did with Zechariah, the Holy Spirit opens our mouths and loosens our tongues to praise Christ and to tell about the wonderful things he has done. Like Mary, we begin to treasure all these things and ponder them in our hearts and minds. Like the shepherds, we join in glorifying and praising him for all the things we have heard and seen.

Because of God's mercy, we are wholly holy—not by our own efforts but entirely because of God's mercy in Christ Jesus.

⁓⊙⊙⁓

Lord God, you have declared me to be holy and righteous for Jesus' sake. Lead me to serve you in holiness all my days. Amen.

This is how the birth of Jesus Christ came about: His mother Mary was pledged to be married to Joseph, but before they came together, she was found to be with child through the Holy Spirit. Because Joseph her husband was a righteous man and did not want to expose her to public disgrace, he had in mind to divorce her quietly. But after he had considered this, an angel of the Lord appeared to him in a dream and said, "Joseph son of David, do not be afraid to take Mary home as your wife, because what is conceived in her is from the Holy Spirit." (Matthew 1:18-20)

The promised Savior comes

Mary was going to have a child, even though Joseph had not yet taken her as his wife. Righteous Joseph—not yet knowing of the miraculous intervention of God in Mary's and his lives—planned to break off their engagement. But God did not let that happen. Jesus would be born within a legal marriage, and Joseph, a descendant of King David, would be recognized in law as the father of Jesus. No virgin except Mary was ever told, "You will be with child and give birth to a son" (Luke 1:31).

The prophet Isaiah had foretold this miracle: the promised Savior, the Son of God, would be born of a virgin. And so Jesus entered history as the Son of a mother who was "with child through the Holy Spirit." His birth came as the fulfillment of God's prophecy and promise.

How did this happen? Only by the power of the Highest, the Creator of heaven and earth; only by the working of the Holy Spirit, with whom "nothing is impossible" (Luke 1:37). This was the revelation granted to Joseph in a dream in which the angel of the Lord appeared to him and said, "Joseph son of David, do not be afraid to take Mary home as your wife, because what is conceived in her is from the Holy Spirit."

God himself suspended his natural law. Though this Child was a true human being, born of a woman, he was different from every other child. The Creator seems to be saying, "See here, world, here is a very special child, born in a special way to do a special work. This is my Son, conceived by the Holy Spirit, born of the virgin Mary. He is your Savior. He is your Lord. Accept him in faith. Worship him. Obey him."

At this Christmastime, heavenly Father, give us the humble faith of your servants, Mary and Joseph. Help us accept your wondrous revelation of our Lord and Savior; help us believe in him and follow him. Amen.

21

"The virgin will be with child and will give birth to a son."
(Matthew 1:23)

The promised Savior—
his home away from home

Mary's time had come. The Son prophesied by Scripture and promised by the angel was born! Luke describes the circumstances more graphically for us: "She gave birth to her firstborn, a son. She wrapped him in cloths and placed him in a manger, because there was no room for them in the inn" (Luke 2:7).

Luther writes, "When they came to Bethlehem, . . . they were the lowliest and most despised; they were obliged to yield to everyone until they, shown into a stable, had a common inn, a common table, a common room, and a common bed, with beasts. In the meantime, many an evil person occupied the place of honor in the inn and permitted himself to be honored as a lord. There no one perceives or knows what God performs in the stable."

The Savior of the world, heaven's great King, was born in extreme poverty. No palace, no gorgeous bed, no soft downy blankets, no obstetrics ward with doctors, nurses, and attendants coming and going—but a stable, a manger, and swaddling clothes. It was great humiliation for the Son of God to descend from his rightful place on heaven's throne, to be born as a child, to take on himself the form of a servant. He, who was to die an outcast "despised and rejected by men" (Isaiah 53:3), began his life of service in deepest humility, shunted aside at the very start because "there was no room . . . in the inn."

Well might we marvel that he whom we confess to be Lord of lords and King of kings should have chosen such a birth and to make this little village, this stable, this manger his first home away from his real home, heaven.

But we know the reason for such humility. This was God's marvelous grace in action. The very circumstances suited his purpose. The eternal Son of God had left the glory of heaven to be born a humble child so that he might fulfill all righteousness for us and bear the curse of our disobedience. He assumed our humility to remove our shame and make it possible for us to inherit the glory that belongs to the children of God. "Though he was rich, yet for your sakes he became poor, so that you through his poverty might become rich" (2 Corinthians 8:9).

We, as the children of God, are indeed rich because Jesus came to this earth and because Jesus dwells in our hearts.

❧⊙⊙☙

O holy Christ Child, we praise your wondrous grace in humbling yourself to become our Savior. May we fully appreciate the rich gifts you have given us. Amen.

In those days Caesar Augustus issued a decree that a census should be taken of the entire Roman world. (This was the first census that took place while Quirinius was governor of Syria.) And everyone went to his own town to register. (Luke 2:1-3)

Who is this newborn King?— he is the ruler of history

A television news flash: "Flight 1440 from Atlanta has crashed. No survivors." The wail of a police siren: What violent act has shattered someone's life? Dad's cracking voice: "Mom has cancer."

Tragedies break into our lives in many ways. Some hit us personally; others tug at our hearts as we feel the grief of other people. Any tragedy can raise these questions: Why does God let this happen? Isn't he in control?

Maybe Joseph had similar questions when he heard of the census decree from Caesar Augustus: Why now when Mary is so far along in her pregnancy? Will the trip harm her or the child? How will I provide for her in Bethlehem?

Whatever questions or doubts Joseph had, he also had the Lord's promise. Through an angel the Lord had promised Joseph, "[Mary] will give birth to a son, and you are to give him the name Jesus" (Matthew 1:21). God was watching over them.

In fact, centuries earlier through the prophet Micah, the Lord had foretold that the Savior would be born in Bethlehem (5:2). Joseph and Mary were not pawns moved around at the whim of a Roman emperor. Rather, the Lord used the Roman emperor to fulfill Micah's prophecy and the Lord's eternal plan. The Lord is always in control. The newborn King is the ruler of history.

Next time tragedy strikes you, remember Jesus, the ruler of history. If he can use a pagan emperor to bring Mary and Joseph to Bethlehem, can he not use the small and great tragedies in your life for your good? You have the Lord's promise: "We know that in all things God works for the good of those who love him, who have been called according to his purpose" (Romans 8:28). You also have the Lord's promise of complete freedom from tragedy in heaven: "He will wipe every tear from [your] eyes. There will be no more death or mourning or crying or pain" (Revelation 21:4).

Often when we look at life, it's like looking at a tapestry too close-up. We see only a chaotic jumble of colors. Yet as we step back, we begin to see the marvelous design that God's love has worked out. And the golden thread running through it all is our Savior Jesus Christ, the ruler of history.

⸎

Lord Jesus, lead me to trust in your love to turn tragedy into blessing. Amen.

So Joseph also went up from the town of Nazareth in Galilee to Judea, to Bethlehem the town of David, because he belonged to the house and line of David. He went there to register with Mary, who was pledged to be married to him and was expecting a child. (Luke 2:4,5)

Who is this newborn King?— he is David's son

Isn't it easy to make promises? "Yes, Mom, I'll clean up my room." "Yes, Son, I'll make it to your baseball game." "Yes, Dear, we'll go out for dinner Friday night." But how easy is it to keep our promises? Work runs late. Friends stop by. Or we simply find ourselves too tired.

Jesus' birth reminds us that the Lord was not too busy or too tired to keep his promise. Right after Adam and Eve sinned, God promised that the woman's offspring would crush Satan's head (Genesis 3:15). Throughout the Old Testament, God repeated and expanded his promise. He promised King David that the Savior would come from his royal line and would establish his throne forever (2 Samuel 7:12-16). The prophets echoed the Lord's promise that the Savior would be David's son. Through Jeremiah the Lord said, "I will raise up to David a righteous Branch, a King who will reign wisely. . . . This is the name by which he will be called: The LORD Our Righteousness" (Jeremiah 23:5,6).

Notice how Luke calls to mind the promise that the Savior would be King David's son: "So Joseph also went up . . . to Bethlehem the town of David, because he belonged to the house and line of David." This newborn King is David's son.

What a difference this makes for you! Without the Lord's promise, you and everyone else would be headed straight for hell. Eternal death in hell is the wage we earn by our sin.

But the Father kept his promise and sent his eternal Son to be born from David's line. Since Jesus is David's son, he is a true human being. He was made like us in every way yet was without sin (Hebrews 2:17; 4:15). Therefore, he is our brother and our substitute.

God's promise makes a difference for you because Jesus is your substitute. Like you, he was "born under law" (Galatians 4:4). Unlike you, he kept that law perfectly in your place. As your substitute, Jesus died for you. He suffered your hell on the cross in your place. Since Jesus is David's son, he is the substitute whom the Lord promised for you. Now live a life of thanks to God for him keeping his promise.

୧ଓ୬ଡ଼

Lord Jesus, keep burning in my heart your promise that you are my substitute. Amen.

While they were there, the time came for the baby to be born, and she gave birth to her firstborn, a son. She wrapped him in cloths and placed him in a manger, because there was no room for them in the inn. (Luke 2:6,7)

Who is this newborn King?— he is the lowly King

Most births in the United States happen in hospitals. That's usually the safest place. The rooms are clean, trained professionals monitor mother and child, and if complications arise, the best tools of modern medicine are close by.

What was Jesus' birthplace like? We know the cleanliness of hospitals and might assume a similar atmosphere. The beautiful nativity scenes painted to honor the birth of our King may also color our minds' pictures.

For a moment, erase these pictures from your mind, and see the picture the Holy Spirit paints for us: "She wrapped him in cloths and placed him in a manger," a feed box for animals. Jesus was not born in a sanitary hospital or in a clean house. He was born in a dirty barn; he was laid where farm animals were fed. Can you imagine a more lowly birth?

Although we can honor our King with marvelous pictures of his birth, we do well to remember its lowliness. This lowliness shows the seriousness of our sin and the greatness of God's love. God's Son chose to leave his heavenly throne and to be born in the most degrading place. Here he began his difficult, lowly life. Then "he humbled himself and became obedient to death —even death on a cross" (Philippians 2:8).

In the lowliness of his birth, we see the purpose of his coming. He came to suffer for the sins of the world. He came to ransom sinners. He came to humble himself even to death on a cross.

So we see the seriousness of sin. My sin led God's Son to enter this world through a most lowly birth. His lowly life ended in a godforsaken death because of my sin. But what unsurpassed love! I deserved only his hate. Yet in love for me, God's Son willingly came. He was born in a lowly manger for me. He laid down his life on the cross for me. How true it is when Paul writes, "Though [our Lord Jesus Christ] was rich, yet for your sakes he became poor, so that you through his poverty might become rich" (2 Corinthians 8:9). This is what you and every Christian confess: Jesus was born in a lowly manger for me; he is my newborn King.

෴

Lord Jesus, thank you for the riches you won for me by your poverty. Amen.

There were shepherds living out in the fields nearby, keeping watch over their flocks at night. An angel of the Lord appeared to them, and the glory of the Lord shone around them, and they were terrified. But the angel said to them, "Do not be afraid. I bring you good news of great joy that will be for all the people. Today in the town of David a Savior has been born to you; he is Christ the Lord. This will be a sign to you: You will find a baby wrapped in cloths and lying in a manger." (Luke 2:8-12)

Who is this newborn King?— he is Christ the Lord

Babies capture people's affections. Grown-ups ooh and aah over them. Parents cuddle and caress them. Brothers and sisters gently kiss them. Oh, the sweetness of a newborn baby!

The newborn Christ Child inspires the same affection in us. Yet so many people see only a cute, cuddly baby in a manger. For them Christmas, at best, arouses a desire to try to help others. They feel inspired by the gentle baby.

Sometimes we also fail to look past the little baby of the Christmas story. We approach the Christ Child as if he were only a cute, cuddly baby. We forget who he is. He is Christ the Lord.

Imagine that you were one of the shepherds out in the fields. How would you have approached the Christ Child? The glory of the Lord and the sight of his heavenly messenger have just dazzled your eyes; the angel's words, "He is Christ the Lord," are still ringing in your ears; your heart is pounding in fear and excitement and wonder. How would you have approached the Christ Child?

He is no ordinary child. He is the Christ, the Anointed One. The Father has anointed, or appointed, him to save sinners. To do this work, he is no less than the Lord himself. He is true God, the eternal Son of the Father. "Through him all things were made" (John 1:3). Even as he lies in the manger, in him "all the fullness of the Deity lives in bodily form" (Colossians 2:9).

As we approach the manger with the shepherds, we approach in humble awe. There lies the Lord, the holy God, our Creator. We are wretched sinners by nature. We come as beggars dressed in filthy rags. Yet we approach in joyful awe. There lies the Christ, our Savior. He washes us in his blood and clothes us with his life. This newborn King is no ordinary child. He is Christ the Lord.

❦

Lord Jesus, all praise and thanks to you for being born for me, for being my Savior and Lord. Let me always cradle you in the arms of faith as I confess my sin and trust in your forgiveness. Amen.

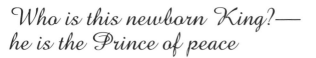

Suddenly a great company of the heavenly host appeared with the angel, praising God and saying, "Glory to God in the highest, and on earth peace to men on whom his favor rests." (Luke 2:13,14)

Who is this newborn King?— he is the Prince of peace

"I believe it is peace for our time . . . a peace with honour." British Prime Minister Neville Chamberlain announced this judgment after returning from conferences with Hitler in 1938. Less than a year later, the bloodiest war in history killed this peace. Is there peace on earth?

As we reflect back on this past year, we see another year filled with conflicts, crime, and bloodshed. Closer to home, each one of us has suffered through our own personal unrest: a loved one's death, financial woes, medical problems, family strife, emotional turmoil. Is there peace on earth?

The angels declared that there was peace on earth. They were not simply wishing for it or dreaming about the future. They proclaimed peace right then and there. How could they be so bold? The Prince of peace was born.

Jesus brings a different kind of peace. The night before his death he told his disciples, "Peace I leave with you; my peace I give you. I do not give to you as the world gives. Do not let your hearts be troubled and do not be afraid" (John 14:27).

What is the peace he gives? It is peace with God. Adam and Eve fired the opening shots in mankind's war against God. Since then all their children have been born in Satan's trenches. Everyone has battled against God.

God could easily have destroyed all of us sinners in hell. But his grace, his undeserved favor that rested on the world, planned a way to rescue us from Satan's trenches. He sent his Son, the Prince of peace.

Jesus willingly took on the guilt of the world's sin. He became the target of God's hatred against sin. He absorbed the full assault of God's wrath. Because his death satisfied divine justice, he rose from the dead and proclaimed peace with God. "Your sins are forgiven" (Luke 5:20), he says. "Peace be with you!" (John 20:19).

Do peaceful feelings fly away from you? Does life harass you? Do you wonder, "Is there peace on earth?" Don't despair. Hear the angels' song. Your Prince of peace is born. He forgives your sins even if you don't have peaceful feelings. He has won peace with God for you even if life keeps harassing you. Regardless of your inner feelings or outward circumstances, cling to Jesus' words: "Your sins are forgiven. Peace be with you!"

cᴓᴒᴅ

Lord Jesus, in this coming year, give me, your servant, the peace that the world cannot give. Amen.

When the angels had left them and gone into heaven, the shepherds said to one another, "Let's go to Bethlehem and see this thing that has happened, which the Lord has told us about." So they hurried off and found Mary and Joseph, and the baby, who was lying in the manger. When they had seen him, they spread the word concerning what had been told them about this child, and all who heard it were amazed at what the shepherds said to them. (Luke 2:15-18)

Who is this newborn King?— he is the Savior for all

Dalton's hands trembled as he unfolded the letter. Three colleges had already turned him down. His test scores had been too low. Was this another rejection letter? He read. Soon his fears disappeared. He exclaimed, "Yes!" and ran home shouting, "I've been accepted!"

Good news gushes out. We can't hold it in. The shepherds couldn't hold it in. They spread the word. The angel had told them, "I bring you good news of great joy that will be for all the people. Today in the town of David a Savior has been born to you" (Luke 2:10,11). The shepherds believed the angel's words, and their faith shared the good news: this newborn King is the Savior for all.

This Christmas you have again listened with the shepherds to the angel's message. You have hurried to the manger with the shepherds. Are you now going to spread the good news with the shepherds?

This can be a scary thought for many of us. Fears well up within us, and Satan uses those fears to keep our mouths shut, even though we want to spread the Word. How can we calm our fears and drive Satan away? Remember about whom you are speaking. You are speaking about the Savior for all. "God so loved the world that he gave his one and only Son" (John 3:16). Jesus "gave himself as a ransom for all" (1 Timothy 2:6). If Jesus came and died for all, he came and died for you and for your neighbors. He is the Savior for you and for your neighbors.

You have eternal life in Jesus through faith in him. How can your neighbors believe and be saved unless someone tells them about their Savior?

As you make your New Year's resolutions, remember those who do not know their Savior. Pray that the Lord gives you the courage and the opportunity to speak to them about the Savior. Be ready when the opportunity comes. With the shepherds, spread the joyful news: The Savior for all is born.

⟨∘⊙∘⟩

Lord Jesus, give me the words and the courage to tell others of your love. Amen.

Mary treasured up all these things and pondered them in her heart. The shepherds returned, glorifying and praising God for all the things they had heard and seen, which were just as they had been told. (Luke 2:19,20)

Who is this newborn King?— he is your heart's treasure

Cameras and camcorders capture slices of our lives. Old pictures sharpen fading memories. Parents relive the happy moments of raising a family. Maybe this past holiday season you added photos and footage to your treasured collections.

Mary photographed and videotaped on her heart the events of the first Christmas. She treasured them up. She did not simply cherish them as a new mother watching her new baby; she cherished them as the Lord's servant watching God's saving plan unfold. What a priceless treasure to ponder!

The Holy Spirit has shown this tape to us. God's Word pictures Jesus Christ, our heart's treasure. We watch his birth. We follow his ministry. We stare in horror and amazement at his death. We witness his victorious resurrection. We gaze into the sky at his ascension. Do we watch in numb disinterest as we would watch a movie that we've seen too many times already? Or do we treasure up each scene from Jesus' life and ponder it in our hearts?

As the Christmas gospel presents your Savior to you, remember he is your heart's treasure. Your heart was a barren wasteland, filled with sin and hate. Through Baptism, Jesus came and made his home in you, bringing you to faith and washing away the guilt of all your sins. Now your heart is a treasure trove filled with Jesus and all the riches his mercy brings. Ponder this treasure.

The more we ponder what a treasure Jesus is, the more we praise him as the shepherds did. Although Grandma treasures her photo album, she does not hide it away or lock it up. She displays it on the living room table. She eagerly shows it to whomever she can so that she can praise her children and grandchildren.

When we treasure Jesus in our hearts, we don't keep him hidden away and locked up. We praise and glorify him by our words and actions. His blood has purchased the riches of heaven for you and me. He gives us this treasure in the gospel free of charge. Do we need any more reasons to praise and glorify God in worship and every day of our lives? This newborn King is our hearts' treasure.

এ৩৬৯

Lord Jesus, you are my priceless treasure. Lead me every day to ponder your riches as I meditate on your Word, and lead me to praise your grace as I live for your glory. Amen.

When the time had fully come, God sent his Son, born of a woman, born under law, to redeem those under law, that we might receive the full rights of sons. (Galatians 4:4,5)

The time had arrived

In homes where the practice of placing gifts beneath the Christmas tree is still observed, children have to be kept from unwrapping them before the appointed time. For some this means waiting until Christmas Eve; for others, Christmas morning; for still others, until after dinner on Christmas Day or some other time set by the family.

Similarly, our heavenly Father waited. He waited several thousand years for the proper time before revealing his gift of love, Jesus Christ. As God allowed 120 years for repentance before sending the flood, so he permitted 400 years to elapse after the last prophecy of Malachi before sending the Messiah so that his people might be prepared to accept him.

But the world, generally speaking, did not prepare itself. Spiritually, even the people of Israel fell to an all-time low. Hence the time of fulfillment was not brought about by the spiritual aspirations of man but by the will of a loving God. God saw our desperate need for a mediator who would satisfy the stern demands of God's law, for a Savior who would pay the debt of sin for fallen mankind.

To pave the way for announcing this gospel, the Lord permitted a vast expansion of the Roman Empire, the wide usage of the Greek language, and a comparative ease of travel throughout the empire. And there were other conditions that helped the circulation of the gospel—like the extensive dispersion of the Jews, the conversion of many Gentiles, and the general military peace that prevailed at the time of the Redeemer's birth.

The message of forgiveness in Christ is still sorely needed because we are still sinners and by nature under the wrath of God. To date, our forgiving Father has allowed 20 centuries of grace for the preaching of Christ, the only hope for fallen mankind. Moreover, he has determined a time when he will judge the world. But that time is not known to a single creature.

Therefore, before the second time of fulfillment arrives, our God, who wants all people to be saved, wants us to use the time allotted to carry his good news into all the world. So let us work while it is still day. The time for Christ's second coming is at hand.

❧◎◗◗

Come, Lord Jesus, come quickly! Amen.

[He came] to redeem those under law, that we might receive the full rights of sons. Because you are sons, God sent the Spirit of his Son into our hearts, the Spirit who calls out, "Abba, Father." (Galatians 4:5,6)

Adopted as sons

One of the points made in the parable of the prodigal son is that the younger son did not realize the blessings of his sonship. Can't you hear him saying as he enviously watched the swine feeding themselves, "I never had it so good as when I was home with my father and family. If only I wouldn't have left!"

Even so, we can also lose sight of our high position as God's children. This happens most often when Satan ambushes us and causes us to fall into sin. Then nothing seems important except to enjoy the sinful gain or grasp the pleasure he dangles before us. The devil does his best to persuade us that our sonship with God is a fairly dispensable thing.

Let us pray that God will bring us to our senses in time so that we realize anew that we are his adopted children. We could not become God's children through our efforts. Yet we are God's children because God has adopted us. But this adoption took place only because God's own Son paid a terrific ransom to free us from the guilt and curse of sin. Because of our sins, we deserved to be forever rejected from God's house, but for Jesus' sake, God has made us members of the household of heaven.

As you value your adoption, so value also your blessings as God's child. Being a child of God means safety and protection against the howling winds of spiritual adversity and the storms of sin and temptation. It means being fed with the precious Bread of Life for the nourishment of your soul. It means being sure of God's love. The God who gave his only begotten Son into death for you—his love cannot leave you or forsake you! And "the Spirit himself testifies with our spirit that we are God's children. Now if we are children, then we are heirs—heirs of God and co-heirs with Christ, if indeed we share in his sufferings in order that we may also share in his glory" (Romans 8:16,17).

Moreover, as his own true child, you have the privilege of bringing all your needs before him, confident that he will help you because he loves you.

It is no mere coincidence that in his model prayer, Jesus taught us to pray, "Our Father," because we are indeed his children. As such, "we may pray to him as boldly and confidently as dear children ask their dear father."

తితిం

Father, we pray that you would keep us as your children until we inherit the glory you have in store for us, for Jesus' sake. Amen.

So you are no longer a slave, but a son; and since you are a son, God has made you also an heir. (Galatians 4:7)

Heirs of God through Christ

Yesterday's meditation reminded us of our blessings and privileges as God's adopted children. The crowning point of our relationship with God, our Father, is that as his beloved children, we are in line for an inheritance, which is none other than a gift of eternal glory in heaven. It is a foregone conclusion that if we are the children of God and not the servants of sin, we are the heirs of his heaven.

And what a glorious inheritance this is! Indescribable in its nature, it includes freedom from pain and woe, grief and death, punishment and everlasting suffering in hell. It offers instead peace and joy, perfect life, eternal praise and glory, and, most glorious of all, dwelling forever in the presence of our divine Creator, Redeemer, and Sanctifier.

The apostle Peter speaks of this inheritance as being perfect in every way, lasting forever, and reserved for all who continue to believe in Christ. He describes it as a "living" hope. He says, "Praise be to the God and Father of our Lord Jesus Christ! In his great mercy he has given us new birth into a living hope through the resurrection of Jesus Christ from the dead, and into an inheritance that can never perish, spoil or fade—kept in heaven for you" (1 Peter 1:3,4). That is in striking contrast to the hopes of this world.

For many years, California has had a higher percentage of suicides than any other state. At first that seems strange when one reflects upon its beautiful scenery, blue skies, and bright sunlight. One would think that life ought to be easier there than anywhere else. Why, then, are there so many suicides? The reason ascribed is that many go to California with a last hope, either for their health or their personal fortune; and when this hope fades, life holds nothing for them.

But Peter says that the believer has been born again, into a family that has a "living" hope. The Lord Jesus has promised, "Heaven and earth will pass away, but my words will never pass away" (Matthew 24:35). His promise of life in heaven, therefore, stands sure.

With such a glorious inheritance absolutely assured, we can conclude this year without fear and face the coming 365 days with courage. We can be confident that no matter what is in store for our world, our nation, our communities, our families, or ourselves, our inheritance of eternal life and glory cannot be taken from us.

༄⊙☾

Unending praise be yours, O Father, Son, and Holy Spirit, for the countless blessings throughout this past year, which is now drawing to a close. Amen.

Scripture Index